I0754165

THE

LIFE

OF

WILLIAM H. SEWARD

WITH

SELECTIONS FROM HIS WORKS

EDITED BY

GEORGE E. BAKER

NEW YORK:
J. S. REDFIELD, NASSAU STREET.
AUBURN AND BUFFALO:
MILLER, ORTON, & MULLIGAN.
1855.

STEREOTYPED BY C. C. SAVAGE,
13 Chambers Street, N. Y.

C. A. ALVORD, Printer,
29 Gold-street.

PREFACE.

"The Works of William H. Seward" are already before the public in three large volumes. They have been received with much favor. At the same time they have increased the demand for an edition in a more reduced and economical form. The present volume is intended to meet that want. The Memoir which follows is substantially the same as that contained in the larger edition. Its faithfulness has been generally acknowledged. Two new chapters have been added to it in the present volume. They recite the history of the Compromises of 1850, the defeat of the Whig party in 1852, and the abrogation of the Missouri Compromise in 1854. A number of extracts from Mr. Seward's Speeches have also been introduced to illustrate the text.

A portion of the volume has been appropriated to Selections from Mr. Seward's Works. Among these Selections will be found extracts from most of his Addresses and Orations, his Executive Messages, his Forensic Arguments, and his Speeches in the Senate. Although comparatively few and brief, they embrace a great variety of topics under the heads of Agriculture, Internal Improvements, Education, Freedom, Commerce, and Miscellaneous. Besides

CHAPTER XIX.

CHAPTER XX.

CHAPTER XXI.

CONTENTS OF THE SELECTIONS.

AGRICULTURE.

INTERNAL IMPROVEMENTS.

EDUCATION.

FREEDOM.

COMMERCE.

MISCELLANEOUS.

ORATIONS AND SPEECHES.

MEMOIR.

CHAPTER I.

THE SEWARD FAMILY.

THE ancestors of WILLIAM HENRY SEWARD were of Welsh extraction. The first of that name in America emigrated from Wales during the reign of Queen Ann, and settled in Connecticut. A branch of the family, from which Mr. Seward is descended, removed to Morris county, N. J., about the year 1740. This branch again divided, one portion of which removed to Virginia, where it is still found in considerable numbers, as well as in Georgia and Kentucky. His paternal grandfather, John Seward, resided in Sussex county, in that state, where he sustained a high reputation for enterprise, integrity, and ability. On the breaking out of the Revolution, he became a prominent leader of the whig party, and on more than one occasion during the long struggle, was engaged in active service. His dwelling is defined on all the maps of the American colonies of that period. Being a zealous partisan he became the object of especial jealousy on the part of the loyalists. The following anecdote is among the traditions of the family. While General Washington's headquarters were at Morristown, Colonel Seward's residence was on the lines. Various plots were resorted to by the tories to circumvent and capture him. One day a man of rather suspicious appearance, on a horse without saddle or bridle, approached the house and upon being hailed by Colonel Seward replied that he brought a message from General Washington requiring Colonel Seward to hasten to headquarters. He was asked if he had a written order. His reply was in the negative. Colonel Seward then charged him with being a tory, whereupon he applied his whip to his horse and rode off at full speed. Colonel Seward seized his rifle and with unerring aim brought him to the ground. He lived long enough to confess that he was sent by a party of loyalists to decoy the colonel from his house that he might be waylaid and his house destroyed. He died in 1799, leaving a family of ten children. His son, Samuel S. Seward, received an academic and professional education, instead of a share in the paternal inheritance. Having completed his studies, he established himself in the practice of medicine in his native place, and soon after became connected in marriage with Mary Jennings, the daughter of Isaac Jennings, of Goshen, New York.

Removing to Florida, a village in the town of Warwick, in Orange county, N. Y., in the year 1795, he combined a large mercantile business with an extensive range of professional practice, both of which he carried on successfully for the space of twenty years. He retired from active business in 1815, and devoted himself to the cultivation of the estate, of which, by constant industry and economy, he had become the owner. Dr. Seward was a man of more than common intellect, of excellent business talents, and of strict probity. After his withdrawal from business, he was in the habit of lending money to a considerable extent among the farmers in his neighborhood; and it is said that no man was ever excused from paying the lawful interest on his loans—that no man was permitted to pay him more than that interest—and that no man who paid his interest punctually was ever required to pay any part of the prin cipal. He was a zealous advocate of republican principles, and exerted a leading influence in the affairs of the party. In 1804, he was elected to the legislature, and during the continuance of the republicans in power, he was never without one or more offices of public trust. Although not a member of the legal profession, he was appointed first judge of Orange county, in 1815, which office he held for seventeen years. His exercise of the judicial functions was marked by discretion, impartiality, and promptness, and he is remembered to this day as one of the best judges the county ever had. After a visit to Europe, he lived in the enjoyment of universal respect until 1849, when he died in a ripe old age. Dr. Seward was the friend of religion, education, and public improvement. He founded the "S. S. Seward Institute," at Florida, an excellent high school for young persons of both sexes. He endowed this seminary with a permanent fund of $20,000, and continued its steadfast friend until the close of his life.

The wife of Dr. Seward was Mary Jennings, whose family had emigrated from Ireland at an early day. She was a woman of a clear and vigorous understanding, with singular cheerfulness of temper, and while devoted with untiring industry to the interests of her family, was a model of hospitality, charity, and self-forgetfulness. She died in 1843.

The subject of this memoir never forgot that he had Irish blood in his veins. This fact serves to explain, in part, the strong attachment he has always cherished for the Irish population of our country. While travelling through Ireland in 1833, his indignation was greatly aroused by the sight of the oppressions inflicted on the people by the British government. He ascribed a large share of the miseries of that unhappy country to its political mismanagement, and especially to the annihilation of its parliament, by the act of union. In writing home from Ireland, he expresses himself in the following terms :—

"But all this glory has departed. The very shadow (and for a long time the Irish parliament was but the shadow) of independence has vanished; Ireland has surrendered the individuality of her national existence, to share, like a younger sister, that of England. The walls of the parliament-house remain in all their primitive grandeur, to reproach the degeneracy of her statesmen. While traversing its apartments, I reverted to the debate when the degenerate representatives surrendered their parliament; and I thought that had I occupied a place there, I would have seen English armies wade in blood over my country, before I would have assented to so disgraceful a union. Something might have been spared, after the deed was consummated, to the wounded pride of the Irish people. The parliament-house ought to have been closed, and left in gloomy solitude, a monument to remind the people that they once had a country. But this was too great a concession for the economy of the English administration of affairs in Ireland. They who build palaces and monuments with a profuse hand, on the other side of the channel, sold the Irish Capitol, and it was forthwith converted into a hall for money-changers. I confess that overleaping all the obstacles which are deemed by many well-wishers of Ireland insurmountable, I wish the repeal of the union. I will not believe that if relieved of that oppressive act, she does not possess the ability to govern herself."

In a private letter written by Mr. Seward in 1840, to a gentleman who had taken strong exceptions to his sentiments in relation to Irishmen, the following passage occurs, in regard to the Irish lineage of his mother. After defending the character of the Irish from some severe charges made by his correspondent, and alluding to their many virtues, he says:—

"If this confession of faith seems strange to you, permit me to explain that I could not believe otherwise, without doing dishonor to a mother eminent for many virtues, and to the memories of humble ancestors, whose names will not be saved from obscurity by the record of any extraordinary vices."

CHAPTER II.

WILLIAM HENRY SEWARD.

WILLIAM HENRY SEWARD was born in Florida, Orange Co., N. Y., May 16, 1801. The house in which his parents then resided is still standing; but the village-church and schoolhouse, where his youthful feet were wont to tread, have given place to more modern structures. A venerable forest-tree on the ancient homestead still overshadows a clear, bubbling spring of water, which William was in the habit of frequenting in his school-boy days, with his books, for the purpose of reading and study in its cool and pleasant retirement. His boyhood is well remembered by the aged inhabitants of his native village. They love to recall their predictions of the future eminence of the studious lad, whose diligence and zeal had already attracted their attention. The colored servant, then a slave of his father's, who led him in infancy, and shared his juvenile sports, still lives to rejoice in the bounty of her young companion, who has given a comfortable home for her old age, in memory of their early attachment.

The subject of our narrative entered upon life amid external circumstances adapted to cherish and develop the higher elements of his nature. Orange county contains within its borders West Point, Fort Putnam, Fort Montgomery, Minisink, Newburgh, Washington's headquarters, and other places famous in the annals of the Revolution. It has also been the birthplace or residence of many distinguished men, among whom may be named George Clinton, James Clinton, De Witt Clinton, Cadwallader C.

Colden, General Belknap, James Burt, Robert Armstrong, John Duer, Ogden Hoffman, Samuel R. Betts, Samuel J. Wilkin, and others. The town of Warwick originally with several other towns composed a part of the town of Goshen, having been set off from that town in 1788. It was settled directly or indirectly as early as 1703. A part of the town was called Florida or Floriday as early as 1738. The origin of this name is not clearly known, but it was probably derived from the Latin word *Floridus* signifying covered or red with flowers. The local scenery of Florida is scarcely surpassed in the country for beauty and magnificence. On each side, mountains of impressive grandeur rear their blue summits into the skies, while the broad and fertile valleys, watered by numerous rivulets and miniature lakes, enriched by genial and appropriate culture, and smiling in joyous abundance, complete the majestic and lovely panorama. The people of Florida, unlike the inhabitants of most other towns in that part of the state, were originally emigrants from New England. They were accordingly imbued with much of the stern and lofty spirit of the Puritans, while their descendants still retained many of their habits and feelings. Brought up amidst such sublime and ennobling scenes of nature—inheriting from a worthy ancestry the purest sentiments of honor and patriotism—imbibing, with his mother's milk, the love of truth, freedom, and equality—the mind of young Seward early received a powerful impulse toward the career of beneficent greatness, which has amply fulfilled the prophetic anticipations of his youthful associates and admirers.

One of the first acts remembered by the friends of young William Henry, was in no small degree significant of his juvenile tendencies. He ran away *to* school—most truants run in the opposite direction. His taste for books was displayed at an early age. They were his favorite companions, and he was seldom seen without a volume in his hands. His thirst for knowledge, once nearly cost him his life.

When about twelve years of age, returning near nightfall from a pasture on his father's farm, driving home the cows, he read a book as he walked, giving an occasional look to his charge, that was travelling quietly before him. A party of boys espied the abstracted herdsman, and disturbed his studious reveries with a volley of small stones. Resolved not to be disturbed in his reading by the missiles of his thoughtless companions, he turned his back toward them, and walked backward with his eye intently fixed upon his book. In a short time, he insensibly diverged from the path, and missing the bridge over a small creek, was thrown into the water. An elder brother, who had witnessed the accident, drew him from the stream in a state of unconsciousness, and he was fortunately restored without serious injury.

His precocious intellect, and his docile, cheerful disposition, led his parents to decide on giving him a superior education to that received by the other members of the family. The common school system had not yet been established in the state of New York, and he attended several different schools in the vicinity of his father's residence, until the age of nine years. At this period, he was sent to Farmers' Hall Academy, at Goshen, which then boasted of having had the celebrated Aaron Burr and Noah Webster among its pupils. The records of the "Classical Society" of Goshen, and of the "Goshen Club," still exist, showing young Seward to have been an active member of each—the constitutions and minutes of proceedings being mostly in his handwriting. Among the principal exercises of these two societies, were declamation, debates, and compositions. In nearly all the debates which are noticed, Seward has a part, and then as now he was generally found on the right side. He pursued his studies at this seminary, and at an academy afterward established in Florida, until the year 1816. He was now but fifteen years of age, when he was presented for admission to Union College, Schenectady. The thin, pale, sandy-visaged boy was found qualified for the junior class, but on account of his extreme youth was persuaded to enter the sophomore.

CHAPTER III.

HIS COLLEGE LIFE—VISIT TO THE SOUTH—DR. NOTT.

THE college career of young Seward, as related by his contemporaries, gave brilliant indication of the rare qualities for which he has since become distinguished. The traits of the future legislator and statesman were foreshadowed in the character of the modest youth during his period of academic retirement. Even then he displayed the manly originality of conception—the sturdy independence of purpose—the firm adherence to his convictions of right—the intrepid assertion of high moral principles—the careful examination of a cause before appearing in its defence—the sympathy with the weak and oppressed—and the intellectual vigilance and assiduity in the pursuit of truth—which have formed such conspicuous and admirable features in his public career.

His favorite studies in college were rhetoric, moral philosophy, and the ancient classics. It was his custom to rise at four o'clock in the morning, and prepare all the lessons of the day. At night, while the other students were engaged in getting ready the exercises of the next morning, he devoted his leisure to general reading, and literary compositions for class declamation or debates in society meetings.

In the year 1819, Seward, who was then in the senior class, and in the eighteenth year of his age, withdrew from college for about a year, passing six months of the time as a teacher at the south. The spectacle of slavery could not fail to make a deep impression on his mind. He witnessed scenes which aroused him to reflection on the subject, and produced the hostility to every form of oppression, which has since become ingrained in his character. One of the many incidents which occurred to him may be related in this place.

While travelling in the interior of the state, he approached a stream spanned by a dilapidated bridge, that had become almost impassable. He forded the river with no little difficulty, and met on the opposite side a negro woman with an old blind and worn-out horse, bearing a bag of corn to mill. The poor slave was in tears, and manifested great distress of mind. She was afraid to venture on the bridge, and the stream seemed too rapid and violent for the strength of her horse. She was reluctant to return to her master, without fulfilling her errand, being fearful of punishment. The heart of the young northerner was moved. He went to her assistance, and attempted to lead the horse across the bridge. But the wretched beast was not equal to the effort. He made a false step, and falling partly through, became wedged in among the plank and timbers. Seward tried in vain to extricate him. Despairing of success, he mounted his own horse, rode to the master's residence, and informed him of the accident, and attempted to excuse the slave. In return for his kindness, he was met with a volley of imprecations on himself, the slave, the horse, the bridge, and all parties and things concerned. His disgust at this adventure taught him a lesson of wisdom, which he never forgot.*

* Another incident is related in one of his speeches as having occurred during a subsequent visit to the south, and he has been heard to remark that it contains the whole story of slavery: "Resting one day at an inn in Virginia, I saw a woman blind and decrepit with age, turning the ponderous wheel of a machine on the lawn, and overheard this conversation between her and my fellow-traveller: 'Is not that very hard work?'—'Why yes, mistress, but I must do something, and this is all I can do now I am so

Returning to college in 1820, he found the students in state of great excitement. They had hitherto been divided into two literary societies, the Philomathean and the Adelphic, between which an earnest, but not unfriendly rivalry subsisted. The former was the most popular with the students, while the latter claimed the most diligent scholars. Young Seward was a member of the Adelphic, and entered into the interests of the society with characteristic zeal. During his absence, some twenty or thirty students from the southern states had left Princeton college and entered Union. These attached themselves to the Philomathean society, giving it a great superiority in numbers over its rival. Questions soon arose in the society, on which the members divided geographically. The southern students were left in a minority, and obtaining a charter from the college faculty, organized a third society called the Delphian institute. Their secession weakened the Philomathean, and was generally regarded by the older members of the rival society as a triumph on their side. The younger Adelphics, however, took a different view, favoring the Philomatheans, on the ground that the secession was factious and sectional. Seward, whose experience at the south, and popularity with all classes in college, served to qualify him for the office, virtually became umpire between the two parties. After an impartial hearing of the question, he decided in favor of the Philomatheans, and against the Delphian institute — thus siding with the sophomores and freshmen, in opposition to the views of his own classmates. He thereby incurred no small odium. The faction, which he

old.'—'How old are you?'—'I don't know; past sixty they tell me.'—'Have you a husband?'—'I don't know, mistress.'—'Have you ever had a husband?'—'Yes, I was married.'—'Where is your husband?'—'I don't know; he was sold.'—'Have you children?'—'I don't know; they were sold.'—'How many?'—'Six.'—'Have you never heard from any of them since they were sold?'—'No, mistress.'—'Do you not find it hard to bear up under such afflictions as these?'—'Why yes, mistress, but God does what he thinks best with us.'"

had condemned, caused him to be arraigned, with a view to his expulsion from the Adelphic society. The members resolved themselves into a court, while a prominent member of his own class acted as public prosecutor. Seward conducted his own defence. After the testimony was completed, he summed up the merits of the case, closing a powerful argument with a thrilling recital of his course throughout the controversy. Declaring that he was indifferent to what might be said of him by the public prosecutor—that he had no wish to know who voted for and who against him—and that he would not embarrass the vote of any member by his presence, or by inquiry about his vote at any time afterward—he abruptly left the chamber in which the trial was held. In half an hour, the rush of students from the hall showed that the case was decided. Soon his room was crowded with sophomores and freshmen, ardent with victory, and loud in congratulations that the prosecution had been voted down. The cause of law and order was sustained against the seceders, and the integrity of the union in Union college fully vindicated.

There was still another trial in college for the young student. Three commencement orators were to be appointed by the Adelphic society. This appointment was deemed the highest college honor. Seward was a prominent candidate. His scholarship, his eloquence, and his character, presented equally strong claims in his favor. But the hostile faction among the friends of the Delphian institute, established a vigorous opposition. An earnest canvass was maintained for several weeks. No pains were spared to defeat the election of Seward. The choice was at length made, and he gained a decided triumph. The subject of his oration was, "The Integrity of the American Union." This was a chaste and manly performance, replete with vigorous sense and patriotic feeling. It was listened to with enthusiasm by an intelligent audience, and called forth warm commendations in the public prints.

Seward graduated among the most distinguished scholars in his class. He shared his academic honors with several, who have since arisen to eminence in different walks of literature and public life. Of these, we need only mention the names of Hon. William Kent, who inherits the legal mind and rare attainments of his father, the celebrated chancellor; Rev. Dr. Hickok, now vice-president of Union college, and as an erudite and profound metaphysician, without an equal among American scholars; and Rev. Tayler Lewis, professor of Greek in Union college, distinguished no less as an adroit and energetic controversialist, than as a classical scholar of consummate accomplishments.

An incident, showing his standing in the college, and his early development of talent, was thus described by a public journal, many years since:—

"The year 1820 was, as our readers will remember, the epoch of the great contest between Tompkins and Clinton. The interest excited by this struggle pervaded all classes and ages of the community, and it was not in the glowing temperament of William H. Seward to remain neutral. He was naturally from his education and early association, on the side of Tompkins, and his zeal was quickened by personal intercourse with this amiable and fascinating man, with whom to have an interview with an individual was to acquire and fix a friend. Seward was appointed to address the vice-president on his visit to Schenectady on behalf of the young republicans of the college. His speech was so much above the common run of political harangues, as to excite general and lasting interest. He lived in the remembrance of Daniel D. Tompkins, until he himself ceased to live; and his friends will recollect the fervent kindness with which he was wont to recur to this eloquent and generous effort of his youthful champion."

The relations of young Seward with Dr. Nott, the venerable and excellent president of Union college, were intimate and cordial, throughout his academic course, and have continued to be of affectionate confidence to the present time. It is believed that Mr. Seward has seldom acted on any important public question, without availing himself of the experience and sagacity of his venerated friend, whose counsels, we need not say, have always been on the side of nobleness and humanity. Nor, we may add, has Mr. Seward failed to preserve the attachment of his early friends. The companions of his school and college days, as well as those of his professional life, have ever been among his foremost supporters, as a public man. And he never forsakes a friend or a cause, that he has once espoused. No reproach can shake his fidelity to objects, of whose worth he has become persuaded.

CHAPTER IV.

LAW STUDIES—REMOVAL TO AUBURN—FAMILY—RELIGIOUS PRINCIPLES—CHARACTER AS A LAWYER.

Soon after taking his degree at Union college, Mr. Seward entered the office of John Anthon, Esq., of the city of New York, as a student at law. He carried the habits of early rising and faithful application, which he had maintained during his college life, into his professional studies. He thoroughly mastered every elementary book which was put into his hands, making a written analysis of its contents. Completing his legal preparation with John Duer and Ogden Hoffman, Esquires, in Goshen, N. Y., he was admitted to the bar of the supreme court at Utica in 1822. For six months previous to his admission he had been associated in practice with Mr. Hoffman.

In January, 1823, Mr. Seward took up his residence in Auburn, and formed a connection in business with the Hon. Elijah Miller, a distinguished member of the legal profession, and at that time first judge of Cayuga county. Judge Miller, who had acquired a competency in a large and successful practice, was desirous of retiring from active professional pursuits, and discovering signs of great promise in young Seward, took him into his confidence, and proved a devoted and efficient friend.

Mr. Seward, in 1824, married his youngest daughter, Frances Adeline Miller. As this lady is still living, we can only say that the connection has been a singularly fortunate one in all respects. Four children compose their family; Augustus, a lieutenant in the United States army, and devoted to its scientific pursuits, Frederick, who has chosen the editorial profession, and a boy and girl yet in childhood. One daughter, "fondly loved," was therefore, perhaps, "early lost."

The town of Auburn, which Mr. Seward selected as a residence, is in the heart of one of the most fertile and delightful regions in central New York. Its growth has been rapid and healthful. Within a few years the primeval forest has given place to a populous city. Its inhabitants are distinguished for their intelligence, enterprise, and refinement. Free from the pride of wealth and the pretensions of aristocracy, they present an attractive example of genuine republican equality. In some degree these characteristics are no doubt due to the influence of Mr. Seward and his estimable family. During a residence of more than thirty years, he has won the unqualified respect and confidence of his townsmen. Moving in the highest circles of society, he has never avoided friendly intercourse with the most obscure and lowly. The patron of struggling merit—cherishing a deep interest in all social and philanthropic movements—watchful to aid the unfortunate and forsaken—and ever ready to devote his time, his talents, and his pecuniary means, to the defence of the wronged and oppressed of every caste and color—he has gained the lasting gratitude and love of the people with whom, for over a quarter of a century, he has lived as a neighbor and fellow-citizen.

Although free from all taint of sectarianism, Mr. Seward cherishes a strong attachment to the protestant episcopal church, of which he became a member in 1837. He has been frequently called to attend ecclesiastical conventions of that body. At the anniversary of the American Bible Society in 1839, he was called to act as one of the vice-presidents, and in his address on that occasion he expresses the following sentiment in regard to the Bible:—

"I know not how long a republican government can flourish among a great people who have not the Bible; the experiment has never been tried: but this I do know that the existing government of this country never could have had existence but for the Bible. And further I do in my conscience believe that if at every decade of years a copy of the Bible could be found in every family of the land its republican institutions would be perpetual."

With his devotion to the cause of public improvement, he has been the patron of churches, schools, and benevolent institutions, liberally contributing his money for their support, and his counsels for their direction.

After establishing himself in Auburn, Mr. Seward became interested in the military affairs of the neighborhood, and was soon honored with various military offices. Accepting the colonelcy of a regiment, he acquired wide distinction and still higher promotion by his zeal and discipline. Without personal military ambition, he was an ardent friend of a well-regulated militia system for the preservation of order and the defence of the country. He was an excellent tactician, and an accomplished commander, while his winning qualities as a man secured the friendship of all around him, who were engaged in the same department of public service.

From the commencement of his practice as a lawyer, Mr. Seward was always in the habit of arguing his own cases, instead of employing older counsellors, as is often done by young advocates. In the management of a case he sparingly refers to the authority of recorded decisions, but stating the general principles of law applicable to the question, and arranging the facts in the simplest order, enforces his arguments by *à priori* reasonings, and shows the basis of his position in natural equity. As a professional rule, he gives his aid to a weaker party against a stronger, even without compensation, whether his client be right or wrong; but if a stronger party claims his services against a weaker, he does not engage in the suit without a clear conviction of its justice, whatever be the compensation. During the whole course of his practice he has never been known to act for a man against a woman; and was never but once engaged in a cause against the accused; and that was an instance of extreme outrage by a man upon a young woman.

The legal career of Mr. Seward is illustrated with no less justice than vigor in the following sketch of his early professional life, written several years since for one of the periodicals of the day:—

"The practice of the law in the country must not be estimated by the practice in the city. Each has its own advantages and difficulties; it is the peculiarity of the former, that it at once brings to the test, and to the public view, the intrinsic qualities of the man. The crowded bar, the long-deferred opportunity, the deference to age and experience, the overshadowing reputation of the seniors of the profession, and the innumerable natural or conventional impediments, which so long keep back, and so often depress the young aspirant with us, are felt in a very mitigated degree in the interior. The candidate for distinction is there summoned at once to the arena: '*naked steel is around him;*' he is thrown upon his own talents, energies, and resources, and he stands and falls as in his native and unaided strength. To have stood this trial successfully, and, after eleven years of arduous labors, to have risen to the very foremost rank of his profession, as did Mr. Seward, is in itself an unerring indication of the high character of the object of these remarks. In all our courts, and in causes of every description, his talents have been exercised and admired. He has stood forward and distinguished himself with such men as John C. Spencer, Joshua A. Spencer, Albert H. Tracy, and their contemporaries of the West, for whom competition, if not pre-eminence, may be challenged with the *Athletes* of the bar in any other section of the state or of the country. Property, liberty, and life, have been committed to the integrity and ability of 'this young man of thirty-three,' and he has never faltered in his trust, nor failed in an emergency, nor left unfulfilled an expectation."

His most formidable competitors at the Auburn bar, during the commencement of his practice, were Hon. John M. Hulbert and William Brown, Esqs. Both these distinguished men were accomplished scholars, erudite jurists, and powerful advocates. At this time they were in the dazzling flush of professional success. The brilliancy of their fame threw most of their rivals into the shade. Many excellent members of the bar had been deterred by their eminence from attempting to vie with them in the courts. But upon a man like Mr. Seward, their influence was of a contrary nature. Their intellectual predominance only aroused his emulation; nor did he suffer by the comparison. Possessing a native independence of mind, he was early accustomed to original thought. This habit was strengthened by severe discipline. Attaching a due value to the suggestions of others, he still relied upon himself. Connected with this trait of character, was a rigid habit of industry; he studied while others slept. The time which most men give to recreation he devoted to strenuous toil. With such qualifications, Mr. Seward soon entered upon an extensive and successful practice. His fame grew with his years, until he fills a sphere which is surpassed in brilliancy and importance by that of few of his contemporaries, incontestably ranking with the first lawyers of the Union

---

CHAPTER V.

POLITICS—SLAVERY—YOUNG MEN'S CONVENTION—ANTI-MASONRY—STATE SENATOR.

THE attention of Mr. Seward was early drawn to political affairs. His father was an ardent champion of the Jeffersonian democracy. The traditionary instincts and early prepossessions of the son were strongly in favor of the same principles. Mr. Seward, accordingly, sympathized with the democratic party, believing that it embodied the spirit of popular freedom to a greater extent than any other party of the day. He was early undeceived by experience. Discovering that, under the pretence of democracy, the leaders of the party were bent on personal interests, irrespective of the rights of humanity and the public good, he left them at once and for ever. He has attached but slight importance to mere party names. The diffusion of genuine republican sentiments among the people, and their practical realization in the institutions and laws of his country, have been the leading objects of his political life.

Mr. Seward first had occasion to express his convictions on the subject of slavery during the protracted struggle on the admission of Missouri into the Union. He perceived, at that early period, the subserviency to southern influence and dictation which prevailed in the democratic party in the state of New York. From that day to the present, his life has been devoted to the principles of liberty. In his view, freedom is national, and slavery sectional. With him the purpose of the Union is to establish the blessings of equality, justice, and humanity; not to enlarge the area of bondage and oppression. His hostility to slavery has not been the result of policy, but of principle—of the strongest conviction of its inherent injustice, and its tendency to corrupt and destroy the noblest institutions of the country. His rule of action on the subject has been uniform from the commencement of his political career. He has never suffered the fear of consequences to silence his voice in defence of freedom, when any practical benefit was at stake; but he has strictly avoided every act that was adapted to inflict a needless wound upon an opponent, or to foment an unprofitable excitement.

In his measures with regard to slavery, Mr. Seward has been no fanatic. Detesting the institution, he has waged against it an honorable warfare. But he has refrained, with scrupulous care, from infringing on the constitutional rights of slaveholders, or depriving them of any privilege to which they are entitled by law. This is the extent of his concessions. He refuses to accord any advantage beyond legal enactment to an institution which violates the first principles of natural right.

His position on this subject was clearly defined in his California speech.*

"I feel assured that slavery must give way, and will give way, to the salutary instructions of economy, and to the ripening influences of humanity; that emancipation is inevitable, and is near; that it may be hastened or hindered; and that whether it be peaceful or violent depends upon the question whether it be hastened or hindered; that all measures which fortify slavery or extend it, tend to the consummation of violence; all that check its extension and abate its strength, tend to its peaceful extirpation. But I will adopt none but lawful, constitutional, and peaceful means, to secure even that end; and none such can I or will I forego. Nor do I know any important or responsible political body that proposes to do more than this. No free state claims to extend its legislation into a slave state. None claims that Congress shall usurp power to abolish slavery in the slave states. None claims that any violent, unconstitutional, or unlawful measure shall be embraced. And on the other hand, if we offer no scheme or plan for the adoption of the slave states, with the assent and co-operation of Congress, it is only because the slave states are unwilling as yet to receive such suggestions, or even to entertain the question of emancipation in any form."

Mr. Seward's first public action of a political character was in 1824. In October of that year, he drew up the address of the republican convention of Cayuga county to the people.† In this document, he gave a brief history of the origin and designs of the Albany regency—a clique of political leaders, which once exerted a great and most injurious influence in the state of New York. He exposed its system of machinery—its opposition to the electoral law, placing the appointment of presidential electors in the hands of the people, although solemnly pledged to its support—and its intrigues to prevent the election of John Quincy Adams to the presidency, and to secure the ultimate election of Martin Van Buren. The opposition to the Albany regency, thus boldly commenced by the young politician, was finally crowned with complete success. The sources of its influence were destroyed, and the power,

* See "Works of William H. Seward," Vol. I., p. 51. † See Vol. III., p. 335.

which had been centralized in its organization, was restored to the possession of the people.

On the 4th of July, 1825, Mr. Seward delivered an anniversary oration at Auburn.* The Missouri Compromise and the Tariff of 1824 had recently elicited threats of nullification at the south. In this oration, Mr. Seward took the same position on several important political questions, which he has maintained to the present day. He argued the capacity of the government for the extension of empire, asserting the perpetuity of the Union on the same grounds that have been advanced in his later productions. Anno̊uncing his devotion to the great principles of emancipation, he insisted that the United States should be a "city of refuge" for the oppressed and down-trodden of every nation.

In 1826 and 1827, the Greek revolution awakened a general sympathy in the United States. A meeting of citizens of Auburn was held in February, 1827, for the purpose of rendering aid to the struggling Greeks. Mr. Seward was invited to deliver a speech on this occasion.† The subject was congenial to his feelings, and he gladly consented to the request. With characteristic eloquence, he defended the cause of liberty in other lands—asserting its claims on American sympathy, in the same line of argument which he afterward reproduced in behalf of Ireland and Hungary. His vigorous and glowing appeal was met by the people to whom it was addressed with a munificent liberality which was elsewhere without a parallel.

In July, 1828, Mr. Seward was invited by the members of the Adelphic society of Union college, to deliver a eulogy on David Berdan,‡ a member of the society, who died on his passage from London to Boston, July 20, 1827. It was a sincere and eloquent tribute to the memory of an esteemed companion and friend. The monument erected to young Berdan, still forms an interesting object to those who visit the college grounds at Schenectady.

* See Vol. III., p 193. † See Vol. III., p. 197. ‡ See Vol. III., p. 117

The year 1828 is distinguished as the period when the young men of our country first made an effort to exert a personal influence on national politics. A convention of the young men of New York in favor of the re-election of John Quincy Adams to the presidency was held at Utica, on the 12th of August. It was one of the largest political conventions ever assembled in the Empire state. Four hundred delegates, in the flower and freshness of youth, were present at the session, which continued for several days. Mr. Seward was called to preside over its deliberations. He fulfilled the duties of the office with marked ability. Though only twenty-seven years of age, he exhibited a dignity, decision, and courtesy, which would have done honor to an experienced statesman. He left a singularly favorable impression on the minds of his colleagues, who, with scarcely an exception, have adhered to the political principles of that convention, until the present time. Many of the most prominent men in New York date their interest in politics from the young men's state convention, and have since exerted an influence which led to a decisive change in the policy and relation of parties in the state.

The election of General Jackson to the presidency in 1828 dissolved the national republican party in Western New York, with which Mr. Seward, as an ardent supporter of John Quincy Adams, had been identified. Meantime, the anti-masonic party had risen into consequence, and though of local origin, and acting in a limited field, for several years, it formed the only opposition in Western New York to the Albany regency and the Jackson administration. In 1828, this party tendered a nomination as member of Congress to Mr. Seward, which he declined, on account of the obligation that he felt to support the national republican party. On the overthrow of the latter party, Mr. Seward and his friends, sympathizing with the citizens who were engaged in vindicating the supremacy of the laws, naturally united with the anti-masons, as affording the best position for a successful resistance of the national and state administrations. Among his political associates at that time, were Frederic Whittlesey, Thurlow Weed, Francis Granger, John C. Spencer, Millard Fillmore, and other distinguished public men of the present day.

In 1830, Mr. Seward was nominated by the anti-masonic party as a candidate for the state senate, from the seventh district, comprising, at that time, the counties of Onondaga, Cayuga, Cortland, Seneca, Ontario, Wayne, and Yates. The nomination was unexpected, but he did not feel at liberty to decline it. Although the district had given a large Jackson majority the preceding year, and the anti-masonic candidate for governor, Francis Granger, was defeated, at the same election, by a majority of eight thousand, Mr. Seward was elected to the senate by the handsome majority of two thousand votes. In Cayuga county, where he resided, the democratic party had long enjoyed a decided ascendency, but still a majority of the senatorial votes were cast for Mr. Seward.

CHAPTER VI.

STATE SENATOR—THE ALBANY REGENCY—CANALS—BANKS—MILITIA—UNITED STATES BANK—PRISONS—CORPORATIONS.

Mr. Seward took his seat in the state senate, in January, 1831. This was his first election to civil office. He had always regarded the career of a statesman, as affording scope for the accomplishment of noble deeds in behalf of freedom and humanity. Hence, he cheerfully exchanged the routine of legal practice for the functions of the legislator. He was, probably, the youngest member that ever entered the New York senate, having not yet completed his twenty-ninth year. In spite of his youth, he soon attained an honorable distinction among his colleagues. With an almost juvenile ardor of temperament, inspired with a generous ambition, cherishing the deepest sentiments of patriotism and philanthropy, a champion of liberty and popular rights, despising the vulgar arts of hackneyed politicians, and filled with an enthusiastic faith in the ultimate triumph of truth and justice—Mr. Seward came into the senate of his native state, a new man, fresh from the living masses of the people, and breathed over that body a spirit of vitality and progress, of which the influence remains to the present day. His course at once assumed the character of boldness and originality which it still sustains. It was not shaped in accordance with traditional prescriptions, but following the impulses of an inventive mind, sought to develop new measures of public good, and larger enfranchisements for the people.

The circumstances, however, under which Mr. Seward entered the senate were adapted to discourage an ingenuous and earnest spirit. The Jackson party were in possession of unlimited sway. Wielding the vast patronage of the federal and state governments, their influence was as extensive as it was pernicious. The Albany regency, knit into a unit by the passion for office and its attending emoluments, ruled the state with an iron rod. With the appointing power, to a great degree, in their hands—controlling the currency by their connection with the banks—retaining well-disciplined emissaries in every county and town to carry their plans into effect—this central junta had but to touch the springs at Albany, to produce any desired movement in the remotest corner of the state. A large majority of the legislature were the supple tools of the regency, ready to enact such measures as might be deemed necessary to maintain the preponderance already secured.

Mr. Seward threw himself fearlessly into the opposition. He soon became its acknowledged leader. Among the debates in which he took a prominent part, were those relating to internal improvements and universal education. He labored strenuously in behalf of the common school system. He urged the abolition of imprisonment for debt, the melioration of prison discipline, and the establishment of a separate penitentiary for female convicts. The construction of the Chenango canal received his efficient support. He opposed the transfer of the salt duties from the canal fund to the general fund, but voted for their reduction. He sustained the bill for making the stockholders in commercial companies personally liable, but not in manufacturing companies. He opposed increasing the salaries of the higher judicial officers, and introduced important amendments of the law in relation to surrogates. But few bank charters obtained his vote. Governor Marcy's great loan law* met with his vehement opposition. He made a powerful speech against executive interference with the United States bank, and against the removal of the deposites;† while he supported General Jackson's measure in regard to southern nullification. Mr. Seward was one of the earliest friends of the New York and Erie railroad;‡ lending it his aid in all its vicissitudes, until it was at length brought to a triumphant completion.

Mr. Seward's first parliamentary effort was his speech on the militia bill,§ delivered on the 7th of February, 1831. In this speech, he proposed a thorough revision of the militia system, substituting volunteer uniformed companies for the general performance of military duty. His views were characterized by the far-reaching wisdom, the lively sense of the progressive wants of the age, which have often placed him in advance of his compeers, as an advocate of beneficent reforms. At first his suggestions failed to command assent; but they awakened discussion; and nearly twenty years afterward were adopted in substance.

* See Vol. I., p. 37. † See Vol. I., p. 14.
‡ See Vol. III., p. 306. § See Vol. I., p. 1, also p. 307 of this volume.

In March of the same year, a bill was introduced authorizing an appropriation to collect materials for a colonial history of New York. It was supported by Mr. Seward in a brief but earnest speech. He maintained that the official documents, relating to the early history of the state, contained in the archives of several European governments, especially of Great Britain, Holland, and France, should be collected by competent agents and embodied in a colonial history. His plan was adopted, and subsequently carried into effect during his administration as governor. The result was the publication of four large volumes of the Documentary History of New York, which appeared during the administration of his successors, Governors Fish and Hunt.

The next important speech of Mr. Seward was on the election of mayor of the city of New York.* This was delivered on the 23d of April. Under the first constitution the mayors and recorders of cities were chosen by the council of appointment at Albany. Under the new constitution of 1821, mayors were chosen by the common council, and recorders were appointed by the governor and senate. The new charter of New York gave the mayor a veto on the acts of the common council. A petition was presented to the legislature by the citizens for a change in the constitution, giving the election of mayor directly to the people. This was opposed by the dominant party. They brought in a resolution providing that mayors should be chosen in such manner as the legislature should direct. Mr. Seward took decided ground in favor of the New York petition. Arguing on the merits of the question, he contended that not only in New York, but in all cities, the mayors should be chosen by the people. This was in accordance with his democratic principles, which have always led him to claim the largest extent of privilege for the people. His views were finally adopted in the legislature of the state.

During the same session he materially aided the bill for

* See Vol. I., p. 10.

the abolition of imprisonment for debt, which at length passed; while the measure was fully completed, as will be seen in the sequel, under his subsequent administration.

At the close of the session Mr. Seward was appointed to draw up the address to the people of the minority of the legislature. In this address* he reviewed the financial condition of the state, and exposed the mismanagement of the treasury. He showed the radical defects of the safety fund system, which under partisan control gave the government of the state to the Albany regency. This monopoly was overthrown by the whigs on their accession to power in 1837, and the freedom of banking, under suitable safeguards, permitted to all citizens. The controversy between New York and New Jersey was at that time a source of much excitement. The address exposed the conduct of the executive, showing that it amounted to virtual nullification.

On the 4th of July, 1831, Mr. Seward delivered an anniversary oration† before the citizens of Syracuse. He took for his subject, The Prospects of the United States. In a strain of masculine eloquence, he defended the American people against the charge of national vanity and presumption, and uttered a stirring appeal for the cultivation of public virtue and the spirit of devotion to the Union.

The meeting of the legislature in 1832 again found Mr. Seward at his post. He entered, with his habitual zeal, upon the great questions which then agitated the public mind. Relying upon the soundness of his principles, he boldly maintained the conflict against a majority so overwhelming, that, to a less ardent temperament than his own, opposition would have seemed hopeless.

A resolution was brought into the senate, at the commencement of the session, against renewing the charter of the United States bank. Soon after, a substitute was proposed, declaring the necessity of a national bank for the collection of the public revenue, and the preservation of a

* See Vol. III., p. 338. † See Vol. III., p. 200.

sound and uniform currency. On the 31st of January, Mr. Seward delivered a speech in support of the proposed substitute. This was his first elaborate effort in the legislature. Having given a minute history of the United States, he discussed the fiscal system of the government, and exposed the fallacy of Gen. Jackson's objections to the renewal of the bank charter. His line of argument was substantially the same as that pursued by Mr. Clay and Mr. Webster in the United States senate. His speech produced a marked sensation throughout the country. The question was new and exciting; it took strong hold of public feeling, and great satisfaction was expressed by the opponents of the federal administration on the appearance of this powerful appeal in its favor. Combined with the discussions on internal improvements and state banks, the speech of Mr. Seward and that of Mr. Maynard, on the same subject, had the effect of concentrating the opposition to the Albany regency and Jackson's administration, in an organized system. This was the origin of the political body which two years afterward, took the name of the Whig Party.

On the 20th of March, the question came up on the establishment of a separate penitentiary for female convicts. In his speech on this subject, Mr. Seward took the broadest grounds of Christian philanthropy. He argued that the imprisonment of women in penitentiaries adapted only to the other sex, and under the exclusive management of men, was inhuman, and at war with the benevolent spirit of the age. He showed the benefits which the convicts would derive from the kind and judicious care of persons of their own sex. The prison, he maintained, should be made a house of refuge, rather than a place of punishment, where its unfortunate inmates might find protection from the wrongs they had received, in most cases at the hands of men; where they might receive instruction and guidance—be inspired with new hopes, and prepared to return to society with the prospect of honor and happiness. The measure, which was carried, owed its success to the exertions of Mr. Seward, greatly aided, however, by the efficient co-operation of Mr. M'Donald of Westchester county.

In a speech during this session on granting a charter to a whaling company, Mr. Seward made a vigorous attack on the tendency of legislation to corporate monopolies for banking, canals, railroads, and similar purposes. His efforts were not supported, and for a time proved unavailing. But the good seed has since ripened. The present system of opening every branch of business to voluntary association, without legislative interference, is the fruit of the principles he then maintained, and is an ample vindication of their soundness and utility.

At the close of the session of 1832, Mr. Seward was again appointed to prepare the address of the minority of the legislature to their constituents. In this document he resumed the discussion of the fiscal affairs of the state, showing the abuses of the administration in management of the public funds for political purposes, exposing the misconduct of the legislature in the incorporation of banking monopolies, and predicting the ruin of the banks from the policy pursued. His prophecy was in due time fulfilled.

CHAPTER VII.

STATE SENATOR—PRESIDENTIAL ELECTION—VISIT TO EUROPE—RETURN TO THE SENATE—REMOVAL OF DEPOSITES—COURT OF ERRORS—LAFAYETTE.

In the presidential campaign of 1832, Mr. Seward gave his support to the electors who were to vote for either Mr. Wirt or Mr. Clay as their vote should prove effective. He has since repeatedly supported Mr. Clay as a candidate for the presidency, although it is known that he always foresaw his defeat, and it is therefore questionable whether that eminent statesman was ever his first choice.

At the legislative session for this year, Mr. Seward took a still more prominent share in the proceedings of the senate. The nomination of Mr. Tallmadge, then a member of the senate, to the office of United States senator, called forth the discussion of an important constitutional question. A clause in the state constitution prohibited any member of the legislature from receiving office at the hands of that body, during the term for which he was elected. The attorney-general, to whom the question of eligibility had been submitted, decided in favor of Mr. Tallmadge. This decision was controverted by Mr. Seward in a speech of remarkable power of logic and eloquence. He was overruled by a strictly party vote; but one can hardly read his speech without being convinced that the appointment, made for temporary political purposes, was a violation of the constitution.

The nullification movements in the South were brought before the attention of the senate in February, 1833. On the 16th of that month, Mr. Seward introduced a series of resolutions, maintaining that Congress should be governed by a strict construction of the powers intrusted to the general government. In his speech sustaining the resolutions, he rebuked the democratic party in the state for their disposition to tamper with the principles of nullification, while professing to support Gen. Jackson's measures, which threatened the nullifiers with the penalty of treason.

During this session, Mr. Seward took part in the discussions on the navigation of the Hudson, and on the increase of judicial salaries.

On the 1st of June, 1833, Mr. Seward sailed for Europe in company with his father. They made a rapid tour through parts of the United Kingdom, Holland, Germany, Switzerland, Sardinia, and France. During his absence he wrote home a series of letters,* describing the countries that he visited, which were afterward published anonymously in the Albany Evening Journal. After about forty of the series had appeared, their publication was arrested, under circumstances which can not, perhaps, be better explained than by inserting the following extract from the Journal of that date:—

"LETTERS FROM EUROPE.—In reply to numerous inquiries for these letters, it is proper to say that their publication was arrested by the 'veto' of the gentleman who wrote them. It is already known to some of our readers that the author of these letters is the whig candidate for governor. They were hastily written to several of his intimate friends, while making a tour upon the continent. On his return, the friends of Mr. Seward earnestly desired the publication of these letters in a more durable form, but this was declined. After much importunity, however, he yielded a reluctant consent to their anonymous publication in the 'Evening Journal.' The series, thus commenced, were continued, contributing to the interest of our readers, and adding new names to our subscription, until the whig state convention placed their author in a new relation to the public; when, unwilling, we suppose, to superadd to other offences the heinous one of writing 'Letters from Europe,' he desired us to suspend their publication.

"From this decision of the author, our readers have appealed to the editor. Having read a portion of these letters, they insist upon the publication of the entire series. They do not, nor can we discover, in the whig nomination for governor, a sufficient reason for cutting off this source of interest and instruction. And besides, the assent of the author to the publication of the whole series, having been obtained *before* his nomination for governor, we insist that he has not now the right to revoke it.

"Under these circumstances, and at the general solicitation of our readers, we *take the responsibility* of resuming the publication of our 'Letters from Europe.' It is due, however, to Mr. Seward, to say, that they were written solely for the gratification of his own family and a few intimate friends, without the slightest expectation that they would ever be given to the public. If any of his political opponents should think proper to find fault with these letters, we shall respectfully inquire who among them possesses the industry and the talent to have travelled through England, Ireland, Scotland, Holland, Switzerland, Germany, and France, within a period of *less than three months*, and produce nearly eighty letters (filling upward of nine hundred manuscript pages) of equal interest and intelligence?"

These letters exhibit a refined taste, great acuteness of observation, and a genial sympathy with the grand and

* See Vol. III.

beautiful in nature. The reputation of the writer was enhanced by the avowal of their authorship.

Mr. Seward returned from his European tour in season to take his seat in the senate, at the opening of the session of 1834. The public attention was occupied with important questions both of national and of state politics. In the controversy relating to the United States bank, Mr. Seward took a leading part, and by his vigorous and eloquent appeals produced a strong impression upon the public mind.

The removal of the deposites by Gen. Jackson took place in September, 1833. Mr. Van Buren was then vice-president, and in order to promote his claims to the presidency, it was deemed essential to obtain the approval of the New York legislature for the measures of Gen. Jackson. Joint resolutions were accordingly introduced by the administration party in January, 1834, approving the removal of the deposites, instructing the senators and representatives in Congress to oppose the renewal of the bank charter, and ascribing the financial distress of the country to the influence of that institution. These resolutions passed the assembly by a large majority. Not a voice was raised in opposition to them. In the senate, however, they met with a different reception. With a deep conviction of duty, and in spite of the remonstrance of his friends, Mr. Seward broke the ominous silence, and, in an elaborate speech,* opposed the passage of the resolutions. This speech, which was, on the whole, the most powerful effort of his intellect and legislative experience during his career in the New York senate, occupied a part of two days in the delivery. It was forcible and conclusive in argument, pointed and brilliant in expression, and adorned with the appropriate embellishments of historical and classic illustration. Its effect, not only on the senate, but throughout the state, was of so decided a character, that several sen-

* See Vol. I., p. 14.

ators of the opposite party attempted to set aside its influence by formal replies. This called forth Mr. Seward in a rejoinder on the 24th of January, on which occasion he indulged in a severity of remark to which he was not accustomed, and for the only time in his public life, noticed the personal attacks of which he had been made the subject.

The evils which Mr. Seward had predicted in consequence of the removal of the deposites, spread over the country with fearful rapidity. Before the close of the session, a severe financial pressure was felt everywhere. Commencing among the mercantile classes, it soon extended to every department of business and industry. Public meetings were called to express the prevailing dissatisfaction, and to avert further calamity. Committees were appointed to implore relief of the president and Congress. As a suitable measure to alleviate the general pecuniary distress, Governor Marcy recommended the issue of six millions of stock, to be sold on account of the state. A bill to this effect was introduced into the legislature, providing that four millions of the avails of this stock should be loaned to safety-fund banks, and the remainder to individuals, on bond and mortgage. Mr. Seward denounced the measure in an admirable speech,* delivered on the 10th of April, 1834. The design of the bill was to operate favorably for the administration at the ensuing fall election. This resulted in the re-election of Gov. Marcy; no stock was issued, and the measure, having accomplished its purpose, passed into oblivion.

The last speech of Mr. Seward in the senate related to the chartered rights of the city of Albany. It was a temperate and logical performance, but failed to prevent the passage of a law, which in his view, was a violation of the rights of the city. At the close of the session, he was for the third time designated to draw up the usual address† of the minority of the legislature to the people of the state.

* See Vol. I., p 37. † See Vol. III., p. 349.

The two great parties on national and state questions were now fully organized. A general trial of strength was to be made in the approaching election. The result of this struggle would indicate the probable issue of the presidential election which was to take place in 1836. The address, accordingly, went into a thorough exposition and defence of the whig policy, and with this document, were concluded the services of Mr. Seward in the legislature of New York.

The court of errors, which was the court of final appeal in New York, from 1775 to 1846, was an institution copied from the English house of lords. It consisted of the chancellor, the judges of the supreme court, and the members of the senate. In the case of appeals from chancery, the chancellor gave his reasons for the decree he had made, but did not vote. In acting on judgments of the supreme court, the judges explained the grounds of their decision, but did not vote. Mr. Seward, although at that time the youngest member of the court, took a leading part in its proceedings. His course was distinguished for its independence, although he never forgot the courtesy due to his seniors. With remarkable power of analysis and accuracy of research, he made himself master of every case, that was presented for decision. An opinion pronounced by him in the case of Parks *vs.* Jackson affords an illustration of his character as a judge. In that case,* a technical rule had been applied by the supreme court, in such a manner as to deprive tenants of valuable estates for which they had contracted and paid in good faith. The reasons for this decision were assigned by Mr. Justice Nelson, of the supreme court, afterward chief justice, and now a judge of the United States supreme court. Chancellor Walworth followed in an opinion, in which he defended the judgment of the supreme court. Mr. Seward then arose and delivered an adverse opinion, and on the question being taken on reversing the judgment, all the members of the court, with the

* Wendell's Reports, Vol. XI., p. 456.

exception of the chancellor, voted in the affirmative. This seems to have been a case where the technicalities of the law came in conflict with justice. Mr. Seward, prompted by a noble sentiment of right, vindicated the claims of justice, against the arbitrary rules of law, carrying the whole court with him, in spite of their previous intentions.

On the 16th of July, 1834, Mr. Seward delivered a eulogy* on the life and character of Lafayette, before the citizens of Auburn. This was a chaste and beautiful production. It presented an admirable analysis of the character of Lafayette, with a discriminating review of the principles of the American Revolution, and of the successive phases of French politics from the death of Louis XVI. An account of a recent personal conversation between Mr. Seward and Lafayette, added greatly to the interest of the discourse.

CHAPTER VIII.

CANDIDATE FOR GOVERNOR—DEFEAT—AGENT OF HOLLAND LAND COMPANY—EDUCATION—INTERNAL IMPROVEMENTS—THE NEW YORK AND ERIE RAILROAD—CANDIDATE FOR GOVERNOR—ELECTION.

As the autumn of 1834 approached, when the election of governor was to be made by the people, the whig party were in anxious search of a suitable candidate for the important crisis. They were not wanting in men, whose political experience, distinguished ability, and brilliant reputation, eminently qualified them for the office. Of these, some had already been candidates and had suffered defeat. Others lacked the elements of popularity that were essential to success. The general impression of the party favored the selection of a new man. The younger portion of

* See Vol. III., p. 25.

the whigs were earnestly desirous that the candidate should be taken from their ranks. Mr. Seward's distinguished senatorial career had made him prominent before the party and the state. His bold attacks on the policy of the administration had won the gratitude and the admiration of the whigs. It was mainly through his efforts, that the party had been organized, and no one was better fitted than himself to take the position of their acknowledged leader.

Accordingly, at the whig state convention held in Utica, September 13, 1834, Mr. Seward was nominated as a candidate for governor. The election came, and he was defeated. The result showed that the whig party had not been able to put forth its full strength. It had not yet gained confidence in its own power to cope with a party that had never been overthrown, and was sustained by the monetary influence of the state and the vast patronage of the national government. Mr. Seward received a flattering vote, and led his ticket in all the counties, but Governor Marcy was re-elected by a majority of about ten thousand.

Mr. Seward, having escaped the claims of public life, resumed the practice of his profession at the commencement of the year 1835. Nor did he lose his interest in the great political questions of the day. He still labored, with unshrinking fidelity, in support of the party to which he was attached, and of which, by a large proportion, he was regarded as the head.

On the 3d of October, 1835, he delivered an address* at Auburn on Education and Internal Improvements. This production was remarkable for its anticipations of the progress of the state, and its lucid exposition of the principles of government, which he afterward carried into effect, during his administration as chief magistrate.

In July, 1836, Mr. Seward established himself in Westfield, Chautauque county, for the purpose of assuming an agency to quiet the troubles between the landlords and ten-

* See Vol. III., p. 128.

ants of the Holland company. Serious difficulties had arisen among the settlers on the tract of the company, and the services of Mr. Seward seemed important for the restoration of tranquillity. A change of scene also it was hoped, would prove favorable to his health, which had become impaired by his assiduous professional labors. The manner in which he conducted this agency subjected him to much reproach in a subsequent political canvass. But of this we shall have occasion to treat in another place.*

The election for governor in 1836 resulted in favor of Mr. Marcy, who received a majority of nearly 40,000 votes over the whig candidate, Mr. Jesse Buel. Meantime, Mr. Seward continued his agency, and his professional toil, with extraordinary success. His growing fame produced no abatement of his industry, and he devoted himself to the interests of his clients with the same earnestness and zeal which he had exhibited in his political efforts on the floor of the senate. During this period he prepared several essays, which display genuine literary merit, no less than a spirit of enlarged and comprehensive statesmanship.

Mr. Seward received an invitation to deliver a discourse on Education† at Westfield in July, 1837. He accepted the service, which he performed with signal ability. The discourse was a clear and eloquent defence of the principle of universal education. It maintained the duty of giving public instruction to all classes of the people, irrespective of condition or circumstances. In regard to the education of females, it claimed for woman the highest standard of literary attainment, challenging for her the same intellectual advantages that were enjoyed by the other sex.

At a meeting of the whigs of Cayuga county, October 11, 1837, Mr. Seward delivered a speech of masterly ability. The state of the country called forth his most vigorous eloquence. The commercial revulsion, which he had so long

* See Letters to the citizens of Chautauque county., Vol. III.

† See Vol. III., p. 136.

predicted, was sweeping over the land. Disastrous experience gave ample confirmation to the principles of the whigs. In his speech on this occasion, Mr. Seward earnestly appealed to the people to redress their wrongs at the ballot-box. This was only one of many efforts during the canvass. He was indefatigable in his exertions, which were now crowned with the most brilliant success. The election resulted in the total overthrow of the Albany regency. The whigs gained a triumphant victory throughout the state, electing six out of eight new senators, and one hundred of the one hundred and twenty-eight members of the assembly.

The New York and Erie railroad was originally undertaken by a company chartered while Mr. Seward was a member of the senate. He voted against the charter, not through hostility to the construction of the road, but on the ground that so great an enterprise could not be effected by a corporation, and that the road when completed should pass into the hands of the state, like the Erie canal, for the public benefit. His vote being misrepresented in the election of 1834, he corrected the error in a letter to a committee,* declaring himself unreservedly in favor of that great work. As he had predicted, the enterprise languished until 1837, when it was abandoned by the regency and its party in the legislature. It was still sustained by the whig majority in the assembly, whose policy, however, was rejected by a regency senate.

A convention of the friends of the railroad was held at Elmira on the 17th of October, 1837, at which Mr. Seward was present. He was the first citizen, living in a portion of the state not immediately interested in the enterprise, who gave it his personal support. At the request of the convention, he prepared an address† on the subject to the people of the state of New York, in which he gave a brief history of the road, and urged the adoption of efficient measures for its speedy completion. He placed the resump-

* See Vol. III., p. 417. † See Vol. III., p. 306.

tion of the work on the same broad principles of policy which pervaded his subsequent administration. On the strength of such reasonings, the whig party throughout the state gradually yielded their aid to the project, and at length rejoiced in the completion of the truly magnificent structure.

At the whig state convention in 1838, the names of William H. Seward and Luther Bradish were presented to the electors of the state for governor and lieutenant-governor. The previous defeat of Mr. Seward had not in the least degree weakened the confidence of his friends. They knew that it was not owing to personal causes, but to the position of parties; and hence were anxious again to present his claims for the suffrages of the people. Great importance was attached to the election by both political parties, on account of its bearing on the presidential campaign of 1840. The canvass labored under peculiar difficulties. During a season of great pecuniary embarrassment, Mr. Seward had conducted the affairs of the Holland Land Company to the eve of a prosperous close. His agency in Chautauque county had been managed with discretion and kindness; but it did not fail to be used by his political opponents as an instrument of reproach. Hoping to alienate the whigs from their favorite candidate, they charged him with fraud, injustice, and oppression, in his treatment of the settlers, averring that he had employed his official power in the agency for his own private emolument, and the benefit of land speculators. Mr. Seward was silent in regard to these calumnies, until they had awakened a painful anxiety toward the close of the canvass. He then published his letter to the citizens of Chautauque county,* which, by its clear and cogent statements, put an effectual stop to the slanders that were in circulation and gave him popular strength never enjoyed before.

The slavery question was another perplexing element in

* See Vol. III., p. 457.

this canvass. The yet distant prospect of the annexation of Texas was viewed with alarm by the friends of liberty at the north. It renewed the discussion of slavery, which had not entered into political movements since the Missouri compromise in 1820. A portion of the citizens of New York, headed by William Jay and Gerrit Smith, had addressed letters to the several candidates for office, intended to draw out their views on the subject of slavery. The mass of all parties at that time regarded this course of action with profound disgust. The candidates of the regency party did not hesitate to give a negative answer to the questions that had been propounded. The whigs were thought to be placed in an inconvenient dilemma. Mr. Seward's answer* was at once frank and sagacious. While he expressed without reserve his devotion to human freedom, he limited his aims by a regard to prevailing opinions, and a sense of what was practicable in the attainment of right. His reply did not compromise his popularity, as had been hoped by his opponents.

The election was warmly contested. With the regency the struggle was for life or death. No measures were neglected on their part to defeat the candidates of the whigs. Every species of objection was urged against Mr. Seward. The gravest and the most trivial charges were alike brought to bear on the canvass. Among other things he was accused of the "atrocious crime" of being a young man, as he was but thirty-three when first nominated for governor, and at this time but thirty-seven. The election took place in November, and in spite of unexpected disasters to the whig cause in all other states, the "young man" was triumphantly elected. Mr. Seward's majority reached to 10,421. The whig party carried the state in every department, and secured a complete ascendency of political power.

* See Vol. III., p. 426.

CHAPTER IX.

GOVERNOR — CIRCUMSTANCES — MEASURES — SCHOOLS — CATHOLICS — NATIVE-AMERICANS — FOREIGNERS — LAW REFORM — DECENTRALIZATION — BANKING — IMPRISONMENT FOR DEBT

MR. SEWARD was the first whig governor of New York. With the exception of De Witt Clinton, he was the only one who had ever been elected in opposition to the Albany regency. The party which had virtually dictated the pol icy of the state for nearly fifty years was thus effectually destroyed, and a new development of principles was to be realized under the administration of William H. Seward.

In entering upon the executive office, Gov. Seward was surrounded with peculiar difficulties. The business of the country had been prostrated by the revulsions of 1836. His political friends looked with confidence to his administration for the financial relief of the public. The whigs, moreover, were in power for the first time. Numerous and excited applicants eagerly pressed their claims for office. In this crisis, Gov. Seward conducted with great moderation and impartiality. Cautious in making promises, he rejected no application without substantial reasons, which he never took pains to conceal. His frankness in rendering all necessary explanations to a disappointed candidate was equal to the wise reserve with which he abstained from giving undue encouragement.* In this judicious course, however, he did not avoid offence. Applicants were more numerous than offices. Of course, some must be disappointed. And of these, some rallied around rival statesmen. Gov. Seward thus incurred the opposition of several

* See Official Correspondence, Vol. II., p. 589.

prominent members of the whig party, who, naturally enough, adopted principles different from his own.

Nor did his election bring the political contest in the state of New York to a close. An important battle had been won, but the campaign was not completed. Never did party zeal run to a greater height than during the period of his administration. In describing his official career, we shall do little more than indicate the principles by which it was inspired, as delivered in his messages and other executive papers.

Among the measures to which the attention of Gov. Seward was early directed, was the completion of a lunatic asylum, and the adoption of a judicious and humane system for the treatment of the insane. Before his retirement from office, his suggestions in this behalf were carried into successful operation. Frequently visiting this and other charities of the state, he recommended them to the patronage of the legislature, as well by his example as his counsels.

In the exercise of the pardoning power, Gov. Seward exercised, we think, a greater degree of wisdom than most of his predecessors. At the same time he labored for the introduction of milder forms of punishment in the penitentiaries, substituting moral discipline for the lash. These reforms were afterward adopted by the legislature.

The interests of agriculture always received the fostering care of Gov. Seward. He was anxious for the establishment of an agricultural department in the state, with a view to the especial promotion of that important source of public prosperity. His efforts for that measure, however, were not seconded by the legislature, and have remained to this day without direct fruit.

Upon the accession of Gov. Seward to office, the system of normal schools, in connection with academies and common-school libraries, had been partially established. These measures received his cordial and efficient support. At his suggestion, a system of visitation and inspection of common schools was adopted by the legislature, although it has failed to be carried into full effect, much to the detriment of the cause of popular education.

In his messages, Gov. Seward took the ground that the welfare of the state demanded the education of all its children,* not as a matter of charity, but of justice and public safety. The defects in the public schools of New York city led him to recommend a modification of the system, and the ultimate substitution of the plan which prevailed in the rest of the state. A prejudice, partaking of both a national and religious character, had come down from the colonial period against foreigners, and especially against catholics. It was this class of the population that would be most directly benefited by the change in the city schools. It was proposed to admit catholic teachers with the same facilities as others. An alarm was at once raised throughout the state. The protestant cause was declared to be in danger, from the undue ascendency of the catholics. Religious bigotry was thus excited. The hostility of both protestant clergy and laity was arrayed against the governor. He was labelled in effigy in New York. The press teemed with abuse of his person and measures. Meantime his political opponents, who had always professed to be more friendly to foreigners and catholics than the whigs, did not fail to take advantage of the popular jealousy for the promotion of their views. The whigs, on the other hand, who were accustomed to contend with naturalized foreigners at the polls, were unwilling to accord them any privileges. Between the two parties, Gov. Seward was obliged to maintain the contemplated reform on its own merits. His influence was greatly impaired by the general impression that the measures in question were not only untenable in themselves, but that they had their origin in sinister political purposes. This impression, however, was

* See Ann. Messages, Vol. II., pp. 206, 216, 278; also page 212 of this vol.

wholly unfounded, and did great injustice to Gov. Seward. His efforts in behalf of the children of catholics sprang from a deep conviction of the importance of education to all men, without regard to condition or circumstances.* During his travels in Ireland in 1833, he saw the effect of British policy in depriving the catholic population of the means of instruction. The people, thus kept in abject ignorance, were more easily made the victims of oppression and tyranny, and more liable to become seditious and treasonable. This spectacle produced a strong impression on his mind. He became anxious that the catholics in America should be put in possession of the advantages of education, and so be assimilated to the native population.†

The controversy on the school question continued throughout the whole of Gov. Seward's administration. It affected his popularity so much as to deprive him of about two thousand votes on his re-election. The result, however, has shown his far-reaching sagacity. Like many other measures proposed by Gov. Seward, this was in advance of public opinion, but has since commended itself to the good sense of the people. At the first session of the legislature, after his retirement from office, his plan for the education of all classes of children, not excluding those of foreigners and catholics, was adopted by decisive majorities. No doubt has since arisen as to the utility of the measure, except on the part of those whose religious scruples had led them to decline a participation in its advantages.

His attention was first called to this question by the fact, that the annual school returns from New York showed that there were about twenty-five thousand children in that city who did not attend school, and were thus left exposed to the allurements of vice and crime.

* See General Correspondence. Letters to Bishop Hughes and others, Vol. III.

† See Letters from Europe, Vol. III.

Along with these efforts of Gov. Seward in behalf of educational reform, he was also actively engaged in the removal of the prejudices between native Americans and adopted citizens. His recommendations to successive legislatures for abolishing the legal disabilities under which foreigners labored were, with more or less reluctance, ultimately adopted.*

The city of New York was at that time just beginning to be crowded with immigrants, who poured into the country from foreign lands. Overtaken by poverty and disease, they served to fill the almshouses and the prisons. Their overflowing numbers increased the amount both of wretchedness and of crime. In order to lessen the evil, a tax upon immigrants was recommended by the mayor of New York. The proposal met with general favor. Under these circumstances, the public was astounded by the suggestions of Gov. Seward for the encouragement of immigration. He maintained that the surplus labor of foreign lands should be employed to advantage in developing the natural resources of this country. Instead of shutting our doors upon the down-trodden immigrant, he insisted that we should welcome him to a share in our industry and citizenship. This generous and humane policy, however, was vehemently condemned. It subjected its author to great reproach. Still, as in the case of the school reform, his measures were finally adopted by the state. In 1847 they were made the subject of discussion in the legislature, and, having passed that body, have since been a part of the established policy of New York.

The courts of law and of chancery in the state of New York had, from time immemorial, been subject to a variety of expensive delays. Organized on the model of the English system, the higher courts consisted of judges, a chancellor, and a vice-chancellor, appointed by the governor and senate, and holding office until sixty years of age. In

* See Annual Messages, Vol. II.

the common-pleas the judges were appointed for five years by the same power. The legal practice was marked by all the prolixity, technicalities, and superfluous expense of the English courts. The judiciary and the banking powers were combined with overpowering and overshadowing influences by the Albany regency. Gov. Seward exerted all his influence in favor of reform. He was opposed by both the bar and the judiciary. In opposition to their combined efforts, he secured the passage of bills in the legislature for reducing the expenses, and simplifying the practice in all the courts of the state. Nor did he stop with this measure for the relief of the public. He urged a complete reform in the constitution of the courts. His plan involved the abolition of the court of chancery, and a new organization of the supreme courts and the common pleas. The legislature did not receive his suggestions with favor; but they did not fail to exert a salutary influence on the public mind. No one can doubt that they prepared the way for the radical change in the constitution effected in 1846. Under this arrangement, the court of chancery, after an existence of over one hundred and fifty years, was abolished, and all judicial offices made elective by the people.

It was the desire of Governor Seward from the commencement of his official career, to effect the decentralization of the political power in the state. By the existing laws, the judges of common pleas were associated in the respective counties with the board of supervisors in the appointment of commissioners of deeds, superintendents of the poor, and other county officers. The boards of supervisors were usually divided in politics, and hence the appointments were in fact decided by the central power at Albany, from which the judges received their offices. At the recommendation of Governor Seward the appointing power was withdrawn from the judges, and the election of most of these offices given to the people. His efforts for reducing the emoluments of several favorites in public office were partially sanctioned by the legislature. But his recommendation to abolish the offices of inspector of various branches of produce and manufacture was not adopted until after the close of his administration.

The safety-fund system, of which Governor Seward had always been a decided opponent, exploded in 1837. A general banking law, passed by the whig assembly of 1838, gave the liberty of banking to any voluntary association of citizens. The new system, however, was at first defective in its details. Many of the banks under this organization failed, producing a loss to the bill-holders. During Governor Seward's administration, the law was revised, and with successive improvements, has become the settled policy of the state, and has also been adopted by several other states of the Union.

A warm discussion arose during this period, in regard to the minimum denomination of bank paper to be used as a circulating medium. In accordance with the views of General Jackson, bills under five dollars were prohibited by the legislature of 1837. The senate of 1838 refused to repeal this law. At the recommendation of Governor Seward in 1839, the act was repealed by the whig legislature and no attempt has been made to restore it since.

The geological survey of the state, which had been commenced pursuant to an act of the legislature in 1836, was brought to a completion, under the auspices of Governor Seward. At his suggestion, the legislature appropriated funds from time to time for its prosecution, and established a depository for the preservation of specimens illustrative of the natural history of the state. This, he recommended should be made the foundation for a system of popular instruction in the natural sciences, with a view to the improvement of agriculture. The spirit of his suggestion has been carried into effect by the state agricultural society, in its system of popular lectures and discussions which are held in the Geological museum at Albany.

The results of the geological survey were embodied in a series of quarto volumes, which ultimately reached the number of thirteen. Governor Seward prepared an elaborate introduction to the work, consisting of a review of the settlement, progress, and condition of the state of New York, somewhat on the plan of Mr. Jefferson's "Notes on Virginia." This historical essay is written in a style of admirable clearness and fluency, abounding in recondite and valuable information, and pervaded by an elevated tone of patriotism and humanity. It appears in the Works of Mr. Seward under the title of "Notes on New York."*

The abolition of imprisonment for debt, effected in 1832, did not reach the class of non-resident debtors, or those held by process issuing from the United States courts. Governor Seward was opposed, both from feeling and principle, to depriving unfortunate debtors of their liberty and of the opportunity to provide for their families. He had not been long in the executive office, when he procured the passage of laws, which swept away these relics of barbarism from the jurisprudence of the state.

* See Vol. II., p. 9 to 180.

CHAPTER X.

GOVERNOR, CONTINUED — ANTI-RENT TROUBLES — ELECTIONS — REGISTRY ACT — CANADIAN DISTURBANCES — THE M'LEOD CASE — EXCITEMENT.

In general, the laws of the state were faithfully executed during Governor Seward's administration. There was, however, an exception. In the counties of Albany and Rensselaer, was a tract of land, fifty miles square, lying on both sides of the Hudson river, which was claimed to have been granted by the Dutch government, at an early day to the Van Rensselaer family, and which was originally denominated the manor of "Rensselaerwyck." The lands on this tract had not been granted in fee to settlers, as elsewhere, but had been farmed out on perpetual leases, securing annuities to the proprietor (denominated the *Patroon*), payable in kind and in labor, and containing covenants, raising charges upon alienation. The late patroon, Hon. Stephen Van Rensselaer, had allowed numerous arrearages of rent to remain uncollected for many years. At his decease, his heirs demanded payment of these arrearages. The tenants refused to comply. Differences growing out of these matters, which extended back through a period of near fifty years, ripened, in 1839, into discontents, popular outbreaks, and open resistance of the laws. Refusing to tamper with such violent proceedings for a moment, Governor Seward issued his proclamation,* calling upon the discontented to reflect upon the nature and consequences of their unlawful acts, and apply to the legislature for redress of their grievances, pledging himself to grant them

* See Vol. II., p. 352.

every aid in his power, in bringing their complaints before that body. This proclamation was accompanied by the organization and despatch of a military force, which, acting under the authority of the sheriff, attended him until he had executed the legal processes in his hands, including those against the individuals who had resisted the laws.

In announcing these measures to the legislature in his annual message, in 1840,* Governor Seward discussed the nature of the tenures out of which the disturbances had arisen, and recommended that efforts should be made for the removal of the difficulty which threatened to be lasting and serious in its consequences. He urged a compromise of the conflicting claims of landlord and tenant, with their consent, and without injustice to either party. The recommendation was adopted, and Hugh Maxwell and Gary V. Sackett, Esqs., were appointed commissioners to effect, if possible, a satisfactory adjustment. After examining the subject, and hearing all the parties, the commissioners decided on the basis of an adjustment, which they recommended for the adoption of the litigants. The tenants assented. But the landlord, under mistaken advice, refused the proffered terms, and insisted on the rights secured in his leases. So the settlement failed.

During the residue of Governor Seward's administration, the laws were executed throughout the discontented regions, as in the other parts of the state. But the controversy between the proprietors of the Rensselaer manor and the tenants, still continued, and has not been settled to the present time. Loud complaints were made against the governor for what was alleged to be an unjust concession to the claims of the tenants, in treating the restraints on alienation and other features in these cases, as illegal and inexpedient. Since Governor Seward's retirement from the executive office, armed resistance has been more than once renewed, and a ruinous litigation has never been sus-

* See Vol. II., p. 219

pended. The court of appeals has recently vindicated the views of Governor Seward, by declaring the restraints upon alienation, illegal and void.

This affair furnishes another instance of Governor Seward's clear forecast and sound wisdom, in the adoption of measures for the removal of existing evils. For the time being, owing to a want of equally enlarged views, his recommendations have been discarded. But time vindicates their soundness. In the present case, after the subject had been litigated, discussed, and argued for years, before legislatures and courts, the decision was finally made in conformity with the views he had originally urged upon the parties interested.

In his earlier years, Governor Seward, as we have seen, devoted considerable attention to military affairs. During his administration, he labored for the accomplishment of certain reforms in the militia system, which he had urged while a member of the senate. Its unequal operation was regarded by him as an infringement of personal rights, and a great public evil. He endeavored to relieve the members of the society of Friends, and other persons who declined performing military duty from religious scruples. This measure was not adopted by the legislature. But he did not fail to use the pardoning power of the executive in behalf of those, who had incurred the penalty of the law, in obedience to their consciences. In this course, Governor Seward was true to the enlarged and liberal sentiments, which he had long cherished, in regard to religious freedom.* It was one of his strongest convictions, that no class of citizens should suffer from legal disabilities, on account of matters of conscience. Here, too, his views, at last, received the sanction of public opinion, and the changes in the militia system, which he had urged in his messages, became the policy of the state.

Previously to 1841, the elections in New York occupied

* See Miscellaneous Correspondence, Vol. III., p. 481.

three days — a single board of inspectors receiving all the votes in each town or ward. This arrangement occasioned numerous inconveniences. In the larger cities, especially, it gave rise to a system of frauds and combinations, impairing the purity of elections, and impeding the voter in the exercise of his political rights. Violent contests took place at the polls, which often resulted in the destruction of the ballot-box. Every one acknowledged and deplored the evil. It was not so easy, however, to discover the remedy. The whigs were in favor of an act of registration; but this was regarded by the opposite party as a scheme to deprive the poorer classes of the exercise of suffrage. As the support of both the great political parties of the day was essential to the success of the measure, the whigs modified their demands, limiting the call for a registry to the city of New York. Governor Seward could not give this course his approval. He was opposed to all partial, invidious legislation. Nor could he be convinced of the practicability of the measure, in the existing state of feeling. He accordingly dissuaded his friends from urging the passage of such an act. In its place, he recommended the division of towns and wards into election districts, each containing not more than five hundred voters, and the limitation of the time for holding elections to a single day. These suggestions were accepted by the whigs, who then formed a majority of the legislature. But under the influence of members from New York, they added a provision for a registry act in that city.

Governor Seward was thus again brought into collision with his political friends. He prepared a veto message,* presenting his objections to the feature of the bill establishing a registry. On consultation, however, with the whigs, it was found that even if the bill should not pass in spite of the veto, yet the party would be convulsed by the consequent excitement, and incur the hazard of yielding the control of the state to their political opponents. The governor

* See Vol. II., p. 379.

was thus induced to suppress the veto and approve the bill, frankly stating to the legislature his objections to the feature in question, and predicting its ultimate effect. An election was held under the new law, in the following autumn. The city of New York returned a democratic majority, induced by the new provision. The legislature at once repealed it by a unanimous vote. The other provisions of the law still remain in force.

The patriot disturbance in Canada which occurred in 1837, awakened deep interest among the people of the United States, who lived adjacent to the frontier. A military corps was organized to aid the Canadians in their struggle for independence. The federal government adopted stringent measures to enforce the neutrality laws. During these excitements an event took place which threatened serious embarrassment to the relations of the United States with Great Britain. On the night of December 29, 1837, an armed force from Canada crossed the Niagara river, attacked a party of American citizens, who were then asleep in the steamboat Caroline, lying in the river at Schlosser. One man was killed; the rest were driven ashore. Having cut out the steamboat, the invaders set her on fire, towed her into the current of the stream and sent her flaming over Niagara Falls. This outrage everywhere excited the deepest indignation. In the border counties especially, the people were almost in a frenzy of passion.

Three years after this occurrence, in the winter of 1840, a citizen of Canada, named Alexander M'Leod, while on a visit to Niagara county, was said to have boasted that he was an active member of the party which destroyed the Caroline. As he was known to be a warm loyalist, the assertion was readily believed. He was arrested on the charge of arson, and committed to jail. In due course of law he was subsequently indicted for that crime, and detained for trial. Upon this the British minister at Washington, Mr. Fox, made a reclamation on Mr. Van Buren, then president of the United States, in behalf of the prisoner. He insisted that the destruction of the Caroline was an act of war, for which the British government should be held responsible, and not a private individual. Hence he protested against the trial of M'Leod, and demanded his release from imprisonment. The president did not assent to the position of Mr. Fox; he maintained that the act was a violation of the jurisdiction of New York, and of the United States in time of peace. Even assuming the views of Mr. Fox to be correct, the matter belonged to the courts of New York for judicial examination, with which the federal government could not interfere.

The decision of Mr. Van Buren was immediately communicated to Governor Seward, while Mr. Fox, on the other hand, submitted the subject for instruction to his government at home. Governor Seward promptly and dispassionately replied to the president accepting his decision on the part of New York. This reply did not reach Washington until after the 4th of March, 1841, when the administration had passed into the hands of General Harrison. The affair was accordingly intrusted to Mr. Webster, the secretary of state under the new president.

Meantime Governor Seward had despatched the attorney-general of the state, Hon. Willis Hall, to Niagara, in order to ascertain the facts relative to the transaction. The result of the investigation convinced the governor that the evidence was insufficient to sustain the indictment, as it appeared that M'Leod was not even on the American side of the river during the night on which the Caroline was destroyed.

Mr. Fox was instructed by his government to insist on the positions which he had assumed. He accordingly demanded the surrender of M'Leod, menacing the president with hostilities in case of non-compliance. In reply to Mr. Fox, General Harrison conceded that M'Leod could not be held to trial for the alleged offence, thus confirming the views of the British government. This decision was communicated to Governor Seward, in a letter from the secretary of state, through Mr. Crittenden, the attorney-general of the United States, who announced the wish of the president that a *nolle prosequi* should be entered, and a stop put to further proceedings. Mr. Crittenden was despatched by the president to Niagara county, with directions to appear in court in behalf of M'Leod, and to urge upon Governor Seward the entering of a *nolle prosequi*. In conversing upon the subject, Mr. Crittenden informed Governor Seward, that Great Britain would declare war against the United States unless the surrender of M'Leod took place. It appeared, however, on further explanation, that the retaliation threatened by Great Britain was made contingent not on the detention, nor on the trial, nor even on the conviction of M'Leod, but on his *execution*. This view was sustained by the correspondence with Mr. Fox. Governor Seward then informed Mr. Crittenden of the course he should pursue. In the first place, it was not probable that M'Leod would be convicted, as there was no proof of his guilt—but if convicted, he could not be executed without the governor's consent; and inasmuch as both governments agreed that his conviction would be an infringement of international law, however he might differ from that opinion, he should feel bound to release the prisoner from his sentence. He added, moreover, that all the questions belonging to the case, must come under the cognizance of the state court, and therefore it was necessary for the trial to proceed. But this course involved no risk of compromising our relations with Great Britain, for the reasons already stated.

The trial, accordingly, was postponed. Mr. Crittenden returned to Washington to lay the views of Governor Seward before the president and his cabinet. It was understood that, if these views were not approved, the subject should receive further examination. But the sudden death of General Harrison, and the consequent dissolution of the cabinet, left the matter as it was.

Meantime, Joshua A. Spencer, Esq., who had been already retained as counsel for M'Leod, was appointed United States district attorney for the northern district of New York, although against the earnest remonstrances of Governor Seward. At the succeeding term of the supreme court, Mr. Spencer appeared with instructions from the president, and demanded M'Leod's discharge from the indictment, without the formality of a trial. The motion was resisted by Willis Hall, Esq., in behalf of the state, under the direction of the governor. After elaborate arguments on both sides, the demand for M'Leod's release was denied, sustaining the ground taken by President Van Buren and Governor Seward in opposition to the views of President Tyler.

In spite of the fact that war was suspended, not on the trial, but on the execution of M'Leod, the public mind was greatly excited by the fear of a collision with Great Britain. Governor Seward was reproached, in many political and commercial circles, with pursuing recklessly a course that tended to plunge the two nations in war. But this had no effect on his determination. He was convinced of the justice of his measures, and resolutely proceeded to carry them into effect.

At length the time for holding the court arrived. It was convened at Utica, remote from the immediate scene of excitement. On trial before a learned and impartial judge, M'Leod was acquitted, for want of evidence that he was concerned in the outrage. He was then sent into the British territory by Governor Seward, under an escort, and safely delivered on the north side of the Niagara river.

This critical transaction affords a fresh illustration of Governor Seward's firmness and sagacity. Had he listened to the advisers whose fears dictated to their judgment, and followed the cowardly policy of President Tyler, he would have disgraced both the state and the nation in the eyes of the world. But his bold and manly course sustained the honor of the country. The fortunate conclusion of the affair restored the public mind to tranquillity, and strengthened the administration of the state in the esteem of the people.*

CHAPTER XI.

GOVERNOR, CONTINUED — CANALS — ENLARGEMENT — FINANCIAL CRISIS — PANIC — SUSPENSION OF PUBLIC WORKS — RAILROADS.

THE Erie and Champlain canals were completed in 1825. This great enterprise of internal improvements had been brought to a prosperous completion by De Witt Clinton, against the strenuous opposition of the Albany regency. But even before these works were finished, it was seen that they could not attain the objects of their construction without the addition of lateral canals, connecting with the Susquehanna and other rivers on the south, and with Lake Ontario on the north. The Erie canal was but forty feet wide, and four feet deep. It was soon evident, that, instead of a canal of such limited capacity, a ship-canal was necessary to unite the navigation of the lakes with that of Hudson river. As early as 1835, it was found necessary to replace the locks and other structures of the Erie canal. At the same time, the state debt incurred in its construction, and that of the Champlain canal, had been virtually paid. Under these favorable circumstances, the legislature voted the enlargement of the Erie canal, on a scale to be fixed by the canal board. The scale adopted was seventy feet wide and seven feet deep, with double instead of single locks, as before used. But the act limited the expenditures for the enlargement to the annual surplus of the tolls after deducting a large amount for the general purposes of the state treasury.

* See Correspondence, Vol. II., pp. 547–586.

In 1836, the construction of the Genesee Valley and the Black River canals was decided on by the legislature. These works were intended as branches of the system of internal improvements which had previously been completed, including the Oswego, Seneca, and Cayuga and Crooked Lake and Chenango canals. A loan of three millions of dollars had been made, during the same year, to the New York and Erie Railroad Company, for the aid of their enterprise. The next year saw the progress of all these works, while the canal commissioners recommended a more vigorous prosecution of the enlargement of the Erie canal. The recommendation was urgently renewed by Governor Marcy and the canal commissioners in 1838. But the state was then suffering from a commercial revulsion. The comptroller, Mr. Flagg, indirectly opposed the recommendations, in a report insisting on the necessity of taxation for the support of the treasury. This report was answered by Hon. Samuel B. Ruggles, chairman of the committee of ways and means in the assembly, who showed that the increase of tolls on the canals would sustain a loan of thirty millions of dollars, reimbursing it in twenty years, or of forty millions of dollars, reimbursing it in twenty-eight years. In accordance with this estimate, the legislature, in 1838, made an appropriation of four millions of dollars for the prosecution of the enlargement, and authorized the loan of eight hundred thousand dollars on the credit of the state, in aid of the Central and other railroads.

Such was the condition of internal improvements in the state, when Mr. Seward entered upon the executive office on the first of January, 1839. The state debt was then eleven millions of dollars; but there were four millions of dollars in the treasury available for the public works, reducing the actual debt to about seven millions of dollars. Governor Seward vigorously followed up the legislative policy of 1838. He recommended that measures should be adopted to secure the enlargement of the Erie canal, and the completion of the lateral canals, before the year 1845.

The report of Mr. Flagg, the comptroller, who retired on the coming in of the whig administration, presented an alarming picture of debt, taxation, and bankruptcy, as the consequences of perseverance in the public works. Mr. Flagg was supported by the opposition party in the legislature and throughout the state, while Governor Seward was sustained by the whigs with great unanimity.

To increase the embarrassments of the whig administration, and to shake the public confidence in the ability of the state to complete the system in which it was engaged, it was now discovered that the canal commissioners who had recommended the new enterprises had made too low an estimate of their cost, which, instead of fifteen millions, three hundred and seventy-five thousand dollars, for the enlargement of the Erie and the construction of the Genesee Valley and the Black River canals, would amount to thirty millions, four hundred and forty-four thousand dollars.

The people were alarmed by this unexpected announcement. Oppressed by pecuniary difficulties in every department of business, the public was divided in opinion. The whigs maintained the wisdom and necessity of completing the public works in spite of the errors of the estimate. But the opposing party condemned the policy in very decided terms. They predicted an insupportable burden of taxation, and ultimate repudiation as its inevitable consequence. This was the great issue between the two parties during the whole of Governor Seward's administration.

A crisis at length came. The failure of Pennsylvania, Michigan, Illinois, Mississippi, Maryland, and other states which had largely engaged in schemes of internal improvement, produced in 1841 a general depreciation of American credit in Europe. The stocks of New York, which had been pledged abroad, were returned, glutting the market in our commercial cities. The capitalists became alarmed.

With a view to prevent a further decline in securities, they combined with the opposition party against the prosecution of the public works. Their measures were met by Governor Seward with decided resistance. In his messages to the legislature, he forcibly remonstrated against suspending the improvements already commenced. Maintaining that, in spite of the fall of public credit abroad, the true policy of the state was unchanged, he clearly set forth the evils that would ensue from the abandonment of the enterprise. But it was all in vain. Political managers took advantage of the prevailing panic to counteract the policy of the governor. The moneyed interest chimed in. His sagacious admonitions were unheeded, and the legislature, in 1842, put a stop to the progress of internal improvement. In his message, at the extra session of 1842, he thus alludes to the sudden and humiliating close of these prosperous and well-directed enterprises:—

"For the first time in the quarter of a century which has elapsed since the ground was broken for the Erie canal, a governor of the state of New York, in meeting the legislature, finds himself unable to announce the continued progress of improvement. The officers charged with the care of the public works have arrested all proceedings in the enlargement of the Erie canal and the construction of the auxiliary works. The New York and Erie railroad, with the exception of forty-six miles from the eastern termination, lies in unfinished fragments throughout the long line of southern counties stretching four hundred miles from the Walkill to Lake Erie. The Genesee Valley canal, excepting the portion between Dansville and Rochester, lies in hopeless abandonment. The Black River canal, which was more than two thirds completed during the last year, has been left wholly unavailable. As if this were not enough, two railroads, toward the construction of which the state had contributed half a million of dollars, and public-spirited citizens large sums in addition, have been brought to a forced sale, and sacrificed with almost total loss to the treasury, without yielding any indemnity to the stockholders, and without even securing a guaranty that the people would be permitted to enjoy the use of the improvements."

Such was the condition of affairs on the first of January, 1843, when Governor Seward resigned the administration of the state into the hands of his successor. A convention was called in 1846 to revise the constitution, containing a large democratic majority. It incorporated provisions in the constitution, prohibiting the enlargement of the public works, except under stringent, and, as it was thought at the time, impracticable conditions. Still the canals, exceeding the largest estimates of the late whig administration, furnished the means for a gradual prosecution of the contemplated improvements until 1850. The whigs being in power at that time, it was ascertained that the sum of nine millions of dollars would suffice to complete the public works on the original plan. It was also ascertained that this object could be accomplished without pledging the credit of the state, by a simple transfer of the surplus tolls of the canals for a short term of years. Daniel Webster, John C. Spencer, and other eminent jurists, to whom the question had been submitted, expressed the opinion that such a measure would be in accordance with the provisions of the constitution. After a vehement party struggle, the legislature of 1851 decided on its adoption. The adverse party brought the question before the state courts, which finally declared that the law was unconstitutional. Still, few can now doubt the wisdom of the policy maintained by Governor Seward.* It only remains to determine how the constitutional prohibitions of 1846, as expounded by the court of appeals, shall be modified so as to allow the speedy attainment of the great object.†

The agency of Governor Seward in behalf of internal im-

* See Vol. II., pp. 183–212.

† Since the above was written, Governor Seward's views have been signally vindicated by the legislature and the people, and his policy re-established. By an amendment of the constitution, the proposed enlargement is to be speedily accomplished, the legislature of 1854 having passed the amendment by an almost unanimous vote. In the senate the ayes were twenty-nine, and the nays none; absent three. In the assembly there were one hundred and fifteen ayes, and one nay; absent twelve. The voice of the people, sanctioning the act of the legislature, was no less emphatic. The amendment, having been submitted to the people at a special election, was confirmed by the following vote: for the amendment, 185,802; against the amendment, 60,556.

provements was by no means limited to the canal system. Upon his accession to the executive office, railroads were a recent invention. They had been adopted only to a comparatively small extent in any part of the United States. They still met with a strenuous opposition from many of the leading New York politicians. The only railroads in the state were the Harlem, eight miles in length, and the Albany and Utica, ninety-five miles in length. Great efforts had been made to extend the latter road from Utica toward the west; but popular prejudice and pecuniary embarrassment were too strong for the corporations. The construction of the New York and Erie railroad had been abandoned; but Governor Seward from the first was an earnest advocate of the improvement. With almost prophetic sagacity, he constantly predicted the success of this new mode of locomotion. His zeal in its behalf excited alarm in the conservative, commercial, and political circles.

In his annual message in 1839,* he expressed himself in the following words:—

"This wonderful agent [steam] has achieved, almost unobserved, a new triumph, which is destined to effect incalculable results in the social system. This is its application to locomotion upon the land. Time and money are convertible. Husbandry of the one is economy of the other, and either is equivalent to the economy of labor. Railroads effect a saving of time and money; and, notwithstanding all the incredulity and opposition they encounter, they will henceforth be among the common auxiliaries of enterprise. Happily it is not in our power to fetter the energies of other states, although we may repress our own. This useful invention, like all others, will be adopted by them, although it gain no favor from us; and they who are willing that New York shall have no railroads, must be ready to see all the streams of prosperity seek other channels, and our state sink into the condition of Venice, prostrate and powerless, among the monuments of her earlier greatness. A glance at the map would render obvious the utility of three great lines of communication, by railroads, between the Hudson river and the borders of the state. One of these would traverse several of the northern counties, and reach with its branches to Lake Ontario and the St. Lawrence. A second, keeping the vicinity of the Erie canal, would connect Albany and Buffalo. A third would stretch through the southern counties, from New York to Lake Erie."

* See Vol. II., p. 183.

These confident predictions have since become magnificent realities. In his messages and speeches, Governor Seward also urged the construction of a railroad on the banks of the Hudson, from New York to Albany. Indeed, they often manifest not a little impatience with the skepticism and want of public spirit which discouraged the undertaking of such an important enterprise.

In a speech delivered at Elmira in 1850, on the completion of the New York and Erie railroad, Governor Seward related some curious personal reminiscences, in regard to the progress of internal improvements. The *chef d'œuvre* of his college life, he remarked, was an essay prepared in 1820 against the Erie canal, then in course of construction under the auspices of De Witt Clinton. He attempted to prove that the canal could never be completed—or, if completed, that it would be the ruin of the state. In five years from that time the canal was finished, and boats placed on its surface, from tide-water to Lake Erie. Just nineteen years after the production of that essay, he found himself in the place of De Witt Clinton, urging the enlargement of the canal to double its original capacity, and the construction of three lines of railroad, between substantially the same *termini*, to supply the deficiency of the canal for transporting the commerce of the state. These recommendations were regarded by the public as even still more visionary than the schemes of Governor Clinton had been in his estimation. But, notwithstanding the popular incredulity, on retiring from office at the end of four years, he had the satisfaction of seeing the aggregate length of the railroads of the state increased from one hundred to eight hundred miles.*

Nor has the devotion of Governor Seward to the cause

* The directors of the New York and Erie railroad company, in token of their appreciation of Governor Seward's services, presented him with a formal vote of thanks on his retirement from office, with a ticket elegantly engraved on silver for the free passage of himself and family on the road during life.

of internal improvements been confined in its operation to the state of New York. He has never failed to cherish a deep interest in whatever was adapted to increase the business advantages, and promote the permanent welfare of the people in every portion of the Union.

In a recent speech in the senate, while advocating a railroad to the Pacific ocean, he thus reviews the progress already made in internal improvements:—

"What are two thousand miles of railroad for the people of the United States to make, who, within eighteen years past, have made twelve thousand miles! The railroads which have been made in the state of New York alone have an aggregate length of two thousand three hundred and one miles, exceeding the distance from Lake Erie to the Pacific ocean. And if you add the canals, the chain would reach from the banks of the Hudson river to the shores of the Pacific ocean. The railroads already made in the United States, if drawn out into one lengthened chain, would reach from Liverpool to Canton. The railroads which have been made, and are now being made, in the United States, if stretched continuously along, would more than encircle the globe. Again, I shall be told of the cost of this railroad. And what will be its cost? One hundred millions of dollars. A cost not exceeding the revenue of the government of the United States for two years only—a cost not exceeding the revenue of the federal and state governments for one year. One hundred millions of dollars; why, we have offered that sum for one island in the Caribbean sea! One hundred millions of dollars; why, New York city spent one sixth of that sum in supplying itself with water, and grew all the while! One hundred millions of dollars; the state of New York has already spent, in making canals and railroads, one hundred and thirteen millions, and prospered while spending it as never state or nation prospered before. That one hundred millions of dollars, if it should never be directly reimbursed, will be indirectly replaced within ten years, by the economy which it would enable us to practise in the transportation of the army, and of the supplies of the army and navy over it, not to speak of the still more important benefits of bringing the public domain into cultivation, and into increased value, and developing rapidly the mineral wealth of California, which can be only imperfectly realized now, because labor on that side of the continent is worth four dollars a-day, while it is worth but one here.

As we write these lines (1854), we see the whole stupendous scheme recommended by Governor Seward on the eve of completion, in spite of commercial and political obstacles.

CHAPTER XII.

GOVERNOR, CONTINUED—THE PARDONING POWER—BENJAMIN RATHBUN—JOHN C. COLT—VETO POWER—D'HAUTEVILLE CASE—THURLOW WEED—REGISTRY ACT.

We have already alluded to the exercise of the pardoning power by Governor Seward. As the subject is one of such deep interest, we will here more fully illustrate the principles which guided his course in this respect.* Combining a natural generosity and tenderness of feeling with a lofty sense of justice, he could not permit his sympathy with the unfortunate to weaken his energy in the execution of laws, which were intimately connected with the order and safety of society. He allowed no conviction, ascertained to be unjust, to stand on any pretence.

An insane man who had committed homicide in Rensselaer county, under circumstances of revolting cruelty, was induced by the court, the public prosecutor, and his own counsel, to plead guilty to an indictment for murder. He was sentenced to be executed, under an arrangement between them, that, in consequence of thus pleading, the sentence of death should be commuted to confinement in the stateprison for life. The court and counsel urged the governor to adopt that course, on the ground that the public safety and public opinion both required the confinement of the offender. The governor answered that a man too insane to be executed was too insane to be imprisoned for life, and discharged the offender at once.

No woman, not abandoned to vice and crime, was suffered to endure the full punishment prescribed by the law.

* See Vol. II., p. 615.

And it must be a pleasant recollection to Governor Seward, that in no instance was a woman so pardoned ever after ward convicted of crime. Juvenile delinquents were pardoned for first offences not very atrocious. But, in these cases, preliminary arrangements were made through the agency of their friends, for their removal from the scenes of their temptations, and their establishment in pursuits favorable to their reformation.

The possession of social advantages, instead of aiding offenders to procure pardon, was always regarded as an objection. On the other hand, great allowance was made for ignorance, orphanage, or social neglect, as presenting incentives to crime.

In the well-known case of Benjamin Rathbun,* whose forgeries were understood to have amounted to the sum of one million five hundred thousand dollars, pardon was earnestly demanded on the ground of extenuating circumstances, and the social position of the criminal. His case was warmly pressed. Petitions for a commutation of punishment were signed by more than ten thousand persons, of all parties and ranks. But, closing his eyes to every consideration but the claims of justice and the integrity of the law, and believing their vindication, in such a case, to be highly important, Governor Seward steadfastly refused all entreaties to extend pardon, although urged by strong political and personal friends. At the same time, pardons were granted to ignorant and obscure persons who had committed forgeries and larcenies for trivial amounts, under the excuse of absolute want, in their own case, or that of their families. The discrimination against John C. Colt,† whose case excited deep interest at the time, proceeded upon similar grounds.

Nor did Governor Seward allow the pardoning power in his hands, to become converted to purposes of oppression. It is gratifying to know, that while the popular approbation

* See Vol. II., p. 630. † See Vol. II., p. 646.

of his administration in other respects, owing generally to political rancor, was delayed until the prejudices and passions of the day had subsided, no such delay occurred in regard to his conduct in the matter of pardons. His acts in this department of his duty, generally received immediate and wide-spread commendation. But what probably was esteemed by him as more important, was the approving testimony of his own mind. We can hardly conceive of a higher pleasure than he must have experienced in writing the following letter to Catharine Wilkins (a convict he had pardoned), unless it was surpassed by his satisfaction in learning how effectual the letter had been in saving her to whom it was addressed.

EXECUTIVE DEPARTMENT, *May* 1, 1839.

You have been convicted of Grand Larceny and have been adjudged to suffer imprisonment in the stateprison for three years. You were made known to benevolent individuals in this city by your crime and the consequent trial upon it. These gentlemen have made unsparing exertions to ascertain your real name and history and to call your distant friends to your aid. Those friends when informed of your unhappy situation have only answered that they were too humble to exercise any influence in your behalf and too poor even to visit you in your distress. Whatever willingness I might have had to interpose for your relief you must be aware that it has been accidental, if it is not rather to be regarded as providential, that those gentlemen were moved to solicit that interference. But you ought also to understand that executive interference was by no means to have been expected, even upon such solicitation as has prevailed in your behalf. Very many applications have been made to me for pardon after conviction and before the sentence was carried into execution. I have granted none under such circumstances where I was not satisfied that the conviction was unjust. Yours is a case of manifest and confessed guilt. You are pardoned. It is because you are young; because this is your first exposure to the law; because you are a woman and a stranger, and it may in charity be believed that your virtue would have resisted temptation had not want and seduction combined to effect your ruin. If confined to a stateprison your good name would be irretrievable and the associates to which you would be exposed would forbid all hope of reformation. I have thought it my duty to accompany the pardon now freely sent to you with my advice that you return as speedily as possible to your aged and afflicted mother: that you justify this extraordinary act of mercy by humble and persevering assiduity in domestic duties which is the only way to regain the respect and confidence of your friends and neighbors. If you will do this you will carry consolation to the hearts of your parents and I shall have the satisfaction of knowing that I have not done injustice to the public in yielding, for once, to the impulses of sympathy.

To Catharine Wilkins.

A gentleman who had interested himself in this case in passing through New Jersey, recently, found this young woman there enjoying the entire respect of the community. She drew the governor's letter from her bosom and said that its advice had saved her from ruin and that it had never been for one moment out of her immediate possession.

Governor Seward no doubt enjoyed a similar pleasure in the surprise exhibited by a slaveholder, who applied for the pardon of his slave, convicted of crime in New York, and sent to the stateprison at Sing-Sing. The master urged his petition on the ground that it would relieve the state of the expense of the slave's imprisonment; and he presented the record of a case where a slave had been thus pardoned by one of the governor's predecessors. Governor Seward answered that notwithstanding the precedent, he did not think it right to pervert a power intrusted to him for purposes of humanity, to accomplish an act of oppression.

The same independence of character was manifested in the case of James Watson Webb.* Colonel Webb had fought a duel with Hon. Thomas F. Marshall, in the state of Delaware, and was convicted under a law of this state, passed as early as 1817, and sentenced to the stateprison. There had been no attempt to enforce this law, except in two cases which occurred immediately after its passage, and in these instances, the offenders were pardoned by the governor who then filled the executive chair. Afterward the law became obsolete, for want of public opinion to sustain it. Duelling was still practised in the state of New York, notwithstanding this law was on the pages of the statute-book, and that too by men enjoying the highest distinctions and honors, including De Witt Clinton himself. It is easy

* See Vol. II., p 661.

to see that if the offender in the duel with Marshall, had been a political editor opposed to Governor Seward, the enforcing of the conviction under such circumstances, would have been regarded as an act of personal and political retaliation. No one can suppose he would have enforced it under such circumstances. But Colonel Webb, the offender in this case, was a personal and political friend of Governor Seward's, and his editorial controversies had made many relentless enemies. Colonel Webb having, like many others, made himself liable to the penalties of this law, probably without being aware of its existence, those enemies, unconscious, without doubt, of the motives which influenced them, demanded the rigorous application of the obsolete statute. The governor showed, in this instance, that he was not afraid to do in the case of a friend, what all men who knew his impartiality and magnanimity, would have expected him to do toward an adversary. He pardoned Colonel Webb. In the case of Rathbun, he would not pardon, because, among other principal reasons, the offender had moved in high circles and had powerful friends. In the case of Webb, he pardoned notwithstanding he occupied an elevated position and was surrounded by influential friends. In both instances he showed his coolness and courage in resisting popular clamor, when satisfied that justice demanded such resistance.

Governor Seward's principles in the exercise of the veto power, may be learned by reference to his messages* delivered on the several occasions when he assumed its exercise. The D'Hauteville case will serve as an illustration.

A lady of large wealth, a resident of Boston, while travelling in Europe, had married a French gentleman, by the name of D'Hauteville, of greater respectability than of fortune. One child was the fruit of this connection. She separated from her husband, and returned to America, in 1840, bringing her child with her. D'Hauteville appeared in Bos-

* See Vol. II., pp. 374, 379, 426, &c.

ton, and demanded her return to Europe, insisting, in case of refusal, on the custody of his child. The friends of the lady, designing that she should take refuge in the state of New York, procured a hurried passage of an act by the legislature of this state, then in session, providing that where an American woman should be married to a foreigner who should propose to require her, with his children, to remove to Europe, the court of chancery should have the power to interpose and take charge of the children and their fortune. A veto from Governor Seward arrested the passage of this bill,* upon the ground that no nation could wisely or justly make a discrimination in its laws regulating parental or other domestic relations, on the ground of the alienage of either of the parties—a decision the wisdom and soundness of which few can doubt.

With the return of an opposition to the legislature, came, of course, a desire for the benefits to be derived from the enjoyment of the state printing. An act was passed removing Thurlow Weed from the office of state printer, which he held, under a contract authorized by law. Governor Seward interposed his veto† promptly, on the ground of the inhibition, in the constitution of the United States, of the passage of laws by the states impairing the obligation of contracts.

But while he thus exercised the veto-power to arrest inconsiderate and unconstitutional legislation, he declined interfering in cases of pure legislative discretion, as has been seen in his action on the New York registry bill, and in his consent, against his own opinions, to the act of 1842, suspending the public works. In such cases, however, he insisted on the right of stating the grounds of his qualified approval of bills, in the message communicating the executive assent. It must be left to impartial public opinion, free from the bias of temporary excitement, to decide between him and the legislature, on their refusal to receive such messages and enter them on their journal.‡

* See Vol. II., p. 374. † See Vol. II., p. 426. ‡ See Vol. II., p. 411.

CHAPTER XIII.

GOVERNOR, CONTINUED—SLAVERY—FUGITIVES—JURY-TRIAL—VIRGINIA CONTROVERSY—COLORED VOTERS—KIDNAPPING—NORTHRUP CASE—ELECTION OF 1840—HENRY CLAY—POLITICAL AFFAIRS—RENOMINATION DECLINED.

IN his administration of the state government, Governor Seward took a firm and dignified attitude against the institution of slavery. He labored to clear the statute-books of every provision which authorized holding a man in slavery, in any form, or on any pretext. His devotion to the principles of freedom at length accomplished the work which had been so nobly commenced by the admirable statesman John Jay, in 1795. The law, which permitted a master, travelling through the state with his slaves, to retain them for the space of nine months, was repealed through his influence. It was this repeal by which the slaves in the recent Lemon case, who had been brought from Virginia to the city of New York, in order to be shipped to Texas, were saved from perpetual bondage.

Governor Seward also procured the passage of an act by the legislature, allowing the benefit of a jury-trial to persons claimed as fugitive slaves. He defended this right with his usual fervid eloquence, and it was mainly through his efforts that it was incorporated in the policy of the state. At a subsequent period, when the fugitive-slave bill was debated in the United States senate, he labored to have a similar provision engrafted in its details.

An act was also passed, at his instance, prohibiting state officers from participating in actions for the recovery of fugitive slaves, and denying the use of the public jails for their detention. He held that these were actions under the constitution and laws of the United States, and should, therefore, be executed only by the United States marshals and judges in United States courts, and that imprisonments they might order should be in United States prisons, if such could be found. Although the supreme court of the United States pronounced these laws to be unconstitutional, they were clearly founded on the eternal principles of right and justice. They will form an enduring memorial of the wise humanity of Governor Seward, and of his heartfelt devotion to the spirit of freedom, as embodied in the Declaration of Independence.

It was through his agency, moreover, that a law was enacted, in 1840, for the recovery of free colored citizens of New York who should be kidnapped into slavery. This law authorized the governor to employ an agent for the aid of such persons, securing their restoration to liberty. It was under the provisions of this act, that H. B. Northrup, Esq., of Washington county, New York, in January, 1853, procured the liberty of Solomon, a colored man, long a member of his family, who twelve years ago had been inveigled to the city of Washington, and there kidnapped and sold into slavery.

Among Governor Seward's last official recommendations to the legislature, was an amendment of the constitution of the state, by which the freehold qualification required of citizens of the African race, as a condition of exercising the right of suffrage, should be abolished. He based this recommendation on the principles of natural justice. And he urged the necessity of granting the right of suffrage to every class of persons subject to the laws of the state, and the safety with which it could be thus extended where a system of universal education had already been established. It is to be regretted that on the revision of the constitution, in 1846, this recommendation was found to have anticipated public sentiment for an indefinite period of time. But that

Governor Seward's recommendation on this point will yet be adopted and incorporated into the constitution of the state, there can not be a doubt.

The course of Governor Seward in regard to these measures was an agreeable surprise to the abolitionists, who had failed to obtain any pledge from him during the preliminary canvass. His noble position in the "Virginia case" was adapted to win the admiration of every lover of freedom.*

The outlines of this case may be briefly given as follows: In 1839, a vessel from Norfolk, Virginia, on arriving near the port of New York, was found to contain a slave, who had secreted himself in the hold. He was taken and conveyed back to bondage. Three colored seamen belonging to the vessel, who had expressed their sympathy with the fugitive, were charged with having conveyed him out of the state by stealth. Affidavits were made to that effect in Norfolk. A requisition, based on these affidavits, was made by the lieutenant-governor of Virginia upon the governor of New York, for the surrender of the accused, in accordance with the provisions of the constitution of the United States, and the act of Congress of 1793, concerning fugitives from justice. Before the requisition was presented to Governor Seward, the parties had been arrested in the city of New York; but, having been brought before Robert H. Morris, the recorder of the city, on a writ of *habeas corpus*, were discharged by him on the ground of the insufficiency of the affidavits to justify their detention. The lieutenant-governor of Virginia, however, persisted in the requisition, demanding that the governor of New York should surrender the persons as fugitives from justice. Governor Seward replied that they had been discharged from arrest in due course of law, and that the affidavits in support of the requisition were informal and insufficient. At the same time, he admitted that these affidavits could be replaced by new affidavits, or a formal indictment. Disdaining, however, to stand upon

* See "Virginia Controversy," Vol. II., pp. 449–516.

mere light technicalities in so grave a case, he met the question on the broad and universal principles which it involved. He took the ground that the crimes contemplated by the constitution of the United States, in its provisions authorizing the demand of fugitives from justice, between the several states, were not such crimes as depended on the arbitrary legislation of a particular state, but such as were *mala in sese*—crimes which could be determined by some common standard, as the concurrent sense of the several states —the common law received by them all alike, or the universal sentiment of civilized nations. No state, he argued, could force a requisition upon another state, founded on an act which was only criminal through its own legislation, but, compared with general standards, was not only innocent, but humane and praiseworthy. Thus, the aiding of a slave to escape from bondage was in itself an act of virtue and humanity. No statute could pronounce such an act a crime, without a perversion of both reason and justice. Still further, though slavery was left by the constitution of the United States to the exclusive jurisdiction of the states where it existed, it was carefully excluded from federal recognition. Hence no state was bound by the constitution to recognise slavery or any of its incidents in another state, so as to create an obligation for the surrendry of persons charged with offences in violation of laws enacted by slaveholding states for the maintenance of slavery. This reasoning was applicable to all cases, and not alone to those which grew out of slavery. By the laws of New York, for instance, as in several other states, there was no legal imprisonment for debt. But in Pennsylvania this barbarous custom was still sanctioned by the laws: hence, in that state, resistance by a debtor to a civil officer charged with process was a felony. The governor of Pennsylvania had made a requisition on Governor Seward, under the federal constitution, for the surrender of a citizen of New York, indicted in Pennsylvania, for resistance to a sheriff charged with an execution against his person. Governor Seward refused to comply with the requisition, on the principles before stated. While the decision was acquiesced in by the state of Pennsylvania, Virginia withheld its assent in the case presented from that state.

A correspondence ensued, which continued during the whole of Governor Seward's administration. The legislature of Virginia appealed from the governor to the legislature of New York. The public mind was profoundly moved by this novel and important discussion. Although not made an affair of strict party division, the whig legislatures of New York, more or less explicitly, sustained the position of the governor.

Upon the election of an opposition legislature in 1842, the assembly took a different ground, and requested Governor Seward to communicate their opinion to the legislature of Virginia. In a firm but respectful manner, he declined to comply with the request.* The soundness of his views on this subject received a striking illustration in subsequent requisitions by the governors of Louisiana and Georgia, demanding the surrendry of fugitive slaves on the most frivolous pretexts as fugitives from justice; in one case, on the indictment of a female-slave for stealing the gown on her back, valued, by the grand jury who found the indictment, at twelve and a half cents: and in the other, on the indictment of a person for stealing a female-slave from her master, and stealing the calico dress and trinkets worn upon her person, when the entire transaction consisted, at most, in his persuading the slave to make her escape from bondage.

The state of Virginia, combined with other states, resorted to retaliatory measures designed to injure the commerce of New York. But this produced no change in the decision of Governor Seward, nor in public opinion, concerning the controversy. The judgment which will ulti-

* See Special Messages, Vol. II., pp. 385–433.

mately be passed upon his conduct in this affair, by the moral sentiment of mankind, is indicated in the construction placed by the British ministry on the article of the recent treaty in regard to the extradition of fugitives from justice—an article of similar purport to the extradition article in the federal constitution. It was stated by them in the house of commons, that they should not deem themselves bound to surrender any person charged with a crime which should appear to have been committed by the offender in effecting his own escape, or that of another from slavery. In connection with this subject, it may be added that Governor Seward always maintained the unconstitutionality of imprisoning colored citizens of the free states in the slaveholding states, when not charged with actual crime. In case of such imprisonment of citizens of New York, he employed agents at the expense of the state to obtain their restoration to freedom.

The condition of Governor Seward's private affairs, which had been affected by the general depreciation of property incident to the financial embarrassment of the country, made his acceptance of a re-election in 1840 a matter of personal sacrifice. But it was deemed necessary by his political friends. His own mind regarded the subject in a different light. He had been elected by a diminished majority. Several hundreds of whig votes were given for other candidates. To him this was a proof of dissatisfaction on the part of no inconsiderable number of persons; many had been disappointed in their hopes of office; others were alienated by his devotion to reform; his policy in regard to universal education was greatly misapprehended: all these causes led him to doubt whether a division of the party would not be produced by his remaining in the executive chair, although no one, in fact, ever possessed a stronger hold on the confidence of a great political party than he did at that moment. Besides, Governor Seward foresaw, more clearly than many of his friends, the progress of reaction in regard to internal improvements. The opponents of the policy were rapidly gaining ground; it would be necessary, at another election, to present a candidate to the whig party against whom there was no considerable prejudice. Accordingly, in January, 1841, Governor Seward announced his determination, under no circumstances, to again become a candidate for the executive office. The announcement took the public by surprise, especially as it was made at a time when he was regarded as having triumphed over all opposition, and gained a firm footing as a leader of the whig party. His last annual message* was considered the ablest official production of his pen. Nor is it too much to say that few, if any, abler documents have ever issued from the executive chair of New York.

The election of General Harrison in 1840, who had been nominated for president, in preference to Mr. Clay, on the ground of superior availability, induced the friends of the latter distinguished leader to believe that he would have been successful if he had received the nomination. This conviction, which became almost universal, produced a settled determination to secure Mr. Clay's nomination for the canvass of 1844. The policy was to foreclose the question by popular movements throughout the United States as early as the spring of 1842. Governor Seward did not assent to the wisdom of the plan. He yielded his private views, however, to the prevailing sentiment of the whig party. But he could not be persuaded to place himself at the head of the movement, with the prospect of a renomination for governor. On the contrary, he frankly pointed out to his friends the reasons against their course. The question of the annexation of Texas, he argued, had become inevitable. Under the excitement produced by its discussion, the anti-slavery interest had grown up in the state, from one thousand in 1838, to two thousand five

* See Vol. II., p. 297.

hundred in 1840, in opposition to General Harrison and himself, neither of whom was regarded with special prejudice by the political abolitionists. It was more than probable that the premature nomination of Mr. Clay, who was already severely censured by the abolitionists, would increase their vote at the state election of 1842, from five thousand to fifteen thousand, at the expense of the whig party. This would insure the loss of the state to the whigs, as well as of the presidential election of 1844.

Other counsels, however, prevailed. Governor Seward persisted in declining a renomination. Mr. Clay was the avowed candidate of the whigs for the presidency. The result was the increase of the abolition vote to sixteen thousand. The whigs were accordingly defeated. Their candidate for governor, Hon. Luther Bradish—a man of unexceptionable character, well known to the public, and universally popular—lost his election by a decided vote.*

On the last day of Governor Seward's second official term, his accounts with the treasury were definitely settled; and on the first day of January, 1843, having occupied the executive chair four years, he introduced his successor, Governor Bouck, to the people of the capitol, exchanging with him appropriate courtesies on the occasion of his inauguration. These courtesies, so well adapted to allay animosities and to cultivate a better tone of feeling, were at that time without precedent. They made a favorable impression upon the public mind. With that successor, and all others in the executive chair, of whatever politics, Governor Seward maintained relations of mutual respect and personal friendship.

How strong a hold his benevolent action, during his official term, had taken upon the classes most generally overlooked, neglected and oppressed, may be seen by referring to his replies to letters and addresses elicited by his retirement.†

* The majority for William C. Bouck was 22,000.

† See Vol. III.

CHAPTER XIV.

PRIVATE LIFE—JOHN QUINCY ADAMS—PROFESSIONAL LABORS—PATENT CAUSES—FREEDOM OF THE PRESS—FUGITIVE SLAVE CASE—O'CONNELL.

On retiring from his official duties, Governor Seward returned immediately to his residence in Auburn. In one week's space of time, he was seen engaged with as much calmness and assiduity in his profession, as if he had never been removed out of it. Having enjoyed the honors of the highest post in his native state, to the full satisfaction of a noble ambition, and in a manner to leave the deep impress of his character on its laws and institutions, he was not only content, but anxious to turn again to the calls of a profession, which he ever pursued with all the ardor of an amateur.

In 1843, Governor Seward, in his retirement at Auburn, had the gratification of a visit from Ex-President John Quincy Adams, between whom and himself the most intimate relations of friendship had long existed. The meeting was one of great cordiality and affection. It has been said, and we believe with truth, that on that, as well as on other occasions, Mr. Adams expressed his confidence that the great work of human rights, which he would be obliged to leave unfinished, would devolve more completely on Governor Seward than on any surviving statesman. Thus far, at least, that expectation, so honorable to Governor Seward, has not been disappointed. His published works contain fragments of correspondence between Mr. Adams and Governor Seward, together with orations and speeches by the latter, which, while they illustrate his own reverence for Mr. Adams, have been regarded as presenting their distinguished subject in his just attitude before the world.

On the occasion of Mr. Adams's death, Governor Seward was invited by the legislature of New York to pronounce a eulogy* on his character and services. It was one of the most faithful and eloquent of the numerous discourses which were prepared on that great national bereavement. Its closing sentences, instituting a comparison between the death scenes of Napoleon and Adams, are scarcely surpassed in pathetic eloquence by any modern production. Believing that a popular biography of that eminent statesman would be more useful, in disseminating and inculcating his principles, than any other contributions that he could make to his memory, Governor Seward applied himself to the preparation of such a work. With the aid of a competent friend,† it was brought out in 1849, in the midst of many absorbing professional engagements. The author's expectations were fully realized. More than thirty-two thousand copies of the work have been already published, and its circulation has been continually increasing.

At the annual commencement of Union College in 1843, Governor Seward was invited to deliver the address before the Phi Beta Kappa Society, of which he is a member. He accepted the appointment, and took for his theme, "The Elements of Empire in America."‡ The address was worthy of his manly and vigorous intellect, and his extensive literary attainments. It presented a comprehensive view of the resources of the American Union, and pointed out the grandeur of its destiny, under the principles of justice and freedom on which it was founded. By special invitation, he repeated the address at the commencement of Amherst College, the same year.

During the ensuing six years, Governor Seward devoted himself to the duties of his profession with brilliant and

* See Vol. III., p. 75. † Rev. J. M. Austin. ‡ See Vol. III., p. 11.

growing success. At first, his practice was confined to the various courts of the state, in which he received liberal retainers for his services. After the lapse of about two years, however, his peculiar aptitude for subjects involving scientific and mechanical principles gained him a large and lucrative practice in the trial of patent cases in the United States courts. He was thus brought into contact with the most distinguished jurists of the country, whom his breadth of intellect and sound legal learning enabled him to meet on equal terms. In one of his arguments he discusses the subject of invention in the following eloquent language:—

"There are two great principles of activity, in regard to the world. One is creation, the other is invention. Creation is the peculiar attribute of Him who made all worlds, all that is on the earth, in the earth, and in the waters under the earth, for the greatness, and the welfare, and the happiness of our race. He created nothing that is not adapted, fit, and useful in some way, to promote our health, welfare, prosperity, and happiness. He made it all, in the counsels of his own will. He spoke it into existence by a word, but he concealed it from his creatures, and made it *their* greatest glory to find out the purposes, principles, and adaptations, of the things by which he surrounded them. Our duty consists in finding them out, and invention is nothing more than finding out what will promote the progress of society, through all time. He has hidden and concealed nothing so deeply that we can not find out, as fast as is best for our welfare and consistent with his providence, the uses and purposes of everything. Invention, then, is worthy of the fostering care of every government. What would society be now, but for the exercise of invention in times past? Where lies our hope of progress in society, but in the exercise of invention for the future? Hope is, in this respect, the spring of youth to mankind and to nations. And, in the exercise of invention, the world is renewing itself, and becoming wiser and better, as it approaches those latter days when our species will have attained a comparative degree of perfection and exaltation.

"Wherein consisted the advantage of the Spaniard over the

Peruvian and the Mexican, when he subverted the empires of America? It was in this, that the invader had invented the power which resides in the combination of sulphur, saltpetre, and charcoal. Wherein our superiority over the enemy, whom we have recently defeated in the centre of this continent, but that we have rewarded invention? Look, too, at the dignity of this principle of invention. It stands in contrast with the power of the Almighty. He creates instantly; man finds out slowly, progressively, laboriously. When you reflect, you will see that there is danger of misapprehension. You have been imagining that somebody made, or created, a railroad-wheel. But no hu man being creates. God alone creates. It is our province, worthy of the patronage of government, and the highest exercise of human power, to follow the clews which lead us to his designs, with regard to matter, for our happiness and welfare. And what is there wrong in this system? Society says to all alike, that, if they will devote talent to the discovery of anything which will contribute to the welfare of society, they shall have the first enjoyment of it for fourteen years, on condition that they will then publish it for the benefit of the world at large, for this and future generations. If, then, there is an honest thought in your hearts, do not your cheeks blush with shame, not because your country has conferred this benefit, here and there, on a struggling inventor, but because you are filled with virtuous indignation that Fulton sleeps in his grave, while his family are mendicants, and while the production he gave to the world has become the engine of your commerce, the great uniting power that binds your confederacy together, and is revolutionizing the East, bringing Africa and Asia into the great fold of the family of civilized man? It is a burning reproach, that he who made the lightning your messenger, and bids it carry for you messages of love, and grief, and joy, and triumph, and trouble, is standing here this day, in this court, a suppliant to the laws of the land, to protect him for fourteen years in the enjoyment of that instrument, the effects of which, to benefit mankind, can not be bounded by lines, and will be felt when time shall have ceased to exist. . . . . .

"The human race is yet enthralled in ignorance, and to a great degree in poverty and suffering. Society is to be disenthralled by finding out the properties which God has conferred on matter.

"If the merit of invention is so great, it must be a pleasing gratification to Him who organized the system on which human society is established, when he sees one of his creatures so employed. And there must have been a beneficent smile from on high, lighting up a halo round the head of Fulton, when he invented a steamboat. No less beneficent must have been the smile when these poor and humble citizens produced an invention which would save the loss of human life on railroads. You are the interpreters of the Omniscient Eye in regard to the aptitude of iron for the purpose which we have been discussing. You must perform your duty under the belief that he sees your hearts, and tries your reins, and that whatever judgment is meted by you, shall be meted to you again. For there is an all-seeing Eye, that renders to us, even in this life, the reward we merit for doing justly. . . . . .

"I ask you, gentlemen, to believe me when I say that you are capable of learning something new in regard to the exercise of this faculty of invention. It is not, like creation, an instantaneous and a perfect thing; but it is a progressive and an imperfect thing. Invention is finding out in the dark. It is groping in a cavern, stored with all things adapted for our purposes. The steam-engine was conceived one hundred years before it floated on the water, or traversed the land. It was described in 1783, an engine as complete as it could be. But the Hudson received, long after that, the first burden of a boat floated by steam. I have seen, in a distant land, a monument to the man who perfected the steam-engine so that it produced motion. And what was the achievement of Fulton? It was, that when the steam-engine had been perfected, he stumbled upon the manner of applying it to move a boat. When was the magnetic telegraph discovered? The germ of it was brought to light by Franklin, when he brought down electricity from the clouds by means of a kite. Yet that was seventy years ago. And it was only within a few years that the manner of applying that principle has been discovered. A cause precedes an effect. One thing always precedes or produces another. The carriage-wheel produced the first railroad-wheel—of course, it was a spoke-wheel. The inventor gropes in a cavern, holding on to a chain that is suspended to the throne of God, who permits him to grasp but a single link at a time. There must be the boll of rotting flax, before there can be the bridal veil. There must be the egg before the eagle, the thought before the thing.

'We learn upon a hint, we find upon a clew,
From the basket and acanthus is modeled the graceful capital;
The shadowed profile on the wall helpeth the limner to his likeness;
The foot-marks stamped on the clay, lead on the thoughts to printing;
The strange skin-garments cast upon the shore, suggest another hemisphere;
A falling apple taught the sage prevailing gravitation;
The Huron is certain of his prey from tracks upon the grass,
And shrewdness, guessing on the hint, followeth the trail;
But the hint must be given, the trail must be there, or the keenest sight is as blindness.' "

At the same time, Mr. Seward's genial and generous disposition, and the natural frankness of his manners, gave him great influence with a jury, and made his services indispensable as counsel in criminal cases. His zeal in the defence of persons unjustly accused was so great, that he has been known not only to give his best efforts gratuitously, but to furnish a large amount of funds from his own means in their behalf.

In 1845, Governor Seward was engaged in a libel-suit in the supreme court of New York, in the case of J. Fenimore Cooper *vs.* Greeley and M'Elrath, publishers of the "New York Tribune." He was counsel for the defendants. It was deemed a case of much importance, involving as it did the rights of newspaper publishers to utter their opinions as to the character and acts of men holding positions of influence before the public. Governor Seward's argument* in this case was a sound and searching production; it sifted thoroughly, and to the bottom, the whole subject of libel, the modifications which that law appears to have undergone by judicial construction in this state, and the rights of the press and the people: the right of free thought and free

* See Vol. I., p. 391.

speech, on the one hand, and the right of exemption from vituperation and libel on the other—all were brought under review, and discussed with clearness and effect. The public and the press will acknowledge their obligations to Governor Seward for the ability and force with which the freedom of speech and of opinion was illustrated and defended on that trial.

At the solicitation of citizens of Cooperstown, New York, Governor Seward left the state fair at Auburn, in 1844, to defend a person of politics adverse to his own, charged with the crime of murder. When he had the pleasure of securing a verdict which reduced the crime to manslaughter, in opposition to the opinion of the court, he declined to receive any compensation for his successful effort in behalf of the prisoner, although it was tendered by the jury, who felt themselves indebted to him for showing how they could rightfully vindicate the laws, and by it save a human life.

In 1847, Governor Seward was solicited by certain humane persons in Cincinnati, with a tender of compensation, to be raised by subscription, to appear before the supreme court at Washington, in behalf of John Van Zandt, who was charged with aiding certain fugitives in an attempt to escape from slavery. He consented to undertake the case. The argument* which he delivered on this occasion presented a masterly and unequalled analysis of the fugitive-slave law of 1793, and the provisions of the federal constitution in regard to the subject. It closed with the following earnest appeal to the court:—

"The act of 1793 is unconstitutional, because, by implication and certain effect, it recognises slavery as a lawful institution, lawfully creating an obligation to labor. All slavery is an open violation of the personal rights guarantied to the people by the constitution. However true it may be that, when Congress finds the institution existing in any state, they have no power to dis-

* See Vol. I., p. 476.

turb it there—it is clear that they have no right to extend it into other states, or compel such states to recognise its peculiar code. Such a power is not expressly conferred by the section which has been considered, nor is it implied by any necessary or reasonable construction. It is manifestly excluded from that portion of the instrument, absolutely interdicted by others which have been recited, and is at war with the spirit of the whole constitution. We need not refer again, minutely, to its provisions to support this argument. Our senses tell us, our happiness assures us, our pride proclaims, the graves and glory of our ancestors, every day and every hour remind us, that we are a FREE people; and that the constitution is a legacy of liberty; and, so far as liberty and slavery depend on that great charter, all men are free and equal. If all this be not evidence enough, we can read the same truth in the severe derision we justly excite throughout the world, and the humiliation we can not conceal, when we attempt to justify the toleration of slavery.

"For myself, an humble advocate in a great cause, I can not hope, I dare not hope, I do not expect, that principles which seem to me so reasonable, so just and truthful, can all at once gain immediate establishment in this tribunal, against the force of many precedents and the weight of many honored names. But I do humbly hope that past adjudications, by which the constitution was unnecessarily declared to recognise, sanction, and guaranty slavery, may be reconsidered. I appeal to the court to restore to that revered instrument its simplicity, its truthfulness, its harmony with the Declaration of Independence—its studied denial of a right of property in man, and its jealous regard for the security of the people. I humbly supplicate, that slavery, with its odious form and revolting features, and its dreadful pretensions for the present and for the future, may not receive in this great tribunal, now, sanction and countenance, denied to it by a convention of the American states more than half a century ago. Let the spirit which prevailed in that august assembly, only find utterance here, and the time will come somewhat more speedily, when throughout this great empire, erected on the foundation of the rights of man, no court of justice will be re-

5

quired to enforce INVOLUNTARY obligations of LABOR, and uphold the indefensible law of PHYSICAL FORCE."

The argument also stated most of the important objections now urged against the present fugitive-slave law. In this case, also, Governor Seward declined all compensation.

In September of the same year, Governor Seward was invited by the Irish citizens of the city of New York, to deliver a eulogy on the life and character of Daniel O'Connell.* An immense assemblage of adopted and native-born citizens, listened to him with the highest admiration. Like all similar efforts from the pen of Governor Seward, it was a production at once chaste and eloquent, full of historical and classical allusions, with many passages of the most thrilling pathos, and did ample justice to the principles and deeds of the great Irish orator. We give only his beautiful exordium:—

"There is sad news from Genoa. An aged and weary pilgrim who can travel no farther, passes beneath the gate of one of her ancient palaces, saying with pious resignation as he enters its silent chambers: 'Well it is God's will that I shall never see Rome. I am disappointed, but I am ready to die.'

"The 'superb' though fading queen of the Mediterranean holds anxious watch through ten long days over that majestic stranger's wasting frame. And now death is there—the Liberator of Ireland has sunk to rest in the cradle of Columbus.

"Coincidence beautiful and most sublime! It was the very day set apart by the elder daughter of the church for prayer and sacrifice throughout the world for the children of the sacred island, perishing by famine and pestilence in their houses and in their native fields, and on their crowded paths of exile, on the sea and in the havens, and on the lakes and along the rivers of this far distant land. The chimes rung out by pity for his countrymen were O'CONNELL'S fitting knell; his soul went forth on clouds of incense that rose from altars of Christian charity: and the mournful anthems which recited the faith and the virtue and the endurance of Ireland were his becoming requiem."

* See Vol. III., p. 44.

CHAPTER XV.

THE WYATT AND FREEMAN CASES—MASSACRE OF THE VAN NEST FAMILY—WILLIAM FREEMAN—WYATT'S TRIAL—TRIAL OF FREEMAN—EXTRAORDINARY PROCEEDINGS.

IN 1845, a convict of the stateprison at Auburn, Henry Wyatt, was indicted for the murder of a fellow-convict. His attempts to procure able counsel, had failed for want of ability to make the usual recompense. On the day but one preceding his trial, he invoked Governor Seward's interposition for his defence. His appeal was promptly accepted. During the trial, many striking incidents were disclosed, which showed that the crime was committed in a morbid state of mind. The case clearly fell within a class which medical writers designate under the general name of moral insanity. Governor Seward procured, at his own expense, the scientific witnesses necessary to present the case fairly to the jury. He followed in his defence with an argument of great power and pathos. The jury divided and could not agree upon a verdict. His second trial at the next circuit court, was eagerly anticipated, with full confidence that he would be acquitted. This event, however, was destined to become the occasion of difficulties such as few advocates have been called to encounter. After the close of the first trial, Governor Seward left Auburn on a professional tour to Washington and the southern states.

While the case of Wyatt was yet the topic of discussion in Auburn and its vicinity, a singularly revolting occurrence took place, which served to increase the agitation of the public mind. This was the massacre of nearly a whole family by William Freeman, a negro of twenty-three years of age, who had been six months before discharged from the Auburn stateprison, after an imprisonment of five years. The bloody scene occurred at the residence of John G. Van Nest, a wealthy and highly respectable farmer, and a friend and former client of Governor Seward's, whose house stood in a secluded grove, near the suburbs of Auburn, on the shores of the Owasco lake. Having armed himself with carefully-prepared weapons, Freeman entered the dwelling at ten o'clock at night, and slew Mr. Van Nest, his wife, then pregnant, a child sleeping in its bed, and the mother-in-law of Van Nest, Mrs. Wyckoff, an aged woman of seventy. The hired man, who came to the defence of the family, was severely injured and left for dead. The murderer, being disabled by a wound from old Mrs. Wyckoff, desisted from further violence, and made his escape. Taking a horse from the stable, he rode him a few miles, when he stabbed the animal, which had become incapable of travelling. He then stole another horse, which proved to be more fleet, and pursuing his flight, rode to the house of a relative about thirty miles from Auburn. There he offered the horse for sale, and proposed to take up his residence, until he should recover from his wound. He was traced and arrested, in a few hours, and brought back to the scene of butchery, and into the presence of the surviving witnesses. On being questioned, he at once confessed the crime, not only without apparent remorse or horror, but with frequent and irrepressible fits of laughter. The public indignation was so excited at this awful tragedy, that it required all the dexterity of the police to keep Freeman from being torn to pieces on the spot. He was at length committed to the jail, by a successful stratagem, but the crowd could with difficulty be prevented from forcing the doors. They were appeased only by the assurance of one of the judges of the county, that Freeman should be tried and executed, and that there should be no plea of insanity and "no Governor Seward to defend him."

None of the usual motives appearing on the part of Freeman for the commission of such a desperate act, it was rumored that he had been present during Wyatt's trial, and had learned from the argument of Governor Seward that responsibilities for crime might be avoided on the ground of insanity. This became the popular explanation of the horrible catastrophe. The public feeling ran high against Governor Seward. Even threats of personal violence were openly made. The excitement became so intense, that when he returned from the south, his family and friends were surprised that on reaching the depot at Auburn, he was permitted to pass to his residence without outrage.

In this state of affairs, the governor, Silas Wright, was induced to issue an order for a special term of the court of oyer and terminer, to be held at an early day, by Judge Whiting, to dispose of the cases both of Wyatt and Freeman. During the interval, public tranquillity was restored by the assurance of Governor Seward's law-partners, while he was absent, that he would not engage in the defence, it being well understood that no other advocate would consent to give his services to so odious a cause.

Governor Seward was unmoved by the tempest of excitement around him. With characteristic courage and calmness, he proceeded to examine the subject, as a philanthropist and lawyer. He felt as keenly as any one, the enormity of the deed. But impelled by a strong sense of duty, he was determined to look thoroughly into the case of the wretched negro. At his solicitation, accordingly, three intelligent and humane citizens of Auburn made several visits to Freeman in jail. They reduced their conversations with him to writing, and submitted them to Governor Seward's inspection. The result of the investigation, together with other facts which had become known to him, convinced him that whatever was the condition of Freeman's mind prior to the homicide, he was then sunk into a state of dementia, approaching idiocy.

The court began with the trial of Wyatt. Governor Seward, aware of the intense and aggravated excitement which prevailed, applied for a postponement of the case, but without effect. A week was consumed without finding a single impartial juror. The attorney-general, John Van Buren, was sent for, with haste. On his arrival, the court reversed the principles by which the trial of jurors had ever been conducted, as laid down by Chief-Justice Marshall, and adopted a standard that permitted jurors to be sworn although they confessed to a bias, or an opinion formed of the prisoner's guilt. The obtaining of a juror, even under this unprecedented decision, was regarded as a triumph, in a controversy in which not only the people of Auburn and its vicinity, but of the whole state took sides for or against Governor Seward.

A trial conducted under such circumstances, could have but one result. At the expiration of a month, Wyatt was convicted and sentenced to be executed. Moral insanity was thus, so far as the verdict of a jury could go, judicially abolished. Governor Seward devoted four weeks of uninterrupted labor to this case, without the slightest pecuniary compensation, and at an outlay of no small sum from his own pocket.*

The Freeman case still remained to be disposed of. It came on immediately after the conclusion of Wyatt's trial. An immense assemblage had convened in the courthouse at Auburn, to witness the opening of the case. Until that moment, it was not known whether Freeman would have any counsel. It was supposed the court would assign him

* Wyatt, after receiving his sentence, anxious to afford Governor Seward some compensation, offered to narrate his "life" for publication, the profits of which should go to Governor S., and it was taken down for that purpose. But on examination it was found to be of doubtful moral bearing and influence, and on that account, Governor Seward refused to permit its publication, or participate in any profits arising therefrom. A spurious copy, however, was afterward surreptitiously obtained, and brought out in a pamphlet, which yielded a net profit of six hundred dollars to the publisher.

some junior member of the bar; but it was considered doubtful if one could be found of sufficient nerve to accept the appointment, and attempt even a formal and weak defence. The excited multitude were not backward in loudly propounding the inquiry, "Who will now dare come forward to the defence of this negro?"—"Let us see the man who will attempt to raise his voice in his behalf!" Nor did they hesitate in uttering threats of vengeance against any member of the bar who would plead the case of so vile a wretch. But there was one seated within the bar in that crowded court-room, who heeded not these menaces. A being in human form was in distress and peril before him. He asked himself, "What does humanity and duty require at my hands, in this case?" And having received from conscience a prompt and decisive reply, he unhesitatingly proceeded to the labor thus enjoined upon him, without delaying to consult interest, or popular favor, or any of the consequences that might ensue. In vain family, personal and political friends, influential citizens, and members of the bar, besought him not to interfere, and call down upon himself the indignation of the populace. In vain was he reminded of the long, weary, and expensive trial to which he had just devoted himself, to the neglect of professional engagements, and the peril of health—in vain was he forewarned of the still more tedious, costly, and exhausting nature of the present case, should he engage in it. A higher law and a louder voice called him to the defence of the demented, forsaken wretch, who stood insensible of the vengeful gaze of a thousand eyes, and he felt that he had no alternative.

Freeman was arraigned on four indictments for murder. When asked whether he pleaded guilty to the first indictment, he replied, "Yes!" "No!" "I don't know!"—"Have you counsel?" was the next inquiry. "I don't know," responded the prisoner, with a stupidity which astonished even those who were most eager for his death.

"Will any one defend this man?" inquired the court. A death-like stillness pervaded the crowded room. Pale with emotion, yet firm and unflinching as steel, Governor Seward, to the amazement of every person present, arose and said, "May it please the court, I appear as counsel for the prisoner!" It would be impossible to describe the excitement which followed this announcement, or the threatening demonstrations which it called forth. David Wright, Esq., of Auburn, a well-known lawyer and philanthropist, volunteered as associate counsel in defence of Freeman. The attorney-general, John Van Buren, conducted the prosecution.

Governor Seward presented to the court in bar of a trial, that the prisoner was then insane. Issue was taken on this plea, and a trial was directed by the court, on the question of Freeman's insanity at that time. After protracted efforts similar to those which took place in Wyatt's case, a jury was empanneled to try this preliminary question, but they were already evidently fixed in their convictions of the sanity and guilt of the prisoner.

Governor Seward's political party, throughout the state, shrinking from the unpopularity in which he had involved himself, in a proceeding universally denounced by the press, abandoned him. While these proceedings were pending, the delegates to the convention called to revise the constitution of the state of New York, assembled at Albany. The whig party was supposed to be compromised by Governor Seward's known bias in favor of extending the right of suffrage to the colored population. The result of the election of delegates had been an overwhelming defeat of the whigs. The exclamation was universal, that whatever might be the fate of the whig party hereafter, Governor Seward was effectually lost.

Still he did not falter, but sternly persevered in what he conscientiously believed to be the line of his duty, and was the only person engaged in these transactions, except his client, who was calm and unmoved. The trial on the question of the prisoner's sanity, continued two weeks, and was contested by Governor Seward with an energy, perseverance, and skill, that drew plaudits from his most violent opposers, and that could not have been exceeded had millions of dollars depended on the issue. His argument at the summing up, for eloquence, pathos, sound legal views, and thorough knowledge of human character, has rarely been excelled at the American bar. At length, when the jury retired, it was at once found that eleven were agreed that the prisoner was sane. The twelfth declared his unchangeable opinion that Freeman, although sane enough to know right from wrong, was yet so unsound in mind as not to be responsible for his actions. The disagreement and discussion in the jury-room being privately communicated to the court, information was returned to the jurors that the verdict would be accepted, although it gave no direct response to the question at issue, and was couched in equivocal language. They accordingly brought in the following verdict—"We find the prisoner at the bar sufficiently sane to distinguish between right and wrong." In an earnest and elaborate argument, Governor Seward protested against the reception of this verdict, as it was illegal, pointless, and irrelevant. But it was pronounced by the court to be sound and satisfactory, and Freeman was forthwith put upon his trial for the murders charged against him.

He was directed to stand up and plead to the indictment. But it was evident to every spectator that the wretched imbecile had not the faintest conception of the nature of an indictment, or of the object of the scenes around him, in which he unconsciously bore so conspicuous a part.

We shall be pardoned for introducing here the following extract from a vivid description of the scene which tran spired at the reading of the indictment, by a clergyman of Auburn, who attended the trial, and was an eye-witness of the proceedings:—

"The district-attorney (Luman Sherwood, Esq.), with the bill of indictment in his hand, called out—'William Freeman, stand up.' He then approached quite near the negro, for he was very deaf, and read the indictment. At the conclusion, the following dialogue ensued:—

"*Dist. Att.*—Do you plead guilty, or not guilty, to these indictments?

"*Freeman.*—Ha?

"*D. A.*—(Repeating the question.)

"*F.*—I don't know.

"*D. A.*—Are you able to employ counsel?

"*F.*—No.

"*D. A.*—Are you ready for trial?

"*F.*—I don't know.

"*D. A.*—Have you any counsel?

"*F.*—I don't know.

"*D. A.*—Who are your counsel?

"*F.*—I don't know.

"At this stage of the proceedings, Governor Seward could no longer restrain himself. He buried his face in his hands, and burst into tears—and seizing his hat, he rushed from the court-room, perfectly overwhelmed with his feelings. And who that had but a common share of sympathy, could fail to be most sensibly moved at witnessing such a procedure on a subject so awful, allowed before one of the highest tribunals of the land. An instrument read to this idiotic creature, pregnant with his death, requiring him to respond to the same, when the wretched being had not *the first glimpse* of what it all meant, or what effect it would have upon him. D. Wright, Esq., who had assisted Governor Seward on the preliminary trial, arose after the reading of the indictment, and declared he could not consent longer to take part in a cause which had so much the appearance of a *terrible farce.* But Governor Seward (who had returned to the room), immediately sprang to his feet and exclaimed—'May it please the court—*I shall remain counsel for the prisoner until his death!*' At the solicitation of the court, Mr. Wright finally consented again to take part in the cause, and assist Governor Seward."

As the commission of the acts charged was not denied by the prisoner's counsel, the only question at issue was his *sanity* at the time of the homicide. Governor Seward labored with unwearied assiduity to establish the insanity or dementia of Freeman, of which he was himself satisfied beyond a possible doubt. At great expense, defrayed by himself, he summoned into court the most eminent medical professors and practitioners from various and extreme parts of the state, whose intelligent and unbiased testimony fully sustained the ground on which he urged the defence.

We can make room here for only a few passages of Governor Seward's thrilling argument in this case:—

"MAY IT PLEASE THE COURT—Gentlemen of the jury: 'THOU SHALT NOT KILL,' and 'WHOSO SHEDDETH MAN'S BLOOD, BY MAN SHALL HIS BLOOD BE SHED,' are laws found in the code of that people who, although distracted and dispersed through all lands, trace their history to the creation; a history that records that murder was the first of human crimes.

"The first of these precepts constitutes a tenth part of the jurisprudence which God saw fit to establish, at an early period, for the government of all mankind, throughout all generations. The latter, of less universal obligation, is still retained in our system, although other states, as intelligent and refined, as secure and peaceful, have substituted for it the more benign principle that good shall be returned for evil. I yield implicit submission to this law, and acknowledge the justness of its penalty, and the duty of courts and juries to give it effect.

"In this case, if the prisoner *be* guilty of murder, I do not ask remission of punishment. If he be guilty, never was murderer *more* guilty. He has murdered not only John G. Van Nest, but his hands are reeking with the blood of other, and numerous, and even more pitiable victims. The slaying of Van Nest, if a crime at all, was the cowardly crime of assassination. John G. Van Nest was a just, upright, virtuous man, of middle age, of grave and modest demeanor, distinguished by especial marks of the respect and esteem of his fellow-citizens. On his arm leaned a confiding wife, and they supported, on the one side, children to whom they had given being, and, on the other, aged and venerable parents, from whom they had derived existence. The assassination of such a man was an atrocious crime, but the murderer, with more than savage refinement, immolated on the same altar, in the same hour, a venerable and virtuous matron of more than threescore years, and her daughter, the wife of Van Nest, mother of an unborn infant. Nor was this all. Providence, which, for its own mysterious purposes, permitted these dreadful crimes, in mercy suffered the same arm to be raised against the sleeping orphan child of the butchered parents, and received it into heaven. A whole family, just, gentle, and pure, were thus, in their own house, in the night-time—without any provocation, without one moment's warning—sent by the murderer to join the assembly of the just; and even the laboring man, sojourning within their gates, received the fatal blade into his breast, and survives through the mercy, not of the murderer, but of God.

"For William Freeman, as a murderer, I have no commission to speak. If he had silver and gold accumulated with the frugality of Crœsus, and should pour it all at my feet, I would not stand an hour between him and the avenger. But, for the innocent, it is my right, my duty to speak. If this sea of blood was *innocently* shed, then it is my duty to stand beside him until his steps lose their hold upon the scaffold.

"'Thou shalt not kill' is a commandment addressed, not to him alone, but to me, to you, to the court, and to the whole community. There are no exceptions from that commandment, at least in civil life, save those of self-defence, and capital punishment for crimes in the due and just administration of the law. There is not only a question, then, whether the prisoner has shed the blood of his fellow-man, but the question whether we shall unlawfully shed his blood. I should be guilty of murder if, in my present relation, I saw the executioner waiting for an insane man, and failed to say, or failed to do in his behalf, all that my ability allowed. I think it has been proved of the prisoner at the bar, that, during all this long and tedious trial, he has had no sleepless nights, and that even in the daytime, when he retires from these halls to his lonely cell, he sinks to rest like a wearied child, on the stone floor, and quietly slumbers till roused by the constable with his staff to appear again before the jury. His counsel enjoy no such repose. Their thoughts by day and their dreams by night are filled with oppressive apprehension that, through their inability or neglect, he may be condemned.

"I am arraigned before you for undue manifestations of zeal and excitement. My answer to all such charges shall be brief. When this cause shall have been committed to you, I shall be happy indeed if it shall appear that my only error has been, that I have felt too much, thought too intensely, or acted too faithfully.

"If error on my part would thus be criminal, how great would yours be if you should render an unjust verdict! Only four months have elapsed since an outraged people, distrustful of judicial redress, doomed the prisoner to immediate death. Some of you have confessed, before you came here, that you approved that lawless sentence. All men now rejoice that the prisoner was saved for this solemn trial. But if this trial, through any wilful fault or prejudice of yours, should prove only a mockery of justice, it would be as criminal as that precipitate sentence. If any prejudice of witnesses, or the imagination of counsel, or any ill-timed jest, shall at any time have diverted your attention, or if any prejudgment which you may have brought into the jury-box, or any cowardly fear of popular opinion shall have operated to cause you to deny to the prisoner that dispassionate consideration of his case which the laws of God and man exact of you, and if, owing to such an error, this wretched man shall fall from among the living, what will be your crime? You will have violated the commandment, 'Thou shalt not kill.' It is not the form or letter of the trial by jury that authorizes you to send your fellow-man to his dread account, but it is the spirit that sanctifies that great institution: and if, through pride, passion, timidity, weakness, or any cause, you deny the prisoner one iota of all the defence to which he is entitled by the law of the land, you yourselves, whatever his guilt may be, will have broken the commandment, 'Thou shalt do no murder.'

"There is not a corrupt or prejudiced witness, there is not a thoughtless or heedless witness, who has testified what was not true in spirit, or what was not wholly true, or who has suppressed any truth, who has not offended against the same injunction.

"Nor is the court itself above that commandment. If these judges have been influenced by the excitement which has brought this vast assemblage here, and under such influence, or under any other influence, have committed voluntary error, and have denied to the prisoner, or shall hereafter deny to him, the benefit of any fact or any principle of law, then this court will have to answer for the deep transgression at that bar at which we all shall meet again. When we shall appear there, none of us can plead that we were insane and knew not what we did; and by just so much as our ability and knowledge exceed those of this wretch, whom the world regards as a fiend in human shape, will our guilt exceed his, if we be guilty.

"I plead not for a murderer. I have no inducement, no motive to do so. I have addressed my fellow-citizens in many various relations, when rewards of wealth and fame awaited me. I have been cheered on other occasions by manifestations of popular approbation and sympathy; and where there was no such encouragement, I have had at least the gratitude of him whose cause I defended. But I speak now in the hearing of a people who have prejudged the prisoner, and condemned me for pleading in his behalf. He is a convict—a pauper—a negro, without intellect, sense, or emotion. My child, with an affectionate smile, disarms my care-worn face of its frown whenever I cross my threshold. The beggar in the street obliges me to give, because he says, 'God bless you,' as I pass. My dog caresses me with fondness if I will but smile on him. My horse recognises me when I fill his manger. But what reward, what gratitude, what sympathy and affection can I expect here? There the prisoner sits. Look at him. Look at the assemblage around you. Listen to their ill-suppressed censures and their excited fears, and tell me where, among my neighbors or my fellow-men—where, even in his heart—I can expect to find the sentiment, the thought, not to say of reward or of acknowledgment, but even of recognition. . . . . . .

"I speak with all sincerity and earnestness; not because I expect my opinion to have weight, but I would disarm the injurious impression that I am speaking, merely as a lawyer speaks for his client. I am not the prisoner's lawyer. I am indeed a volunteer in his behalf; but society and mankind have the deepest interests at stake. I am the lawyer for society, for mankind, shocked, beyond the power of expression, at the scene I have witnessed here of trying a maniac as a malefactor. In this, almost the first of such causes I have ever seen, the last I hope that I shall ever see, I wish that I could perform my duty with more effect. If I suffered myself to look at the volumes of testimony through which I have to pass, to remember my entire want of preparation, the pressure of time, and my wasted strength and energies, I should despair of acquitting myself as you and all good men will hereafter desire that I should have performed so sacred a duty. But, in the cause of humanity, we are encouraged to hope for Divine assistance where human powers are weak. As you all know, I provided for my way through these trials, neither gold nor silver in my purse, nor scrip; and when I could not think beforehand what I should say, I remembered that it was said to those who had a beneficent commission, that they should take no thought what they should say when brought before the magistrate, for in that same hour it should be given them what they should say, and it should not be they who should speak, but the spirit of their Father speaking in them."

After a laborious and exhausting trial of two weeks' duration, aided by the abhorrent nature of the crime, the overwhelming popular clamor, and various decisions of the court, subversive in many instances, of established rules in capital trials, the attorney-general succeeded in procuring from the jury a verdict of *guilty*.

Governor Seward's efforts in behalf of the prisoner were thus defeated. But he had faithfully discharged his duty, and the responsibility of holding an insane or idiotic person responsible for his deeds, rested not with him. Freeman was adjudged and condemned as a sane man. Governor Seward had no more to offer in that place, and the court was suffered to proceed in passing sentence upon the prisoner.

As in reading the indictment, so in the passing of the sentence, a scene occurred unparalleled, we venture to affirm, in any court of justice. Instead of standing in the dock as is customary, the judge directed the prisoner to be brought to his side upon the bench. The judge then said to him: —

"'The jury say you are guilty. Do you hear me?'

"'Yes,' replied Freeman.

"'The jury,' repeated the judge, 'say you are guilty. Do you understand?'

"'No,' said the negro.

"'Do you know which the jury are?' inquired the court.

"'No!' answered the prisoner.

"'Well! they are those gentlemen down there,' continued Judge Whiting, pointing to the jurors in their seats—'and they say you are guilty. Do you understand?'

"'No!'

"'They say you killed Van Nest. Do you understand that?'

"'Yes!'

"'Did you kill Van Nest?'

"'Yes!'

"'I am going to pronounce sentence upon you. Do you understand that?'

"'No.'

"'I am going to sentence you to be hanged. Do you understand that?'

"'No.'"

The prisoner was then led back to the dock, and the judge proceeded to pronounce sentence of death upon him. This he did in the form of an address read to the audience; thus tacitly admitting, what was evident to every person in the immense multitude present, that Freeman knew not a word he uttered, or the strange scene thus transpiring. He was conveyed to his cell as unconscious of the sentence that had been pronounced upon him, as an unborn child.

A bill of exceptions was prepared by Governor Seward, but the judge refused a stay of proceedings. It was, however, subsequently granted by a judge of an appellate court, and in October following, on a full review of the whole case, a new trial was granted. But Freeman, who had proved himself a monomaniac in the committal of the homicide, now sunk so low in dementia, that Judge Whiting, before whom he was tried and convicted, pronounced him incompetent for another trial, and refused to proceed with the case. A few weeks later, the wretched and imbruted William Freeman passed from earth to the presence of a more wise and merciful Judge.

A post-mortem examination was made, by the most eminent physicians in the state, which showed that Freeman's brain was diseased and destroyed. The publication of Governor Seward's second argument* in this remarkable

* See Vol. I., p. 409 to 475.

case, an effort of the highest and most attractive character, unsurpassed in eloquence, logic, and legal ability, had already wrought a reaction in public opinion, which was rendered complete and universal by this post-mortem examination. Now, there is no one act of Governor Seward's life, for which society is more grateful to him than that of having saved the community from the crime of the judicial murder of Freeman — an ignorant colored boy who had been confined in the stateprison for an offence of which he was innocent, and driven to lunacy by a sense of the injustice of his punishment, and by inhumanity in the exercise of penitentiary discipline.

Before leaving this case, it is due to Governor Seward to insert another extract from an article by the clergyman in Auburn, to whom allusion has already been made, written immediately after the conclusion of the trial, and published in the journals of the day. It describes the impression made at the time by the high-minded and humane course of Governor Seward on a class of individuals who did not allow retaliatory emotions to cloud their judgment, or harden their feelings, against the forsaken creature who committed the dreadful homicide. The sentiments it utters in regard to the part taken by Governor Seward in this remarkable case, we are confident will find a response in every unprejudiced and humane heart: —

"The conduct of Governor Seward in this painful affair reflects the highest honor upon him. Shocked, horrified, though he was at the awful tragedy which had been enacted, and which had destroyed a family with whom he was on terms of intimate friendship, yet seeing the blood-stained, wretched negro deserted by all, even those of his own caste and color, and becoming abundantly satisfied that he was an insane, irresponsible being, he nobly volunteered in his defence. Moved alone by the sympathies of his generous soul, and a high sense of duty to the weak and defenceless — in opposition alike to the entreaties of friends ever watchful of his reputation and interests, and the imprecations of an incensed multitude, eager that the blood of a demented creature should be shed — he boldly threw himself between the victim and those who would hurry him in hot haste to an ignominious death! Without fee or compensation of any description, for four weeks he toiled through the sultry hours of the summer day, far into the shades of night — sparing no time, no strength, no ability — contesting every inch of ground, with an industry, a perseverance, an unyielding faithfulness, that wrung commendation even from those most exasperated against his idiotic client. And all this for whom? For a NEGRO! — the poorest and lowest of his degraded caste — and who, though seated directly by his side, did not know that he was his counsel — was not even aware that one of the mightiest intellects of the age, one of the noblest spirits of the world, was taxing his utmost energies in defence of his life!

"In his eloquent appeal on the preliminary trial respecting Freeman's *insanity*, Governor Seward alluded to the excitement which had been kindled against him for the *faithfulness* with which he defended both Wyatt and Freeman, in the following thrilling passage: —

"'In due time, gentlemen of the jury, when I shall have paid the debt of nature, my remains will rest here in your midst, with those of my kindred and neighbors. It is very possible they may be unhonored — neglected — spurned! But perhaps, years hence, when the passion and excitement which now agitate this community shall have passed away — some wandering stranger — some lone exile — some *Indian* — some *negro* — may erect over them an humble stone, and thereon this epitaph: "HE WAS FAITHFUL!"'

"What spectacle more interesting can be witnessed on earth than was presented on this trial? A statesman of the most commanding talents — one who had received the highest honors the people of his native state could bestow upon him — one whose well-known abilities call around him crowds of wealthy clients, able to reward his valuable services with streams of gold — turning from all these, at the call of humanity, and going down unrewarded, yea at great pecuniary expense to himself, to the defence of this forsaken, pitiable son of Africa! Unrewarded, did I say? A richer reward than silver or gold is his! Wherever the tidings of this strange trial shall be wafted throughout this civilized world, they will carry the name of SEWARD to be embalmed as a sacred treasure in the hearts of all lovers of humanity — of all who sympathize with the degraded and enslaved Ethiopian — of all who pity those whom God has deprived of reason!"

An extract from Mr. Seward's argument in this case, containing an enlightened exposition of insanity, will be found among the Selections in this volume.

CHAPTER XVI.

THE TRIAL OF ABEL F. FITCH AND OTHERS FOR CONSPIRACY, AT DETROIT, IN 1851—MR. SEWARD'S DEFENCE.

In May, 1851, an announcement was made by the press of Detroit, that an atrocious conspiracy (embracing fifty citizens of Jackson county, in the state of Michigan), for the destruction of the property of the Michigan Central Railroad Company, and an indiscriminate war against the lives of passengers travelling on the road, had been discovered, through the activity of agents of that company, and of the police, and that the guilty parties had been suddenly surprised, arrested, and conveyed to jail in Detroit.

The accusation took the form of an indictment for arson, in burning the depôt of that company in Detroit, and the proof that of a conspiracy for the commission of that and other great crimes. The prisoners alleged their entire innocence, and declared that the prosecution was itself a conspiracy, to convict them, by fabricated testimony, of a crime that had not even been committed.

The accused parties denied combination with each other, and even all knowledge of the principal, who was alleged to have committed the crime, and who, as they supposed, had been fraudulently induced to confess it and charge them as accomplices. In applying to be admitted to bail, the sums were fixed so high as to practically deny them that privilege.

Public opinion was vehemently and intensely excited against them, by reason of aggressions that had been committed in their neighborhood for a long time, seriously endangering the lives of passengers. Among the accused were persons in every walk of life; and, while the guilt of some seemed too probable, that of all appeared to be quite impossible. The ten most distinguished lawyers of Michigan were retained, before the arrest, by the railroad company, to conduct the prosecution; and it was said that every other counsellor in the city and state qualified to defend them, except one, had been induced to decline to appear in their behalf.

They applied to Mr. Seward, at Auburn, by telegraph, after the trial had begun, stating these facts. He did not hesitate to appear for men whom the public had prejudged and condemned, and whom the legal profession, except for his going to their aid, would have been deemed to have abandoned.

The issues were perplexed. The evidence was of a most extraordinary character. Even now, it is impossible, on reading it, to decide which was most improbable, the existence of the crime, or the truth of the defence. The trial lasted four months, and so was the longest, in a jury-case, that was ever held. The alleged principal died before the trial began. One of the chief defendants, and another more obscure, died during its progress. Twelve of the fifty defendants were convicted, and all the others acquitted. All these circumstances, together with the ability and learning displayed, mark the case as one of the great state trials of this country. Mr. Seward's argument was published at the time. It reviewed, collated, and condensed the testimony of four hundred witnesses, presenting a very complicated series of transactions, private and public.

This speech fills more than one hundred pages in the report of the trial. To that report we refer the reader, regretting that our limits allow us to present only the introduction and the close of so elaborate and interesting a speech:—

"May it please the Court—Gentlemen of the Jury: This is Detroit, the commercial metropolis of Michigan. It is a prosperous and beautiful city, and is worthy of your pride. I have enjoyed its hospitalities liberal and long. May it stand, and grow, and flourish, for ever! Seventy miles westward, toward the centre of the peninsula, in the county of Jackson, is Leoni, a rural district, containing two new and obscure villages, Leoni and Michigan Centre. Here, in this dock, are the chief members of that community. Either they have committed a great crime against this capital, or there is here a conspiracy of infamous persons seeking to effect their ruin, by the machinery of the law. A state that allows great criminals to go unpunished, or great conspiracies to prevail, can enjoy neither peace, security, nor respect. This trial occurs in the spring-time of the state. It involves so many private and public interests, develops transactions so singular, and is attended by incidents so touching, that it will probably be regarded, not only as an important judicial event in the history of Michigan, but also as entitled to a place among the extraordinary state trials of our country and of our times.

"Forty and more citizens of this state were accused of a felony, and demanded, what its constitution assured them, a trial by jury. An advocate was indispensable in such a trial. They required me to assume that office, on the ground of necessity. I was an advocate by profession. For me the law had postponed the question of their guilt or innocence. Can any one furnish me with what would have been a sufficient excuse for refusing their demand? '*Hoc maxime officii est, ut quisquam maxime opus indigeat, ita ei potissimum opitulari,*'* was the instruction given by Cicero. Can the American lawyer find a better rule of conduct, or one derived from higher authority? . . . . .

"Gentlemen, in the middle of the fourth month we draw near to the end of what has seemed to be an endless labor. While we have been here, events have transpired which have roused national ambition—kindled national resentment—drawn forth national sympathies—and threatened to disturb the tranquillity of empires. He who, although He worketh unseen, yet worketh irresistibly and unceasingly, hath suspended neither his guardian care nor his paternal discipline over ourselves. Some of you

* "The clear point of duty is, to assist most readily those who most need assistance."

have sickened and convalesced. Others have parted with cherished ones, who, removed before they had time to contract the stain of earth, were already prepared for the kingdom of heaven. There have been changes, too, among the unfortunate men whom I have defended. The sound of the hammer has died away in the workshops of some; the harvests have ripened and wasted in the fields of others. Want, and fear, and sorrow, have entered into all their dwellings. Their own rugged forms have drooped; their sunburnt brows have blanched; and their hands have become as soft to the pressure of friendship as yours or mine. One of them—a vagrant boy—whom I found imprisoned here for a few extravagant words, that perhaps he never uttered, has pined away and died. Another—he who was feared, hated, and loved, most of all—has fallen in the vigor of life—

——— 'hacked down,
His thick summer-leaves all faded.'

When such a one falls amid the din and smoke of the battle-field, our emotions are overpowered—suppressed—lost, in the excitement of public passion. But when he perishes a victim of domestic or social life—when we see the iron enter his soul, and see it, day by day, sink deeper and deeper, until nature gives way, and he lies lifeless at our feet—then there is nothing to check the flow of forgiveness, compassion, and sympathy. If, in the moment when he is closing his eyes on earth, he declares—'I have committed no crime against my country; I die a martyr for the liberty of speech, and perish of a broken heart'—then, indeed, do we feel that the tongues of dying men enforce attention, like deep harmony. Who would willingly consent to decide on the guilt or innocence of one who has thus been withdrawn from our erring judgment to the tribunal of eternal justice? Yet it can not be avoided. If Abel F. Fitch was guilty of the crime charged in this indictment, every man here may nevertheless be innocent; but if he was innocent, then there is not one of these, his associates in life, who can be guilty. Try him, then, since you must—condemn him, if you must—and with him condemn them. But remember that you are mortal, and he is now immortal; and that, before the tribunal where he stands, you must stand and confront him, and vindicate your judgment. Remember, too, that he is now free. He has not only left behind him the dungeon, the cell, and the chain, but he exults in a freedom compared with which the liberty we enjoy is slavery and bondage. You stand, then, between the dead and the living. There is no need to bespeak the exercise of your caution—of your candor—and of your impartiality. You will, I am sure, be just to the living, and true to your country; because, under circumstances so solemn—so full of awe—you can not be unjust tc the dead, nor false to your country, nor your God."

Of the character of Governor Seward's professional labors and conduct in the department of arguments at the bar, further illustrations will be found in his pleas for the liberty of the press, and against the fugitive-slave law, and for the rights of inventors, contained in the collection of his works.

A single passage from the first-named plea is given here as embodying Mr. Seward's views of resorts to courts of justice in vindication of personal character when assailed:—

"Actions of libel are now at least comparatively unnecessary. A virtuous and humble life carries with it its own vindication. And if this be not enough, the press has the antidote to its own poisons. If it sometimes wounds, it can effectually heal. An eminent citizen who once presided in this court commenced public life with actions in defence of his character. Assailed as he thought in the evening of his life, he appealed to the press, and his vindication was complete and successful. The licentiousness of the press has impaired its power to defame—and the worst libel ever published would be effectually counteracted by a publication in the simple words, 'I am not guilty,' if it bore the signature of James Milnor, or of one who like him walked among his countrymen in the ways of a pure and blameless life."

CHAPTER XVII.

RECALL TO PUBLIC LIFE — RETROSPECT — POLITICAL AFFAIRS — GENERAL TAYLOR'S ELECTION — CLEVELAND SPEECH.

THE retirement of Governor Seward from office, permitting party heats to abate, and freeing his views on public questions from the influence of prejudice, was followed by a growing reaction of popular sentiment in his favor. He had been opposed by the abolitionists, because he withheld his countenance from their extreme measures, and by the enemies of abolition, because of his sympathy with the cause. Adopted citizens had been led to distrust the sincerity of his efforts in their behalf, and protestants saw danger to religion in his zeal for equal justice to the foreigner and native. The friends of internal improvement accused him of lukewarmness, while the opponents of that system predicted the impoverishment of the state from the extravagance of his zeal. But now all these prejudices were softened. His character and his opinions were presented in a truer light. His sincerity was placed above the reach of suspicion. No one questioned his rare abilities. While new friends were constantly won, his old friends adhered to him with affectionate fidelity. Though abstaining from the exercise of political influence, he was regarded as the leader of his party in the state, and his labors were claimed for every movement in behalf of its interests.

Upon the organization of the Native American party, which commenced with the burning of Roman Catholic churches, and aimed at a complete change in the naturalization laws, the adopted citizens, with one accord, appealed to Governor Seward for sympathy and protection. His speeches and letters, during the agitation of this subject, show his vigorous resistance to principles which he had always regarded as political heresies.* In this respect, his course has been uniform and consistent, from the beginning.

Notwithstanding Governor Seward was overruled in his opposition to the nomination of Mr. Clay for the presidency, in 1844, at the instance of the whig party, he took an active part in the canvass of the state, until the day of the election. He spared no pains to remove the objections of the anti-slavery voters, and of the adopted citizens, to the whig candidate. If strenuous energy and powerful eloquence could have insured success, Henry Clay would have received the vote of New York. But the only result of these efforts was to prevent an increase of the desertion from the whig ranks, which was experienced in 1842.

With his uncompromising hostility to the extension of slavery in the United States, Governor Seward opposed the annexation of Texas to the last, and condemned the Mexican war, which he had predicted as its consequence. Still, during the continuance of the war, he urgently maintained the duty of supporting the government by liberal appropriations of men and money.

While the Oregon question was pending between the United States and Great Britain, he agreed with John Quincy Adams that our government should give notice to Great Britain of the termination of the joint occupancy of that territory. Notwithstanding all the threats and alarms of war, he exerted his influence with the members of Congress to sustain the administration in the adoption of that measure.

The subject of internal improvements in the state, together with the conflicts of interest about the patronage of the federal government, produced a division as early as 1843 in the ranks of the so-called New-York democracy. The rival factions came soon to designate each other as

* See Vol. III.

hunkers and barnburners. While each admitted the necessity of some amendments to the constitution, they could not agree on the details. No proposal to that effect, accordingly, could obtain the assent of two successive legislatures, or a two-third vote, which was necessary in the last instance, for submitting a proposition to the people. The barnburners, who sought for more radical reforms than their opponents, were thus led to agitate the call of a convention for the entire revision of the constitution. This measure was discountenanced by leading whigs, who regarded it as revolutionary, and of dangerous tendencies. Governor Seward took the opposite ground. He argued that such a convention would present an opportunity to the whigs to take the sense of the people upon the measures proposed by the barnburners against internal improvements. It might also secure the advantage of decentralizing the political power of the state, by dividing it into single senatorial and assembly districts, and transferring the appointment of all judicial and administrative offices from the governor and legislature to the people, as well as intrusting all matters of local legislation to county boards of supervisors, instead of the legislature at Albany. It would, moreover, permit an attempt to extend the right of suffrage, without a freehold qualification, to the African race. The views of Governor Seward were generally adopted. The convention was called with great unanimity by all parties. Although the whigs had but a small minority in that body, all the proposed reforms were carried, except the latter. The sceptre which had so long been wielded by the Albany regency was broken, and the concentration of political, judicial, and moneyed power, on which their empire was built, was henceforth impossible.

The recurrence of the presidential election in 1848 found Governor Seward consenting to the nomination of General Taylor, whom he regarded, at that time, as the only available candidate. He had greater confidence in the success of General Taylor, as his name had been brought before the people, in connection with the presidency, on account of his brilliant achievements in the Mexican war, to which he was understood to have been opposed. His election, therefore, would serve to rebuke those politicians who had plunged the country in war for selfish purposes, and would thus inculcate lessons of moderation and peace to rulers. Governor Seward favored his nomination, moreover, because the previous course of the candidate warranted the belief that he would veto no act of Congress establishing governments which excluded slavery in our newly-acquired Mexican territory. With these views, Governor Seward devoted himself with great energy to the canvass in the states of New York, Pennsylvania, Ohio, and Massachusetts, in behalf of General Taylor, and of such members of Congress as might be relied upon to support his administration and to extend the ordinance of 1787, on the principle of the Wilmot proviso, over the Mexican territories.

His speech at Cleveland, Ohio, so clearly presents his views of the relative position of parties on the slavery question that we make room for several extracts in this place: —

"The occasion invites to a consideration of many grave subjects. But the time is short. I shall waste little on the prejudices which constitute the chief capital of our political adversaries. The two ancient and obsolete parties originated in the debate upon questions of organic law, and waxed strong in the discussion of the principles of administration proper for a neutral nation during the conflict between European belligerents. Each performed its duties and fulfilled its destiny; each contributed enough to be remembered in lasting gratitude; and each was hurried at times into errors to be forgiven and avoided.

"'The knights are dust,
Their swords in rust,
Their souls in heaven we trust.'

"Our duties are to the generation which is living, and to the generations which are to come into life. It is a living faith, and not a dead one, that yields beneficent fruits. He who acts from prejudice or from passion is a slave. He who persuades another to act so makes him a slave. The ballot-box is an altar of independence, not of slavery:—

> "'Thou of an independent mind,
> With soul resolved, with soul resigned,
> Prepared Oppression's proudest frowns to brave,
> Who will not *be* nor *make* a slave,
> Virtue alone who dost revere,
> Thy own reproach alone dost fear—
> Approach this shrine and worship here.'

"I am to converse with whigs only, and not with all whigs, but with some who propose to secede temporarily if not permanently from the association whose labors, privations, defeats, and triumphs, they have hitherto shared with perseverance and fidelity. I shall speak not for a man, not for men, not even for a party, but for the common cause which thus far has held us together, and which the seceders promise to advance more effectually by separation. To such I may say, perhaps, without presumption—

> "'Hear me for my cause, and be silent, that you may hear; believe me for mine honor, and have respect unto mine honor that you may the better judge.'

"I shall ask you to consider, first, the principles and policy which the interest of our country and of humanity demand; secondly, how we can most effectually render those principles and that policy triumphant.

"We never were, we are not now, and for a long time to come we can not be, a unique and homogeneous people. The colonies which preceded our states were off-shoots from an imperfect European civilization. England, Ireland, Scotland, Wales, France, Spain, Switzerland, Italy, Germany, Holland, and Sweden, contributed the original elements of population; with these were mingled the natives of the continent, and compulsory immigration from the wilds of Africa. The disasters and privations of the Old World cause this flood of immigration to continue with daily-increasing volume, and our settlement on the Pacific will soon become the gate for a similar flow from the worn-out civilization of Asia. Our twenty millions are expanding to two hundred millions—our originally narrow domain into a great empire. Its destiny is to renovate the condition of mankind.

"The first principle of our duty as American citizens is to preserve the integrity of the Union. Without the Union, there would be not only a want of harmony of action, but collisions and conflicts ending in anarchy or probably in despotism. This Union must be a voluntary one, and not compulsory. A Union upheld by force would be despotism.

"The second principle of American citizenship is, that our democratic system must be preserved and perfected. That system is founded in the natural equality of *all* men—not alone all *American* men, nor alone all *white* men, but all MEN of every country, clime, and complexion, are equal—not made equal by human laws, but born equal. It results from this that every man permanently residing in a community is a member of the state, obliged to submit to its rule, and therefore entitled equally with every other man to participate in its government. If it be a monarchy, he has a right to keep a musket to defend himself when the government becomes intolerable. If it be a democracy, where consent is substituted for force, he has a right to a ballot for the same purpose; and each should be placed in his hands (he being a resident) when he is able to speed the bullet or cast the ballot with discretion. Whatever institutions or laws we have existing among us which deny this principle, are wrong, and ought to be corrected.

"A third principle of American citizenship is, that knowledge ought to be diffused, as well for the safety of the state, as to promote the happiness of society.

"A fourth principle is, that our national resources, physical, moral, and intellectual, ought to be developed and applied to increase the public wealth, and enhance the convenience and comfort of the people.

"A fifth principle is, that peace and moderation are indispensable to the preservation of republican institutions.

"A sixth principle is, that slavery must be abolished.

"I think these are the principles of the whigs of the Western Reserve of Ohio. I am not now to say for the first time that they are mine. I imbibed them from the philosophy of the American Revolution—

> "Soon as the charity of my native land
> Wrought in my bosom.'

* * * * * * * *

"There are two antagonistical elements of society in America, freedom and slavery. Freedom is in harmony with our system of government and with the spirit of the age, and is therefore passive and quiescent. Slavery is in conflict with that system, with justice, and with humanity, and is therefore organized, defensive, active, and perpetually aggressive.

"Freedom insists on the emancipation and elevation of labor; slavery demands a soil moistened with tears and blood—freedom a soil that exults under the elastic tread of man in his native majesty.

"These elements divide and classify the American people into two parties. Each of these parties has its court and its sceptre. The throne of the one is amid the rocks of the Allegany mountains; the throne of the other is reared on the sands of South Carolina. One of these parties, the party of slavery, regards disunion as among the means of defence, and not always the last to be employed. The other maintains the Union of the states, one and inseparable, now and for ever, as the highest duty of the American people to themselves, to posterity, to mankind.

"The party of slavery upholds an aristocracy founded on the humiliation of labor, as necessary to the perfection of a chivalrous republic. The party of freedom maintains universal suffrage, which makes men equal before human laws, as they are in the sight of their common Creator.

"The party of slavery cherishes ignorance, because it is the only security for oppression. The party of liberty demands the diffusion of knowledge, because it is the only safeguard of republican institutions.

"The party of slavery patronizes labor which produces only exports to commercial nations abroad—tobacco, cotton, and sugar—and abhors the protection that draws grain from our native fields, lumber from our native forests, iron and coal from our native mines, and ingenuity, skill, and labor, from the free minds and willing hands of our own people.

"The party of freedom favors only the productions of such minds and such hands, and seeks to build up our empire out of the redundant native materials with which our country is blest.

"The party of slavery leaves the mountain ravine and shoal to present all their natural obstacles to internal trade and free locomotion, because railroads, rivers, and canals, are highways for the escape of bondsmen.

"The party of liberty would cover the country with railroads and canals, to promote the happiness of the people, and bind them together with the indissoluble bonds of interest and affection.

"The party of slavery maintains its military defences, and cultivates the martial spirit, for it knows not the day nor the hour when a standing army will not be necessary to suppress and extirpate the insurrectionary bondsmen.

"The party of freedom cherishes peace, because its sway is sustained by the consent of a happy and grateful people.

"The party of slavery fortifies itself by adding new slave-bound domain on fraudulent pretexts and with force.

"The party of freedom is content and moderate, seeking only a just enlargement of free territory.

"The party of slavery declares that institution necessary, beneficent, and approved of God, and therefore inviolable.

"The party of freedom seeks complete and universal emancipation.

"You, whigs of the Reserve, and you especially, seceding whigs, none know so well as you that these two elements exist and are developed in the two great national parties of the land, as I have described them. That existence and development constitute the only reason you can assign for having been enrolled in the whig party, and mustered under its banner so zealously and so long. And now I am not to contend that the evil spirit I have described has possessed the one party without mitigation or exception, and that the beneficent one has on all occasions, and fully, directed the action of the other. But I appeal to you, to your candor and justice, whether the beneficent spirit has not worked chiefly in the whig party, and its antagonist in the adverse party.

* * * * * * * *

"You infer that the whig party have fallen away from their ancient faith. I admit its comparative unsoundness. I confess it, but it is still the truest and most faithful of the two parties, and one or the other of them must prevail. The unsoundness of both arises from the fault of the country and of the age. Neither was ever more sound and faithful than it is now: it is your duty and mine to make them both more faithful.

"Slavery was once the sin, not of some of the states only, but of them all—not of our nation only, but of all nations. It perverted and corrupted the moral sense of mankind, deeply, universally; and this corruption became a universal habit. Habits of thought became fixed principles. No American state has yet delivered itself entirely from those habits. We in New York are guilty of slavery still, by withholding the right of suffrage from the race we have emancipated. You in Ohio are guilty in the same way, by a system of black-laws, still more aristocratic and odious. It is written in the constitution of the United States that five slaves shall count equal to three free men, as a basis of representation; and it is written also, in violation of the Divine law, that we shall surrender the fugitive slave who takes refuge at our fireside from his relentless pursuers. You blush not at these things, because they have become familiar as household words, and your pretended free-soil allies claim particular merit for maintaining these miscalled guaranties of slavery which they find in the national compact.

"Does not all this prove that the whig party has kept up with the spirit of the age—that it is as true and faithful to human freedom as the inert conscience of the American people will permit it to be?

"'What, then!' you say, 'can nothing be done for freedom because the public conscience is inert?' Yes, much can be done—everything can be done. Slavery can be limited to its present bounds, it can be ameliorated, it can be and must be abolished, and you and I can and must do it. The task is as simple and easy as its consummation will be beneficent and its rewards glorious. It requires only to follow this simple rule of action, viz.: to do everywhere and on every occasion what we can, and not to neglect or refuse to do what we can at any time, because at that precise time and on that particular occasion we can not do more. Circumstances determine possibilities. When we have done our best to shape them and make them propitious, we may rest satisfied that superior Wisdom has determined their form as they exist, and will be satisfied with us if we then do all the good that circumstances leave in our power. But we must begin deeper and lower than in the composition and combination of factions and parties. Wherein do the strength and security of slavery lie? You answer that they lie in the constitution of the United States, and the constitution and laws of all slaveholding states. Not at all. They lie in the erroneous sentiment of the American people. Constitutions and laws can no more rise above the virtue of the people than the limpid stream can climb above its native spring. Inculcate, then, the love of freedom and the equal rights of man, under the paternal roof; see to it that they are taught in the schools and in the churches; reform your own code—extend a cordial welcome to the fugitive who lays his weary limbs at your door, and defend him as you would your paternal gods; correct your own error, that slavery has any constitutional guaranty which may not be released, and ought not to be relinquished. Say to Slavery, when it shows its bond and demands the pound of flesh, that if it draws one drop of blood, its life shall pay the forfeit. Inculcate that free states can maintain the rights of hospitality and of humanity; that executive authority can forbear to favor slavery; that Congress can debate; that Congress at least can mediate with the slaveholding states, that at least future generations might be bought and given up to freedom, and that the treasures wasted in the war with Mexico would have been sufficient to have redeemed millions unborn from bondage. Do all this and inculcate all this in the spirit of moderation and benevolence, and not of retaliation and fanaticism, and you will soon bring the parties of the country into an effective aggression upon slavery. Whenever the public mind shall will the abolition of slavery, the way will open for it.

"I know that you will tell me that this is all too slow. Well, then, go faster, if you can, and I will go with you; but remember the instructive lesson that was taught in the words, "These things ought ye to have done, and not to have left the others undone." Remember that the liberty party tried the unattainable, overlooking the attainable, and now has compromised and surrendered the principle of immediate emancipation for a coalition to effect a practicable measure which can only be defeated by that coalition. Remember that no human work is done without preparation. God works out his sublimest purposes among men with preparation. There was a voice of one crying in the wilderness, 'Prepare ye the way,' before the Son of man could come. There was a John before a Jesus; there was a baptism of water before the baptism of the Holy Ghost and of fire."

All Mr. Seward's speeches during this campaign were full of the same sentiments. In the cities of Boston, Philadelphia, and New York as well as among the yeomanry of Pennsylvania, New York, and Ohio, he spoke the same language, and the demonstrations of concurrence were equally hearty and unanimous in city and country.

In one of these speeches he alludes to the nomination of General Taylor in preference to Mr. Clay and Mr. Webster in the following words: —

"What is the presidency of the United States compared with the fame of a patriot statesman who triumphs over popular injustice and establishes his country on the sure foundations of freedom and empire?"*

* See Vol. III., p. 305.

CHAPTER XVIII.

PRESIDENT TAYLOR—MR. SEWARD ELECTED SENATOR—GENERAL TAYLOR'S POLICY—MR. SEWARD'S COURSE AND SPEECHES—THE HIGHER LAW—THE COMPROMISE OF 1850—SPEECHES ON VARIOUS SUBJECTS—VISIT TO VERMONT—AGRICULTURAL ADDRESS—CANADA.

THE election of General Taylor to the presidency seemed to be a favorable indication for the policy of freedom, that had been so earnestly defended by Governor Seward. Connected with the return of a whig majority both in the national house of representatives and the legislature of New York, that event was supposed to guaranty the restriction of slavery within its existing boundaries and the establishment of a free domain along the gulf of Mexico, and across the continent to the Pacific ocean. Under these circumstances, Governor Seward was elected to the senate of the United States, in place of Hon. John A. Dix, whose term was about to expire. The vote of the legislature, which was given in February, 1849, stood—for Governor Seward 121, and for all others 30. This was an unusually large majority, there being no serious opposition to his election. He entered the thirty-first Congress, together with thirty-three other whig members, and one democratic member, from the state of New York, who, in accordance with the prevailing sentiment of the state, were all understood to agree with him in the policy of circumscribing the region of slavery.

On arriving at Washington, in February before the commencement of his senatorial term, Mr. Seward found Congress engaged on an amendment to the civil and diplomatic appropriation bill, proposed by Mr. Walker, of which the effect would be to abrogate the laws of Mexico for the prohibition of slavery. This amendment had already passed the senate, but Mr. Seward, with characteristic energy, exerted himself to secure its defeat in the house. His efforts were successful; the amendment was lost in the house, after a long and excited debate; the senate receded from it, on the last night of the session.*

The sagacity of President Taylor, on his accession to office was signally displayed in his choice of Mr. Seward as one of his most intimate friends and counsellors. Familiar with all the elements of northern society, with every aspect of public opinion, and the feelings and interests of the people — conversant with civil affairs as a jurist and statesman — cherishing a lofty sense of honor and a generous sympathy with popular rights — courteous and tolerant toward his opponents, though rigidly faithful to his convictions — inspired with a glowing sentiment both of patriotism and humanity — and ardently devoted to the support of the federal Union — he was eminently qualified to promote the welfare of his country in the responsible function of adviser to the president. With a delicate sense of propriety, while thus enjoying the confidence of President Taylor, he declined being placed on any important committee of the senate, lest it might be supposed, on some occasions, that he acted authoritatively in his behalf. He was unwilling to embarrass the administration by any sectional prejudices against himself, but wished quietly to bring the aid of his wisdom and experience to the support of its head.

He concurred with President Taylor in his invitation to California and New Mexico to organize state governments and apply for admission into the Union at the next session of Congress. The suggestion of the president was adopted. As Mr. Seward had anticipated, California appeared by her senators and representatives at the commencement of the congressional session in December, 1849, with a

* See Vol. III., p. 443.

constitution excluding slavery. It was understood that New Mexico was preparing to come with a similar constitution.

To Mr. Seward belongs the authorship of the phrase —*the Higher Law*—which has acquired a fame that will never die. It was used by him in his speech in the senate, March 11, 1850, on the admission of California into the Union.*

This speech was unanimously acknowledged to be a bold, manly, and profound production. Lucid and consecutive in argument, learned in historical and philosophical illustrations, with a chaste elegance of diction, it was not surpassed for sound statesmanship and an acute exposition of the principles of natural and constitutional law, by any speech delivered in the senate on the absorbing subject of freedom in the territories.

The enemies of Mr. Seward at once accused him of maintaining the existence of a Higher Law, in *opposition* to the constitution, by which the new domain of California was devoted to justice, liberty, and union. But this was a flagrant misrepresentation of his language, which embodied a truth, that none but the grossest materialists and skeptics can call in question. No enlightened ethical philosopher, no man of ordinary religious feeling and conscientiousness, will deny that there is a law higher than political constitutions and human legislation, "the law which governs all law—the law of our Creator, the law of humanity, justice, equity, the law of nature and of nations." Nor will it be doubted, that in case of a conflict between divine and human law, "we ought to obey God, rather than man." But it was not the purpose of Mr. Seward on that occasion, to repeat a principle so plain as this. The phrase as used by him on the floor of the senate would hardly seem capable of such misconstruction as has been given to it. We quote his words, precisely as they were spoken:—

* See Vol. I., p. 51.

"It is true, indeed, that the national domain is ours. It is true it was acquired by the valor and with the wealth of the whole nation. But we hold, nevertheless, no arbitrary power over it. We hold no arbitrary authority over anything, whether acquired lawfully or seized by usurpation. The constitution regulates our stewardship; the constitution devotes the domain to union, to justice, to defence, to welfare, and to liberty. But there is a Higher Law than the constitution, which regulates our authority over the domain, and devotes it to *the same noble purposes*. The territory is a part, no inconsiderable part, of the common heritage of mankind, bestowed upon them by the Creator of the universe. We are his stewards, and must so discharge our trust as to secure in the highest attainable degree their happiness."

Every intelligent reader will perceive that while Mr. Seward devoutly recognises the law of God, and its paramount claims both on individuals and nations, he was far from asserting a contradiction between that law and the American constitution on the subject in question. On the contrary, he declares that they agree in demanding freedom and justice for the new domain. Can any wise statesman, can any far-seeing patriot, can any friend of human improvement, deny the soundness of this position?

But let us not be misunderstood. In vindicating Mr. Seward from the aspersions which were brought upon him by the expression alluded to, it is far from our intention to disclaim for him a belief that the obligation of human laws is founded on their harmony with the principles of eternal justice. He is no adherent of the superficial and wretched philosophy which derives the distinctions of morality from the caprices of opinion. In common with the greatest thinkers of all ages, he traces the obligation of right to the uncreated wisdom of the Deity. With Plato and Cicero, in ancient times, with Bacon, Hooker, and Cudworth, at a later date, he recognises the bosom of the Deity as the seat and fountain of law—"whose voice is the harmony of the world." This ennobling idea pervades the writings of Mr. Seward—it is the pivot of his personal character, as well as of his public and legislative career. Among other instances of its operation, we find it in an argument, in 1847, relating to the fugitive slave law of 1793, wher) he uses the following striking expression: "Congress has no power to inhibit any duty commanded by God on Mount Sinai, or by his son on the Mount of Olives."*

In a subsequent speech in the senate he alludes to the personal abuse which these sentiments had excited, in the following firm but dignified language:—

"I do not propose to reply to what is personal in the remarks of the honorable senator. I have nothing of a personal character to say. There is no man in this land who is of sufficient importance to this country and to mankind, to justify his consumption of five minutes of the time of the senate of the United States, with personal explanations relating to himself. The speeches which I have made here, under a rule of the senate, are recorded, and what is recorded has gone before the people and will go, worthy or not, into history. I leave them to mankind. I stand by what I have said. That is all I have to say upon that subject.

The senator proposes to expel me. I am ready to meet that trial too; and if I shall be expelled, I shall not be the first man subjected to punishment for maintaining that there is a power higher than human law, and that that power delights in justice; that rulers, whether despots or elected rulers of a free people, are bound to administer justice for the benefit of society. Senators, when they please to bring me for trial, or otherwise, before the senate of the United States, will find a clear and open field. I ask no other defence than the speeches upon which they propose to condemn me. The speeches will read for themselves, and they will need no comment from me."

During the discussion of the "Compromise Bill," Mr. Seward addressed the senate, July 2, 1850, in a speech† remarkable for the vigor of its dialectics, its comprehensive

* See Forensic Arguments, Parks vs. Van Zandt, Vol. I., p. 476.

† See Vol. I., p. 94.

and sagacious statesmanship, and its noble zeal for freedom, as well as for the appositeness of its classical illustrations, and the polished beauty of its style. His exposition of the dangers and evils of the compromise is in a strain of masterly eloquence. After appealing to the wisdom of his auditors to adopt the true principle of conciliation by gradual reform, he closed his remarks with one of those genuine touches of poetry which often flash over the severity of his argumentative discourse. "We shall then realize once more the concord which results from mutual league, united councils, and equal hopes and hazards in the most sublime and beneficent enterprise the earth has witnessed. The fingers of the powers above would tune the harmony of such a peace."

This speech was succeeded by speeches on "New Mexico," and "Freedom in the District of Columbia,"* in which Mr. Seward displayed his usual elevation of thought in applying the principles of universal justice to the maintenance of human rights. In January, 1851, Mr. Seward delivered a speech on the question of "Indemnities for French Spoliations,"† giving a luminous analysis of the whole subject, accompanied with ample historical proofs, and eloquently enforcing the necessity of justice and good faith to national honor. The state that would be prosperous must be free from the burden of violated engagements. The people that would dwell in safety, without fear for fireside, fane, or capitol, must practise an austere and pure morality — must embody in their daily lives the spirit of the eternal law through which "the most ancient heavens are fresh and strong."

The next important topic on which Mr. Seward addressed the senate was the "Public Domain."‡ In his speech on this subject, February 27, 1851, without maintaining the absurdity that the land of any country ought

* See Vol. I., p. 111. † See Vol. I., p. 132.
‡ See Vol. I., p. 156.

to be, or can be, equally divided and enjoyed, he shows the evils arising to the highest interests of society from great inequalities in landed estates. His views of the gratuitous distribution of portions of the public domain to actual settlers, although they may fail to win the sympathy of politicians, are marked by equal humanity and good sense, and will challenge the attention of all intelligent friends of social progress.

In December, 1851, Mr. Seward submitted a resolution to the senate, in favor of a cordial welcome by Congress to Kossuth, to be communicated by the president as the executive organ of the United States. His sentiments in regard to the illustrious champion of Hungary are expressed in two speeches on the subject, which handle the objections of the opponents to the resolution with a good-humored severity of argument, and a remarkable terseness of language, while they present the claims of Kossuth to the admiration of American freemen, in a style of fervid eloquence that is equally touching in its pathos and convincing in its appeals.*

During the following February, the discussion of Mr. Foote's resolution, declaring the sympathy of Congress with the exiled Irish patriots, Smith O'Brien and Thomas F. Meagher, came up in the senate, when Mr. Seward took occasion to express his deep interest in the welfare of Ireland, enforcing his views with his usual vigor of argument and liveliness of illustration.† This was succeeded in March by a speech on "Freedom in Europe," in which he presents an admirable sketch of the Hungarian revolution, discusses the neutral policy of Washington in regard to foreign nations, explains the true character of intervention, and argues at length in its defence. The tone of this speech is lofty and severe, and in some passages rises to an almost Miltonic grandeur.‡

* See Vol. I., p. 172. † See Vol. I., p. 186.
‡ See Vol. I., p. 196.

The next speeches of Mr. Seward in the senate were on "American Steam Navigation,"* "Survey of the Arctic and Pacific Oceans,"† and "The American Fisheries."‡ A peculiar value attaches to these speeches from their eminently practical character, the variety and accuracy of the statistics which they embody, their clear and cogent reasonings on the facts they present, the intimate knowledge which they exhibit of the commercial and industrial relations of the country, and the enlightened and glowing patriotism with which they are inspired. To the admirers of Mr. Seward they are of no less interest, on account of their fine illustrations both of his mental habits and his personal character. In the action of his intellect, patience, and depth of research, a constant aim at the integral unity of the subject, a logical grouping of particulars in reference to a future pregnant inference, and a singular self-possession in the exercise of judgment, ever serve as the basis which underlies the expression of a masculine and generous enthusiasm and an earnest-hearted sympathy with all that is beautiful in the progress, or sacred in the hopes of collective humanity.

Immediately after the adjournment of Congress, Mr. Seward delivered the first anniversary address before the Agricultural Society of the state of Vermont, at Rutland, on the 2d of September, 1852.

As nothing could be more grateful or more just, so we are sure nothing could be more sincere than the following tribute, paid by him to that state, in the opening of this interesting address:—

"Citizens of Vermont:—Ladies and Gentlemen: A schoolmaster from Middlebury taught me to read the glowing praises and simple maxims of Roman agriculture recorded in the pages of Virgil. Natives of Rutland and Bennington were among my youthful companions and early patrons, still affectionately and gratefully remembered. Long ago I seemed to myself to have imbibed—I know not when nor how—many

* See Vol. I., p. 222. † See Vol. I., p. 236. ‡ See Vol. I., p. 254.

principles, sentiments, and sympathies, from fountains of philosophy and feeling which had been opened early, and which are yet flowing freely here in Vermont. Longer than I can recollect, my hopes for my country and mankind have had their anchorage in the ever-widening prevalence of those maxims of political justice and equal liberty which have been always maintained with unyielding constancy in this state, the Tyrol of America. I have wondered often, when such memories as these have come over me, that although I had not been quite unused to travel, and had lived always near, yet I was nevertheless a stranger in Vermont. Long-delayed wishes of mine are now gratified. I am at last in Vermont. I pay to her mountains the homage which the sublime in nature exacts; and to her mountaineers I confess that my motive in coming was not so much to instruct them as to seek their personal acquaintance, and to thank them for precious and cherished instructions which they have long since imparted to me.

"These, then, are 'the grants' sold by New Hampshire without title, and won by force from New York when she perverted title to purposes of oppression. In lime and marble they are rich, and in forest-growth and in pasturage, at least, they are fertile; and the vigorous play of the elastic air upon lungs which had become languid under southern skies, assures me that they are as healthful as they are romantic and beautiful. Nevertheless, it must have been no easy task that the settler performed here when he removed the sturdy trees and massive rocks, and opened the dank and festering soil to the light and heat of the morning sun. It was no common bravery that kept the savage Indian at bay while exterminating the wolf and the panther; and no common heroism that, while engaged in the foremost ranks of the Revolution for the deliverance of New York and the other colonies from British power, effected a revolution also against New York, and established the independence of Vermont herself. I think, indeed, that, at this day, men as hardy, brave, and heroic, as ETHAN ALLEN and his followers—if there be such—would pass by regions as rugged and wild as of old these must have been, to find, with less fatigue and danger, easier and more attractive homes on the Mississippi prairies, or on the golden terraces of California and Oregon.

"Certainly the descendants have carried on with perseverance and success the enterprise their ancestors so bravely began. Their fields are clean, and a stiff stubble shows that they have been covered well with grain; their pasturages carefully drained, and trodden by sheep, horses, and cattle—than which I am sure there are none better; their villages embellished with gardens, and crowned with schools and colleges; and their statesmen discharging useful and honorable functions in the national councils and in foreign courts. I can not, indeed, suppress repining regret that so fair a portion of my native state was lost for ever by the obstinate persistence of her authorities in claims which, although based on royal constitutions, were without necessary foundation in equity. Nevertheless, looking upon the scenes that stretch out before me, as we may suppose an Englishman, who loves his native land well, but loves freedom and humanity still better, may look upon the growing greatness and spreading dominion of our common country, I say again, with cheerfulness and enthusiasm, hail to Vermont! Her independence was justly and bravely won. She has chosen a peaceful and beneficent mission, and she fulfills it faithfully and generously. May her prosperity continue, and her glory increase for ever!"*

After a pleasant sojourn of several days in Vermont, receiving many manifestations of courtesy and respect in various parts of the state, Mr. Seward extended his journey to Montreal and Quebec. The provincial parliament was then in session at Quebec; and he was entertained by its members, as well as by the governor-general (Lord Elgin) and other authorities, in a manner which evinced a high consideration for him as a statesman, and the most fraternal feelings toward the country of which he was regarded as a representative.

* See Vol. III., p. 176.

CHAPTER XIX.

THE PRESIDENTIAL ELECTION OF 1852—THE SLAVERY CONTEST OF 1850—DEATH OF PRESIDENT TAYLOR—HIS SUCCESSOR—OVERTHROW OF THE WHIG PARTY—CAUSES—RESULTS, ETC.

The presidential election of 1852 is yet so recent, that its incidents can be recalled without difficulty. The success of the whig party in the free states, during the contest of 1848, was promoted by the assurance that it would prevent the introduction of slavery into the new territories, where it was already prohibited by the Mexican laws. The representatives of the free states in Congress were understood to be pledged to that wise and beneficent policy. It was assumed that the new president would not interpose the executive veto, should that policy be adopted. Mr. Seward was committed in its favor, both by the circumstances of his election, and the well-known tenor of his political life. On the meeting of Congress in December, 1849, several whig members from the South apprehended the adoption of that policy, and refused to unite with their northern brethren in the choice of a speaker. After delaying the organization of the house for a number of weeks, they finally joined with their political opponents, and elected a democratic speaker from one of the slaveholding states. As soon as the house was organized, the southern party demanded the establishment of the new territories, without any condition as to the introduction of slavery. The representatives of the free states earnestly protested against this course. Mr. Seward took an active part in the opposition. Faithful to their convictions, they insisted on the insertion of the Wilmot proviso (which was identical in its spirit with Mr. Jefferson's proviso in the ordinance of 1787) in any act ordaining the government of the territories. The president took a middle ground in his message to Congress. He recommended that the territories should be left, without any preliminary organization, under the existing Mexican laws, until they should have obtained the requisite population to form voluntary constitutions, and apply for admission as states of the Union. California and New Mexico were already taking measures for this purpose. The recommendation of the president was condemned by the slave states, while it met the approval of the friends of freedom. At an early period it was opposed by Mr. Clay. After great reserve and deliberation, Mr. Webster subsequently declared his hostility to the proposed measure. Mr. Seward, who upheld the recommendation, thus became the leader of the administration party in both houses of Congress. The antagonists of slavery with whom he co-operated, though a minority in the senate, had a decided majority in the house of representatives. Each branch of Congress became the scene of vehement debate. The slaveholding party indulged in such violent and inflammatory language as to threaten the derangement of public business, and even the disorganization of Congress. This party was sustained by the Nashville convention — a body of southern delegates assembled for the purpose of adopting measures for the secession of the slave states from the Union. But neither President Taylor nor Mr. Seward was intimidated by these proceedings. They both persisted in the course, which was sanctioned alike by judgment and conscience. Mr. Clay, on the other hand, believed that the existence of the Union was at stake. Sustained by Mr. Webster, he consented to adopt the non-intervention policy, the avowal of which by General Cass had made him the candidate of the democratic party in the late presidential election. He now brought forward his famous compromise scheme, and urged its adoption with all the force of his glowing and persuasive eloquence. Appealing to the sentiment of patriotism, to the prevailing attachment to the Union, and to the love of peace, he represented the acceptance of his measures as essential to the final settlement of the issues which had grown out of the existence of slavery in the United States. Mr. Clay's views were sustained by the leading advocates of slavery in Congress. For the most part, these belonged to the democratic party. They were pledged to insist on a Congressional declaration of the right of slaveholders to carry their slaves into any of the territories of the United States. But the compromise was opposed by most of the representatives of the free states, who were determined to make no further concessions besides those involved in the position taken by President Taylor. The whigs of the slave states, on the other hand, gave it their hearty support. It was defended also by the more especial friends of Mr. Clay and Mr. Webster, among the whigs of the North, as well as by a large portion of the democratic party in the free states. The more conservative classes in the great northern cities were induced to give it their support, through fear of the loss of southern trade and patronage, and a growing discontent with the policy of the new administration. The friends of the compromise endeavored to arouse the fears of the people, by showing the danger of a dissolution of the Union, which was threatened, as they alleged, by the policy of President Taylor. Mr. Seward, of course, was denounced as a desperate and dangerous agitator. His resistance to the compromise was represented as a contumacy. He was accused of wishing to obtain personal aggrandizement, even upon the ruins of the constitution and the wreck of the Union. These reproaches were not without effect. They produced a partial division of the whig party in the free states, and awakened a prejudice in many quarters against the name of Mr. Seward. But he was not shaken from his steadfastness. With admirable firmness and self-possession, he nobly resisted the current of popular agitation and Congressional excitement. The dignity of his bearing and the wisdom of his counsels, during this stormy period, receive ample illustration from his published "Works," as well as from many pages of the present volume.

The first applicant for admission into the Union was California, which had adopted a free constitution in a general convention. The friends of the compromise refused to grant her demand, except on certain stringent conditions. They insisted that Congress should waive a similar prohibition of slavery in organizing the territories of Utah and New Mexico, and at the same time enact a new and offensive law for the capture of fugitive slaves in the free states. Mr. Seward demanded the admission of California, without condition and without qualification, leaving other subjects to distinct and independent legislation. No fair-minded man, it would seem, could doubt the wisdom or justice of such a course. The partisans of the compromise contended that Utah and New Mexico should be organized, without a prohibition of slavery, at the very moment when the latter was known to have adopted a free constitution, and to have chosen representatives to demand admission into the Union. On this question, Mr. Seward maintained that New Mexico should either be admitted into the Union as a free state, or left to enjoy the protection from slavery afforded by the existing Mexican laws.

The fugitive-slave law, which was proposed as a condition of the admission of California, met with a determined opponent in Mr. Seward, from the first. He clearly foresaw the impolicy, as well as the cruelty of the contemplated measure. He argued with no less humanity than good faith, that no public exigency required a new law on the subject—that the bill in question was as unconstitutional as it was repugnant to every just sentiment—and that the principles and habits of the northern people would place every obstacle in the way of its execution. Admitting the justice of these views, the compromisers demanded that they should be set aside, lest the determination of the slaveholders should lead to a dissolution of the Union. Mr. Seward was incapable of yielding to such unworthy terrors. He constantly passed them by, as too trivial for serious notice. At the same time, he urgently pointed out the danger of quailing before the threats of the South. Knowing the dispositions engendered by slavery, he insisted that any craven truckling on the part of the free states, would lead to unbounded aggressions by the slave power in the future. With prophetic sagacity, he was enabled to cast the horoscope of coming ills, which have since been realized in the legislation concerning Kansas and Nebraska.

The compromisers regarded their measures as essential to the suppression of the slavery agitation in the national councils, and to the permanent tranquillity of the Union. Mr. Seward maintained precisely the opposite views. He insisted that the extension of slavery was too great a price to pay even for the attainment of peace—that a peace purchased on such terms, would be only a hollow truce—that it would soon be disturbed by new and deeper agitations—that freedom and slavery were essentially antagonistic in their nature—and that no reconciliation could be effectual, until the latter should abandon its pretensions to new territories, and new conquests. The soundness of Mr. Seward's opinions have been confirmed by subsequent events. The exciting congressional discussion of the subject continued for several months. Its effect was favorable to the policy of President Taylor and Mr. Seward. It promised to guaranty the establishment of free institutions, unvitiated by the presence of slavery, to the vast possessions between the organized states and the Pacific ocean.

An unforeseen casualty changed the fortunes of the conflict. President Taylor died in the month of July, 1850, and by the terms of the constitution, Millard Fillmore, the vice-president, was advanced to the executive chair of the

United States. A citizen of the state of New York, he had already exhibited symptoms of jealousy, in regard to the influence of Mr. Seward—a feeling which was shared by many of his friends. At the same time, he was understood to concur with Mr. Seward in the general principles of policy, which had guided the course of the latter on the slavery question. Mr. Seward advised the new president to retain the cabinet of General Taylor, and endeavor to carry out his views. But this course was in direct opposition to the plan of the compromisers. They urged the importance of abandoning the policy hitherto pursued, and of appointing a cabinet committed to their own. Mr. Fillmore accepted their advice. His administration was, in reality, founded on the principles of the party, which his election had defeated. Of course, it relied for support on a coalition between the members of that party, and so many of his own, as could be gained to his views. Soon after this change in the executive, many of the opponents of the compromise fell off from the side of Mr. Seward, while others attempted to steer a middle course, expressing themselves in language of moderation, or preserving a total silence. Although the compromise bill itself was defeated, the measures which it embodied were submitted to a separate discussion and successively passed. The whigs of the free states were thrown into perplexity by this sudden change. The coalition demanded the acceptance of the compromise as the final adjustment of the slavery controversy. No favors were to be expected from the administration by those who failed to comply with the terms. A refusal was deemed sufficient evidence of disloyalty to the government, and of hostility to the Union. But Mr. Seward was not influenced by the motives thus held out. His opposition to the compromise measures was unabated. He gave no heed to the denunciations of power. For the present, the vital question had been settled in Congress. It had now passed over to the tribunal of the country. In fact, it waited the judgment of the civilized world. Mr. Seward was unwilling to expose himself for a moment to the danger of misapprehension. He neglected no proper occasion to declare his adherence to the convictions and principles which he had expressed throughout the congressional debates; although he declined to engage in any defence or explanation of his course amid the excitement of popular assemblies.

The question of slavery, in its comprehensive bearings, formed the turning point in the presidential canvass of 1852, which resulted as will be seen in the election of Mr. Pierce, and at a subsequent period, in the abrogation of the Missouri Compromise, and the enactment of the Kansas and Nebraska bill.

The national democratic convention, held in Baltimore, June 1, 1852, unanimously adopted a platform, approving the compromise of 1850, as the final decision of the slavery question. After a vehement and protracted struggle between the friends of prominent candidates, Franklin Pierce, of New Hampshire, who had hitherto not been placed in the ranks of competitors, was nominated for president.

The whig party were widely divided on the question of acquiescence in the compromise measures. They were still more at variance in regard to the claims of rival candidates for the presidency. Mr. Seward's friends in the free states, united in the support of General Scott, who had, to a considerable extent, stood aloof from the agitations of the last few years. Although, as it was understood, General Scott approved of the compromise measures, as acts of political necessity, he was supposed to have no wish to use them as a political test. On the other hand, the exclusive supporters of the compromise as a condition of party allegiance, were divided between Millard Fillmore, at that time the acting president, and Daniel Webster, secretary of state, as candidates for the executive office. The Whig convention met in Baltimore on the 17th of June. A large majority of the delegates from New York, and a considerable number from other states, maintained their opposition to the test resolutions proposed by the other branch of the party. Those resolutions, however, were adopted by a decisive majority. They were voted for by many who may be presumed to have been convinced of their importance, while others doubtless were influenced by fears of a disruption of the party. A platform was thus established, resembling, in its main features, that of the democrats. Supported by several advocates of the new platform, on the ground of his personal popularity, General Scott received the nomination. He was, however, regarded with suspicion by a great number of whigs in the slave-holding states. It was feared, that if he was elected to the presidency, Mr. Seward would be called to the office of secretary of state, and thus exert a leading influence on the administration. General Scott lost no time in attempting to remove these prejudices. In announcing his acceptance of the nomination, he promptly declared his adhesion to the principles of the platform, adopted by the party. At the instance of the friends of the candidate, Mr. Seward disclaimed all personal interest in the election of General Scott. With his characteristic frankness and fidelity to political associates, he publicly announced his determination to accept no office at the hands of the president, in case of General Scott's success. This had hitherto been his course, and it would not be changed under a future administration.*

The democratic party, forgetting its past divisions, at least, for the moment, supported Mr. Pierce with unanimity and zeal. On the contrary, Mr. Webster was nominated by a portion of the whig party, and died not only refusing to decline the nomination but openly avowing his disgust with the action of the party. Many ardent friends of the compromise refused to rally around General Scott, distrusting his fidelity to the platform; while a large number

* See Vol. III., p. 416.

of whigs in the free states, through aversion to the platform, assumed a neutral position, or gave their support to a third candidate. Mr. Seward and his friends could not so far belie their convictions, as to approve the principles of the platform, but yielded their aid to General Scott, in the manner, which, in their opinion, was best adapted to secure his election. The result, however, was what might have been foreseen. The democratic nominees received the electoral votes of twenty-six out of the thirty-one states. The loud exultations of the prevailing party, as well as of those whigs, who had sympathized with them in the canvass, showed their belief, that in the defeat of General Scott, Mr. Seward was not only overthrown, but politically annihilated. The whig party, in their opinion, was also for ever destroyed. Under these discouraging auspices, Mr. Seward resumed his seat in the senate, at the second session of the Thirty-Second Congress, in December, 1852. But neither his speeches nor his public conduct, were colored by the remembrance of the recent struggle. No traces of disappointment were visible in his bearing, and he at once devoted himself to the business of the session with the same calmness and assiduity which had always marked his congressional career.

CHAPTER XX.

XXXIId CONGRESS, SECOND SESSION, 1852-'53—SPEECHES—JOHN QUINCY ADAMS—CUBA—PACIFIC RAILROAD—TARIFF—TEXAS—ORATIONS—JAMES TALLMADGE.

THE speeches of Mr. Seward in the senate during the second session of the thirty-second Congress were on questions of great practical interest. In his remarks in the debate on "Continental Rights and Relations," Jan. 26, 1852, he pays a graceful and feeling tribute to the character of John Quincy Adams, whom he claims as the author of the policy on recolonization generally ascribed to President Monroe. Passing to the discussion of the policy itself, he gives his reasons for holding to its substantial truth, while he protests against the manner in which it was brought in issue on that occasion. The speech is gravely and forcibly argued, though not without incidental touches of effective satire.*

We quote a few passages relating to John Quincy Adams and to Cuba:—

"MR. PRESIDENT: On the 23d day of February, 1848, John Quincy Adams, of Massachusetts, who had completed a circle of public service filling fifty years, beginning with an inferior diplomatic function, passing through the chief magistracy, and closing with the trust of a representative in Congress, departed from the earth, certainly respected by mankind, and, if all posthumous honors are not insincere and false, deplored by his countrymen.

"On a fair and cloudless day in the month of June, 1850, when the loud and deep voice of wailing had just died away in the land, the senator from Michigan, of New England born, and by New England reared—the leader of a great party, not only

* See Vol. III., p. 605.

here, but in the whole country—rose in the senate-chamber, and after complaining that a member of the family of that great statesman of the east, instead of going backward with a garment to cover his infirmities, had revealed them by publishing portions of his private diary, himself proceeded to read the obnoxious extracts. They showed the author's strong opinions, that by the federal compact the slaveholding class had obtained, and they had exercised, a controlling influence in the government of the country.

"Placing these extracts by the side of passages taken from the Farewell Address of Washington, the senator from Michigan said: 'He is unworthy the name of an American who does not feel at his heart's core the difference between the lofty patriotism and noble sentiments of *one* of these documents, and—— but I will not say what the occasion would justify. I will only say, and that is enough, *the other*, for it is *another*.'—'It can not, nor will it, nor should it, escape the censure of an age like this.'—'Better that it had been entombed, like the ancient Egyptian records, till its language was lost, than thus to have been exposed to the light of day.'

"The senator then proceeded to set forth, by contrast, his own greater justice and generosity to the southern states, and his own higher fidelity to the Union. This was in the senate of the United States. And yet no one rose to vindicate the memory of John Quincy Adams, or to express an emotion even of *surprise*, or of *regret*, that it had been thought necessary thus to invade the sanctity of the honored grave where the illustrious statesman, who had so recently passed the gates of death, was sleeping. I was not of New England, by residence, education, or descent, and there were reasons enough why I should then endure in silence a pain that I shared with so many of my countrymen. But I determined that, when the tempest of popular passion that was then raging in the country should have passed by, I would claim a hearing here—not to defend or vindicate the sentiments which the senator from Michigan had thus severely censured, for Mr. Adams himself had referred them, together with all his actions and opinions concerning slavery—not to this tribunal, or even to the present time, but to that after-age which gathers and records the impartial and *ultimate judgment* of mankind—but to show how just and generous he had been in his public career toward all the members of this confederacy, and how devoted to the union of the states, and to the aggrandizement of this republic. I am thankful that the necessity for performing that duty has passed by, and that the statesman of Quincy has, earlier than I hoped, received his vindication, and has received it, too, at the hands of him from whom it was justly due — the accuser himself. I regret only this — that the vindication was not as generously as it was effectually made.

"There are two propositions arising out of our interests in and around the gulf of Mexico, which are admitted by all our statesmen. One of them is, that the safety of the southern states requires a watchful jealousy of the presence of European powers in the southern portions of the North-American continent; and the other is, that the tendency of commercial and political events invites the United States to assume and exercise a paramount influence in the affairs of the nations situated in this hemisphere; that is, to become and remain a great western continental power, balancing itself against the possible combinations of Europe. The advance of the country toward that position constitutes what, in the language of many, is called 'progress;' and the position itself is what, by the same class, is called 'manifest destiny.' It is held by all who approve that progress, and expect that destiny, to be necessary to prevent the recolonization of this continent by the European states, and to save the island of Cuba from passing out of the possession of decayed Spain, into that of any of the more vigorous maritime powers of the old world.

"In December, 1823, James Monroe, president of the United States, in his annual message to Congress, proclaimed the first of these two policies substantially as follows: 'The American continents, by the free and independent condition which they have assumed and maintain, are henceforth not to be considered as subjects for future colonization by any European power; and while existing rights should be respected, the safety and interest of the United States require them to announce that no future colony or dominion shall, with their consent, be planted or established in any part of the North American continent.' This is what is called, here and elsewhere, the Monroe doctrine, so far as it involves recolonization.

"John Quincy Adams and John C. Calhoun were then members, chief members, of Monroe's administration. John Quincy Adams afterward acknowledged that he was the author of that doctrine or policy; and John C. Calhoun, on the 15th of May, 1848, in the senate, testified on that point fully. A senator had related an alleged conversation, in which Mr. Adams was represented as having said that three memorable propositions contained in that message, of which what I have quoted was one, had originated with himself. Mr. Calhoun replied, that 'Mr. Adams, if he had so stated, must have referred to only the one proposition concerning re-colonization [the one now in question]' and then added as follows: 'As respects that, his [Mr. Adams's] memory does not differ from mine. . . . . . It originated entirely with Mr. Adams.'*

"Thus much for the origin of the Monroe doctrine on recolonization. Now, let us turn to the position of John Quincy Adams, concerning national jealousy of the designs of European powers upon the island of Cuba. The recent revelations of our diplomacy on that subject begin with the period when that statesman presided in the department of state. On the 17th of December, 1822, Mr. Adams informed Mr. Forsyth, then American minister in Spain, that 'the island of Cuba had excited much attention, and had become of deep interest to the American Union;' and, referring to reported rival designs of France and Great Britain upon that island, instructed him to make known to Spain 'the sentiments of the United States, which were favorable to the continuance of Cuba in its connection with Spain.' On the 28th of April, 1823, Mr. Adams thus instructed Mr. Nelson, the successor of Mr. Forsyth: —

"'The islands of Cuba and Porto-Rico still remain, nominally, and so far really dependent upon Spain, that she yet possesses the power of transferring her own dominion over them to others. These islands, from their local position, are natural appendages to the North American continent; and one of them, Cuba, almost in sight of our shores, from a multitude of considerations, has become an object of transcendant importance to the commercial and political interests of our Union. Its commanding position, with reference to the gulf of Mexico and the West India seas; *the character of its population;* its situation midway between our southern coast and the island of St. Domingo; its safe and capacious harbor of the Havana, fronting a

* App. Cong. Globe, 1847–'48, p. 631.

long line of our shores destitute of the same advantage; the nature of its productions and of its wants, furnishing the supplies and needing the returns of a commerce immensely profitable and mutually beneficial—give it an importance in the sum of our national interests with which that of no other foreign territory can be compared, and little inferior to that which binds the different members of this Union together. Such, indeed, are, between the interests of that island and of this country, the geographical, commercial, moral, and political relations, formed by nature, gathering in the process of time, and even now verging to maturity, that, in looking forward to the probable course of events, for the short period of half a century, it is scarcely possible to resist the conviction that the annexation of Cuba to our federal republic will be indispensable to the continuance and integrity of the Union itself. It is obvious, however, that for this event we are not yet prepared. Numerous and formidable objections to the extension of our territorial dominions beyond sea, present themselves to the first contemplation of the subject; obstacles to the system of policy by which alone that result can be compassed and maintained, are to be foreseen and surmounted, both from at home and abroad; but there are laws of political as well as of physical gravitation; and if an apple, severed by the tempest from its native tree, can not choose but fall to the ground, Cuba, forcibly disjoined from its own unnatural connection with Spain, and incapable of self-support, can gravitate only toward the North American union, which, by the same law of nature, can not cast her off from its bosom.

"'It will be among the primary objects requiring your most earnest and unremitting attention, to ascertain and report to us every movement of negotiation between Spain and Great Britain upon this subject. . . . . . So long as the constitutional government may continue to be administered in the name of the king, your official intercourse will be with his ministers, and to them you will repeat, what Mr. Forsyth has been instructed to say, that the wishes of your government are that Cuba and Porto-Rico may continue in connection with independent and constitutional Spain.'

"Thirty years afterward, viz.: on the 4th day of January, 1853, the senator from Michigan (Mr. Cass) without one word of acknowledgment of Mr. Adams's agency in instituting those measures of 'progress' toward the 'manifest destiny' of the country, submitted the resolutions which are under consideration, and which are in these words:—

"'*Resolved by the Senate and House of Representatives of the United States of America in Congress assembled*, That the United States do hereby declare, that "the American continents, by the free and independent condition which they have assumed and maintained, are henceforth not to be considered as subjects for future colonization by any European power;" and while "existing rights should be respected," and will be by the United States, they owe it to their own "safety and interests" to announce, as they now do, "that no future European colony or dominion shall, with their consent, be planted or established on any part of the North American continent;" and should the attempt be made, they thus deliberately declare that it will be viewed as an act originating in motives regardless of their "interests and their safety," and which will leave them free to adopt such measures as an independent nation may justly adopt in defence of its rights and its honor.

"'*And be it further resolved*, That while the United States disclaim any designs upon the island of Cuba, inconsistent with the laws of nations, and with their duties to Spain, they consider it due to the vast importance of the subject to make known, in this solemn manner, that they should view all efforts on the part of any other power to procure possession, whether peaceably or forcibly, of that island, which, as a naval or military position, might, under circumstances easy to be foreseen, become dangerous to their southern coast, to the gulf of Mexico, and to the mouth of the Mississippi, as unfriendly acts directed against them, to be resisted by all the means in their power.'

"In bringing together these actions of John Quincy Adams in 1822, and of the senator from Michigan in 1853, and placing them in juxtaposition in the history of the senate, I have done all that the senator from Michigan seems to have left undone, to vindicate the departed statesman from the censures heaped upon him by the living one in 1850."

After this vindication of the sage of Quincy, Mr. Seward availed himself of the opportunity to express his own opinions on the great subjects under review. In regard to the acquisition of Cuba, he says:—

"While I do not desire the immediate or early annexation of Cuba, nor see how I could vote for it at all until slavery shall have ceased to counteract the workings of nature in that beautiful island, nor even then, unless it could come into the Union without injustice to Spain, without aggressive war, and without producing internal dissensions among ourselves, I nevertheless yield my full assent to the convictions expressed by John Quincy Adams, that this nation can never safely allow the island of Cuba to pass under the dominion of any power that is already, or can become, a formidable rival or enemy; and can not safely consent to the restoration of colonial relations between any portions of this continent and the monarchies of Europe."

In February the important question of our "Relations with Mexico, and the Continental railroad," was debated in the senate. The speech of Mr. Seward on that subject abounds in lucid views of national policy.*

On the proposal to abolish or suspend the duty on foreign railroad iron, Mr. Seward addressed the senate in one of his most characteristic speeches.† In this speech we find the following warning to the country of the danger of an approaching revulsion in railroad affairs no less just than, as it now appears, prophetic:—

"I ask, now, what is the apology for this extraordinary measure? It is that it will encourage the making of railroads. Sir, I have spent my life, what there has been of it spent in public action, in encouraging the making of canals and railroads. I am a friend to canals and railroads; but I show my fidelity to them in adhering to them when they are unpopular and need help, and support, and patronage, and not when they have patronage so great as to be alarming for its effect, not only upon enterprises of that class, but upon the country itself. Do you know how many railroads you are making? You are making twelve thousand miles of railroads in the United States already. You are making them so fast, that you do not rely upon your own resources for making them at all, but you are selling the credit of individuals, towns, counties, and states, throughout the Union, in untold amounts, and constituting an aggregate debt greater than any amount which any man ever presumed it would be safe for this country to owe to foreign countries. Your railroads are not now made chiefly by subscriptions to their stock. There are small substratum subscriptions, then mortgages on the road, then second mortgages, then third mortgages, until the credit of whole communities is pledged, and pledged to English capitalists.

"We are pledged in London for the cost of nearly all our railroads. Our capital is being diverted, so that there is no place in the United States where there is not a railroad being made.

"There are already half a dozen railroads from the point of Lake Erie to the city of New York, all converging there, because railroads have become popular and profitable. So it is

* See Vol. III., p. 656. † See Vol. III., p. 623.

throughout New England and throughout the west. Now it is not possible that the railroad enterprise in this country can absorb capital in an exclusive degree without producing an injury, not only to that enterprise and those subservient to it, but also injurious to other enterprises which increase the vigor and promote the progress of the country. Does any man doubt it? What did we do ten years ago, when we embarked in building canals and railroads so deeply, and pledged our credit so far, that the construction of every canal and railroad had to be suspended? What happened in England on a like occasion, but that a great railroad-king projected railroads all over the island; and so much capital was invested in them, that all at once the bubble was pricked, and the whole enterprise collapsed, bringing on general stagnation and bankruptcy? This is the tendency of things here now. I am not by habit a croaker; but I can see that, unless the national government shall act so as to restrain rather than encourage and stimulate this excessive spirit of speculation in railroad investments, just such a collapse will happen here. Railroads do not need protection; iron manufacturers do need it. Through the town in which I live, and the towns adjacent, the people, carried away by railroad enthusiasm, have applied to the legislature for permission to mortgage their whole property for the making of railroads; and yet there is not one railroad which they are thus making, in which foreign capitalists will invest a dollar, except they have collateral, personal, or public security. But you will tell me that Congress has not encouraged railroads. Congress has already encouraged railroads by donations of duties on foreign railroad iron exceeding the sum of three millions of dollars. Congress has already, with almost a unanimous vote in this chamber, given to every western state land enough from the public domain—as much as they said was necessary—to construct a web of railroads now in progress and advancing to its completion, covering over the whole of the territories of the United States from the shores of the Atlantic to the Mississippi river, and even crossing that broad line, and advancing precisely upon the same system and same policy toward the base of the Rocky mountains. We have done enough, unless we have some other resources—some other revenues which we can apply to this great and beneficent enterprise of the age; and we have no other, if the only other one is the sacrifice of the mining interest of iron in the old Atlantic states. Sir, I have voted land by the square league across the continent, and twenty millions of dollars out of the public treasury for railroads. I will not vote one dollar out of the iron-mines of my country, at the cost of the owner, and of the miner who is engaged in drawing its wealth to the surface."

This was followed by a speech on "Texas and her Creditors,"* which closes the list of Mr. Seward's senatorial efforts during that Congress. Both of these speeches are marked by the admirable union of statistics, general reasoning, and lofty sentiments of which the texture of his deliberative eloquence is composed.

After an extra session of several weeks called by the new administration to consider executive appointments, the senate adjourned in April, 1853. Mr. Seward was occupied during the summer in the courts of the United States, but he found time to accept an urgent call to deliver an address at the dedication of Capital University at Columbus the seat of government in the state of Ohio. This address rises to the dignity of an oration and pleads the cause of human nature as especially committed to the care of the people of the United States. It closes with an eloquent showing of the responsibilities, in this respect, of the college or the university as an American institution.†

Mr. Seward's studies during the recess of Congress closed with the delivery of an address before the American Institute at New York on the 20th of October, 1853. This address was a stirring appeal to the American people to rise to a higher tone of individual and national independence, in thought, sentiment, and action. While every part of it was received with distinguished favor, no part was more just or more highly appreciated than the following touching tribute to the memory of James Tallmadge:—

* See Vol. III., p. 667.

† This address will be found among the selections in this volume.

"I have been for many reasons habitually averse from mingling in the sometimes excited debates which crowd upon each other in a great city. There was, however, an authority which I could not disobey, in the venerable name and almost paternal kindness of the eminent citizen, who so recently presided here with dignity and serenity all his own; and who transmitted the invitation of the Institute, and persuaded its acceptance!

"How sudden his death! Only three weeks ago, the morning mail brought to me his announcement of his arrival to arrange this exhibition, and his summons to me to join him here; and the evening despatch, on the self-same day, bore the painful intelligence that the lofty genius which had communed with kindred spirits so long, on the interests of his country, had departed from the earth, and that the majestic form which had been animated by it, had disappeared for ever from among living men.

"I had disciplined myself when coming here, so as to purpose to speak no word for the cause of human freedom, lest what might seem too persistent an advocacy might offend. But must I, therefore, abridge of its just proportions the eulogium which the occasion and the character of the honored dead alike demand?

"The first ballot which I cast for the chief magistracy of my native and most beloved state, bore the name of James Tallmadge, as the alternate of De Witt Clinton. If I have never faltered in pursuing the policy of that immortal statesman, through loud reproach and vindictive opposition during his life, and amid clamors and contentions, often amounting almost to faction, since his death, I have found as little occasion to hesitate or waver in adhering to the counsels and example of the illustrious compeer, who, after surviving him so many years, has now been removed, in ripened age, to the companionship of the just. How does not time vindicate fidelity to truth and to our country! A vote for Clinton and Tallmadge in 1824, what censures did it not bring then? Who will impeach *that* ballot now?

"A statesman's claim to the gratitude of his country rests on what were, or what would have been, the results of the policy he has recommended. If the counsels of James Tallmadge had completely prevailed, then not only would American forests, mines, soil, invention, and industry, have rendered our country, now and for ever, independent of all other nations, except for what climate forbids; but then, also, no menial hand would ever have guided a plough, and no footstep of a slave would ever have been tracked on the soil of all that vast part of our national domain that stretches away from the banks of the Mississippi to the far western ocean.

"This was the policy of James Tallmadge. It was worthy of New York, in whose name it was promulgated. It would have been noble, even to have altogether failed in establishing it. He was successful, however, in part, though only through unwise delays and unnecessary compromises, which he strenuously opposed, and which, therefore, have not impaired his just fame. And so in the end, he more nearly than any other citizen of our time, realized the description of the happiest man in the world, given to the frivolous Crœsus by the great Athenian: 'He saw his offspring, and they all survived him. At the close of an honorable and prosperous life, on the field of civic victory, he was rewarded with the honors of a public funeral by the state that he had enriched, adorned, and enlarged.'"

CHAPTER XXI.

THE XXXIIId CONGRESS—NEBRASKA.

UPON the accession of Mr. Pierce to the presidency, high expectations were formed of great and beneficent legislative action by the first Congress under his administration, which met on the first Monday in December, 1853. Among the measures which, it was anticipated, would come up for consideration were the modification of the tariff, so as to enlarge the field of national industry—the construction of a railroad between the Atlantic states and the Pacific ocean—the substitution of a system of gratuitous allotments of land, in limited quantities, to actual settlers, instead of the policy of sales of the public domain—the improvement and reform of the army and navy—the regulation of the commercial marine in regard to immigrant passengers—the endowment of the states with portions of the public land, as a provision for the care of the insane within their limits—the establishment of steam-mails upon the Pacific ocean—and the opening of political and commercial relations with Japan.

Mr. Seward addressed himself to the accomplishment of these important objects with his accustomed diligence and zeal. Early in the session he introduced a bill for the construction of a railroad to the Pacific, and another for the establishment of steam-mails between San Francisco, the Sandwich Islands, Japan, and China. The times seemed favorable for such legislation. The public treasury was overflowing. The slavery agitation had died away both in Congress and throughout the country. This calm, however, was doomed to a sudden interruption. The prospect of such extended beneficent legislation was destroyed by the introduction of a measure, which at once supplanted all other subjects in Congress, and in the political interest of the people. This was the novel and astounding proposal of Mr. Douglas of Illinois, in relation to the Kansas and Nebraska territories. The country saw with regret and mortification, the homestead bill transformed into one of mere graduation of the prices of the public lands. The bills for the improvement of the army and navy, and the bill for regulating the transportation of immigrants were dropped, before coming to maturity. The bill for a grant of lands to the states in aid of the insane, was defeated in the senate for want of a constitutional majority, after having been vetoed by the president. The bill for establishing the Pacific railroad was lost for want of time to debate it; and the bill for opening steam communication with the East, after passing the senate failed for want of consideration in the house. The administration had a majority of nearly two to one in both branches of Congress. The opponents of introducing slavery into the free territories, were in a decided minority in the house, while they constituted less than one fifth of the senate.

The measure, already alluded to, which produced this sudden derangement in Congress, was a provision in the bill for the organization of a territory in Nebraska, declaring that the states which might, at any future time, be formed in the new territory, should leave the question of slavery to be decided by the inhabitants, on the adoption of their constitution. This provision, as explained by the bill itself, was the application to Nebraska of the policy established in regard to Utah and New Mexico by the compromise of 1850. It was evident that the Missouri compromise of 1820 was thus virtually repealed. By that arrangement, it was provided that slavery should be excluded from the whole unorganized portion of the public domain, acquired from France, and lying north of the parallel of 36° 30′ north latitude. The territory of Nebraska was comprised within these limits.

Mr. Dixon, a senator from Kentucky, however, desirous to bring the supporters of prohibition, to a still more decided test, moved an amendment to the bill, expressly annulling the portion of the Missouri compromise, which related to the subject. After some deliberation, Mr. Douglas accepted the amendment, and modified his plan, so far as to introduce a new bill for the organization of Nebraska and Kansas, within the same limits, instead of the territory of Nebraska alone, according to the original programme. The administration lost no time in adopting this policy as their own. It was at first proposed to hasten the passage of the bill through both houses so rapidly, as to prevent any remonstrance on the part of the people. But the opponents of the measure, including Mr. Seward, Mr. Everett, Mr. Chase, Mr. Sumner, Mr. Truman Smith, Mr. Wade, Mr. Bell, Mr. Houston, and Mr. Fessenden, presented such an earnest and effective resistance, that the attention of the country was aroused, and an indignant protest called forth from the people of the free states. The bill, however, passed the senate by a majority of more than two to one, and after a protracted struggle was carried through the house, in an amended form by a vote of 113 to 100.

On its return to the senate, it was met by Messrs. Seward, Sumner, and Chase, with a continued and powerful opposition. But it was all to no effect. The bill finally passed that body, and amid the firing of cannon and the shouts of its friends, it was sent to the president for his signature, at three o'clock in the morning of May 26, 1854. The approval of the president was promptly given, and the odious measure became the law of the land. Thus was abrogated the celebrated Missouri compromise—a law enacted thirty years before with all the solemnity of a compact between the free and slave states—and a territory opened to slavery as large as the original thirteen states, and nearly equal in extent to all the existing free states. The act was consummated by the co-operation of the North. Originating with a senator from a free state—it was passed by a Congress containing in each branch a majority of members from the free states, and was sanctioned by the approval of a free state president.

The friends of this legislation attempted to defend it on the pretence that it was not an original act, but only declaratory of the true intent and significance of the compromise measures of 1850. For his resistance to those measures, Mr. Seward had been vehemently denounced. But at the very commencement of the Nebraska struggle, the friends of freedom at the North turned their eyes toward him, as its devoted champion. He was beset with appeals from all sides to awaken the country to the atrocity of the proposed transaction. In no quarter were these appeals more urgent than in the city of New York, where his opposition to the compromise of 1850 had been most severely condemned. With his usual sagacity and confidence in the popular impulse, and faithful to his innate sense of personal dignity, he kept aloof from these overtures, and was content with the zealous discharge of his senatorial duties on the floor of Congress. The following characteristic letter illustrates the coolness and decision of his bearing at this time:—

WASHINGTON, *Saturday, January* 28, 1854.

"GENTLEMEN: The invitation to a meeting to be held in the city of New York, to protest against any repeal or violation of the Missouri Compromise, with which you have honored me, has been received. My constant attendance here is required by the interest which the city of New York and the state of New York have in the great projects of a railroad to San Francisco, and the extension of our commerce to the islands and continents divided from us by the Pacific ocean, which are now being matured in committees to which I belong. Moreover the day designated for the meeting is one upon which the senate may be brought to a vote upon the bold and dangerous measure which has so justly excited the patriotic apprehensions of the citizens of the metropolis. I could not be safely absent from the capital under these circumstances, even if my attendance in New York would otherwise be proper.

"You have kindly asked me, in view of this inability, to give you such an expression of my 'sentiments as may help to arouse the North to the defence of its rights, and the South to the maintenance of its plighted honor.' Permit me to say, in response to the appeal, that when the slavery laws of 1850 were under discussion in the senate, I regarded the ground then demanded to be conceded by the North as a vantage ground, which, when once yielded, would be retrieved with infinite difficulty afterward, if, indeed, it should not be absolutely irretrievable; and that I, therefore, in my place as a representative here, said and did all that it was in my power to do and say, and all that I could now do and say, to 'help to rouse the North to the defence of its rights, and the South to the maintenance of its honor.' When, afterward, eminent members of Congress, who had been engaged in passing those laws, carried an appeal against those who had opposed them before the people in their primary assemblies, I declined to follow them then, and I have ever since refrained from all unnecessary discussions of the slave laws of 1850, and of matters pertaining to slavery, even here, as well as elsewhere, because I was unwilling to injure so just a cause by discussions which might seem to betray undue solicitude, if not a spirit of faction. We have only now arrived at a new stage in the trial of that appeal. For it is quite clear that if the slavery laws had not been passed in 1850, for the territories acquired from Mexico, there would have been no pretence for extending such slavery laws now, over the territories before acquired from Louisiana, and that if we had maintained our ground on the laws of freedom, which then protected New Mexico and Utah, we should not now have been attacked in our stronghold in Nebraska. It is equally evident, also, that Nebraska is not all that is to be saved or lost. If we are driven from this field, there will yet remain Oregon and Minnesota, and we who thought only so lately as 1849 of securing some portion at least of the shore of the Gulf of Mexico and all of the Pacific coast to the institutions of freedom, will be, before 1859, brought to a doubtful struggle to prevent the extension of slavery to the shores of the great lakes, and thence westward to Puget's sound. I hope, gentlemen, that for one, I may be allowed to continue to the end that abstinence from popular agitation which I have heretofore practised, less from considerations of self-respect than from my confidence in the sagacity and virtue of the people I represent. Nevertheless, I beg you to be assured that, while declining to go into popular assemblies, as an agitator, I shall endeavor to do my duty here with as many true men as shall be found in a delegation, which, if all were firm and united in the maintenance of public right and justice, would be able to control the decision of this great question. But the measure of success and effect which shall crown our exertions must depend now, as heretofore, on the fidelity with which the people whom we represent shall adhere to the policy and principles which are the foundation of their own unrivalled prosperity and greatness.

"I am, gentlemen, with great respect and esteem, your obedient servant, "WILLIAM H. SEWARD."

The pledges given in this letter were nobly fulfilled. The first of his speeches* on the Nebraska bill was a profound and dispassionate statement of the whole argument against the measure in question. Though it failed of preventing the accomplishment of the measure in Congress, it acted, with magnetic power, on the people of the free states, arousing them to a spirit of unconquerable resistance to the aggressions of slavery. It was a gloomy night for the lovers of freedom in those states, when the telegraphic despatches flashed throughout the country, announcing that the ill-omened bill was on its final reading in the senate, and that its inevitable enactment was near at hand. Mr. Seward chose that hour of intense excitement to close the debate on his part. He commenced his speech with these solemn and impressive words:—

* See page 351 of this volume.

"The sun has set for the last time upon the guarantied and certain liberties of all the unsettled and unorganized portions of the American continent that lie within the jurisdiction of the United States. To-morrow's sun will rise in dim eclipse over them.* How long that obscuration shall last, is known only to the Power that directs and controls all human events. For myself, I know only this—that now no human power will prevent its coming on, and that its passing off will be hastened and secured by others than those now here, and perhaps by only those belonging to future generations. . . . .

"We are on the eve of the consummation of a great national transaction—a transaction which will close a cycle in the history of our country—and it is impossible not to desire to pause a moment and survey the scene around us and the prospect before us. However obscure we may individually be, our connection with this great transaction will perpetuate our names for the praise or for the censure of future ages, and perhaps in regions far remote. If, then, we had no other motive for our actions but that of an honest desire for a just fame, we could not be indifferent to that scene and that prospect. But individual interests and ambition sink into insignificance in view of the interests of our country and of mankind. These interests awaken, at least in me, an intense solicitude."

He then proceeded to review the sophistries which had been offered in defence of the bill, and pointed out its calamitous tendencies, with a clearness and power that might almost have arrested its progress even on the verge of enactment. Presenting to the free states the evidences of their ability to procure a repeal of the law, he urged, by conclusive arguments, the importance of such a step, and at the same time luminously expounded the methods of excluding slavery from Nebraska, and the vast, unsettled regions of the West, by promoting a wide and rapid emigration into the territories in question. The effect of this speech† was cheering in the extreme. It threw a rainbow

* It will be remembered that an almost total eclipse of the sun actually occurred on that day—the 26th of May, 1854.—Ed

† See p. 384 of this volume.

over the dark cloud that hung over the country. The auspicious omen was accepted. And the faith of the people has been rewarded by the most gratifying results in the recent elections.

Beside these two important speeches, Mr. Seward made several other elaborate efforts in the senate, addressing that body on the bills which have been already enumerated.

During the discussion of the Kansas and Nebraska bill in the house of representatives, a memorial remonstrating against the repeal of the Missouri compromise, signed by three thousand and fifty clergymen of New England, was presented to the senate by Edward Everett. Mr. Douglas and other senators attacked this memorial with great violence, severely criticising its language, calling in question its propriety, and denying the claim of its authors to a hearing in the senate. Mr. Seward defended the course of the memorialists, and maintained the right of petition on its broadest grounds. A reference to his remarks on this subject will show the character of his positions, and the vigor and acumen with which they were sustained.*

Two unusually important treaties were ratified by the senate in executive or secret session, during this meeting of Congress. One is known as the "Gadsden Treaty," for the settlement of our relations with Mexico and the other, as the "Reciprocity Treaty" for the regulation of trade between Canada and the United States. Mr. Seward is understood to have opposed the former, while he gave his support to the latter.

It will be seen that Mr. Seward has not been an idle spectator of the proceedings of the senate. His voice has been raised on the most momentous questions in those halls "where debate either wins a great influence or utterly wastes the speaker's power." No one can doubt the effect of his active participation in the senatorial strife on his own fame. His speeches have not only been heard with

* See p. 223 of this volume.

profound respect in the august forum, where they were delivered, but they will be read with instruction and delight by the most intelligent portion of our republican population.

Rich in significant lessons of statesmanship, abounding in the treasured wisdom of years of study and practice in affairs, breathing a spirit of the most expansive humanity, and adorned with the classic embellishments of a susceptible and refined taste, they form an interesting memorial of the progress of American letters. Mr. Seward, we are persuaded, will henceforth occupy as enviable a place among the writers of his country, as he has long held among her practical statesmen.

In addition to his elaborate speeches in the senate, Mr. Seward has often taken an incidental part in important debates, a record of which is preserved in the collection of his works. After the decease of Henry Clay and Daniel Webster, he delivered a tribute to the memory of each of those illustrious statesmen, in chaste and discriminating sketches of their characters. For justness and vigor of conception, elevation of feeling, and felicity of diction, these are scarcely inferior to the best specimens of mortuary eloquence in our language.*

Just before the adjournment of Congress (on the 26th of July), Mr. Seward delivered the annual oration before the Phi Beta Kappa society of Yale college, on which occasion he received the honorary degree of Doctor of Laws. The subject of his discourse was "The Physical, Moral, and Intellectual Development of the American People," which he treated with a masterly discrimination and vigorous eloquence that commanded the admiration of a highly intellectual audience, and strengthened his well-earned title to oratorical fame.†

Mr. Seward has now been nearly six years in the senate of the United States. Of his conduct in that exalted station, the speeches and debates now published, afford the

* See Vol. III., p. 104. † See p. 291 of this volume.

most authentic illustration. Amid the heated excitements of the day, he has been found calm, watchful, and earnest, on the post of duty. Trustfully biding his time, he has cherished no anxiety to vindicate his reputation from the aspersions of his opponents, save by a uniform course of well-doing. In the most ardent zeal of senatorial debate, he has never lost sight of the decorum belonging to the place. Often the subject of violent personalities, he has preserved the courtesy of the gentleman and the dignity of the legislator. No provocation has induced him to violate the amenities of refined social life, nor to reply to ill-mannered abuse by a retort in kind.

His fidelity to his political associates has often been the subject of remark. During the administration which followed that of President Taylor, to be a friend of Mr. Seward was to be proscribed. The price of such partiality, to an office-holder, was invariably removal. But that administration came into power through the action of the whig party, from which he derived his trust. Hence, it never failed to receive the support of Mr. Seward. He has neglected no suitable occasion to defend it: he has never been one of its assailants. It is said, and we believe truly, that he promptly sustained all its nominations to office.

But the most remarkable feature in his public career is his consistent adherence to principle. Guided not by a low worldly policy, or motives of secular expediency, but by the radiant light of ideal truth, his course has been like the path of a noble ship on the ocean, faithfully steering by celestial luminaries. His past history presents the best assurance of his future activity. Whatever the sphere in which he may be placed, it is certain that he will bring exalted talents to the performance of the humblest as well as the noblest duties, postponing all private interests to his love of humanity, and seeking as the highest boon of a manly life, the realization of truth, justice, and love, in the institutions of society.

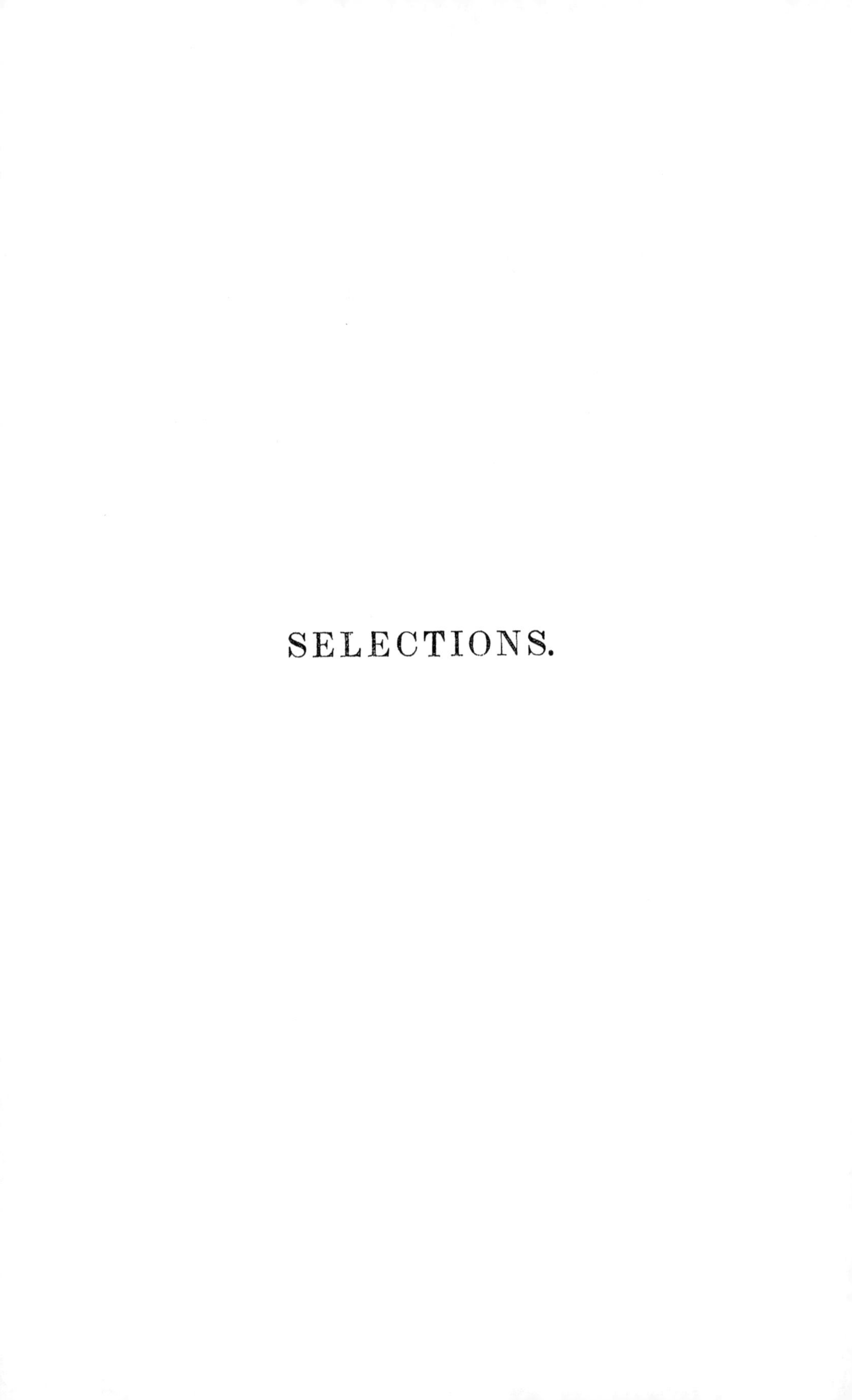

SELECTIONS.

INTRODUCTORY NOTE.

THE SELECTIONS which follow have been made partly for their literary merits, and partly on account of the sentiments they contain, as well as for the purpose of illustrating the preceding Memoir.

The arrangement of the extracts under the several heads of AGRICULTURE, INTERNAL IMPROVEMENTS, EDUCATION, FREEDOM, COMMERCE, and MISCELLANEOUS, has been adopted for the greater convenience of reference. It need not be remarked, perhaps, that these selections embrace but small portions of Mr. Seward's Speeches or Writings on any of those topics. The limits of the volume have excluded much that might have been considered equally pertinent and valuable. It is believed, however, that they present a fair and faithful exposition of his views.

The difficulty of making the wisest selections, where so much must necessarily be omitted, will readily occur to the reader. Neither is it necessary to say, here, that more or less injustice must always be done to any author by detaching portions of his writings from their original connections. For this reason, as well as for a want of room, we have forborne to make even the briefest extracts from some of Mr. Seward's most eloquent and important productions. Among these may be named his "Notes on New York"—his "Virginia Correspondence"—his "Letters from Europe"—and his Eulogiums on Lafayette, John Quincy Adams, Daniel Webster, and Henry Clay.

Room has been made, however, for his Oration at Columbus, on the "Destiny of America," and for his two Speeches in the Senate on the "Nebraska Question," entire. They were deemed too important to be omitted or abridged. His defence of the Right of Petition, on the occasion of the reception of the Memorial from the Clergy of New England in the Senate, has also been retained, substantially, in full. Beside these and others, in the following pages, a number of extracts of especial interest and of considerable length, it will be observed, have been included in the Memoir; among which are several Arguments at the bar, on Invention, on the Fugitive-Slave Law, in defence of William Freeman, and of Abel F. Fitch and others; the Speech at Cleveland on the relative position of parties on the Slavery question; the vindication of John Quincy Adams; and the Eulogium on James Tallmadge.

Among the Selections, also, the following may be particularly referred to as especially interesting, and therefore quoted at more than usual length: Address at Springfield, Mass., on the completion of the Western Railroad; Annual Messages relating to the Education of the Children of Exiles; Address at Yale College on the American People, their Moral, Intellectual, and Physical Development; Argument in the Freeman Case, on Insanity; and Address before the American Institute on the True Basis of American Independence.

EDITOR.

AGRICULTURE.

Improvement of Agriculture Essential to the Security of Republican Institutions.

THE science which involves the physical laws most open to our investigation, and to which the primeval law of our existence compels us, and the art which precedes all other inventions and whose cultivation leads to plenty and is cheered by health and contentment, are the last which receive the patronage of philosophy or attain the favor of government. Mankind learned the distances and laws of planets, and even the periods of comets before they conceived the mysteries of vegetation; and the fine arts were perfected in ages when agriculture, loaded with the superstition of centuries, was confined to slaves. It may easily be explained why this should have been the experience of other ages and other countries. The powers of government have always been vested in classes or individuals farthest removed from the tillers of the soil; and ambition and pride have sought gratification in conquests and in homage of the fine arts. But it must not, it can not, be so here where the agricultural interest is sovereign, and as it furnishes all the means, so also it rightfully supplies the motives and directs the action of the government. . . . Agriculture appeals to us as republicans, therefore with peculiar earnestness not only by our desire to increase the public wealth, enlarge the public intelligence, and elevate the standard of public virtue; but also by our solicitude to preserve the ascendency of that policy of peace and improvement which is identified with the existence of democratic institutions.—*Annual Message*, 1839.

The Homestead of the American Citizen should be Exempted from Involuntary Sale.

I RESPECT all lawful contracts, and I would not unnecessarily interfere with even rigorous remedies which existed when such contracts were made. But it is wise as it is just and humane, to alleviate prospectively the relations between debtor and creditor, Within the last twenty years, imprisonment for debt, a system which had prevailed for more than two thousand years before, has been safely abolished by every state in this Union, and I believe by every commercial nation in Europe. New York, the most commercial state, has with equal safety abolished the rigorous remedy of distress for rent, and has exempted certain portions of estates from liability to sale for debts contracted after such laws were passed. Other states have adopted the policy of protecting the homestead from compulsory sale. A home is the first necessity of every family; it is indispensable to the education and qualification of citizens. Can not society justly withdraw it from the hazards of commercial contracts, and from exposure to the accidents following disease and death? We bestow pensions upon decayed soldiers who have served their country in her wars; we protect such annuities against involuntary assignment; and the policy is as wise as it is generous. But he who reclaims an acre of land from the sterility of nature, and brings it into a productive condition, confers a greater benefit upon the state than valor has often the power to bestow. Sir, all that is movable in property may be used as a security for credits—and that security is adequate to supply all the wants of commerce. The home of the farmer, the asylum of the children of the republic, may be safely reserved and protected.—*Speech in U. S. Senate, Feb.* 27, 1851.

Popular Prejudices against Improvement of Agriculture Unreasonable and Pernicious.

WHO does not desire that the generation to which he belongs shall be wiser and greater than those which have gone before it? Fellow-citizens, if you would thus distinguish the generation to which you belong, of which you are a part, you must have a wiser and more enlightened system of agriculture than that of your predecessors. I appeal to the learned men whom I see around me—is the science of agriculture peculiarly difficult to explore and perfect? Quite the contrary. Chemistry, mineralogy, botany, and physiology, the ancillary sciences, have already given up the secrets of the composition of the soil and of the atmosphere, and the laws which regulate the germination and growth of vegetable and animal organisms. What remains seems to be little more than the reduction of truths already known into methodical forms, for the purposes of instruction, with guides to their application under the widely-varying circumstances of soils, climates, and seasons. Notwithstanding these obvious truths, and notwithstanding that agriculture, as it was the first, has also always been the most general pursuit of civilized men, yet it is nevertheless true that it has been, more than all other sciences and arts, neglected. We generally plough, we sow, and we reap, not with enlightened knowledge of the processes we prosecute, but by habit, and with a blind following of customs established before that knowledge had been gained. We suffer disappointments which we might have prevented, and, charging the misfortune to accident and destiny, we perseveringly renew our culture in the same—I had almost said wilful—ignorance, and at the risk of the same ever-recurring disasters.

Permit me to say plainly and with some emphasis, that this indifference to agricultural science can not be suffered to continue. While commerce, aided by vigorous and well-sustained invention, is reducing the dangers and diminishing the cost of navigation, and thus bringing the similar productions of various nations into competition in common markets, population is crowding on subsistence in many countries, so rapidly as to oblige them to study intensely how to increase the fruits of the earth which constitute that subsistence. The statesmen of Great Britain and continental Europe have already employed science to check the tide of an impoverishing and exhausting emigration. Even, therefore, if we should continue to neglect agricultural improvement, England, Ireland, France, Spain, Italy, Germany, and Russia, would not. They must improve, are improving, and will continue to improve, agriculture; and if we neglect to follow—

ay, and if we fail to keep up with them in that improvement, they will not only exclude us from foreign markets, but will even ultimately undersell us in our own. A pretty figure we should make in that case. This is what they are already doing in manufactures, and by the process I have indicated.

I think that there is no lack of schools and seminaries and professorships, adapted and qualified for advancing and disseminating agricultural science. Our present seminaries, and the teachers of natural science in them, are quite sufficient; and text-books, guides to experiment, and laboratories, are not wanting in the country. What then is wanting? Only pupils. The students in all our seminaries, intent on — not agricultural pursuits, but what are called the learned or liberal professions — rush by the agricultural chair, to attend to instructions in mathematics, rhetoric, and classical literature. Certainly the professor ceases to explore for new acquisitions, when no one will listen to his expositions of what he already has. A desire to communicate to others, is always combined with the passion for the pursuit of knowledge.

Why then are there no pupils? The fault — again I pray you — pardon my boldness — the fault is chiefly with the farmers themselves. A farm, of course, is necessary to him who is to be a farmer. Generally, only farmers' sons have or expect farms, and so they are the class who must supply the candidates for the profession of farming. But the farmers' sons are generally averse from scientific study. There is a general prejudice that agriculture is a simple, easy art or trade, which can be taken up and practised without academic instruction or systematical apprenticeship, and that theoretic precepts serve only to mislead and bewilder.

On the contrary, Nature has left all the human faculties in one sense incomplete, to be perfected by general education and by training for special and distinct pursuits. She has left those faculties not less incomplete, and without adaptation, in the farmers' case than in any other. Her laws are general and inflexible. Brutes only have perfect instincts. Man can do nothing well, and indeed can do nothing at all, but by the guidance of cultivated reason. Notwithstanding admitted differences of natural capacity, and of tastes and inclinations, it is nevertheless practically and generally true, that success, and even distinction and eminence, in any vocation, are proportioned to the measure of culture, training, industry, and perseverance, brought into exercise. So he will be the best farmer, and even the best woodsman or well-digger, as he will be the best lawyer, the greatest hero, or the greatest statesman, who shall have studied most widely and most profoundly, and shall have labored most carefully and most assiduously.

There is another prejudice even more injurious than that which I have thus exposed. The farmer's son is averse from the farmer's calling. He does not intend to pursue it, and is always looking for some gate by which to escape from it. The prejudice is hereditary in the farmhouse. The farmer himself is not content with his occupation; nor is the farmer's wife any more so. They regard it as an humble, laborious, and toilsome one; they continually fret about its privations and hardships, and thus they unconsciously raise in their children a disgust toward it. Is not this at least frequently so? Is there a farmer here who does not desire, not to say seek, to procure for his son a cadet's or midshipman's warrant, a desk in the village-lawyer's office, a chair in the physician's study, or a place behind the counter in the country-store, in preference to training him to the labors of the farm? I fear that there is scarcely a farmer's son who would not fly to accept such a position, or a farmer's daughter who would not prefer almost any settlement in town or city, to the domestic cares of the farmhouse and the dairy.

Whence is this prejudice? It has come down to us from ages of barbarism. In the savage state, agricultural labor is despised, because bravery in battle, and skill in the chase, must be encouraged; and so heroism is still requisite for the public defence in the earlier stages of civilization, and the tiller of the soil, therefore, rises slowly from the condition of a villein, a serf, or a slave. Nevertheless, ancient, and almost universal, as this prejudice is, I am sure that it is unnatural to mankind in ripened civilization, such as that at which we have arrived. Of all classes of men, we practically have the least need of hunters; and we employ very few soldiers, while the whole structure of society hinges on the agricultural interest. A taste, nay, a passion for agriculture, is inherent and universal among men. The soldier or the sailor cares little for learning, mechanism, or music; but the solaces of his weary watchings and his midnight dreams are recollections and hopes of a cottage-home. The merchant's anxieties and the lawyer's studies are prosecuted patiently for the ultimate end of graceful repose in a country-seat; and lunatics, men and women, are won back to the sway of reason by the indulgence of labor in the harvest-field, and the culture of fruits and flowers in the gardens of the asylum.

I know that frivolous persons, in what is called fashionable society, who sleep till noon, still continue to depreciate and despise rural pursuits and pleasures. But what are the opinions of such minds worth? They equally depreciate and despise all labor, all industry, all enterprise, and all effort; and they reap their just reward in weariness of themselves, and in the contempt of those who value human talents, not by the depth in which they are buried, but by the extent of their employment for the benefit of mankind.

The prejudice, however, must be expelled from the farmer's fireside: and the farmer and his wife must do this themselves. It is as true in this case as in the more practical one which the rustic poet had in view: —

> "The wife too must husband, as well as the man;
> Or farewell thy husbandry, do what thou can."

Let them remember, that, in well-constituted and highly-advanced society like ours, intellectual cultivation relieves men from labor, but it does not at all exempt them from the practice of industry; that, on the contrary, it obliges the universal exercise of industry; and that, notwithstanding the current use of the figures of speech, "wearied limbs, sweating brows, hardened sinews, and rough and blackened hands," there is no avocation in our country that rewards so liberally with health, wealth, and honor, a given application of well-directed industry, as does that of the farmer. If he is surpassed by persons in other pursuits, it is not because their avocations are preferable to his own, but because, while he has neglected education and training, they have taken care to secure both.

When these convictions shall have entered the farmhouse, its respectability and dignity will be confessed. Its occupants will regard their dwellings and grounds, not as scenes of irksome and humiliating labor, but as their own permanent homes, and the homesteads of their children and their posterity. Affections unknown before, and new-born emulation, will suggest motives to improvement, embellishment, refinement, with the introduction of useful and elegant studies and arts which will render the paternal roof, as it ought to be, attractive to the young, and the farmer's life harmonious to their tastes and satisfactory to their ambition. Then the farmer's sons will desire and demand education as liberal as that now chiefly conferred on candidates for professional life, and will subject themselves to discipline, in acquiring the art of agriculture, as rigorous as that endured by *those who apprentice themselves to other vocations.*

Then, with the certain improvement of agriculture, we shall have the improvement and elevation of the agricultural class of American society. Have you considered how much that class renounce in denying themselves the self-improvement I have urged? Have you considered that in practice they widely renounce the functions of representation in the conduct of the government in favor of other classes, no more privileged than their own? This is unnecessary, unwise, unsafe; indeed, it is not republican—it is not American. In nearly all civilized states, the farmers, or those who cultivated the soil, have constituted far the greater part of the population. The chief control of society and government, then, it would seem, should, of right, have been vested in them. Yet, in truth, they have never, since the age of the patriarchs, attained any such control, except just here, and just now. In Great Britain they divide authority, but are overbalanced by merchants, manufacturers, and privileged classes. Notwithstanding modern constitutional concessions to them in France, they are nevertheless ruled there alternately by the city population and the army. In Germany, by the army. In parts of Italy, by the church; and in Russia they are slaves.

It has always been otherwise here. Farmers planted these colonies—all of them—and organized their governments. They were farmers who defied the British soldiery on Bunker hill and drove them back from Lexington. They were farmers—ay, Vermont farmers, who captured the fortress at Ticonderoga, and accepted its capitulation in the name of the "Great

Jehovah and the Continental Congress," and thus gave over the first fortified post to the cause of the Revolution. They were farmers who checked British power at Saratoga, and broke it in pieces like a potter's vessel at Yorktown. They were farmers who reorganized the several states and the federal government, and established them all on the principles of equality and affiliation. In every state, and in the whole Union, they constitute the broad electoral faculty, and by their preponderating suffrages, the vast and complex machine is perpetually sustained and kept in regular motion and operation. That it is in the main well administered, we all know by experienced security and happiness; that it might be better administered, our perpetual and intense passion for change fully proves; that it is administered no better, results from what? From the fact that the electoral body, the farmers, intelligent and patriotic as they are, may nevertheless become more intelligent and more patriotic than they now are. The more intelligent and patriotic they become, the more effective will be their control, and the wiser their direction of the government. Is there not room? Nay, is there not need for more activity, energy, and efficiency, on their part, for their own security and welfare? In the federal government, commerce has its minister and department, the law its organ and representative, and the arts their commissioner and bureau. But the vast interest of agriculture has only a single desk and a subordinate clerk in the basement of the patent-office. It is scarcely better in the states. An empty charter of incorporation, with a scanty endowment, constitutes substantially all that has been anywhere done for agriculture. Gentlemen, I like not that it should be so. Our nation is rolling forward in a high career, exposed to shocks and dangers. It needs the utmost wisdom and virtue to guide it safely; it needs the steady and enlightened direction which, of all others, the farmers of the United States can best exercise, because, being freeholders invested with equal power of suffrage, they are at once the most liberal and the most conservative element in the country.—*Address before Vermont Agricultural Society, Rutland, Sept.* 2, 1852.

The Same.

But, gentlemen, in whatever direction your efforts may be made, you will encounter difficulties and discouragements. You will be opposed by that contented spirit which regards every improvement as innovation, and which perpetually, though falsely, complains that mankind degenerate without making an effort to check the progress of error. You will be regarded as visionary by those who consider skill in acquiring, and success in retaining wealth, as the perfection of human wisdom; but you will remember that such as these seldom bestow their countenance upon the benefactors of mankind, nor does Fortune always distinguish them by her favors. Robert Morris, a financier of the Revolution, died a bankrupt. Christopher Colles, our efficient advocate of inland navigation in the last century, was interred by private charity in the Strangers' burying-ground. The essays of Jesse Hawley, which demonstrated the feasibility and importance of a continuous canal from Lake Erie to the Hudson river, were sent forth from a debtor's prison; and De Witt Clinton, whose name is written upon the capital of every column of our social edifice, was indebted to private hospitality for a tomb. It is the same generous and patriotic spirit which animated those philanthropists, and sustained them in their struggles with the prejudices of the age in which they lived, that I desire to invoke in favor of agriculture. This spirit, wisely directed, can not fail, for it has been irresistible in every department it has hitherto entered. But let us all remember that the only true way to begin reform is to find the source of error; and that if we cultivate man, the improvement of the animal and vegetable kingdoms will surely follow.—*Address before N. Y. State Agricultural Society, Albany, Sept.* 29, 1842.

INTERNAL IMPROVEMENTS.

Internal Improvement the Policy of the Founders of the Republic.

THE principle of internal improvement derives its existence from the generous impulses of the revolutionary age. It regards the future welfare, prosperity, and happiness of the people. Its agency is everywhere salutary in encouraging emigration and the settlement and improvement of new lands, in augmenting national wealth, in promoting agriculture, commerce, manufactures, and the diffusion of knowledge, and in strengthening the bonds of our national Union. It is recited in the Declaration of Independence as one of the wrongs committed by the king of England, that he had endeavored to prevent the population of these states, and for that purpose had obstructed the laws for the naturalization of foreigners, had refused to pass others to encourage their migration hither, and had raised the condition of new appropriations of lands. The father of his country could have had none of the modern skepticism when in his first message to Congress he recommended a facilitation of the intercourse between distant parts of the country by a due attention to the postoffice and postroads. The population of the United States was confined for almost two centuries to the Atlantic coast, but the mighty mind of Washington perceived that a region far more extended, fertile, and salubrious, lay beyond the borders of the thirteen states; that inasmuch as the sovereignty of the Union was distributed among the cultivators of the earth, the political power of the government would find a centre in that region; that if the natural barriers between that region and the East should remain unchanged the West would at no distant pe riod cast off its union with the maritime states: but that if the natural barriers could be surmounted by roads and pierced by canals, connecting the inland navigation of lakes and rivers with tidewater, the wealth and population of the whole country would be vastly increased, and the states be bound together in an indissoluble union of interest and affection. Imbued with these sentiments, he stopped not in his farewell address to discuss or to recommend his favorite policy, but boldly predicted as a certain event that progressive improvement of interior communication by land and water, the auspicious results of which are only just beginning to be realized. It is a fact as interesting as it is instructive that the solicitude of the father of his country knew no rest after the achievement of her independence, but passed directly from the cares of that great struggle to the greater and even more glorious work of strengthening the union of the states and perpetuating their liberties. In 1783, immediately after the close of the war, he proceeded up the difficult navigation of the Mohawk to Fort Stanwix, now the site of the town of Rome, and crossed to Wood creek, which empties into Oneida lake and affords an imperfect communication with Lake Ontario. The noble and patriotic sentiments inspired by his observations were thus expressed: "Taking a contemplative and extensive view of the vast inland navigation of the United States, I could not but be struck with the immense diffusion and importance of it, and the goodness of that Providence who had dealt his favors to us with so profuse a hand. Would to God we may have wisdom to improve them!" The connection of Lake Ontario with the Hudson by perfect canals instead of the difficult and obstructed navigation of the Mohawk and Wood creek, the mingling of the waters of Lake Erie with those of the same noble river by means of a canal, the conversion of Fort Stanwix into the centre of a constellation of cities and villages, with all the consequent benefits of those improvements, reflect additional glory upon the fame of Washington, and prove that the efforts of this state in fulfilment of his noble aspiration have been crowned with the blessing of that Great Being to whom it was addressed. His contemporary, Jefferson, one of the most sagacious of American statesmen as well as one of the most ardent votaries of liberty, pronounced roads, canals, and rivers, to be great foundations of national prosperity and union, and recommended to Congress the policy of applying the surplus revenues arising from imposts upon luxuries and from the sale of the public lands, to the great purposes of public education, the improvement of the navigation of rivers, the construction of roads and canals, and such other objects of public improvement as it might be thought proper to add to the constitutional enumeration of the federal powers: operations by which, as he well remarked, new channels of communication would be opened between the states, the lines of their separation would disappear, their interests would be identified, and their union cemented by new and indissoluble ties.

It is worthy of remark, that none of the distinguished founders of American liberty stopped to calculate the question of revenue when they recommended this enlightened policy, designed to increase the prosperity and cement the Union of the states. The distinction between internal improvements and measures of public defence upon the ground that the former can not as rightfully be carried on with the revenues of the state, or with the use of its credit, as the latter is a refinement of modern times. The statesmen of the Revolution evidently regarded free intercommunication as one of the means of national defence. Had it been then understood as is now asserted, that internal improvement is a departure from the legitimate power of government, the opposition of the British king to emigration and his raising the conditions of new appropriations of land, would have found no reprobation in the Declaration of Independence, and the improvement of roads and rivers at the public expense would not subsequently have obtained an equal place with the promotion of public education in the executive recommendations of Washington and Jefferson. No such absurdity was then conceived as the proposition that while a nation may employ its revenues and credit in carrying on war, in suppressing sedition, and in punishing crime, it can not employ the same means to avert the calamities of war, provide for the public security, prevent sedition, improve the public morals, and increase the general happiness.—*Annual Message*, 1840.

Internal Improvement Wise and Beneficent.

When we look abroad through our country, and regard the improvements already completed, and the struggling efforts which are put forth by intelligent and patriotic men, with little of popular support or sympathy, in favor of others—and when we mark how surely and how speedily increased wealth and prosperity, and moral, social, and intellectual refinement, have followed the accomplishment of every enterprise which has been consummated—it seems passing strange that every advance of the system should have been contested against the incredulity of the people, and with a consent wrung from a hesitating and reluctant government. Hitherto the merit of the founders and advocates of the system has been enhanced more by their triumphs over popular prejudice and legislative repugnance than by their forecast of the rich blessings they called down upon their country. We will not question either the necessity or the wisdom of the decision by which the great system of internal improvement has, with the apparent consent of the people, been rejected from among the responsibilities of the general government, interested as that government is to secure the union of the states, and enriched as it is with the entire national domain and the exhaustless resources of the commerce which owes its prosperity to that very system. But it is manifestly our right, as it is our duty, to carry forward the system with such agency and under such patronage and sanction as the popular will recognises as legitimate for that purpose. It seems now to be settled that the agency consists in the combination of individual effort, under the sanction and patronage of the state government. To every region of our state the legislature owes a paternal care in this respect; and its obligations are only limited by the condition of its resources, and the question whether such improvements as are contemplated will advance the public weal. We must expect to encounter local prejudices; but these, when disclosed, are seldom able to defeat a meritorious enterprise. We must be prepared, by generous and lofty motives, and patriotic and expanded views, to overcome the more formidable opposition which arises from an honest but often unwise application of republican economy.

It is well to remember that the experience of human government affords not a solitary instance in which a state or nation became impoverished or subjected to an irredeemable debt by works of internal improvement. Ambition, revenge, and lust for extended territory, have been the only causes, and war almost the sole agent in entailing those calamities upon nations. Palaces and pyramids, the luxurious dwellings of living tyrants, and the receptacles of their worthless ashes when dead, have in every country, but our own, cost more than all its canals and roads. Ancient Egypt and ancient Rome, modern Netherlands, England, and France, and even our own peace-loving country (and these include the lands where art has expended the greatest effort in internal improvement), have severally disbursed more in a single war than was required to complete a system of improvements sufficient to perfect their union, wealth, and power, and enable them to defy invasion or aggression. Internal improvement, then, is the antagonist cause of national luxury and of war. It commands the support of those who would benevolently advance the greatest happiness of the greatest number, as well as the efforts of those who would increase the national power, elevate the national glory, and extend the sway of public virtue. A cause so catholic, so enlightened, so benevolent, may well engage the exertions of all good, wise, and patriotic citizens. It may often encounter hinderances, not only in the fluctuations of commerce, but from the drooping of popular feeling, and the diversity of local interests. But it may be maintained by the exercise of that perseverance which alone crowns with success the agency of human powers, and is itself little less than a positive virtue.—*Address, N. Y. and Erie Railroad Convention, Elmira,* 1837.

Internal Improvement the Real Source of the Prosperity of New York, and the only Sure Bond of Union of the States.

WHEN will the people of the state of New York learn to know and comprehend their own strength and their own resources? The New York and Erie railroad, which ought to have been built for eight or ten millions, has been made, by delays and consequent charges and loss of interest, to cost twenty millions!

The Erie canal enlargement, which ought to have been constructed for about the latter sum, is prosecuted with timidity and even distrust, increasing its cost twofold, and postponing its benefits till those who must pay for it shall have gone down to their graves.

Even now they tell us New York must hold in her breath, and forbear from speaking aloud for truth and justice, for fear of losing her trade and commerce. Her trade and commerce came to her, by no suppression of her principles and her sentiments, but were drawn to her by her Atlantic position, and by her rivers, and her canals and railroads. They came not from favor, but because she of all others could pay most for what others had to sell, and could sell cheaper what others wished to buy. Her trade and commerce are held now on this tenure and condition, and in that lies the secret of the commercial supremacy of New York.

What is that secret? Statesmen and citizens of other states, here it is! Here is Lake Erie. Stretching away for thousands of miles to the west lies the continent. Then almost at your feet is the Atlantic, the key of that continent. Far away in the east is the Old World, famishing for the supplies which that new country can supply. Here on the lakes which receive these supplies, and bear them in sloops, schooners, brigs, ships, and steam-vessels, and deposite them here on this isthmus, some three or four hundred miles wide, over which or through which they must be carried to the banks of the Atlantic coast, where other sloops, schooners, brigs, ships, and steamships, are waiting to waft them to Liverpool and London, and bring back the compensation to the cultivator. New York has only to cut a canal across this narrow isthmus, which is almost one continuous plain —a channel broad enough and deep enough to carry across the freight of the west which is to be transported to the east. A channel how large? Manifestly a ship-canal, because the commerce on the lakes and on the sea employs fleets, and nothing less than ship-channels from Lake Erie and Lake Ontario would be adequate.

The Erie canal, the Central railroad, the Northern railroad, and last, but by no means least, this great Southern railroad, all together contribute to that one great channel which New York has opened across the isthmus, enlarging it continually with the growing exactions of commerce, adopting at the same time the improvements suggested by art.

This command of the commerce of this continent is the dowry of New York. All our merchants who were merchants have always understood it; all our statesmen who were statesmen have always labored to realize it. Those merchants who were not merchants have built their enterprises on it unknowingly, and those statesmen who were not statesmen have labored to build the power and greatness of the state on other and unsubstantial foundations. This secret, however, was not the discovery of our own statesmen. It preceded them all. It revealed itself to Washington in 1783, when he had made his way, at the close of the war of the Revolution, up the Hudson and the Mohawk, and along Wood creek, and Oneida lake, and the Mad river, to the shore of Lake Ontario at Oswego. The sea was behind him, the lakes stretched away before him; his feet were on the isthmus. The secret broke upon him, and he gave utterance to it at once in a letter to the marquis of Chastellux, which has long since gone into history. How came the secret to break itself to the father of our country? I will tell you how. He was seeking security for the union of the states which was so soon to cover this continent. He found that guaranty in commercial union, and he saw that commercial union rising out of the canals and roads which New York might construct across the isthmus on which he stood.

Thus it is seen that we have only been executing the plans which wise and patriotic men designed for us long ago. We have only been too timid and too slow. In 1800, Gouverneur Morris predicted that in fifty years ships would sail out of Lake Erie, through the Hudson, to Liverpool. The half century is up, and the prediction is unfulfilled. Shame upon us! It might have been fulfilled, and ought to have been fulfilled in 1845, and would have been, if the public works had not been unnecessarily and unduly abandoned. Gouverneur Morris promised only a revenue of one and a quarter millions of dollars from the whole navigation across the isthmus. One boat-canal and our railroads, which are only the imperfect fulfilment of his plan of navigation, are yielding already nearly five millions.

It is due to the truth of history to confess that the city of New York was slow to comprehend this great policy and her own great destiny. The state forced the Erie canal upon the city in spite of herself. The city of New York never gave a vote for the Erie canal until twelve years after its original construction. But it is equally true that the state then faltered and fell away, leaving the system to fall into ruins; and its wrecks still present themselves to our view along all the routes of the canals and along the route of this great railroad. But then it was that the merchants of New York, who were merchants, came to the rescue. Their city had trebled in population and quadrupled in wealth within twenty-five years by the operation of the Erie canal. They then made returns to the state for this great boon, by the construction of the New York and Erie railroad, which will serve to supply the deficiency of facilities for the commerce which grows faster than we can enlarge its channel.

The suspension of this work in their hands on former occasions was the result of causes beyond their control. The commercial embarrassments of 1837 resulted in the suspension, not of this enterprise alone, but in the suspension of every enterprise of the sort in this state and in all other states, except that indomitable and noble state, Massachusetts. The resumption and completion of it, after it had lost the public confidence and the favor of the state, are worthy to be held in respect and admiration by all men. All honor, then, to the merchants of New York! I, whom they do not flatter, and who do not hesitate to say what I think to be the truth to them, am free to confess and to own before the world that they are the builders of the power and greatness of the state, and the saviors of the union of the states. But they do all this, not by going down to Castle-Garden to resolve in favor of the Union, but by building canals and railroads, to increase the freedom of inland trade, and swell to its utmost limits foreign commerce.

For my part, I have faith and trust in the wisdom and adaptation of this noble system of union established by our fathers. I have faith unbroken in the loyalty of the people of all the states, in any hour of trial. I repose the fullest confidence in their patriotism. Let these bonds of union remain, and let me see this isthmus on which we stand, channelled and furrowed by a river wide enough and deep enough to convey the products of the west with the least cost to the vessels which wait for them on the Atlantic. Let me never fail to see these iron chains forged and cast upon the territory within the several states, binding it together with new and durable links as it grows broader and broader, and I shall care not who may agitate, nor shall I fear the utmost extension. The Union will be safe, for its security will be anchored in the necessities and affections of the states and of the people.—*Remarks at Celebration of Completion of N. Y. and Erie Railroad, Dunkirk, May* 15, 1851.

The Suspension of the Public Works of New York Condemned and their Resumption Recommended.

THE fourth day of July last completed a quarter of a century since the system of internal improvements was undertaken by this state. Within that period artificial navigation has been opened throughout distances equal to eight hundred and three miles: and animal power in transportation has given place to the steam engine on routes seven hundred and fifty-seven miles in length. . . . . Our revenues have been increased from four hundred and nineteen thousand and nine hundred dollars in 1817 to one million, nine hundred and fifty-two thousand in 1841; our school and literature funds have been doubled; the remote districts of the state have become the homes of an intelligent and industrious population; four flourishing cities and upward of a hundred incorporated villages have been called into existence; our commercial emporium has trebled in population and added one hundred and seventy millions to its wealth; the revenues, commerce, and physical strength, of the whole commonwealth have been augmented in almost an equal proportion; and the states are bound together with bands stronger than those of merely political compact, and the danger of dismemberment is happily averted. New York was the projector of the system which, though yet incomplete, has produced these wonderful results; and she may point to it as a column designed and shaped by herself, to strengthen and perpetuate the national structure.

But the high career of prosperous and well-directed enterprise has been brought to a sudden and humiliating close. For the first time in the quarter of a century which has elapsed since the ground was broken for the Erie canal, a governor of the state of New York, in meeting the legislature, finds himself unable to announce the continued progress of improvement. The officers charged with the care of the public works, have arrested all proceedings in the enlargement of the Erie canal and the construction of the auxiliary works. The New York and Erie railroad, with the exception of forty-six miles from the eastern termination, lies in unfinished fragments throughout the long line of southern counties stretching four hundred miles from the Walkill to Lake Erie. The Genesee valley canal, excepting the portion between Dansville and Rochester, also lies in hopeless abandonment. The Black river canal, which was more than two thirds completed during the last year, has been left wholly unavailable. As if this were not enough, two railroads toward the construction of which the state had contributed half a million of dollars, and public-spirited citizens large sums in addition, have been brought to a forced sale, and sacrificed with an almost total loss to the treasury, without yielding any indemnity to the stockholders, and without even securing a guaranty that the people would be permitted to enjoy the use of the improvements.

The painful emotions excited by the condition to which the public works are thus reduced, might be somewhat relieved if there were any well-grounded hope that their prosecution would be resumed within any reasonable period. But the provisions of the law suspending those works, as well as the contemporaneous expositions of the grounds on which it was enacted, with every rational view which can be taken of its tendency forbid any such expectation. The policy of the act plainly is, that the debt of the state shall in no event be increased for the prosecution of improvements; nay, further, that the whole of the existing debts shall be extinguished before any additional sum shall be borrowed, and that the accruing revenues, instead of being appropriated, as heretofore, to the prosecution of the works, shall be henceforth applied exclusively to the establishment of a fund for the extinguishment of the existing debts, although, with small exceptions, those debts are redeemable only at distant periods. It is but too apparent that these provisions render any further progress in our public works wholly impracticable. The present generation, if this law continues, must abandon all hopes of seeing the system resumed, and it will only remain for them to pay the whole cost of the works, in a great degree useless because left unfinished, and hastening rapidly to dilapidation and ruin.

The objects which the legislature had in view, in directing the suspension of the public works were declared to be to pay the debts of the state, and preserve its credit. The means of paying the debts are derived from revenues and taxes. But the state, so far from diminishing, has increased its indebtedness, by becoming liable to contractors for heavy damages which might have been avoided by prosecuting the works; while, by discontinuing the necessary enlargement of the Erie canal, the increase of revenues hitherto so constant and so confidently relied upon for the reimbursement of the debts, is checked, and must ultimately cease. . . . . . Nor has the expectation of restoring the stocks of the state to their former high valuation been adequately realized, and certainly not to any extent commensurate with the sacrifices which have been made. The fiscal officers of the state are not now able to negotiate loans, even at seven per cent., except occasionally for small amounts. Under these circumstances, the inquiry arises whether the policy thus attempted ought to be continued. An imperative sense of duty compels me again to declare my conviction that it is radically wrong, and that erroneous views have been taken of the causes of our embarrassment.

* * * * * * * *

The people, however, look not for temporary or partial relief, but for the re-establishment of the system of internal improvement upon broad and impregnable foundations. Our fellow-citizens urge us to resume the public works, by pleading the distress which their suspension has already produced. They point us to labor unemployed and to masses impoverished; to agriculture unrewarded and burdened; to trade diminished and discouraged; to credit paralyzed; to land and property depreciated, and passing from hands hardened with the labor of production into others that wait to gather the ripened fruits of industry; to disappointed expectations built on the public faith, which no damages can reach or compensate; to dilapidated structures with increasing expenditures; to diminished revenues and protracted taxation; to increasing and hopeless embarrassment and decaying enterprise; and to a long and cheerless decline from a career in which so much has been won for the interests and honor of the state.

But we need no such painful incentives. Progressive physical improvement comprehending the North as well as the South, the East and the West opening every necessary channel and disclosing every resource which nature has bestowed, is emphatically the policy of the state. And we are required to return to the course we have left, by every consideration of duty to ourselves, to posterity, to our country, and to mankind.—*Message, Extra Session*, 1842.

New York and Massachusetts.*

May it please your Excellency, Gentlemen of the Senate and of the House of Representatives of the General Court of Massachusetts:

In the name of the senate and of the assembly of New York, in my own behalf, and as well for the absent as for those present, with whom I have the honor to be associated in the affairs of that state, I tender to you acknowledgments for this cordial and fraternal welcome. Representatives are here from our commercial metropolis and our agricultural districts; from the seacoast and the shores of our lakes; and from the valleys of the Susquehanna, the Delaware, the Hudson, and the St. Lawrence; and their unanimity warrants me in tendering these salutations in the name of the people of New York.

Not to know the wisdom, moderation, and virtue, of your counsels, would argue us unobservant of the prosperity and tranquillity of your commonwealth. I congratulate you, sir, the chief magistrate of that commonwealth [his excellency John Davis], upon this conjunction of two stars in our constellation as an event that will for ever signalize your career of public service.

* The completion of the railroad between Boston and Albany was celebrated by a meeting of the legislatures of Massachusetts and New York at Springfield, Massachusetts, in March, 1842, on which occasion Governor Seward delivered this speech.

Shall I not confess that the invitation which brought us here excited our surprise? We had supposed that *we* were on the very eastern verge, and that all the broad and boundless *West* lay between us and the setting sun. But this improvement, which you have so strangely called the *Western* railroad, has changed our position, and we must now acknowledge ourselves your western brethren.

We of New York are not a unique, or a primitive, or even a homogeneous people. We trace no common lineage to an unmingled ancestry. The colony of New Netherlands, which was the nucleus of our state, has received accumulations from England, from Ireland, Scotland, Germany, France, Poland, and from every other land, in modern Europe, where man has suffered oppression, or arbitrary power has attempted to subject his conscience. The nervous languages of the upper and the lower Rhine, and the softer dialects of the Mediterranean, mingle in our streets and in our distant settlements. Among us, he alone is of peculiar birth whose blood allies him to only one fatherland. It is one of our cares, by the agency of benign and equal institutions, to assimilate all these various masses, and reduce them to one great, harmonious, united, and happy people. Judge, then, with what interest we regard a community to whom such efforts are unnecessary and unknown — a community who, descended from a common stock, have for two centuries remained separate from other portions of their race, and retained throughout all that time the primitive virtues, energies, customs, forms, and habits, of their ancestors.

The impress of the New-England schoolmaster is seen everywhere in our state, and you might obtain an acknowledgment from each one of her representatives here that he has profited by that teacher's instructions. Having thus known the schoolmaster, it was among our motives to this visit that we should see the land whence he went abroad, and become acquainted with the people whose ancestors erected a church simultaneously with their dwellings, and a university within twelve years after their landing at Plymouth.

Nor can we forget that it was Massachusetts that encountered first and suffered most from the tyranny which resulted in our national independence; that the first blood shed in that sacred cause flowed at Lexington; and that Liberty's earliest rampart was established upon Bunker's hill. Nevertheless the struggles and sacrifices of Massachusetts have until now been known to us through traditions not her own, and they still seem to have been those of a distant though an allied people—of a country separated from us by mountain-barriers such as divide every continent into states and empires. But what a change is here! This morning's sun was just greeting the site of old Fort Orange as we took our leave; and now, when he has scarcely reached the meridian, we have crossed our hitherto impassable barrier, and have met you here on the shore of the Connecticut, the battle-ground of King Philip's cruel wars: and before that sun shall set, we might ascend the heights of Charlestown, or rest upon the rock that was wet with the blood that flowed from the weary feet of the pilgrim-fathers.

Sir, you have well set forth the benefits which will result to you, to us, to our country, and to mankind, from the triumph of modern science over the physical obstructions to intercourse between the American communities. I can advert to but one of these results—the increasing strength of the states, and the perpetuity of their union. New York, Massachusetts, and her sister-states of New England, will no longer be merely confederated states. Their interests, their affections, and their sympathies, will now be intermingled—and a common and invisible destiny, whether of good or evil, awaits them all. Had such connections existed when the British throne attempted to abridge the rights of the colonies, what power could have wounded Massachusetts when New York could have rushed to her defence? Could Great Britain and her savage allies have scourged so severely our infant settlements upon the Mohawk and the Susquehanna, if New England could have gone to their relief? How vain will be any attempt hereafter to array us against each other! Since Providence has been pleased to permit these states to be thus joined together, who shall put them asunder?

You have rightly assumed that on this occasion we indulge no jealousies of your prosperity, and no apprehensions of losing our power or influence. The Hudson is beautiful in our eyes, for it flows through the land of our birth, and our institutions and marts overhang its waters. But if its shores be not the true and proper seat of commerce and of empire, or if we have not the virtues and the energies necessary to retain our vantage-ground, we shall not try to check the prosperity or the political ascendency of our sister-states. Far from indulging such unworthy thoughts, we regard this and every other improvement as calculated to promote our own prosperity, and, what is far more important than the advancement of our state or of yours, the union and harmony of the whole American family. The bond that brings us into so close connection is capable of being extended from your coast to the Mississippi, and of being fastened around not only New York and the first thirteen, but all the twenty-six states. This is the policy of New York, and her ambition. We rejoice in your co-operation, and invite its continuance, until alarms of disunion shall be among the obsolete dangers of the republic.

New York has been addressed here in language of magnanimity. It would not become me to speak of her position, her resources, or her influence. And yet I may, without offending the delicacy of her representatives here, and of her people at home, claim that she is not altogether unworthy of admiration. Our mountains, cataracts, and lakes, can not be surveyed without lifting the soul on high. Our metropolis and our inland cities, our canals and railroads, our colleges and schools, and our twelve thousand libraries, evince emulation and a desire to promote the welfare of our country, the progress of civilization, and the happiness of mankind. While we acknowledge that it was your WARREN that offered up his life at Charlestown, your ADAMS and your HANCOCK who were the proscribed leaders in the Revolution, and your FRANKLIN whose wisdom swayed its councils, we can not forget that Ticonderoga and Saratoga are within our borders — that it was a son of New York that fell in scaling the heights of Abraham — that another shaped every pillar of the Constitution and twined the evergreen around its capital — that our FULTON sent forth the mighty mechanical agent that is revolutionizing the world — and that but for our CLINTON, his lofty genius and undaunted perseverance, the events of this day and all its joyous anticipations had slept together in the womb of futurity.

The grandeur of this occasion oppresses me. It is not, as

some have supposed, the first time that states have met. On many occasions, in all ages, states, nations, and empires, have come together. But the trumpet heralded their approach; they met in the shock of war: one or the other sunk to rise no more, and desolation marked, for the warning of mankind, the scene of the fearful encounter. And if sometimes Chivalry asked an armistice, it was but to light up with evanescent smiles the stern visage of war. How different is this scene! Here are no contending hosts, no destructive engines, nor the terrors nor even the pomp of war. Not a helmet, sword, or plume, is seen in all this vast assemblage. Nor is this a hollow truce between contending states. We are not met upon a cloth of gold, and under a silken canopy, to practise deceitful courtesies; nor in an amphitheatre, with jousts and tournaments, to make trial of our skill in arms preparatory to a fatal conflict. We have come here enlightened and fraternal states, without pageantry, or even insignia of power, to renew pledges of fidelity, and to cultivate affection and all the arts of peace. Well may our sister-states look upon the scene with favor, and the nations of the earth draw from it good auguries of universal and perpetual peace.

EDUCATION.

The proper Range of Popular Education.

LET us remember for ourselves, and inculcate upon the people, that our progress thus far has but led us to the vestibule of knowledge. When we see the people content in the belief that they know all that is known or is desirable to be known, let us instruct them that there is a science that will reveal to them the hidden and perpetual fires in which are continually carried on the formation and modification of the rocks which compose this apparently solid globe, and from whose elaborate changes is derived the sustenance of all that variety of vegetable life with which it is clothed: that another will disclose to them the elements and properties of those metals which men combine or shape with varied art into the thousand implements and machines by the use of which the forest-world has been converted into a family of kindred nations; that another solicits their attention, while it will bring in review before them, so that they can examine, with greater care and instruction than did their great progenitor in the primitive garden, all the races of animated beings, and learn their organization, uses, and history; that another will classify and submit to their delighted examination the entire vegetable kingdom, making them familiar with their virtues as well as the forms of every species, from the cedar of Lebanon to the humble flower that is crushed under their feet; that another will decompose and submit to their examination the water which fertilizes the earth, and the invisible air they breathe; will develop the sources and laws of that heat which seems to kindle all life into existence, and that terrific lightning which seems the especial messenger of Divine wrath to extinguish it. Let us teach that the world of matter in which we live, in all its vast variety of form, is influential in the production, support, and happiness, of our own life, and that it is passing strange, that with minds endowed with a capacity to study that influence and measurably direct it, we yield uninquiringly to its action, as if it were controlled by capricious accident or blind destiny. Shall we not excite some interest, when we appeal to the people to learn that science which teaches the mechanism of our own wonderfully and fearfully fashioned frames, and that other science which teaches the vastly more complicated and delicate structure of our immortal minds? Who would not follow with delight that science which elevates our thoughts to the heavens and teaches us the magnitude, forms, distances, revolutions, and laws of the globes that fill the concave space above us? And who, with thoughts thus gradually conducted through the range of the material universe, would not receive with humility, yet with delight, the teachings of that spirit of divine truth which exalts us to the study of the character and attributes of that glorious and beneficent Being, whose single volition called it all into existence? Let us teach the people all this, and let us show them that, while we sit contentedly in comparative ignorance, the arts are waiting to instruct us how to reduce the weary labors of life; philosophy, how to avoid its errors and misfortunes; and eloquence, poetry, and music, how to cheer its way and refine our affections; and that Religion is most efficient when she combines and profits by all these instructions, to conduct us to happiness in a future state. Above all, let us inculcate that the great and beneficent Being who created us and this material universe, has established between each of us, and every part of it cognisable by our minds, relations more or less intimate; that he has impressed not more on the globes that roll through the infinitude of space than on the pebble that lies beneath our feet—not more on the immovable continent than on the rolling sea—not more on the wind and lightning than on the ethereal mind of man; and not more on the human soul than on the dimly-lighted instinct of the glow-worm, or of the insect visible only by microscopic aid—"laws that determine their organization, their duration, time, place, circumstance, and action;

that for our security, improvement, and happiness, he has subjected these laws to our keen investigation and perpetual discovery; and that, vast as is the range of that discovery, so vast and more extended than we can describe, or can yet be conceived, is knowledge; and that to attain all this knowledge—is Education!"—*Address at Westfield, N. Y.*, 1837.

Popular Education a Leveller.

THE aristocracy with which the world has been scourged was never one that was produced by science and learning. That education increases the power of those who enjoy its advantages is true; and in this best sense is education aristocratic. In this sense, science and learning always will create an aristocracy in every country where they are cherished. Not an aristocracy of birth, for it is education that has exploded among us the prejudice in favor of birth. To it we owe our exemption from the error prevalent all over the rest of the world, that no man is so fit, or so well entitled, to be a king as he who is the son of a king; none so brave as he whose father was a warrior; none so well entitled to the enjoyment of wealth as he whose ancestors were rich. Nor is the aristocracy produced by education that of wealth; for knowledge pays no respect to mere wealth: it humbles all pretensions except those of virtue and intellect. But the aristocracy produced by education is the increased power and influence of the most enlightened, and therefore the most useful, members of society. However repugnant we may be to admit the truth, and however glaring may be the exceptions to it, it is nevertheless a sound general principle that knowledge is power. Whatever there is in our lot that distinguishes us from the disfranchised peasantry of continental Europe, or the turbaned followers of the prophet, or the mutually-warring Africans in their native deserts, or their abject offspring here, or the aborigines of our forests, all is knowledge obtained by education; and, compared with all those classes of our common race, we are aristocratic. We exercise greater power, because we are wiser, and therefore better, than they. In every stage of society this tendency of education has been observed. He who first learned the malleable property of iron, and first shaped the axe and the ploughshare, became an aristocrat. He who first attenuated and wove the fleece, he who first smoothed and rendered pliable the skins of beasts, he who first erected the rude huts for his tribe —all these, all classes of mechanics, have in their day been, and all who exercise their callings will be, aristocrats. They all exercise an influence, great in proportion to their knowledge. It is inevitable, because it is the wisdom of Providence that the world shall be governed by ascendant minds. Our own observation shows us daily that knowledge gives the capacity for usefulness; and he who is, or is esteemed, useful, is by consent invested with power. In agriculture, he who adds science to labor is an aristocrat, compared with the drudge who performs an allotted task. He who in the mechanic arts adds skill to patient industry, rises instantly above the uninstructed artisan; and he who to industry and skill adds taste, is far above the competition of the dull and plodding workman. If, at this day, wealth sometimes usurps the place of intellect and appropriates its honors, it is only because public sentiment is perverted, and requires to be corrected by a higher standard of education. But, although education increases the power and influence of its votaries, it has no tendency like other means of power to confine its advantages to a small number: on the contrary, it is expansive and thus tends to produce equality, not by levelling all to the condition of the base, but by elevating all to the association of the wise and good. If, then, we would advance popular education, if we would secure the success of our common schools, and extend their advantages to the whole people, we must remember that education is a catholic cause, and must banish all prejudices that retard improvement in any direction.—*Address at Westfield, N. Y.*, 1837.

The Same.

OUR institutions, excellent as they are, have hitherto produced but a small portion of the beneficent results they are calculated to confer upon the people. The chief of those benefits is *equality*. We do indeed enjoy equality of civil rights; but we have not yet attained, we have only approximated toward, what is even more important—*equality of social condition.*

From the beginning of time, aristocracy has existed, and society has been divided into classes — the rich and the poor — the strong and the dependent — the learned and the unlearned; and from this inequality of social condition have resulted the ignorance, the crime, and the sufferings of the people. Let it excite no wonder when I say that this inequality exists among us, and that aristocracy has a home even in the land of freedom. It does not, indeed, deprive us of our civil rights, but it prevents the diffusion of prosperity and happiness. We should be degenerate descendants of our heroic forefathers did we not assail this aristocracy, remove the barriers between the rich and the poor, break the control of the few over the many, extend the largest liberty to the greatest number, and strengthen in every way the democratic principles of our constitution.

This is the work in which you are engaged. Sunday schools and common schools are the great levelling institutions of the age. What is the secret of aristocracy? It is, that knowledge is power. Knowledge, the world over, has been possessed by the few, and ignorance has been the lot of the many. The merchant — what is it that gives him wealth? The lawyer — what is it that gives him political power? The clergy — what is it that gives them influence so benign for good purposes, so effective for mischievous ends? Knowledge. What makes *this* man a common laborer, and the *other* a usurer — *this* man a slave, and the *other* a tyrant? Knowledge. Knowledge can never be taken from those by whom it has once been attained; and hence the power which it confers upon the few can not be broken while the many are uneducated. Strip its possessors of all their wealth, and power, and honors, and knowledge still remains the same mighty agent to restore again the inequality you have removed. But there is a more effectual way to banish aristocracy from among us. It is by extending the advantages of knowledge to the many — to all the citizens of the state. Just so far and so fast as education is extended, democracy is ascendant.

I wish you, my fellow-citizens, God speed in your benevolent and patriotic labors. Seldom does it happen to any citizen to render to his country any service more lasting or more effectual than that which is accomplished by the teachers of such schools as these. While they are at work throughout the country, we need indulge no fears of extending too widely the privilege of suffrage and the right of citizenship.—*Address at Sunday-School Celebration, July* 4, 1839.

Female Education.

THERE remains to be noticed an error scarcely less extensive, or less pernicious, than any I have mentioned. It is that which limits to a comparatively lower standard the education of the female sex. We may justly boast in this country a higher and more deferential regard, a more chivalrous devotion, to the sex than is exhibited by any other nation. I myself have compared our sentiments and customs, in this respect, with those of western Europe. I have seen, indeed, in some other countries, the more ardent and impassioned devotion that marks the clime where licentiousness assumes the name of love, but is not imbued with any of its sentiment, nor elevated by any of its purity. I have seen, under colder skies, more humble homage paid to individuals, because they were distinguished by learning, accomplishments, birth, wealth, or beauty. But it is in this land only that respect and tenderness are yielded to women because they are women. If the vehement imagination of other countries is here subdued, and passion is modified, the romance and poetry of other lands are here converted into a real and living sentiment. There is no other country where the humblest female receives, from the highest in rank of the other sex, the surrender of the chief place in public assemblies, not more than in the social circle —in accidental meetings by the way, not less than in the ceremonials of fashionable life. In Italy, often described as the land where beauty wields a despotic sway, I have seen women rolling huge stones from the mountain-roads. In France, the land of gallantry and politeness, I have seen them performing the labor of porters: in refined England, the task of scavengers of the streets. And in all those countries, I have seen them employed in field labor, with countenances hardened by exposure to all vicissitudes of weather, and hands familiar with the spade and the plough. It reflects great honor upon our national character that such degradation of the sex is never exhibited here.

But there yet remains a duty toward women to be learned by us all; and that is, to make their education equal always to that of the other sex. He, it seems to me, is a dull observer, who is not convinced that they are equally qualified with the other sex, for the study of the magnificent creation around us, and equally entitled to the happiness to be derived from its pursuits: and still more blind is he, who has not learned that it was the intention of the Creator to commit to them a higher and greater portion of responsibility in the education of the youth of both sexes. They are the natural guardians of the young. Their abstraction from the engrossing cares of life, affords them leisure both to acquire and communicate knowledge. From them the young more willingly receive it, because the severity of discipline is relieved with greater tenderness and affection while their quicker apprehension, enduring patience, expansive benevolence, higher purity, more delicate taste and elevated moral feeling, qualify them for excellence in all departments of learning, except perhaps the exact sciences. If this be true, how many a repulsive, bigoted, and indolent professor will, in the general improvement of education, be compelled to resign his claim to modest, assiduous, and affectionate woman? And how many conceited pretenders who now wield the rod in our common schools, without the knowledge of human nature requisite for its discreet exercise—too indolent to improve, and too proud to discharge their responsible duties, will be driven to seek subsistence elsewhere? It is not, as is generally supposed, the female sex alone who suffer by this exclusion from their proper sphere. Whatever is lost to the other sex, of the advantages of their nurture and cultivation, is an additional loss to our common race. —*Address at Westfield, N. Y.*, 1837.

Improvement of Popular Education must begin not with the Government but with the People.

FELLOW-CITIZENS, it is less the object of this discourse to give practical suggestions for the reform of education, than it is to excite an interest in its behalf; yet I will add, in order that it may not appear altogether without practical tendency, that if we would communicate an effective impulse to the cause, we are not to wait the action of the government. Our government acts only in obedience to popular influence, and in pursuance of popular direction. It is not in its principles to anticipate the one, or resist the other. Like all other reforms, this must be effected by a combination of individual efforts, to stimulate and enlighten the public mind. In the present case public feeling is not to be reached from a distant point. A more practicable course is offered. We must begin at home, with the schools around us, and among that portion of the community in which we reside. Let us revive the system of visitation and examination of our academies and schools. This all-important feature in every plan of public instruction has, during a long period, fallen into desuetude. The officers invested with the responsibility of discharging the duty, unfortunately, are selected as the favorites of some political party, and do not even make a nominal visitation of the institutions subject to their examination. The right of visitation, however, is not divested from parents and patrons of these schools. If, in addition to the examinations heretofore practised, there could be adopted some plan in pursuance of which, institutions of equal rank situated in the same vicinity could be brought into comparative examination, competition would at once be produced between instructors, and emulation among pupils; increased interest would be excited on the part of parents, and a lively concern in the whole community.

I appeal to all patriots and Christians to consider the subject upon which I have presented these hasty remarks, and adopt such measures as shall be found expedient to discharge the responsibility they owe to their children, to the church of our Savior, to our common country, and to the great family of mankind.—*Address at Westfield, N. Y.*, 1837.

Education preferable to Conquest.

THE distinguished senator from Kentucky [Mr. CLAY], several years since, by his great influence in the councils of the nation, secured the distribution among the several states of this Union of a portion of the surplus revenues of this government. I was at a distance, an humble follower and approver of that policy. The result of it in other states I do not know. But you, Mr. President [Mr. FILLMORE], can testify with me the result, the beneficent result, in the state of New York, from which we come. The share which was allotted to us was six millions of dollars; the amount we received was four millions, five hundred thousand dollars. Every dollar of that four and a half millions, sir, more than ten years ago, went to the foundation of public schools, academies, seminaries, and other higher institutions of learning, and of libraries for the common people. And, sir, I will now state to the senate—and I am proud that, in behalf of the state of New York, I am here this day to state it to the praise and honor of the distinguished senator from Kentucky—the condition of the state of New York, of the people, bond and free—I might say, if we had any of the former class—native and foreigner, to which they have been brought by this act of justice—I will not call it benevolence. Sir, the state of New York, having a population of three millions of people, has not in it one child of citizen or foreigner that is not educated, from the age of five years to the age of twenty years, at the public cost and expense. Again, sir: at the distance of every mile and a half on every main road, railroad, canal, and cross-road—separated by only a mile and a half—is the schoolhouse of New England. The schoolmaster is at home everywhere in New York, and all the time; and New York has made a trial of the blessed example of Massachusetts and Connecticut. This is what has been done in my day, since my and your experience began; and more than that: in every one of these schoolhouses is a public library of two hundred and fifty volumes, containing all that is interesting in ancient or modern history or science, literature, geography, and every other branch of human knowledge, open and accessible to every citizen—man, woman, and child—in the state of New York. Yes, sir, these four millions and a half have supplied us with libraries which, taken collectively, contain more than one million of volumes.

More than that, sir: there has not been left in the state of New York the blind person who has not been taught to read his bible—there has not been left in the state the deaf and dumb, the mute, who has not been brought to be able to give expression of his gratitude and praise to God, and to the state which has brought him from ignorance and degradation below his race. More than that, sir; we have not neglected that other unfortunate class. I have been asked, why not consider the free negroes? Sir, the free negroes have been considered. This fund has been appropriated to their advancement, also; to raise their condition; to cultivate them to exercise the rights of self-government, and to carry on the great work of the emancipation of their race wherever they are found in bondage. Yes, sir, five thousand children of the African race are educated out of this great fund of national benevolence. What becomes of the reproach, then, that this is a charity? What would have been the disposition of this fund if it had been left here, sir? It would have been expended as the revenues of this country, always too large, too liberal, have been expended, in improvidence. It is therefore that I have always claimed that it should be distributed among the states, that they might apply it to works of advancement — progress — humanity.

Now, sir, there has been no diminution of the fund all this time. While we have been enjoying this four and a half millions, there is not one dollar of it gone. Every dollar is there yet. It is still in the treasury of the state of New York; and all that has been done has been only by the *use* of the money. Tell me, sir, is it not wiser to make such a distribution of this fund than it would be to employ it in encouraging prodigality in the government; than to encourage that lust of conquest in which the Mexican war had its origin, by which were brought into this Union seven hundred and sixty-three millions of acres of public domain, to be added to the one thousand millions we had before? What has it wrought? It has proved, in the words of an honorable senator here, but a Pandora's box of evils; and we are entertained here, day after day, with the intelligence that the Union must be dissolved — that it is really now dissolved — even to-day. We employed the revenues of the public domains in extending our dominions, that were too large — unnecessarily large — already. Sir, I want no more Mexican wars, no more lust of conquest, no more of seizing the unripened fruit, which, if left alone, would of itself fall into our hands. — *Speech in U. S. Senate, Jan.* 30, 1850.

The Bible the Basis of Republican Institutions.

WHAT is that which has enabled the Scriptures of the Jews to supplant all other writings of antiquity, and to maintain an authority and veneration unapproachable by even modern learning? It is the fact that they describe the Creator and man more accurately according to the standard of enlightened reason, and define the relations between them more justly according to the suggestions of the human heart. I am asked, what is my opinion of the influence of the Holy Scriptures on human society? I answer, that I do not believe human society, including not merely a few persons in any state, but whole masses of men, ever has attained, or ever can attain, a high state of intelligence, virtue, security, liberty, or happiness, without them; and that the whole hope of human progress is suspended on the ever-growing influence of the Bible. . . . . .

The constitution of the United States established a republican form of government for the free people of this Union; and it has ordained that once in every ten years the number of souls under the protection of that constitution, and in the enjoyment of the freedom which it secures, shall be ascertained, in order that their political rights shall be secured, and that each portion of the country shall enjoy its just and proper proportion of power. I know not how long a republican form of government can flourish among a people who have not the Bible: the experiment has never been tried; but this I do know, that the existing government of this country never could have had an existence but for the Bible. And further: I do in my conscience believe, that if at every decade of years a copy of the Bible shall be found in every family of the land, its republican institutions will be perpetual.—*Address before Am. Bib. Society*, 1839.

The System of Public Schools Defective.—Amendment Proposed.

THE colleges, academies, and common schools, constitute our system of public instruction. The pervading intelligence, the diminution of crime, the augmented comforts and enjoyments of society and its progressive refinement, public order, and the supremacy of the laws, testify that the system has been by no means unsuccessful.

It must nevertheless be admitted, that its usefulness is much less than the state rightfully demands, both as a return for her munificence and a guaranty of her institutions. Some of our colleges and academies languish in the midst of a community abounding in genius and talents impatient of the ignorance which debases and the prejudices which enslave. The common school system, but partially successful in agricultural districts, is represented as altogether without adaptation to cities and populous villages. The standard of education ought to be elevated, not merely to an equality with that attained in other states, but to that height which may be reached by cultivating the intellectual powers with the aid of modern improvements during the entire period when the faculties are quick and active, the curi osity insatiable, the temper practicable, and the love of truth supreme. The ability to read and write, with the rudiments of arithmetic, generally constitute the learning acquired in common schools. To these our academies and colleges add superficial instruction in the dead languages without the philosophy of our own; scientific facts without their causes; definitions without practical application; the rules of rhetoric without its spirit; and history divested of its moral instructions. It is enough to show the defectiveness of our entire system that its pursuits are irksome to all except the few endowed with peculiar genius and fervor to become the guides of the human mind, and that it fails to inspire either a love of science or a passion for literature. Science is nothing else than a disclosure of the bounties the Creator has bestowed to promote the happiness of man, and a discovery of the laws by which mind and matter are controlled for that benignant end. Literature has no other object than to relieve our cares and increase our virtues. That the pursuits of either should require monastic seclusion, or be enforced by pains and penalties upon reluctant minds, is inconsistent with the generous purposes of both. Society can not be justly censured for indifference to education, when those who enjoy its precious advantages manifest so little of the enthusiasm it ought to inspire. All the associations of the youthful mind in the acquisition of knowledge must be cheerful; its truths should be presented in their native beauty and in their natural order; the laws it reveals should be illustrated always by their benevolent adaptation to the happiness of mankind; and the utility and beauty of what is already known should incite to the endless investigation of what remains concealed. If education could be conducted upon principles like these, the attainments of our collegiate instruction might become an ordinary measure of acquirement in our common schools; and our academies and colleges would be continually enjoying new revelations of philosophy and attaining higher perfection in the arts which alleviate the cares of human life.

If these reflections seem extravagant, and the results they contemplate unattainable, it need only be answered that the improvability of our race is without limit, and all that is proposed is less wonderful than what has already been accomplished. I do not hesitate to invite efforts to establish the standard I have described. Postponed, omitted, and forgotten, as it too often is amid the excitement of other subjects and the pressure of other duties, education is, nevertheless, the chief of our responsibilities. The consequences of the most partial improvement in our system of education will be wider and more enduring than the effects of any change of public policy, the benefit of any new principle of jurisprudence, or the results of any enterprise of physical improvement we can accomplish. These consequences will extend through the entire development of the human mind, and be consummated only with its destiny.—*Annual Message*, 1839.

Education of the Children of Exiles.

THE children of foreigners, found in great numbers in our populous cities and towns, and in the vicinity of our public works, are too often deprived of the advantages of our system of public education, in consequence of prejudices arising from difference of language or religion. It ought never to be forgotten that the public welfare is as deeply concerned in their education as in that of our own children. I do not hesitate therefore to recommend the establishment of schools in which they may be instructed by teachers speaking the same language with themselves, and professing the same faith. There would be no inequality in such a measure, since it happens from the force of circumstances, if not from choice, that the responsibilities of education are in most instances confided by us to native citizens, and occasions seldom offer for a trial of our magnanimity by committing that trust to persons differing from ourselves in language or religion. Since we have opened our country and all its fullness to the oppressed of every nation, we should evince wisdom equal to such generosity by qualifying their children for the high responsibilities of citizenship.—*Annual Message*, 1840.

The Same.

WHEN the census of 1850 shall be taken, I trust it will show that within the borders of the state of New York there is no child of sufficient years who is unable to read and write. I am sure it will then be acknowledged that when, ten years before, there were thirty thousand children growing up in ignorance and vice, a suggestion to seek them wherever found, and win them to the ways of knowledge and virtue by persuasion, sympathy, and kindness, was prompted by a sincere desire for the common good. I have no pride of opinion concerning the manner in which the education of those whom I have brought to your notice shall be secured, although I might derive satisfaction from the reflection, that, amid abundant misrepresentations of the method suggested, no one has contended that it would be ineffectual, nor has any other plan been proposed. I observe, on the contrary, with deep regret, that the evil remains as before; and the question recurs, not merely how or by whom shall instruction be given, but whether it shall be given at all or shall be altogether withheld. Others may be content with a system that erects free schools and *offers* gratuitous instruction; but I trust I shall be allowed to entertain the opinions that no system is perfect that does not accomplish what it proposes; that our system is therefore deficient in comprehensiveness in the exact proportion of the children that it leaves uneducated; that knowledge, however acquired, is better than ignorance; and that neither error, accident, nor prejudice, ought to be permitted to deprive the state of the education of her citizens. Cherishing such opinions, I could not enjoy the consciousness of having performed my duty, if any effort had been omitted which was calculated to bring within the schools all who are destined to exercise the rights of citizenship ; nor shall I feel that the system is perfect or liberty safe until that object be accomplished. Not personally concerned about such misapprehensions as have arisen, but desirous to remove every obstacle to the accomplishment of so important an object, I very freely declare that I seek the education of those whom I have brought before you, not to perpetuate any prejudices or distinctions which deprive them of instruction, but in disregard of all such distinctions and prejudices. I solicit their education less from sympathy, than because the welfare of the state demands it, and can not dispense with it. As native citizens, they are born to the right of suffrage. I ask that they may at least be taught to read and write ; and in asking this, I require no more for them than I have diligently endeavored to secure to the inmates of our penitentiaries, who have forfeited that inestimable franchise by crime, and also to an unfortunate race, which, having been plunged by us into degradation and ignorance, has been excluded from the franchise by an arbitrary property qualification incongruous with all our institutions. I have not recommended nor do I seek the education of any class in foreign languages or in particular creeds or faiths ; but fully believing with the author of the Declaration of Independence, that even error may be safely tolerated where reason is left free to combat it, and therefore indulging no apprehensions from the influence of any language or creed among an enlightened people, I desire the education of the entire rising generation in all the elements of knowledge we possess, and in that tongue which is the universal language of our countrymen. To me the most interesting of all our republican institutions is the common school. I seek not to disturb in any manner its peaceful and assiduous exercises, and least of all with contentions about faith or forms. I desire the education of all the children in the commonwealth in morality and virtue, leaving matters of conscience where, according to the principles of civil and religious liberty established by our constitution and laws, they rightfully belong.—*Annual Message*, 1841.

The Same.

It was among my earliest duties to bring to the notice of the legislature the neglected condition of many thousand children, including a very large proportion of those of immigrant parentage, in our great commercial city; a misfortune then supposed to result from groundless prejudices and omissions of parental duty. Especially desirous at the same time not to disturb in any manner the public schools, which seemed to be efficiently conducted, although so many for whom they were established, were unwilling to receive their instructions, I suggested, as I thought in a spirit not inharmonious with our civil and religious institutions, that if necessary it might be expedient to bring those so excluded from such privileges into schools rendered especially attractive by the sympathies of those to whom the task of instruction should be confided. It has since been discovered that the magnitude of the evil was not fully known, and that its causes were very imperfectly understood. It will be shown you in the proper report, that twenty thousand children in the city of New York, of suitable age, are not at all instructed in any of the public schools, while the whole number in all the residue of the state not taught in common schools, does not exceed nine thousand. What had been regarded as individual, occasional, and accidental prejudices have proved to be opinions pervading a large mass, including at least one religious communion equally with all others entitled to civil tolerance—opinions cherished through a period of sixteen years, and ripened into a permanent, conscientious distrust of the impartiality of the education given in the public schools. This distrust has been rendered still deeper and more alienating by a subversion of precious civil rights of those whose consciences are thus offended.

Happily in this as in other instances, the evil is discovered to have had its origin no deeper than in a departure from the equality of general laws. In our general system of common schools, trustees, chosen by tax-paying citizens, levy taxes, build schoolhouses, employ and pay teachers, and govern schools which are subject to visitation by similarly-elected inspectors, who certify the qualifications of teachers; and all schools thus constituted participate in just proportion in the public moneys, which are conveyed to them by commissioners also elected by the people. Such schools are found distributed in average spaces of two and a half square miles throughout the inhabited portions of the state, and yet neither popular discontent, nor political strife, nor sectarian discord, has ever disturbed their peaceful instructions or impaired their eminent usefulness. In the public school system of the city of New York, one hundred persons are trustees and inspectors, and, by continued consent of the common council, are the dispensers of an annual average sum of thirty-five thousand dollars received from the common-school fund of the state, and also of a sum equal to ninety-five thousand dollars derived from an indiscriminating tax upon the real and personal estates of the city. They build schoolhouses chiefly with public funds, and appoint and remove teachers, fix their compensation, and prescribe the moral, intellectual, and religious instruction which one eighth of the rising generation of the state shall be required to receive. Their powers, more effective and far-reaching than are exercised by the municipality of the city, are not derived from the community whose children are educated and whose property is taxed, nor even from the state, which is so great an almoner, and whose welfare is so deeply concerned, but from an incorporated and perpetual association, which grants, upon pecuniary subscription, the privileges even of life membership, and yet holds in fee simple the public school edifices, valued at eight hundred thousand dollars. Lest there might be too much responsibility even to the association, that body can elect only one half the trustees, and those thus selected appoint their fifty associates. The philanthropy and patriotism of the present managers of the public schools, and their efficiency in imparting instruction, are cheerfully and gratefully admitted. Nor is it necessary to maintain that agents thus selected will become unfaithful, or that a system that so jealously excludes popular interference must necessarily be unequal in its operation. It is only insisted that the institution, after a fair and sufficient trial, has failed to gain that broad confidence reposed in the general system of the state, and indispensable to every scheme of universal education. No plan for that purpose can be defended except on the ground that public instruction is one of the responsibilities of the government. It is therefore a manifest legislative duty to correct errors and defects in whatever system is established. In the present case the failure amounts virtually to an exclusion of all the children thus withheld. I can not overcome my regret that every suggestion of amendment encounters so much opposition from those who defend the public school system of the metropolis, as to show, that in their judgment it can admit of no modification, neither from tenderness to the consciences, nor from regard to the civil rights of those aggrieved, nor even for the reclamation of those for whose culture the state has so munificently provided; as if society most conform itself to the public schools instead of the public schools adapting themselves to the exigencies of society. The late eminent superintendent, after exposing the greatness of this public misfortune, and tracing it to the discrepancy between the local and general systems, suggested a remedy which, although it is not urged to the exclusion of any other, seems to deserve dispassionate consideration.

I submit, therefore, with entire willingness to approve whatever adequate remedy you may propose, the expediency of restoring to the people of the city of New York—what I am sure the people of no other part of the state would upon any consideration relinquish—the education of their children.

For this purpose, it is only necessary to vest the control of the common schools in a board to be composed of commissioners elected by the people; which board shall apportion the school moneys among all the schools, including those now existing, which shall be organized and conducted in conformity to its general regulations and the laws of the state, in the proportion of the number of pupils instructed. It is not left doubtful that the restoration to the common schools of the city of this simple and equal feature of the common schools of the state, would remove every complaint, and bring into the seminaries the offspring of want and misfortune presented by a grand jury on a recent occasion as neglected children of both sexes who are found in hordes upon wharves and on corners of the streets, surrounded by evil associations, disturbing the public peace, committing petty depredations, and going from bad to worse, until their course terminates in high crimes and infamy.

This proposition to gather the young from the streets and

wharves into the nurseries which the state, solicitous for her security against ignorance, has prepared for them, has sometimes been treated as a device to appropriate the school fund to the endowment of seminaries for teaching languages and faiths, thus to perpetuate the prejudices it seeks to remove; sometimes as a scheme for dividing that precious fund among a hundred jarring sects, and thus increasing the religious animosities it strives to heal; and sometimes as a plan to subvert the prevailing religion and introduce one repugnant to the consciences of our fellow-citizens; while, in truth, it simply proposes by enlightening equally the minds of all, to enable them to detect error wherever it may exist, and to reduce uncongenial masses into one intelligent, virtuous, harmonious, and happy people. Being now relieved from all such misconceptions, it presents the questions whether it is wiser and more humane to educate the offspring of the poor than to leave them to grow up in ignorance and vice; whether juvenile vice is more easily eradicated by the court of sessions than by common schools; whether parents have a right to be heard concerning the instruction and instructors of their children, and tax-payers in relation to the expenditure of public funds; whether, in a republican government, it is necessary to interpose an independent corporation between the people and the schoolmaster; and whether it is wise and just to disfranchise an entire community of all control over public education, rather than suffer a part to be represented in proportion to its numbers and contributions.

Since such considerations are now involved, what has hitherto been discussed as a question of benevolence and universal education, has become one of equal civil rights, religious tolerance, and liberty of conscience. We could bear with us in our retirement from public service no recollection more worthy of being cherished through life than that of having met such a question in the generous and confiding spirit of our institutions, and of having decided it upon the immutable principles on which they are based.—*Annual Message*, 1842.

FREEDOM.

John Quincy Adams.*

THE capitol is deserted! The legislature have suspended their labors; the city is in mourning; a sudden blow has fallen on the master-chord in the heart of this nation, and grief is diffusing itself throughout the Union. The voice of JOHN QUINCY ADAMS has died away on earth, and he has resumed converse with John Adams and Jefferson, with La Fayette and with Washington, in heaven.

Death found the statesman where he wished to meet it—in the capitol; in his place; in the performance of his duty; in defending the cause of peace and of freedom. He submitted to the inevitable blow as those who loved and honored him foretold and desired that he would—saying only, "This is the last of earth—I am content."

I will not suffer myself to speak all I feel on this sad occasion. While the American people have lost a father and a guide—while Humanity has lost her most eloquent, persevering, and indomitable advocate—I have lost a patron, a guide, a counsellor, and a friend—one whom I loved scarcely less than the dearest relations, and venerated above all that was mortal among men.

I speak in behalf of my associates. Great as he was, illustrious as his achievements were, he was one of us. He was a civilian, a lawyer, a jurist. His great mind was imbued with the science of our noble profession, and enriched with all congenial learning; and to these he added the ornaments of rhetoric

* Remarks before the Court of Chancery, Albany, Feb. 25, 1848.

and eloquence. Trained in constitutional law, in the school of its founders, Washington called him in precocious youth to the kindred field of diplomacy. That mission discharged, he returned to his profession, and devoted himself to it with assiduity until the people called him from the duty of expounding laws to the higher department of making laws.

Rising through various and very responsible departments of public service, he became chief magistrate of the republic. There he impressed on its history an enduring illustration of a wise, peaceful, and enlightened administration, devoted to the cultivation of peace, to its arts and its interests, and to extending the sway of republican institutions over the continent, and yet in all things subordinate to the law and regulated by the law.

When he had thus filled the measure of the world's expectation and of his own generous ambition, he resumed his place in the national legislature, and devoted what remained of life to a long, arduous, and finally-successful vindication of the constitutional liberty of speech, and of the universal inalienable right of petition. Nor can we forget that, while thus engaged, he set a noble example for us, by returning again to the field of his early labors, the unpaid, unrivalled advocate of the Amistad captives. Those unhappy fugitives, rescued by him from the oppression of two great nations, were restored to Africa, the first of the many millions of her people of whom she had been despoiled by the avarice of our superior race. Whatever difference of opinion there may be concerning the principles and policy of the deceased, all men will now agree that he won among American statesmen, and eminently more than any other, the fame accorded to the most illustrious chevalier of France—the fame of a statesman—*sans peur et sans reproche.*

It is fit that the death of such a citizen should be marked with all the testimonials of public grief, in order that his life may have its just influence on mankind. It is fit that it should be honored in this tribunal, the fame of which is not unknown throughout the world, and the records of which will remain for ever.—*Remarks before Court of Chancery, Albany, Feb.* 25, 1848.

NOTE.—Another and more elaborate eulogy on Mr. Adams will be found n the third volume of Mr. Seward's complete Works.

Mutual Rights and Duties of Nations.

WRITERS on law teach us that states are free, independent, equal, moral persons, existing for the objects of happiness and usefulness, and possessing rights and subject to duties defined by the law of nature, which is a system of politics and morals founded in right reason; that the only difference between politics and morals is, that one regulates the operations of government, while the other directs the conduct of individuals, and that the maxims of both are the same; that two sovereign states may be subject to one prince, and yet be mutually independent; that a nation becomes free by the act of its ruler when he exceeds the fundamental laws; that when any power, whether domestic or foreign, attempts to deprive a state of independence or of liberty, it may lawfully take counsel of its courage, and prefer before the certainty of servitude the chances of destruction; that each nation is bound to do to every other in time of peace the most good, and in time of war the least harm possible, consistently with its own real interests; that while this is an imperfect obligation, of which no state can exact a performance, any one has nevertheless a right to use peaceful means, and even force, if necessary, to repress a power that openly violates the law of nations, and directly attacks their common welfare; and that, although the interests of universal society require mutual intercourse between states, yet that intercourse can be conducted by those only who in their respective nations possess and exercise in fact adequate political powers. . . . . .

It is time to protest. The new outworks of our system of politics in Europe have all been carried away. Republicanism has now no abiding place there, except on the rock of San Marino and in the mountain-home of William Tell. France and Austria are said to be conspiring to expel it even there. In my inmost heart, I could almost bid them dare to try an experiment which would arouse the nations of Europe to resist the commission of a crime so flagrant and so bold.

I have heard frequently, here and elsewhere, that we can promote the cause of freedom and humanity only by our example, and it is most true. But what should that example be but that of performing not one national duty only, but all national duties; not those beginning and ending with ourselves only, but those also which we owe to other nations and to all mankind? No dim eclipse will suffice to illuminate a benighted world.

I have the common pride of every American in the aggrandizement of my country. No effort of mine to promote it, by just and lawful means, ever was or ever will be withheld. Our flag, when it rises to the topmast or the turret of an enemy's ship or fortress, excites in me a pleasure as sincere as in any other man. And yet I have seen that flag on two occasions when it awakened even more intense gratification. One was when it entered the city of Cork, covering supplies for a chivalrous and generous but famishing people. The other was when it recently protected in his emigration an exile of whom continental Europe was unworthy, and to whom she had denied a refuge. Sir, it raised no surprise and excited no regret in me, as it did in some, to see that exile and that flag alike saluted and honored by the people, and alike feared and hated by the kings of Europe.

Let others employ themselves in devising new ligaments to bind these states together. They shall have my respect for their patriotism and their zeal. For myself, I am content with the old ones just as I find them. I believe that the Union is founded in physical, moral, and political necessities, which demand one government, and would endure no divided states; that it is impregnable, therefore, equally to force or to faction; that secession is a feverish dream, and disunion an unreal and passing chimera; and that, for weal or wo, for liberty or servitude, this great country is one and inseparable. I believe, also, that it is righteousness, not greatness, that exalteth a nation, and that it is liberty, not repose, that renders national existence worth possessing. Let me, then, perform my humble part in the service of the republic, by cultivating the sense of justice and the love of liberty which are the elements of its being, and by developing their saving influences, not only in our domestic conduct, but in our foreign conduct also, and in our social intercourse with all other states and nations.

It has already come to this—that whenever in any country an advocate of freedom, by the changes of fortune, is driven into exile, he hastens to seek an asylum here; that whenever a hero falls in the cause of Freedom on any of her battle-fields, his eyes involuntarily turn toward us, and he commits that cause with a confiding trust to our sympathy and our care. Never, sir, as we value the security of our own freedom, or the welfare and happiness of mankind, or the favor of Heaven, that has enabled us to protect both, let that exile be inhospitably repulsed. Never let the prayer of that dying hero fall on ears unused to hear, or spend itself upon hearts that refuse to be moved.—*Speech in U. S. Senate, March* 9, 1852.

The Right of Petition.

EVERY man who is a citizen of the United States, and, according to my theory, every man who, although he may not be a citizen, yet is a subject of the government of the United States, has a right to petition the Congress of the United States upon any subject of national interest, or which can be legitimately the subject of legislation. Then, is there any well-grounded objection to the fact that these memorialists* describe themselves as clergymen? Certainly not; because it is the right and the privilege of a citizen, if he can petition at all, to present his petition in his own way. If he thinks there is anything in his character or position which entitles his opinions to higher consideration, or which leads to the belief that he understands the subject more thoroughly than others, it is his right to describe himself by the appellation which designates his profession, his character, or his office. It is only on this principle that the legislatures of the states make their voices known to Congress, by describing themselves as the legislatures of the states. They come here with their resolutions in the character of petitioners or remonstrants, under that provision of the constitution which guaranties the right of petition, and upon no other ground of constitutional right whatever.

Is there any well-grounded objection to the language or tone of this memorial? I think not. While, on the other hand, it is such a memorial as a secular person like myself would not be apt to dictate or sign, because there is a solemnity of tone, a

* The New England Clergy.

seriousness, and religious consideration which secular men do not indulge or affect; yet, on the other hand, it is professional, and natural on the part of the memorialists; it is in the character of those who make it. It is said, indeed, that they assume to speak the will and judgment of the Creator and Judge of men and nations. I do not understand them as assuming to speak any such thing. I understand them as saying simply, in substance, "We, citizens of the United States, subscribing ourselves as clergymen in the presence of Almighty God, and in his name, address the Congress of the United States." Sir, what is unusual or wrong in this? You do not commence your proceedings here on any day of your whole session without acknowledging and declaring that they are begun in the presence, and in the name, and with an invocation of the blessing of Almighty God. * * * * * * * * * *

I have said, sir, that they come here declaring that they come in the presence of Almighty God. It is that universal and eternal presence in which we all are every day and hour of our lives, and from which we can never for even a moment escape.

Again, sir, it is objected that they say they address us in the name of Almighty God. What is that but a mode of arresting or calling attention to their solemn prayer and earnest remonstrance? Sir, while there are occasions on which we never forget, never suffer ourselves to forget that we are responsible to Almighty God, it is equally true that all our action is, or ought to be, in the name of the Supreme Being. Sir, we may put off, we may lay aside the thoughts of that awful presence during our secular labors, and even during our life of confusion and toil, and turmoil and care; but when we come to close our eyes upon this world, we can not shut them without the reflection that we are ever here in the sight of the Judge of all men. Every man of us, when he comes to write his will, or his instructions, for those who are to come after him, recites that it is done in the name of God. Sir, as I have said, I should not adopt this mode of addressing the senate or Congress. It is not my habit to do so; but I know that it is the habit, that it is in the character, in the way of those who have signed this memorial. I see no ground of objection to it. Is it disrespectful to the senate of the United States, or to Congress, that men should say they speak to them in the name of God, and in his presence? If it be so, it must be because we claim to be here exempt from the superintending government and providence of that Being, in whom and by whom we walk, and act, and through whom we exist upon the earth.

But, sir, it is said that at the close of this remonstrance, there is another remark which is offensive, and that is, that the memorialists think the measure against which they protest is immoral in its nature. Sir, the great measure proposed is either moral or immoral. There is no neutrality between morality and immorality. It may be that we may conscientiously differ in ascertaining which is the moral side, but nevertheless it is of one character or the other—either moral or immoral. These persons tell us they think it is of one character, others think it is of another character. It is our right to act. Let them think what they will, it is their right to tell us that, in their opinion, it is either one thing or the other, just as they understand and believe.

Then, again, it is complained that the memorialists allege that the act will draw after it the judgments of Almighty God. Sir, by the judgments of Almighty God, I understand simply this: that every human act of any importance or magnitude is connected with preceding causes, and with subsequent effects; that there is connected with a right act the consequence of usefulness, of beneficence, of happiness, and all the blessings of a just Ruler; and that, on the other hand, to those acts which, whether we deem them moral or immoral, whether intentionally wrong or not, are unwise, there are connected consequences of error, danger, peril, unhappiness, wretchedness, ruin. This, in my judgment, is all that that expression means.

And now, sir, I come to the close of what I have to say on this whole matter; and that is, that I regard this as a question of no idle importance. The right of petition is a constitutional right, and a useful and invaluable one, and I shall never be found criticising the language of petitioners or remonstrants, to see whether I can not find cause for cavil or for rejection, and petitioners and remonstrants may say precisely what they please, and precisely what they think, in whatever tone or language they think proper. They may utter against me any epithet which they please. They may invoke on my head any judgment they please. Still, sir, with a conscience void of offence against God and man, I can go on here performing my duties, leaving them in the enjoyment of their rights, and listening to all that they say, precisely as if it had been rendered into the language of courtesy, or compliment, or of praise, which would be acceptable under other circumstances. It is because I wish that this right of petition may take no injury from the debate of this morning, that I have risen to vindicate the memorial, and to do justice to those from whom it has come.—*Speech in Senate on Reception of Remonstrance from* 3050 *Clergymen of New England against Repeal of Missouri Compromise, March* 14, 1854.

Political Equality.

I AM in favor of the equality of men—of ALL men, whether they be born in one land or born in another. I am in favor of receiving the whole. I acknowledge them all to constitute one great family, for whom it is the business of statesmen and the business of man to labor and to live. And, sir, when I do have occasion to ask the votes of those distinguished senators and friends in behalf of the alien and the foreigner, it will not be the exile, merely, who is commended to our sympathies for the sufferings he has sustained in the cause of liberty in Europe; but it will be for the melioration of the laws of naturalization, which put a period of five years and an oath in the way of any man of any country in becoming a citizen, which raise a barrier between ourselves and those who cast their lot among us. There is where they will find me; and they will find that to the extent that humanity bears the semblance which is impressed upon us by the hand of our Maker, it is my design and my purpose to labor to bring about that equality in the land in which I live, and as far as may be, in all other lands.

And, going upon this broad principle, I have no hesitation in saying that there is no distinction in my respect or affection between men of one land and of another; between men of one clime and another; between men of one race and another; or between men of one color and another; no distinction but what is based, *not upon institutions of government,* not upon the consent of society, but upon their *individual and personal merit.* If the senator from Georgia [Mr. DAWSON] will test this, if he has this sympathy for free negroes which I am rejoiced to hear him proclaim, let him bring in his bill, and the first ay that shall respond to it will be mine—if none should so respond to it before my name should be alphabetically reached. More than that; if his sympathies embrace a class that deserve them still more—the slave—let him bring in his bill for the slave, and my voice for emancipating the slave in any district or territory shall go for it. Nay, more; let him show me a way in which I can give a vote, an effectual vote, for the emancipation of the slave in his own state, or any state, and I shall feel honored to participate in the movement; and my vote shall be given to sustain it, with more gladness, more gratitude, and more joy, than it was ever given upon any occasion in my life.

Sir, neither here nor elsewhere will I admit, as a rule for the government of my own conduct, that there is a distinction between men. But on the contrary, I will walk up to the mark, assigned in the Declaration of Independence, that "ALL MEN ARE CREATED EQUAL." Sir, the first vote given by me to keep any man, or any class of men, in a condition below my own, is yet to be given. It never will be given in this place.—*Speech, U. S. Senate, Jan. 30, 1850.*

Religious Intolerance.

WITHIN a few months a portion of the American community, men, women, and children, were compelled by American citizens to flee from burning dwellings in the night-time, and found their way to the woods and fields by the light of the flames which consumed not only their dwellings, but also their libraries, their hospitals, their churches, and their altars. The offence was that they or their ancestors were born in Ireland, and that they worshipped God according to the creed and ritual of the Roman Catholic church. And this has happened in the city that was founded by William Penn, and endowed by Benjamin Franklin —in the city where the Declaration of American Independence was promulgated, and where the American constitution was established.

These great wrongs, the outbreak of long-cherished religious and political intolerance, were not its most fearful and alarming incident. Emboldened by popular forbearance, the spirit of proscription has approached Congress, with a demand for the full disfranchisement in America of all men not born on the American soil. I say disfranchisement—for twenty-one years' residence, which is now insisted on, as a condition of naturalization, would be virtual disfranchisement. . . . . .

I have not heard the loud and deep-toned censures upon the Philadelphia wrongs, and upon the recent acts of British oppression, which I expected from the American press and from the leaders of mind in America. Therefore in this hour of trial I come here freely to declare before my countrymen — and if my voice could reach the region of thrones, to declare before principalities and powers — that the injuries inflicted upon the Irishmen in America are a flagrant violation of law, of constitution, of liberty, and of humanity. I know, indeed, what this declaration costs. It may, indeed, give comfort to the poor and desponding exile, and awaken feelings of kindness toward me in his bosom, but it will offend very many of my own countrymen. Be it so. I desire the respect and regard of my own countrymen; but I would rather have the gratitude of one desponding and depressed fellow-man, than the suffrage of the whole American people given to me in consideration of denying any true principle of free government, or repressing any impulse of humanity. . . . . . .

Believe not, fellow-citizens, that this is a question which interests or concerns only the voluntary citizen. The work of disfranchisement once effectually begun, would not cease with the debasement of one class or condition of men; other classes would follow, and oligarchy be succeeded by despotism. Nor is this all. Let the wise men who favor this disfranchisement tell us how they expect to secure the subordination of the disfranchised classes. They can not be expelled; they must increase — they increase by virtue of the irresistible and unchangeable laws of God. They can not be degraded to domestic slavery, and unless so degraded, they can not be held in subjection to authority, except in one of two ways, by their own voluntary consent, or by military force. Standing armies no man dare defend: disfranchised men will not yield voluntary obedience.—*Address at Utica, July*, 1844.

Intolerance.

I GREATLY fear that the American people do not know how highly they are respected and venerated by the down-trodden masses of Europe. Some among us are ambitious of the favorable judgment of the privileged classes in the old world. *Their* respect and sympathies are not to be expected. We are disturbers, innovators; and the affection we gain in Europe must proceed from those to whom the progress of democratic principles brings hope not terror. To the oppressed masses in France, in Greece, in Poland, in Italy, in England, and Ireland, the United States of America is the Palestine from which comes a revelation effectual to political salvation. Thence, therefore, come pilgrims of hope, ardent and enthusiastic in the faith they have received from us, and they expect naturally and justly to be received and welcomed as brethren. Strange that any native American citizen should repel those pilgrims, and justly sad is their disappointment when repulsed. Not even the Christian knights who penetrated to the Holy City by crusade were more grieved when they discovered that the Christians of Jerusalem had relapsed into the superstition of the Moslem faith, and forgotten the place of the tomb in which the Savior had reposed.

So, too, when a revolution occurs in Europe, whether tempestuous and convulsive like those in France, Greece, and Poland, or moral and pacific like that in your own native land, the uprising masses turn at once to the United States of America for succor and for support; and such is the mysterious fellowship produced by the love of liberty, that the sympathies of the American people have always been found irrepressible. Ought it to be otherwise? Who would not blush for his country if it were not so? The spirit of freedom, like that of Christianity, is expansive and comprehensive. The church that sends forth no missionaries, need take heed, for its light is about to be darkened. The republic that desires no proselytes, must take warning, for its downfall is at hand.

These sentiments, derived, I trust, from the teachings of the

American Revolution, seem to me as wise as they are generous. If there be any petition which mankind might wish added to the formula given by the Savior, it would be that the scourge of war might cease, and that peace and good will might prevail among men. But peace and good will can never prevail until mankind learn and feel the simple truth, that however birth or language or climate may have made them differ—however mountains, deserts, rivers, and seas, may divide states—the nations of the earth are nevertheless one family, and all mankind are brethren, practically equal in endowments, equal in national and political rights, and equal in the favor of the common Creator.

Exclusion of foreigners and hostility to foreign states always were elements of barbarism. The intermingling of races always was, and always will be, the chief element of civilization. Japan and China are exclusive states. Great Britain and the United States are social nations. So inconsistent is exclusiveness with progress, that, sooner or later, Providence wills the subjugation of unsocial states, thus securing the advancement of civilization compulsively, when nations obstinately resist it. The conquest of Mexico in the west, of India in the east, and the present humiliation of China, are illustrations of this great truth.

If at St. Petersburg you seek the exchange, where the Russian "merchants most do congregate," the native understands not your inquiry, until you ask for the "Dutch" exchange. Thus do the subjects of the czar unwittingly perpetuate the memory of the fact that they owe their rising commerce to immigration from the Netherlands. I remember that in Clinton's time the Erie canal then in progress was stigmatized as the "Irish ditch." Had we been as generous as the natives of St. Petersburg, we should have persevered in that designation, and we should now confess for the instruction of mankind, that not only the Erie canal, but its numerous and far-reaching veins and arteries, and our railroads, harbors, and fortifications, were chiefly constructed by hardy, joyous, light-hearted, liberty-loving immigrants from Ireland.

We emulate the sway of ancient Rome; but Rome was wiser than those who affect an exclusive monopoly of American citizenship. Provinces and nations as soon as subjugated, became parts of the Roman empire, and although its eagles threatened conquest wherever they advanced, they nevertheless bore on their wings charters of Roman citizenship.

Love for their native land is common to all men, but it exceeds its just bounds when it leads men to despise or hate their fellow-men. This excess is the prejudice of ignorance. The native American can not half so heartily despise the Irishman, as the Chinese despises the American. He who has left his native land to seek an asylum here, has made a sacrifice to liberty which ought to commend him to our respect and affection. His children born here will be native Americans as we are; the parent is a foreigner only as our own parents or ancestors, near or remote, also were.

Do we excel, because the foreigner can not speak our language. We can not speak his. It were well if each knew the language of the other, for it is stored with treasures which would add immeasurably to his knowledge and the elements of his happiness.

The battle-cry of liberty is as animating when sounded in French, in German, or in Spanish, as in English, and the accents of love and affection are tender in whatever dialect they may have utterance. Should differences of religious belief divide us? Washington invoked the Divine blessing on our army in a protestant ritual—Lafayette employed the Roman formulary. Would the prayers of either have been answered, if they had carried into council quarrels from the altar? We ought never to forget that, various as are the expositions of our holy faith, they all agree in this, that without charity there is no Christianity.—*Letter, March* 15, 1844.

Louis Kossuth.

I AM a lover of peace. I shall never freely give my consent to any measure which I shall think will tend to involve this nation in the calamities of foreign war. I believe that our mission is a mission of republicanism. But I believe that we shall best execute it by maintaining peace at home and with all mankind; and if I saw in this measure a step in advance toward the bloody field of contention in the affairs of Europe, I, too, would hesitate long before adopting it. But I see no advance toward any such danger in doing a simple act of national justice and magnanimity. I believe that no man will deny the principle, that a nation may do for the cause of liberty in other nations whatever the laws of nations do not forbid. I plant myself upon that principle. What the laws of nations do not forbid, any nation may do for the cause of civil liberty in any other nation, in any other country. Now, the laws of nations do not forbid hospitality. The laws of nations do not forbid us to sympathize with the exile—to sympathize with the overthrown champion of freedom. The laws of nature demand that hospitality, and from the very inmost sources of our nature springs up that sympathy. What is that great epic poem which has filled the second place in the admiration, I had almost said in the affections, of mankind for two thousand years, but the history of an exile flying from the walls of his burning city and devoted state? Sir, the laws of nature require—the laws of nations command hospitality to those who fly from oppression and despair. And this is all that we have done, and all that we propose to do. We have invited Kossuth—we have procured his release from captivity—we have brought him here—and we propose to say to him, standing upon our shores with his eye directed to us, and while we know that the eyes of the civilized world are fixed upon him and us, "Louis Kossuth, in the name of the American people we bid you a cordial welcome." * * * *

I will suppose now that the opposition made to this resolution is effective. I will suppose that the measure is defeated. Let us look to the consequences beyond. What are they? Kossuth, admitted here to be the representative of the down-trodden constitutional liberties of his own country, and the representative of the up-rising liberties of Europe, shakes from his feet the dust that has gathered upon them on American shores, and returns to the eastern continent—returns upon a point of honor with the United States of America, and therefore, in a practical view, returns, as he will say, and those devoted to his cause will say, repulsed, driven back. Where then, sir, shall he find welcome and repose? In his own beautiful native land, at the base or on the slopes of the Carpathian hills? No! the Austrian despot reigns absolutely there. Shall he find it in Germany, east or west, north or south? No sir; the despot of Austria and the despot of Prussia reign absolutely there. Shall he find it under the sunny skies of Italy? No, sir; for the Austrian monarch has crushed Italy to the earth. Shall he find it in Siberia, or in the frozen regions of the North? No, sir; for the Russian czar, who drove him from his native land and forced him into exile in Turkey, will be ready to seize the fugitive. The scaffold awaits him there. Where shall he go? Shall he seek protection again from the sceptred Turk? The Turk would say, 'You have eaten my salt as a voluntary captive, and I sheltered you until you left me under the seductions of the republic of the United States. If you come now, the laws of my country and of my God will not oblige or allow me to hazard the peace of my own people again to extend protection over you.' Where, then, shall he go? Where else on the face of broad Europe can he find refuge but in the land of your forefathers, in Britain? There, God be thanked, there would be a welcome and a home for him. Are you prepared to give to the world evidence that *you* can not receive the representative of liberty and republicanism, whom England can honor, shelter, and protect?

But, Mr. President, will this transaction end there? I fancy that I see the exile wending his lonely way, with downcast look, along the streets and thoroughfares of the great metropolis of Britain and the world, forsaken and abandoned, but not forgotten. Will it end in that? No, sir. Beyond us, above us, there is a tribunal, higher and greater than the Congress of the United States. It is a tribunal whose existence and jurisdiction and authority we have acknowledged, and to whose judgment-seat we have already called the Turk, the Austrian, and the Russian, to account for their action in regard to Hungary and to Kossuth. It is the tribunal of the public opinion of the world—the public opinion of mankind. Sir, that tribunal is unerring in its judgments. It is constituted of the great, the wise and the good of all nations—not only of the great, and wise, and good, who are now living, but of the great, the wise, and the good of all ages. Before that tribunal, states, great and small, are equal. Ay, before that tribunal the proudest empire is equalled by its humblest citizen or subject. Yes, the Indian and the serf are equal there to the American republic and to the Russian empire. I know no living man entitled by the consent of Christendom to preside in that august tribunal. But there is a venerable form that seems to rise up before me, and all the congregated nations and people deferentially make way as he advances and takes the judgment-seat. It is the shade of Franklin. And there I see the parties opposed. On the one side stands Hungary, downcast and sorrowful, but she is surrounded by the people of many lands, who wait her redemption and their own. On the other side I see the United States of America, sustained—most singular conjunction!—by the youthful and impatient Bonaparte, the sickly successor of the Romans, and the czar of all the Russias. I hear the impeachment read. It is, that the United States have dishonored and insulted the unfortunate representative of unfortunate Hungary; that they found him a captive in Asia Minor, under the protection of the Turk, but subjected to the surveillance of the Russian tyrant; that they addressed to him words of sympathy and hope, and that they brought to the doors of his captivity a national vessel, with their time-honored flag, and bade him to come upon its deck and be conveyed to a land of constitutional freedom—a land where the advocates and champions of universal liberty were sure to enjoy respect and sympathy, and fraternal welcome; and that when they had so seduced him from a place of obscurity, but of safety, and had thus brought him to their own shores, and when he stood waiting there for one simple word of welcome, one simple look of recognition, they turned away from him, spurned him from their presence, and cast him back upon the charities of Christian or Turk, in whatever land they might be found.

That is the impeachment. And the United States hold up the right hand and answer, "Not guilty." I see the books of testimony opened on behalf of Hungary. Here they are. A resolution of the Congress of the United States of America, passed in the year 1850, tendering the hospitalities of the nation, and the use of a national ship, to Louis Kossuth; then the message of the president of the United States, in 1851, calling upon Congress to say what shall be the ceremonial of receiving him who has been brought here under their authority; and then the record of this senate, that upon a division of its members, a resolution of welcome was rejected. That constitutes the case on the part of Hungary. Sir, the United States appear in that august tribunal by learned and eloquent defenders and advocates. I see there my ardent and enthusiastic young friend from Alabama [Mr. CLEMENS], and the candid and learned senator from Kentucky [Mr. UNDERWOOD], the impulsive and generous senator from Georgia [Mr. DAWSON], the very learned and astute advocate, the honorable senator from North Carolina [Mr. BADGER], and, lastly, he who holds the first place in our veneration of living senators, save only one [Mr. CLAY], the honorable senator from Georgia [Mr. BERRIEN]. I listen to the long, elaborate, and earnest defence which they make against this impeachment. Hungary declines to reply; and Kossuth, the orator of modern times, upon whom she leans for support, for the first time overcome by a sense of cruel insult, is silent, dumb.

The defence is weighed by that august Shade, in whose placid countenance I read at once the sagacity of the lightning hunter and the common sense of Poor Richard: "You say, that your invitation to the Magyar 'justified on his part and on the part of Hungary no expectation of a welcome.' How, then, came Kossuth, how came Hungary, how came the world, how came your president, to misunderstand the invitation which was addressed to the exile? When did you first revise your diplomacy to ascertain to what extent you might abridge the hospitalities to which you had invited him? Not until you were committed before the world. You say that 'Kossuth was invited to be a resident, to become a citizen of the United States, and yet that he came, on the contrary, as a transient guest.' Grant it; what then? Is a welcome less due to him whom you have invited as a perpetual guest, when he comes to thank you and decline the courtesy, than if he had accepted it and had become a perpetual charge upon your hospitalities? You say that the honors to Kossuth 'were moved in your senate by ambitious aspirants for place and distinction.' Has, then, my country degenerated so much that there are no true, genuine patriots in the senate of the United States who could lead that illustrious body in the discharge of so great a national obligation? You plead that the Hungarian chief 'was a noble by birth, an aristocrat by education and association, and that he had devoted himself in an effort not to disseminate the spirit of universal liberty, but to fortify the privileges of the Magyar race.' If that be so, did you not know it when you invited him? If you did not, how can you justify your ignorance of a character that was blazoned to the world? But it is not true. Kossuth's first public action in early youth, was an effort, through the Hungarian Diet, to extend equal privileges of representation, of suffrage, and of taxation, to all the people of Hungary, without distinction of rank, or caste, or race. For his fidelity to the great cause of human equality and freedom, he was imprisoned three long years in a dungeon in the castle of Buda, by the hand of the Austrian despot. When he came out from that captivity, he commenced that career of agitation for the restoration of the constitution of his country, which ended with success in the year 1848. When he had wrung that charter from the emperor of Austria, his constitutional king, the first exercise of Hungarian authority by the legislature which he directed, was an act which abolished all the feudal tenures, that brought land within the reach of all, and put the Croat, the Wallachian, the Illyrian, the Jew, and the Magyar, upon the same platform of equality before the law, equality before the government, equality in representation, equality in suffrage, and equality in enduring the burdens of government. It was for this that he was hunted from his native land and came an exile to your shores. Who pursued him there with reproaches of falsehood to freedom? Not the Jew, the Croat, or the Sclave, but the tyrant of Austria, who has reduced all the people of Hungary, of whatever rank or race or caste, to the level of slaves. You say that you were willing to give Kossuth a welcome, but that he demanded more. How did you know that he 'demanded more'? How did you learn that Kossuth demanded more than a cordial welcome? Where did he ask of you even so much as a welcome? Was it in your capital? To whom did he address his extravagant and offensive reclamation? Was it to your president? to your ministry? to your Congress? No; all alike refused to receive him, refused even to hear him speak, and yet you say he demanded too much. You closed his mouth before he had time to tell you what he thought, and what he wanted, or whether he wanted anything. But you reply, he was overheard to say that he expected arms, men, money, 'material aid, and intervention.' Overheard? What! did you deliver Kossuth from Russian surveillance in Turkey to establish an espionage over him of your own? Shame! shame to the country that so lightly regards the sanctity of the character of a stranger and an exile! But you say that he would have demanded *intervention*. Suppose he should have demanded intervention? Would you have been less able to have met that unreasonable demand after having accorded to him the exact justice which was his due, than you are now when you have done him injustice, and thus clothed him with the sympathies of your people and of mankind? But you aver that he spoke irreverently of your authority: he was overheard to say, in the outgushing of his gratitude to the generous people who received him on Staten Island, that the people were the sovereigns of the government of the United States, and you can not pardon that offence. What if he did say that? Are not the people the sovereigns of the government of the United States? Which one of your senators or representatives dare deny in his place that the people are his sovereigns? But you say that you had a precedent; that you once took offence at a minister of France who assumed the same position. You refer to Genet. But there is no parallel. Genet was a minister of a government actually hostile, almost belligerent. He was in negotiation, and his demands were denied. He took an appeal from the decision of your government to the people. But Kossuth is no minister. He is your guest. He went to you not to negotiate, or to demand a right. He went by your invitation to enjoy your hospitalities. You have decided nothing against him. He has submitted no appeal. I do not say that you ought to have granted intervention had it been demanded. But I do say this, that the Hungarian would have demanded no more of you than, in a strait less severe than his, I solicited and obtained for the United States of America from the Bourbon of France. Could you not have pardoned him for asking what you had once asked and obtained for yourselves? Was it so great a fault in him to suppose that now, in the day of your greatness, prosperity, and power, you might not be unwilling to do for Hungary what, in the day of your infancy, poverty, and weakness, France had done for yourselves? You say you stand upon precedent. Precedent? By whom established? By yourselves. Was Hungary concluded by such a precedent? And what precedent? The precedent of the reception given to Lafayette? Was not even that reception grudgingly given by the Congress of the United States? If the ashes of Lafayette could be reanimated, and he could present himself again upon your shores, would you not now willingly accord him a greater than the welcome he before received at your hands—a welcome such as it was proposed to give to Kossuth? Wherein does the parallel between Kossuth and Lafayette fail? Lafayette began his career as a soldier of liberty in the cause of your country; but he pursued it through life in an effort to establish a republic in his own beloved land. Kossuth found the duty which first devolved upon him was to wage a struggle for freedom in his own country. When overborne there, he became, like Lafayette, a champion of liberty throughout the world. You say that the Russian might have taken offence. Is America, then, brought so low that she fears to give offence when commanded by the laws of nature and of nations? What right had Russia to prescribe whom you should receive and whom reject from your hospitalities? Let no such humiliation be confessed."

Thus in the tribunal of the public opinion of mankind, all our pleas are disallowed. We have exposed ourselves to the *censure*—I will not say the *derision of the world.*—*Speeches in U. S. Senate, December,* 1851.

Congressional Compromises.

IT is insisted that the admission of California shall be attended by a COMPROMISE of questions which have arisen out of SLAVERY!

I AM OPPOSED TO ANY SUCH COMPROMISE, IN ANY AND ALL THE FORMS IN WHICH IT HAS BEEN PROPOSED; because, while admitting the purity and the patriotism of all from whom it is my misfortune to differ, I think all legislative compromises, which are not absolutely necessary, radically wrong and essentially vicious. They involve the surrender of the exercise of judgment and conscience on distinct and separate questions, at distinct and separate times, with the indispensable advantages it affords for ascertaining truth. They involve a relinquishment of the right to reconsider in future the decisions of the present, on questions prematurely anticipated. And they are acts of usurpation as to future questions of the province of future legislators.

Sir, it seems to me as if slavery had laid its paralyzing hand upon myself, and the blood were coursing less freely than its wont through my veins, when I endeavor to suppose that such a compromise has been effected, and that my utterance for ever is arrested upon all the great questions — social, moral, and political — arising out of a subject so important, and as yet so incomprehensible.

What am I to receive in this compromise? Freedom in California. It is well; it is a noble acquisition; it is worth a sacrifice. But what am I to give as an equivalent? A recognition of the claim to perpetuate slavery in the District of Columbia; forbearance toward more stringent laws concerning the arrest of persons suspected of being slaves found in the free states; forbearance from the *proviso* of freedom in the charters of new territories. None of the plans of compromise offered demand less than two, and most of them insist on all of these conditions. The equivalent, then, is, some portion of liberty, some portion of human rights in one region for liberty in another region. But California brings gold and commerce as well as freedom. I am, then, to surrender some portion of human freedom in the District of Columbia, and in East California and New Mexico, for the mixed consideration of liberty, gold, and power, on the Pacific coast.

This view of legislative compromises is not *new*. It has widely prevailed, and many of the state constitutions interdict the introduction of more than one subject into one bill submitted for legislative action.

It was of such compromises that Burke said, in one of the loftiest bursts of even his majestic parliamentary eloquence: —

"Far, far from the commons of Great Britain be all manner of real vice; but ten thousand times farther from them, as far as from pole to pole, be the whole tribe of spurious, affected, counterfeit, and hypocritical virtues! These are the things which are ten thousand times more at war with real virtue, these are the things which are ten thousand times more at war with real duty, than any vice known by its name and distinguished by its proper character.

"Far, far from us be that false and affected candor that is eternally in treaty with crime—that half virtue, which, like the ambiguous animal that flies about in the twilight of a compromise between day and night, is, to a just man's eye, an odious and disgusting thing. There is no middle point, my lords, in which the commons of Great Britain can meet tyranny and oppression."—*Speech in U. S. Senate, March* 11, 1850.

The Recaption of Fugitive Slaves in the Free States.

I ADVERT to the proposed alteration of the law concerning fugitives from service or labor. I shall speak on this as on all subjects with due respect, but yet frankly and without reservation. The constitution contains only a compact, which rests for its execution on the states. Not content with this, the slave states induced legislation by Congress; and the supreme court of the United States have virtually decided that the whole subject is within the province of Congress, and exclusive of state authority. Nay, they have decided that slaves are to be regarded not merely as persons to be claimed, but as property and chattels, to be seized without any legal authority or claim whatever. The compact is thus subverted by the procurement of the slave states. With what reason, then, can they expect the states, *ex gratia*, to reassume the obligations from which they caused those states to be discharged? I say, then, to the slave states, you are entitled to no more stringent laws; and that such laws would be useless. The cause of the inefficiency of the present statute is not at all the leniency of its provisions. It is a law that deprives the alleged refugee from a legal obligation not assumed by him, but imposed upon him by laws enacted before he was born, of the writ of *habeas corpus*, and of any certain judicial process of examination of the claim set up by his pursuer, and finally degrades him into a chattel which may be seized and carried away peaceably wherever found, even although exercising the rights and reponsibilities of a free citizen of the commonwealth in which he resides, and of the United States—a law which denies to the citizen all the safeguards of personal liberty, to render less frequent the escape of the bondman. And since complaints are so freely made against the one side, I shall not hesitate to declare that there have been even greater faults on the other side. Relying on the perversion of the constitution, which makes slaves mere chattels, the slave states have applied to them the principles of the criminal law, and have held that he who aided the escape of his fellow-man from bondage was guilty of a larceny in stealing him. I speak of what I know. Two instances came within my own knowledge, in which governors of slave states, under the provision of the constitution relating to fugitives from justice, demanded from the governor of a free state the surrender of persons as thieves whose alleged offences consisted in constructive larceny of the rags that covered the persons of female slaves, whose attempt at escape they had permitted or assisted.

We deem the principle of the law for the recapture of fugitives, as thus expounded, therefore, unjust, unconstitutional, and immoral; and thus, while patriotism withholds its approbation, the consciences of our people condemn it.

You will say that these convictions of ours are disloyal. Grant it for the sake of argument. They are, nevertheless, honest; and the law is to be executed among us, not among you; not by us, but by the federal authority. Has any government ever succeeded in changing the moral convictions of its subjects by force? But these convictions imply no disloyalty. We reverence the Constitution, although we perceive this defect, just as we acknowledge the splendor and the power of the sun, although its surface is tarnished with here and there an opaque spot.

Your constitution and laws convert hospitality to the refugee from the most degrading oppression on earth into a crime, but all mankind except you esteem that hospitality a virtue. The right of extradition of a fugitive from justice is not admitted by the law of nature and of nations, but rests in voluntary compacts. I know of only two compacts found in diplomatic history that admitted EXTRADITION OF SLAVES. Here is one of them. It is found in a treaty of peace made between Alexander, Comnenus, and Leontine, Greek emperors at Constantinople, and Oleg, king of Russia, in the year 902, and is in these words: —

"If a Russian slave take flight, or even if he is carried away by any one, under pretence of having been bought, his master shall have the right and power to pursue him, and hunt for and capture him wherever he shall be found; and any person who shall oppose the master in the execution of this right, shall be deemed guilty of violating this treaty, and be punished accordingly."

This was in the year of grace 902, in the period called the "Dark Ages," and the contracting powers were despotisms. And here is the other: —

"No person held to service or labor in one state, under the laws thereof, escaping into another, shall, in consequence of any law or regulation therein, be discharged from such service or labor, but shall be delivered up, on claim of the party to whom such service or labor is due."

This is from the constitution of the United States in 1787, and the parties were the republican states of this Union. The law of nations disavows such compacts; the law of nature, written on the hearts and consciences of freemen, repudiates them. Armed power could not enforce them, because there is no public conscience to sustain them. I know that there are laws of various sorts which regulate the conduct of men. There are constitutions and statutes, codes mercantile and codes civil; but when we are legislating for states, especially when we are founding states, all these laws must be brought to the standard of the laws of God, and must be tried by that standard, and must stand or fall by it. This principle was happily explained by one of the most distinguished political philosophers of England in these emphatic words: —

"There is but one law for all, namely, that law which governs all law; the law of our Creator, the law of humanity, justice, equity, the law of nature and of nations. So far as any laws fortify this primeval law, and give it more precision, more energy, more effect by their declarations, such laws enter into the sanctuary and participate in the sacredness of its character; but the man who quotes as precedents the abuses of tyrants and robbers, pollutes the very fountains of justice, destroys the foundations of all law, and therefore removes the only safeguard against evil men, whether governors or governed; the guard which prevents governors from becoming tyrants, and the governed from becoming rebels."

There was deep philosophy in the confession of an eminent English judge. When he had condemned a young woman to death, under the late sanguinary code of his country, for her first petty theft, she fell down dead at his feet. "I seem to myself," said he, "to have been pronouncing sentence, not against the prisoner, but against the law itself."

To conclude on this point. We are not slaveholders. We can not, in our judgment, be either true Christians or real freemen, if we impose on another a chain that we defy all human power to fasten on ourselves. You believe and think otherwise, and doubtless with equal sincerity. We judge you not, and He alone who ordained the conscience of man and its laws of action can judge us. Do we then, in this conflict of opinion, demand of you an unreasonable thing in asking that, since you will have property that can and will exercise human powers to effect its escape, you shall be your own police, and, in acting among us as such, you shall conform to principles indispensable to the security of admitted rights of freemen? If you will have this law executed, you must alleviate, not increase, its rigors.—*Speech in U. S. Senate, March* 11, 1850.

The Fugitive Slave Law of 1793 Unconstitutional and Void.

THE law is based upon the second section of Article IV. of the constitution: "No person held to service or labor, in one state, under the laws thereof, escaping into another, shall, in consequence of any law or regulation therein, be discharged from such service or labor; but shall be delivered up, on claim of the party to whom such service or labor may be due."

If we admit, for the purpose of the argument, that this section furnishes ground for the exercise of legislation, by the Congress of the United States, to carry the section into execution, we may, nevertheless, confidently assert, that such legislation must be confined to the very object and purpose of the section, and can not be extended further. If any state should pass any law, or establish any regulation adapted to work a discharge of persons escaping into its jurisdiction from lawful obligation of labor or service, existing in the state whence they fled, or to prevent their delivery to proper claimants, Congress might abrogate such law or regulation. But such an act of abrogation would be unnecessary, because the offensive law or regulation would be unconstitutional, and *ipso facto* void. Here the constitutional power reposed in Congress to legislate on this subject must end; for the object of the second article is attained when such action or legislation by the several states, is effectually prohibited or defeated. We admit that the section provides that the fugitive "shall be delivered up, on claim of the party to whom such service or labor may be due." But these are merely words of explanation, giving precision, force, and effect, to the inhibition of the passage of laws or adoption of regulations by the states for the discharge of fugitives. Any law or regulation of a state, which may work the discharge of the fugitive, shall be so absolutely void, that not only such consequence shall not take effect, but the right of recaption shall not be at all affected by such law or regulation. The section would have full, complete, and satisfactory effect through judicial action. If a person in any court of any state claimed that another who had escaped into its jurisdiction was lawfully held in the state whence he fled, to labor for the claimant, and if the defendant being either the person against whom the claim was made, or any other person, or even the state within whose jurisdiction the fugitive was found, should interpose by plea any law or regulation affecting to discharge him from such obligation imposed by the law of the other state, that plea should be overruled. The second section would necessarily receive this complete effect by the adjudication of the courts of law of the United States, and of every state, without any interposition by Congress whatever. No law of Congress could give to the section any greater force, effect, or power; because all laws must be tried by the constitution before the judiciary. It results from this that the court in which such a claim should be asserted, would be confined to try the questions first, whether the alleged fugitive from labor was held to labor to the claimant in another state by the laws of that state, and secondly, whether he had escaped from that state into the state where he was found. And the court would have a right to decide upon the validity of the laws of the other state, by which the fugitive was alleged to be held to labor, and be obliged to decide upon them as courts now do in all cases of conflict of laws. The court would be restricted in this judicial proceeding, only in two respects; first, they must not allow a plea of any law or regulation of the state where the fugitive was found, to work his discharge from an obligation created by the laws of the state from which he fled; and secondly, the court might perhaps be obliged, by the last clause of the section, to pronounce judgment, that the fugitive should be delivered to the party who had established the claim to the labor or service of the fugitive. If it be assumed that the courts of the state, or of the United States, might disregard the constitutional inhibition: we reply, first, that Congress can not presume, nor can this court presume that any court would be guilty of a dereliction; and secondly, that the remedy could always be applied in a revision of the proceedings of inferior courts by the supreme court of the United States, whose power on questions of constitutional law is higher than that of the legislature. . . . .

Again. It is a duty of the citizen, and a duty of man, in every social state, and even in savage life, to give necessary shelter, comfort, and sustenance, to the wayfaring man, the stranger, and the fugitive. Such exiles have a natural right to demand protection and charity. That right is sustained by divine laws. The act of 1793, however necessary, or even just its provisions, by forbidding hospitalities to a class excepted from among all other men, is in derogation of the rights of citizenship, and of manhood.—*Argument, U. S. Supreme Court, Dec.*, 1847.

Extradition of Fugitives.

"No person held to service or labor, in one state, under the laws thereof, escaping into another, shall, in consequence of any law or regulation *therein, be discharged from such service or labor, but* shall be delivered up on claim of the party," &c. This is a mere announcement of a principle which shall be paramount, in courts of justice, to any local laws or regulations.

Nor is the origin of the principle of this latter clause, in any degree the same, with the source to which we have traced the principle of extradition of fugitives from *justice.* The latter is found in the comity of nations, and in the necessity of maintaining the cause of justice, of order, of law, and of government. The former has no such foundation. If by the words "persons held to service or labor" are meant, as some suppose, persons held by contract, we shall look in vain throughout the history of every civilized state, for a principle so much at war with human liberty, as the surrender of fugitive debtors. Some modern states allow to citizens, or subjects of other states, access to courts of justice, to enforce obligations of debt by the remedies given in similar cases to their own citizens. None ever surrendered—and none ever will surrender a fugitive debtor, to be conveyed to the state where the obligation was incurred.

Another opinion exists, which is thus expressed by the late and lamented Justice Story: "The object of this clause was 'to secure to the citizens of the slave-holding states the complete right and title of ownership in their slaves as property in every state in the Union, into which they might escape from the state where they were held in servitude.'" If this opinion be adopted, the very shadow of analogy between the two constitutional powers will vanish. For, by the general law of nations, none is bound to recognise the state of slavery as to foreign slaves, found within its territorial dominions, when it is in opposition to its own policy and institutions, in favor of the subjects of other nations, where slavery is recognised. There is not now, and never was, any such comity of nations, as dictated compacts for the surrender of fugitive slaves. No Christian nation would ever make such a compact. Every state has denied an obligation to surrender persons claimed to be slaves. It was truly said, by the distinguished judge last mentioned, that "if the constitution had not contained the clause now under consideration, every non-slaveholding state in the Union would have been at liberty to have declared free all runaway slaves coming within its limits, and to have given them entire immunity, and protection against the claims of their masters." Therefore the clause is an abridgment of state sovereignty—it conflicts with the principles of natural and civil liberty, and contrasts, at least, strongly with the rights and privileges guarantied to the citizens of all the states by the constitution. It is, therefore, to be strictly construed. If strictly construed, the clause spends its whole force in an inhibition of laws and regulations calculated, in one state, to work a discharge of fugitives held to labor in other states, by the laws thereof, and neither needs nor contemplates, legislation by Congress, but relies for its execution, upon the judicial authorities of the states and of the Union.

The work of usurpation once begun, derives strength from precedent and fearful force from judicial acquiescence. Thus it has happened in regard to the claim under consideration. The very structure of the provision shows that it was designed merely to limit and restrict the legislative power of the states, not to deprive them of all power to legislate concerning fugitives from slavery. No person held to labor by the laws of one state, and escaping into another, shall be discharged in *consequence* of any law or regulation of that state. This language plainly implies that any state may pass what laws, and establish what regulations it may deem expedient, and those laws will be valid and effectual, save only in one respect, namely, that no person shall, in consequence thereof, be discharged from labor or service due, in another state, by the laws thereof. It was so understood throughout the Union. Accordingly, at a very early period, every state, or almost every state, enacted laws regulating the proceedings on the claim of fugitives, in harmony, as was believed, with the constitutional provisions. But after a lapse of fifty years, and after acquiescence during that period by nearly all the states in this system of legislation, it was decided in the case of Prigg *vs.* Pennsylvania, that the restriction of state legislative power was an absolute inhibition of its exercise. With the most profound deference, we submit that the error of that adjudication need not be exposed by argument, but is apparent and rendered palpable, by bringing the constitution and the *adjudication* into simple juxtaposition and contrast.—*Argument in U. S.Supreme Court*, 1847.

Emancipation in the District of Columbia.

We of the free states are, equally with you of the slave states, responsible for the existence of slavery in this district, the field exclusively of our common legislation. I regret that, as yet, I see little reason to hope that a majority in favor of emancipation exists here. The legislature of New York, from whom, with great deference, I dissent, seems willing to accept now the extinction of the slave-trade, and waive emancipation. But we shall assume the whole responsibility if we stipulate not to exercise the power hereafter when a majority shall be obtained. Nor will the plea with which you would furnish us be of any avail. If I could understand so mysterious a paradox myself, I never should be able to explain to the apprehension of the people whom I represent, how it was that an absolute and express power to legislate in all cases over the District of Columbia was embarrassed and defeated by an implied condition not to legislate for the abolition of slavery in this district. Sir, I shall vote for that measure, and I am willing to appropriate any means necessary to carry it into execution. And, if I shall be asked what I did to embellish the capital of my country, I will point to her freedmen, and say, "These are the monuments of my munificence!"

* * * * * * * *

I think it wrong to hold men in bondage at any time and under any circumstances. I thing it right and just, therefore, to abolish slavery when we have the power, at any time, at all times, under any circumstances. Now, sir, so far as the objection rests upon the time when this measure is proposed, I beg leave to say that if the present time is not the right time, then there must be, or there must have been, some other time, and that must be a time that is already past, or time yet to come. Well, sir, slavery has existed here under the sanction of Congress for fifty years, undisturbed. The right time, then, has not passed. It must, therefore, be a future time. Will gentlemen oblige me and the country by telling us how far down in the future the right time lies? When will it be discreet to bring before Congress and the people the abolition of slavery in the District of Columbia? Sir, let not senators delude themselves. The right time, if it be not now, will never come. Sir, each senator must judge for himself. Judging for myself, I am sure the right time has come. Past the middle age of life, it has happened to me now, for the first time, to be a legislator for slaves. I believe it to be my duty to the people of this district, to the country, and to mankind, to restore them to freedom. For the performance of such a duty, the *first* time and the *first* occasion which offers is the *right* one. The people who sent me here knew my opinions and my principles on that subject. If I should waive this time and this occasion, such is the uncertainty of human life and human events, that no other may offer themselves to me. I could not return to the people who sent me here, nor could I go before my Maker, having been here, without having humbly, but firmly, endeavored to discharge that great obligation.

Sir, I can spare one word of reply, not to the wretched imputation that I seek by this measure to dissolve the union of these states, but to the argument that the measure itself tends to so disastrous a consummation. This Union is the feeblest and weakest national power that exists on the earth, if with twenty millions of freemen now it can not bear the shock of adding two thousand to their number. The Union stands, as I have demonstrated at large on former occasions, not upon a majority of voices in either or both houses of Congress upon any measure whatever, but upon enduring physical, social, and political necessities, which will survive all the questions and commotions and alarms of this day, and will survive the extinction of slavery, not only in the District of Columbia, but throughout the world. Others may try to save it from imaginary perils, by concessions to slavery. I shall still seek to perpetuate it by rendering the exercise of its power equal, impartial, and beneficent, to all classes and conditions of mankind. — *Speeches in U. S. Senate,* 1850.

Admission of New Slaveholding States.

I SAID I would have voted for the admission of California even as a slave state, under the extraordinary circumstances which I have before distinctly described. I say that now; but I say also, that before I would agree to admit any more states from Texas, the circumstanees which render such an act necessary must be shown, and must be such as to determine my obligation to do so; and that is precisely what I insist can not be settled now. It must be left for those to whom the responsibility will belong.

Mr. President, I understand, and I am happy in understanding, that I agree with the honorable senator from Massachusetts, that there is no obligation upon Congress to admit four new slave states out of Texas, but that Congress has reserved her right to say whether those states shall be formed and admitted or not. I shall rely on that reservation. I shall vote to admit no more slave states, unless under circumstances absolutely compulsory — and no such case is now foreseen.

Mr. WEBSTER. What I said was, that if the states hereafter to be made out of Texas choose to come in as slave states, they have a right so to do.

Mr. SEWARD. My position is, that they have not a right to come in at all, if Congress rejects their institutions. The subdivision of Texas is a matter optional with both parties, Texas and the United States.

Mr. WEBSTER. Does the honorable senator mean to say that Congress can hereafter decide whether they shall be slave or free states?

Mr. SEWARD. I mean to say that Congress can hereafter decide whether any states, slave or free, can be framed out of Texas. If they should never be framed out of Texas, they never could be admitted.

Another objection arises out of the principle on which the demand for compromise rests. That principle assumes a classification of the states as northern and southern states, as it is expressed by the honorable senator from South Carolina [Mr. CALHOUN], but into slave states and free states, as more directly expressed by the honorable senator from Georgia [Mr. BERRIEN]. The argument is, that the states are severally equal, and that these two classes were equal at the first, and that the constitution was founded on that equilibrium; that the states being equal, and the classes of the states being equal in rights, they are to be regarded as constituting an association in which each state, and each of these classes of states, respectively, contribute in due proportions; that the new territories are a common acquisition, and the people of these several states and classes of states, have an equal right to participate in them, respectively; that the right of the people of the slave states to emigrate to the territories with their slaves as property is necessary to afford such a participation on their part, inasmuch as the people of the free states emigrate into the same territories with their property. And the argument deduces from this right the principle that, if Congress exclude slavery from any part of this new domain, it would be only just to set off a portion of the domain — some say south of 36° 30′, others south of 34° — which should be regarded at least as free to slavery, and to be organized into slave states.

Argument ingenious and subtle, declamation earnest and bold, and persuasion gentle and winning as the voice of the turtle dove when it is heard in the land, all alike and all together have failed to convince me of the soundness of this principle of the proposed compromise, or of any one of the propositions on which it is attempted to be established.

How is the original equality of the states proved? It rests on a syllogism of Vattel, as follows: All men are equal by the law of nature and of nations. But states are only lawful aggregations of individual men, who severally are equal. Therefore, states are equal in natural rights. All this is just and sound. But assuming the same premises, to wit, that all men are equal by the law of nature and of nations, the right of property in slaves falls to the ground; for one who is equal to another can not be the owner or property of that other. But you answer, that the constitution recognises property in slaves. It would be sufficient, then, to reply, that this constitutional recognition must be void, because it is repugnant to the law of nature and of nations. But I deny that the constitution recognises property in man. I submit, on the other hand, most respectfully, that the constitution not merely does not affirm that principle, but, on the contrary, altogether excludes it.

The constitution does not *expressly* affirm anything on the subject; all that it contains is two incidental allusions to slaves. These are, first, in the provision establishing a ratio of representation and taxation; and secondly, in the provision relating to fugitives from labor. In both cases, the constitution designedly mentions slaves, not as slaves, much less as chattels, but as *persons*. That this recognition of them as persons was designed is historically known, and I think was never denied. I give only two of the manifold proofs. First, JOHN JAY, in the *Federalist*, says:

"Let the case of the slaves be considered, as it is in truth, a peculiar one. Let the compromising expedient of the constitution be mutually adopted which regards them as *inhabitants*, but as debased below the equal level of free inhabitants, which regards the slave as divested of two fifths of the man."

Yes, sir, of two fifths, but of only two fifths; leaving still three fifths; leaving the slave still an *inhabitant*, a person, a living, breathing, moving, reasoning, immortal man.

The other proof is from the debates in the convention. It is brief, and I think instructive:—

AUGUST 28, 1787.

"Mr. BUTLER and Mr. PINCKNEY moved to require fugitive slaves and servants to be delivered up like convicts.

"Mr. WILSON. This would oblige the executive of the state to do it at public expense.

"Mr. SHERMAN saw no more propriety in the public seizing and surrendering a slave or a servant than a horse.

"Mr. BUTLER withdrew his proposition, in order that some particular provision might be made, apart from this article."

AUGUST 29, 1787.

"Mr. BUTLER moved to insert after article 15: 'If any person bound to service or labor in any of the United States shall escape into another state, he or she shall not be discharged from such service or labor in consequence of any regulation subsisting in the state to which they escape, but shall be delivered up to the person justly claiming their service or labor.'"

"After the engrossment, September 15, page 550, article 4, section 2, the third paragraph, the term 'legally' was struck out, and the words, 'under the laws thereof' inserted after the word 'state,' in compliance with the wishes of some who thought the term 'legal' equivocal, and favoring the idea that slavery was legal in a *moral view*. —*Madison Debates*, pp. 487, 492.

I deem it established, then, that the constitution does not recognise property in man, but leaves that question, as between the states, to the law of nature and of nations. That law, as expounded by Vattel, is founded on the reason of things. When God had created the earth, with its wonderful adaptations, he gave dominion over it to man, absolute human dominion. The title of that dominion, thus bestowed, would have been incomplete, if the lord of all terrestrial things could himself have been the property of his fellow-man.

The right to *have* a slave implies the right in some one to *make* the slave; that right must be equal and mutual, and this would resolve society into a state of perpetual war. But if we grant the original equality of the states, and grant also the constitutional recognition of slaves as property, still the argument we are considering fails. Because the states are not parties to the constitution as states; it is the constitution of the people of the United States.

But even if the states continue under the constitution as states, they nevertheless surrendered their equality as states, and submitted themselves to the sway of the numerical majority, with qualifications or checks; first, of the representation of three fifths of slaves in the ratio of representation and taxation; and, secondly, of the equal representation of states in the senate.

The proposition of an established classification of states as *slave states* and *free states*, as insisted on by some, and into *northern* and *southern*, as maintained by others, seems to me purely imaginary, and of course the supposed equilibrium of those classes a mere conceit. This must be so, because, when the constitution was adopted, twelve of the thirteen states were slave states, and so there was no equilibrium. And so as to the classification of states as northern states and southern states. It is the maintenance of slavery by law in a state, not parallels of latitude, that makes it a southern state; and the absence of this, that makes it a northern state. And so all the states, save one, were southern states, and there was no equilibrium. But the constitution was made not only for southern and northern states, but for states neither northern nor southern, namely, the western states, their coming in being foreseen and provided for.

It needs little argument to show that the idea of a joint stock association, or a copartnership, as applicable even by its analogies to the United States, is erroneous, with all the consequences fancifully deduced from it. The United States are a political state, or organized society, whose end is government, for the security, welfare, and happiness, of all who live under its protection. The theory I am combating reduces the objects of government to the mere spoils of conquest. Contrary to a theory so debasing, the preamble of the constitution not only asserts the sovereignty to be, not in the states, but in the people, but also promulgates the objects of the constitution:—

"We, the people of the United States, in order to form a *more perfect union*, establish *justice*, insure *domestic tranquillity*, provide for the *common defence*, promote the GENERAL WELFARE, and secure the *blessings of liberty*, do ordain and establish this constitution."

Objects sublime and benevolent! They exclude the very idea of conquests, to be either divided among states or even enjoyed by them, for the purpose of securing, not the blessings of liberty, but the evils of slavery.—*Speech in U. S. Senate*, 1850.

Uses of the National Domain.

It is true, indeed, that the national domain is ours. It is true it was acquired by the valor and with the wealth of the whole nation. But we hold, nevertheless, no arbitrary power over it. We hold no arbitrary power over anything, whether acquired lawfully or seized by usurpation. The constitution regulates our stewardship; the constitution devotes the domain to union, to justice, to defence, to welfare, and to liberty.

But there is a higher law than the constitution, which regulates our authority over the domain, and devotes it to the same noble purposes. The territory is a part, no inconsiderable part, of the common heritage of mankind, bestowed upon them by the Creator of the universe. We are his stewards, and must so discharge our trust as to secure in the highest attainable degree their happiness. How momentous that trust is, we may learn from the instructions of the founder of modern philosophy:—

"No man," says Bacon, "can by care-taking, as the Scripture saith, add a cubit to his stature in this little model of a man's body; but, in the great frame of kingdoms and commonwealths, it is in the power of princes or estates to add amplitude and greatness to their kingdom. For, by introducing such ordinances, constitutions, and customs, as are wise, they may sow greatness to their posterity and successors. But these things are commonly not observed, but left to take their chance."

This is a state, and we are deliberating for it, just as our fathers deliberated in establishing the institutions we enjoy. Whatever superiority there is in our condition and hopes over those of any other "kingdom" or "estate," is due to the fortunate circumstance that our ancestors did not leave things to "take their chance," but that they "added amplitude and greatness" to our commonwealth "by introducing such ordinances, constitutions, and customs, as were wise." We in our turn have succeeded to the same responsibilities, and we can not approach the duty before us wisely or justly, except we raise ourselves to the great consideration of how we can most certainly "sow greatness to our posterity and successors."

And now the simple, bold, and even awful question which presents itself to us is this: Shall we, who are founding institutions, social and political, for countless millions—shall we, who know by experience the wise and the just, and are free to choose them, and to reject the erroneous and unjust — shall we establish human bondage, or permit it by our sufferance to be established? Sir, our forefathers would not have hesitated an hour. They found slavery existing here, and they left it only because they could not remove it. There is not only no free state which would now establish it, but there is no slave state which, if it had had the free alternative as we now have, would have founded slavery. Indeed, our revolutionary predecessors had precisely the same question before them in establishing an organic law under which the states of Ohio, Indiana, Michigan, Illinois, and Wisconsin, have since come into the Union, and they solemnly repudiated and excluded slavery from those states for ever. I confess that the most alarming evidence of our degeneracy which has yet been given is found in the fact that we even debate such a question. — *Speech in U. S. Senate*, 1850.

Slavery in the New Territories.

SIR, there is no Christian nation, thus free to choose as we are, which would establish slavery. I speak on due consideration, because Britain, France, and Mexico, have abolished slavery, and all other European states are preparing to abolish it as speedily as they can. We can not establish slavery, because there are certain elements of the security, welfare, and greatness of nations, which we all admit, or ought to admit, and recognise as essential; and these are, the security of natural rights, the diffusion of knowledge, and the freedom of industry. Slavery is incompatible with all of these; and, just in proportion to the extent that it prevails and controls in any republican state, just to that extent it subverts the principle of democracy, and converts the state into an aristocracy or a despotism. I will not offend sensibilities by drawing my proofs from the slave states existing among ourselves; but I will draw them from the greatest of the European slave states. The population of Russia in Europe, in 1844, was fifty-four millions, two hundred and fifty-one thousand. Of these, fifty-three millions and five hundred thousand were serfs, and the remaining seven hundred and fifty-one thousand, nobles, clergy, merchants, etc.

The imperial government abandons the control over the fifty-three and a half millions to their owners; and these owners, included in the seven hundred and fifty-one thousand, are thus a privileged class, or aristocracy. If ever the government interferes at all with the serfs, who are the only laboring population, it is by edicts designed to abridge their opportunities of education, and thus continue their debasement. What was the origin of this system? Conquest, in which the captivity of the conquered was made perpetual and hereditary. This, it seems to me, is identical with American slavery, only at one and the same time exaggerated by the greater disproportion between the privileged classes and the slaves in their respective numbers, and yet relieved of the unhappiest feature of American slavery, the distinction of castes. What but this renders Russia at once the most arbitrary despotism and the most barbarous state in Europe? And what is its effect, but industry comparatively profitless, and sedition, not occasional and partial, but chronic and pervading the empire. I speak of slavery not in the language of fancy, but in the language of philosophy. Montesquieu remarked upon the proposition to introduce slavery into France, that the demand for slavery was the demand of luxury and corruption, and not the demand of patriotism. Of all slavery, African slavery is the worst, for it combines practically the features of what is distinguished as real slavery, or serfdom, with the personal slavery known in the oriental world. Its domestic features lead to vice, while its political features render it injurious and dangerous to the state.

I can not stop to debate long with those who maintain that slavery is itself practically economical and humane. I might be content with saying that there are some axioms in political science that a statesman or a founder of states may adopt, especially in the Congress of the United States, and that among those axioms are these: That all men are created equal, and have inalienable rights of life, liberty, and the choice of pursuits of happiness; that knowledge promotes virtue, and righteousness exalteth a nation; that freedom is preferable to slavery, and that democratic governments, where they can be maintained by acquiescence, without force, are preferable to institutions exercising arbitrary and irresponsible power.

It remains only to remark that our own experience has proved the dangerous influence and tendency of slavery. All our apprehensions of dangers, present and future, begin and end with slavery. If slavery, limited as it yet is, now threatens to subvert the constitution, how can we, as wise and prudent statesmen, enlarge its boundaries and increase its influence, and thus increase already-impending dangers? Whether, then, I regard merely the welfare of the future inhabitants of the new territories, or the security and welfare of the whole people of the United States, or the welfare of the whole family of mankind, I can not consent to introduce slavery into any part of this continent which is now exempt from what seems to me so great an evil.—*Speech in U. S. Senate*, 1850.

Apprehensions of Disunion Groundless.

AND this brings me to the great and all-absorbing argument that the Union is in danger of being dissolved, and that it can only be saved by compromise. I do not know what I would not do to save the Union; and therefore I shall bestow upon this subject a very deliberate consideration.

I do not overlook the fact that the entire delegation from the slave states, although they differ in regard to the details of the compromise proposed, aud perhaps in regard to the exact circumstances of the crisis, seem to concur in this momentous warning. Nor do I doubt at all the patriotic devotion to the Union which is expressed by those from whom this warning proceeds. And yet, sir, although such warnings have been uttered with impassioned solemnity in my hearing every day for near three months, my confidence in the Union remains unshaken. I think they are to be received with no inconsiderable distrust, because they are uttered under the influence of a controlling interest to be secured, a paramount object to be gained; and that is an equilibrium of power in the republic. I think they are to be received with even more distrust, because, with the most profound respect, they are uttered under an obviously high excitement. Nor is that excitement an unnatural one. It is a law of our nature that the passions disturb the reason and judgment just in proportion to the importance of the occasion, and the consequent necessity for calmness and candor. I think they are to be distrusted, because there is a diversity of opinion in regard to the nature and operation of this excitement. The senators from some states say that it has brought all parties in their own region into unanimity. The honorable senator from Kentucky [Mr. CLAY] says that the danger lies in the violence of party spirit, and refers us for proof to the difficulties which attended the organization of the house of representatives.

Sir, in my humble judgment, it is not the fierce conflict of parties that we are seeing and hearing; but, on the contrary, it is the agony of distracted parties — a convulsion resulting from the too narrow foundations of both the great parties, and of all parties — foundations laid in compromises of natural justice and of human liberty. A question, a moral question, transcending the too narrow creeds of parties, has arisen; the public conscience expands with it, and the green withes of party associations give way and break, and fall off from it. No, sir; it is not the state that is dying of the fever of party spirit. It is merely a paralysis of parties, premonitory however of their restoration, with new elements of health and vigor to be imbibed from that spirit of the age which is so justly called Progress.

Nor is the evil that of unlicensed, irregular, and turbulent faction. We are told that twenty legislatures are in session, burning like furnaces, heating and inflaming the popular passions. But these twenty legislatures are constitutional furnaces. They are performing their customary functions, imparting healthful heat and vitality while within their constitutional jurisdiction. If they rage beyond its limits, the popular passions of this country are not at all, I think, in danger of being inflamed to excess. No, sir; let none of these fires be extinguished. For ever let them burn and blaze. They are neither ominous meteors nor baleful comets, but planets; and bright and intense as their heat may be, it is their native temperature, and they must still obey the law which, by attraction toward this solar centre, holds them in their spheres.

I see nothing of that conflict between the southern and northern states, or between their representative bodies, which seems to be on all sides of me assumed. Not a word of menace, not a word of anger, not an intemperate word, has been uttered in the northern legislatures. They firmly but calmly assert their convictions; but at the same time they assert their unqualified consent to submit to the common arbiter, and for weal or wo abide the fortunes of the Union.

What if there be less of moderation in the legislatures of the south? It only indicates on which side the balance is inclining, and that the decision of the momentous question is near at hand. I agree with those who say that there can be no peaceful dissolution — no dissolution of the Union by the secession of states; but that disunion, dissolution, happen when it may, will and must be revolution. I discover no omens of revolution. The predictions of the political astrologers do not agree as to the time or manner in which it is to occur. According to the authority of the honorable senator from Alabama [Mr. CLEMENS], the event has already happened, and the Union is now in ruins. According to the honorable and distinguished senator from South Carolina [Mr. CALHOUN], it is not to be immediate, but to be developed by time.

What are the omens to which our attention is directed? I see nothing but a broad difference of opinion here, and the excitement consequent upon it.

I have observed that revolutions which begin in the palace seldom go beyond the palace-walls, and they affect only the dynasty which reigns there. This revolution, if I understand it, began in this senate-chamber a year ago, when the representatives from the southern states assembled here and addressed their constituents on what were called the aggressions of the northern states. No revolution was designed at that time, and all that has happened since is the return to Congress of legislative resolutions, which seem to me to be only conventional responses to the address which emanated from the capitol.

Sir, in any condition of society there can be no revolution without a cause, an adequate cause. What cause exists here? We are admitting a new state; but there is nothing new in that; we have already admitted seventeen before. But it is said that the slave states are in danger of losing political power by the admission of the new state. Well, sir, is there anything new in that? The slave states have always been losing political power, and they always will be while they have any to lose. At first, twelve of the thirteen states were slave states; now only fifteen out of the thirty are slave states. Moreover, the change is constitutionally made, and the government was constructed so as to permit changes of the balance of power, in obedience to changes of the forces of the body politic. Danton used to say, "It's all well while the people cry Danton and Robespierre; but wo for me if ever the people learn to say, Robespierre and Danton!" That is all of it, sir. The people have been accustomed to say, "the South and the North;" they are only beginning now to say, "the North and the South."

Sir, those who would alarm us with the terrors of revolution have not well considered the structure of this government, and the organization of its forces. It is a democracy of property and persons, with a fair approximation toward universal education, and operating by means of universal suffrage. The constituent members of this democracy are the only persons who could subvert it; and they are not the citizens of a metropolis like Paris, or of a region subjected to the influences of a metropolis, like France; but they are husbandmen, dispersed over this broad land, on the mountain and on the plain, and on the prairie, from the ocean to the Rocky mountains, and from the great lakes to the gulf; and this people are now, while we are discussing their imaginary danger, at peace and in their happy homes, as unconcerned and uninformed of their peril as they are of events occurring in the moon. Nor have the alarmists made due allowance in their calculations for the influence of conservative reaction, strong in any government, and irresistible in a rural republic, operating by universal suffrage. That principle of reaction is due to the force of the habits of acquiescence and loyalty among the people. No man better understood this principle than MACHIAVELLI, who has told us, in regard to factions, that "no safe reliance can be placed in the force of nature and the bravery of words, except it be corroborated by custom." Do the alarmists remember that this government has stood sixty years already without exacting one drop of blood?—that this government has stood sixty years, and yet treason is an obsolete crime? That day, I trust, is far off when the fountains of popular contentment shall be broken up; but, whenever it shall come, it will bring forth a higher illustration than has ever yet been given of the excellence of the democratic system; for then it will be seen how calmly, how firmly, how nobly, a great people can act in preserving their constitution, whom "love of country moveth, example teacheth, company comforteth, emulation quickeneth, and glory exalteth."

When the founders of the new republic of the south come to draw over the face of this empire, along or between its parallels of latitude or longitude, their ominous lines of dismemberment, soon to be broadly and deeply shaded with fraternal blood, they may come to the discovery then, if not before, that the natural and even the political connections of the region embraced forbid such a partition; that its possible divisions are not northern and southern at all, but eastern and western, Atlantic and Pacific; and that nature and commerce have allied indissolubly for weal and wo the seceders and those from whom they are to be separated; that while they would rush into a civil war to restore an imaginary equilibrium between the northern states and the southern states, a new equilibrium has taken its place, in which all those states are on the one side, and the boundless west is on the other.

Sir, when the founders of the republic of the south come to draw those fearful lines, they will indicate what portions of the continent are to be broken off from their connection with the Atlantic, through the St. Lawrence, the Hudson, the Delaware, the Potomac, and the Mississippi; what portion of this people are to be denied the use of the lakes, the railroads, and the canals, now constituting common and customary avenues of travel, trade, and social intercourse; what families and kindred are to be separated, and converted into enemies; and what states are to be the scenes of perpetual border warfare, aggravated by interminable horrors of servile insurrection? When those portentous lines shall be drawn, they will disclose what portion of this people is to retain the army and the navy, and the flag of so many victories; and, on the other hand, what portion of the people is to be subjected to new and onerous imposts, direct taxes, and forced loans, and conscriptions, to maintain an opposing army, an opposing navy, and the new and hateful banner of sedition. Then the projectors of the new republic of the south will meet the question—and they may well prepare now to answer it—What is all this for? What intolerable wrong, what unfraternal injustice, have rendered these calamities unavoidable? What gain will this unnatural revolution bring to us? The answer will be: All this is done to secure the institution of African slavery.

And then, if not before, the question will be discussed, What is this institution of slavery, that it should cause these unparalleled sacrifices and these disastrous afflictions? And this will be the answer: When the Spaniards, few in number, discovered the western Indies and adjacent continental America, they needed labor to draw forth from its virgin stores some speedy return to the cupidity of the court and the bankers of Madrid. They enslaved the indolent, inoffensive, and confiding natives, who perished by thousands, and even by millions, under that new and unnatural bondage. A humane ecclesiastic advised the substitution of Africans reduced to captivity in their native wars, and a pious princess adopted the suggestion, with a dispensation from the head of the church, granted on the ground of the prescriptive right of the Christian to enslave the heathen, to effect his conversion. The colonists of North America, innocent in their unconsciousness of wrong, encouraged the slave traffic, and thus the labor of subduing their territory devolved chiefly upon the African race. A happy conjuncture brought on an awakening of the conscience of mankind to the injustice of slavery, simultaneously with the independence of the colonies. Massachusetts, Connecticut, Rhode Island, New Hampshire, Vermont, New York, New Jersey, and Pennsylvania, welcomed and embraced the spirit of universal emancipation. Renouncing luxury, they secured influence and empire. But the states of the south, misled by a new and profitable culture, elected to maintain and perpetuate slavery; and thus, choosing luxury, they lost power and empire.

When this answer shall be given, it will appear that the question of dissolving the Union is a complex question; that it embraces the fearful issue whether the Union shall stand, and slavery, under the steady, peaceful action of moral, social, and political causes, be removed by gradual, voluntary effort, and with compensation, or whether the Union shall be dissolved, and civil wars ensue, bringing on violent but complete and immediate emancipation. We are now arrived at that stage of our national progress when that crisis can be foreseen, when we must foresee it. It is directly before us. Its shadow is upon us. It darkens the legislative halls, the temples of worship, and the home and the hearth. Every question, political, civil, or ecclesiastical, however foreign to the subject of slavery, brings up slavery as an incident, and the incident supplants the principal question. We hear of nothing but slavery, and we can talk of nothing but slavery. And now, it seems to me that all our difficulties, embarrassments, and dangers, arise, not out of unlawful perversions of the question of slavery, as some suppose, but from the want of moral courage to meet this question of emancipation as we ought. Consequently, we hear on one side demands—absurd, indeed, but yet unceasing—for an immediate and unconditional abolition of slavery—as if any power, except the people of the slave states, could abolish it, and as if they could be moved to abolish it by merely sounding the trumpet loudly and proclaiming emancipation, while the institution is interwoven with all their social and political interests, constitutions, and customs.

On the other hand, our statesmen say that "slavery has always existed, and, for aught they know or can do, it always must exist. God permitted it, and he alone can indicate the way to remove it." As if the Supreme Creator, after giving us the instructions of his providence and revelation for the illumination of our minds and consciences, did not leave us in all human transactions, with due invocations of his holy spirit, to seek out his will and execute it for ourselves.

Here, then, is the point of my separation from both of these parties. I feel assured that slavery must give way, and will give way, to the salutary instructions of economy, and to the ripening influences of humanity; that emancipation is inevitable, and is near; that it may be hastened or hindered; and that whether it shall be peaceful or violent, depends upon the question whether it be hastened or hindered; that all measures which fortify slavery or extend it, tend to the consummation of violence; all that check its extension and abate its strength, tend to its peaceful extirpation. But I will adopt none but lawful, constitutional, and peaceful means, to secure even that end; and none such can I or will I forego. Nor do I know any important or responsible political body that proposes to do more than this. No free state claims to extend its legislation into a slave state. None claims that Congress shall usurp power to abolish slavery in the slave states. None claims that any violent, unconstitutional, or unlawful measure shall be embraced. And, on the other hand, if we offer no scheme or plan for the adoption of the slave states, with the assent and co-operation of Congress, it is only because the slave states are unwilling as yet to receive such suggestions, or even to entertain the question of emancipation in any form.

But, sir, I will take this occasion to say that, while I can not agree with the honorable senator from Massachusetts in proposing to devote eighty millions of dollars to remove the free colored population from the slave states, and thus, as it appears to me, fortify slavery, there is no reasonable limit to which I am not willing to go in applying the national treasures to effect the peaceful, voluntary removal of slavery itself.

I have thus endeavored to show that there is not now, and there is not likely to occur, any adequate cause for revolution in regard to slavery. But you reply that, nevertheless, you must have guaranties; and the first one is for the surrender of fugitives from labor. That guaranty you can not have, as I have already shown, because you can not roll back the tide of social progress. You must be content with what you have. If you wage war against us, you can, at most, only conquer us, and then all you can get will be a treaty, and that you have already.

* * * * * * * *

I do not say that there may not be disturbance, though I do not apprehend even that. Absolute regularity and order in administration have not yet been established in any government, and unbroken popular tranquillity has not yet been attained in even the most advanced condition of human society. The machinery of our system is necessarily complex. A pivot may drop out here, a lever may be displaced there, a wheel may fall out of gearing elsewhere, but the machinery will soon recover its regularity, and move on just as before, with even better adaptation and adjustment to overcome new obstructions.

There are many well-disposed persons who are alarmed at the occurrence of any such disturbance. The failure of a legislative body to organize is to their apprehension a fearful omen, and an extra-constitutional assemblage to consult upon public affairs is with them cause for desperation. Even senators speak of the Union as if it existed only by consent, and, as it seems to be implied, by the assent of the legislatures of the states. On the contrary, the Union was not founded in voluntary choice, nor does it exist by voluntary consent.

A union was proposed to the colonies by Franklin and others, in 1754; but such was their aversion to an abridgment of their own importance, respectively, that it was rejected even under the pressure of a disastrous invasion by France.

A union of choice was proposed to the colonies in 1775; but so strong was their opposition, that they went through the war of independence without having established more than a mere council of consultation.

But with independence came enlarged interests of agriculture—absolutely new interests of manufactures—interests of commerce, of fisheries, of navigation, of a common domain, of common debts, of common revenues and taxation, of the administration of justice, of public defence, of public honor; in short, interests of common nationality and sovereignty—interests which at last compelled the adoption of a more perfect union—a national government.

The genius, talents, and learning of Hamilton, of Jay, and of Madison, surpassing perhaps the intellectual power ever exerted before for the establishment of a government, combined with the serene but mighty influence of Washington, were only sufficient to secure the reluctant adoption of the constitution that is now the object of all our affections and of the hopes of mankind. No wonder that the conflicts in which that constitution was born, and the almost desponding solemnity of Washington, in his farewell address, impressed his countrymen and mankind with a profound distrust of its perpetuity! No wonder that while the murmurs of that day are yet ringing in our ears, we cherish that distrust, with pious reverence, as a national and patriotic sentiment!

But it is time to prevent the abuses of that sentiment. It is time to shake off that fear, for fear is always weakness. It is time to remember that government, even when it arises by chance or accident, and is administered capriciously and oppressively, is ever the strongest of all human institutions, surviving many social and ecclesiastical changes and convulsions; and that this constitution of ours has all the inherent strength common to governments in general, and added to them has also the solidity and firmness derived from broader and deeper foundations in national justice, and a better civil adaptation to promote the welfare and happiness of mankind.

The Union, the creature of necessities—physical, moral, social, and political—endures by virtue of the same necessities; and these necessities are stronger than when it was produced—stronger by the greater amplitude of territory now covered by it—stronger by the sixfold increase of the society living under its beneficent protection—stronger by the augmentation ten thousand times of the fields, the workshops, the mines, and the ships, of that society; of its productions of the sea, of the plow, of the loom, and of the anvil, in their constant circle of internal and international exchange—stronger in the long rivers penetrating regions before unknown—stronger in all the artificial roads, canals, and other channels and avenues essential not only to trade but to defence—stronger in steam navigation, in steam locomotion on the land, and in telegraph communications, unknown when the constitution was adopted—stronger in the freedom and in the growing empire of the seas—stronger in the element of national honor in all lands, and stronger than all in the now settled habits of veneration and affection for institutions so stupendous and so useful.

The Union, then, IS, not because merely that men choose that it shall be, but because some government must exist here, and no other government than this can. If it could be dashed to atoms by the whirlwind, the lightning, or the earthquake, to-day, it would rise again in all its just and magnificent proportions to-morrow. This nation is a globe, still accumulating upon accumulation—not a dissolving sphere.

I have heard somewhat here, and almost for the first time in my life, of divided allegiance—of allegiance to the South and to the Union—of allegiance to states severally and to the Union. Sir, if sympathies with state emulation and pride of achievement could be allowed to raise up another sovereign to divide the allegiance of a citizen of the United States, I might recognise the claims of the state to which, by birth and gratitude, I belong—to the state of Hamilton and Jay, of Schuyler, of the Clintons, and of Fulton—the state which, with less than two hundred miles of natural navigation connected with the ocean, has, by her own enterprise, secured to herself the commerce of the continent, and is steadily advancing to the command of the commerce of the world. But for all this, I know only one country and one sovereign—the United States of America and the American people. And such as my allegiance is, is the loyalty of every other citizen of the United States. As I speak, he will speak when his time arrives. He knows no other country and no other sovereign. He has life, liberty, property, and precious affections, and hopes for himself and for his posterity, treasured up in the ark of the Union. He knows as well and feels as strongly as I do, that this government is his own government; that he is a part of it; that it was established for him, and that it is maintained by him; that it is the only truly wise, just, free, and equal government, that has ever existed; that no other government could be so wise, just, free, and equal; and that it is safer and more beneficent than any which time or change could bring into its place.

You may tell me, sir, that although all this may be true, still the trial of faction has not yet been made. Sir, if the trial of faction has not been made, it has not been because faction has not always existed, and has not always menaced a trial, but because faction could find no fulcrum on which to place the lever to subvert the Union, as it can find no fulcrum now; and in this is my confidence. I would not rashly provoke the trial: but I will not suffer a fear, which I have not, to make me compromise one sentiment, one principle of truth or justice, to avert a danger that all experience teaches me is purely chimerical. Let, then, those who distrust the Union make compromises to save it. I shall not impeach their wisdom, as I certainly can not their patriotism; but, indulging no such apprehensions myself, I shall vote for the admission of California directly, without conditions, without qualifications, and without compromise.

For the vindication of that vote, I look not to the verdict of the passing hour, disturbed as the public mind now is by conflicting interests and passions, but to that period, happily not far distant, when the vast regions over which we are now legislating shall have received their destined inhabitants.

While looking forward to that day, its countless generations seem to me to be rising up and passing in dim and shadowy review before us; and a voice comes forth from their serried ranks, saying: "Waste your treasures and your armies, if you will; raze your fortifications to the ground; sink your navies into the sea; transmit to us even a dishonored name, if you must; but the soil you hold in trust for us — give it to us free. You found it free and conquered it to extend a better and surer freedom over it. Whatever choice you have made for yourselves, let US have no partial freedom; let us all be free; let the reversion of your broad domain descend to us unencumbered, and free from the calamities and from the sorrows of human bondage."— *Speech in U. S. Senate*, 1850.

Slavery.

PROPERTY and possession, in common speech, are predicated as incidents belonging to the relation of master and slave; but the terms are inaccurate, without foundation in law, and essentially false. . . . . The institution of slavery accustoms us to confound the broadest distinctions in nature, not less than to subvert the plainest principles of justice. The right of individual property is derived from the consent of the Creator. When he had finished a world, and filled it with bounties, he gave to the last being created to inhabit, and the only one capable of governing it, DOMINION, or the right of property, and that dominion was universal; and yet man was excepted from it. The right of dominion by man over inert matter and irrational beings could not be complete, if one man could be made the property of another man, or could be reduced into his possession. Happily, God has deprived us of the power to abridge this great dominion in such a way, by making the mind, the soul, the heart, the affections of every man, more truly independent of all human power than the subtlest and most elastic substance unendowed with life. . . . .

A great diversity of opinion exists in the United States, concerning the proper construction of the constitution of the United

States, in relation to slavery. Some receive it as a gospel of universal emancipation, and others as a covenant of perpetual toleration of slavery. Those who maintain the latter opinion fortify themselves with arguments derived from the condition of the country and the spirit of the times when the constitution was established. It seems to me that truth is found on both sides of the controversy. The constitution of the United States, in its general scope and spirit, recognises the absolute natural rights of mankind, and it contemplates an ultimate condition of perfect democratic liberty and equality. On the other hand, it contains provisions (adopted doubtlessly by way of compromise) which have served but too well to fortify an institution whose existence nearly all reflecting and candid men deplore. Slavery is only the negation or privation of that liberty which is the birthright of all men. It results from an ascendency of physical force which always obtains in rude communities, and never finally disappears in any state, until intellectual and moral agencies are fully developed. Let slavery receive what name or form it may, it is always the same—subjection of the weak to the strong. The progress of our race is so slow, that liberty never all at once achieves an absolute triumph, and every advantage gained is followed by reaction. Thus African slavery, unjust as it is conceded to be, long as it has endured, and long as it may be yet destined to endure, is only the reaction of the principle of physical force by which it has compensated itself for the loss of feudal villeinage, in the sixteenth century in western Europe. So the emancipation of Europe seems to have mysteriously drawn after it the desecration of a new continent, with a darker, more degrading, and severer system of oppression. Labor was needed to reclaim, suddenly, a wide domain from the sovereignty of Nature. Voluntary labor stood upon terms too high for contract, and therefore physical force sought and subjugated involuntary labor. Slavery, wherever found, was not created by law, but obtained its establishment by evasion or subversion of law. It spread at an early period throughout Virginia, although the charter secured to all whom the colonial corporation should lead thither "all the liberties, franchises, and immunities of free denizens, and natural subjects within any of the British dominions, to all intents and purposes. as if they had been abiding at home, within the realm of England, or in others of his majesty's dominions."* Slavery was thus excluded by royal inhibition from the territory now included within the state of Kentucky, and yet it took root and flourished in defiance of law, until it overshadowed the state. The cause of human liberty, however baffled, never rests, and in the eighteenth century it had borrowed new vigor from philosophy and the diffusion of Christianity. The movement for the abolition of slavery, which now excites so much apprehension in portions of our country, is by no means as modern as those who think it can be suppressed suppose. It began in a meeting of Friends, in London, in 1727, and proceeded so slowly that it did not expel the institution from the British dominions until after the lapse of one hundred and seven years. Fifty-six years were spent before the abolitionists could obtain a reading in the British parliament of a petition for the suppression of the slave-trade, and that trade was not finally abolished within what were the British colonies on this continent until 1807. The agitation of abolition in England reached and sensibly affected the colonies previously to the Revolution, and the Declaration of American Independence bears memorable testimony of the high tone which the American mind had then assumed. The representatives who assumed to pronounce, in 1776, a separation of this country from the parent state, were so deeply imbued with the sentiment of abolition, that they confided the task of preparing the immortal declaration to John Adams, an obstinate hater of slavery, and Thomas Jefferson, a young, enthusiastic, and open abolitionist. But emancipation was destined, in its turn, to suffer reaction.—*Argument, U. S. Supreme Court, Dec.,* 1847.

The Slavery Question can never be settled by Compromises.

STILL it is replied that the slavery question must be settled. That question can not be settled by this bill. Slavery and freedom are conflicting systems, brought together by the union of the states, not neutralized, nor even harmonized. Their antagonism is radical, and therefore perpetual. Compromise continues conflict, and the conflict involves, unavoidably, all questions

* Charter of Virginia, by James II., 1609, Littell's Laws of Ky., vol. i., p. 11.

of national interest—questions of revenue, of internal improvement, of industry, of commerce, of political rivalry, and even all questions of peace and of war. In entering the career of conquest, you have kindled to a fiercer heat the fires you seek to extinguish, because you have thrown into them the fuel of propagandism. We have the propagandism of slavery to enlarge the slave-market, and to increase slave representation in Congress and in the electoral colleges—for the bramble ever seeks power, though the olive, the fig, and the vine, refuse it; and we have the propagandism of freedom to counteract those purposes. Nor can this propagandism be arrested on either side. The sea is full of exiles, and they swarm over our land. Emigration from Europe and from Asia, from Polynesia even, from the free states and from the slave states, goes on, and will go on, and must go on, in obedience to laws which, I should say, were higher than the constitution, if any such laws were acknowledged here. And I may be allowed here to refer those who have been scandalized by the allusion to such laws to a single passage by an author whose opinions did not err on the side of superstition or of tyranny:—

> "If it be said that every nation ought in this to follow their own constitutions, we are at an end of our controversies; for they ought not to be followed, unless they are rightly made; they can not be rightly made if they are contrary to the universal law of God and nature."—*Discourses on Government, by Algernon Sidney.*

You may slay the Wilmot proviso in the senate-chamber, and bury it beneath the capitol to-day; the dead corse, in complete steel, will haunt your legislative halls to-morrow.

When the strife is ended in the territories you now possess, it will be renewed on new fields, north as well as south, to fortify advantages gained, or to retrieve losses incurred, for both of the parties well know that there is "Yet, in that word Hereafter."

This compromise is rendered doubly dangerous by the circumstance that it is a concession to alarms of disorganization and faction. Such concessions, once begun, follow each other with fearful rapidity and always increasing magnitude. It is time, high time, that panics about the Union should cease; that it should be known and felt that the constitution and the Union, within the limits of human security, are safe, firm, and perpetual.

Settle what you can settle; confide in that old arbiter, Time, for his favoring aid in settling for the future what belongs to the future, and you will hereafter be relieved of two classes of patriots whose labors can well be spared — those who clamor for disunion, either to abolish slavery or to prevent emancipation, and those who surrender principles or sound policy to clamors so idle.

Sir, the agitations which alarm us are not signs of evils to come, but mild efforts of the commonwealth for relief from mischiefs past.

There is a way, and one way only, to put them at rest. Let us go back to the ground where our forefathers stood. While we leave slavery to the care of the states where it exists, let us inflexibly direct the policy of the federal government to circumscribe its limits and favor its ultimate extinguishment. Let those who have this misfortune entailed upon them, instead of contriving how to maintain an equilibrium that never had existence, consider carefully how at some time — it may be ten, or twenty, or even fifty years hence — by some means, by all means of their own, and with our aid, without sudden change or violent action — they may bring about the emancipation of labor and its restoration to its just dignity and power in the state. Let them take hope to themselves, give hope to the free states, awaken hope throughout the world. They will thus anticipate only what must happen at some time, and what they themselves must desire if it can come safely, and as soon as it can come without danger. Let them do only this, and every cause of disagreement will cease immediately and for ever. We shall then not merely endure each other, but we shall be reconciled together, and shall realize once more the concord which results from mutual league, united councils, and equal hopes and hazards in the most sublime and beneficent enterprise the earth has witnessed. The fingers of the Powers above would tune the harmony of such a peace. — *Speech in U. S. Senate, July* 2, 1850.

Moderation.

THE cause of emancipation has now reached an interesting crisis. The sentiment of justice to the African race has at length become a political element too important to be overlooked or disregarded by either of the great political parties. The expediency of practical emancipation is directly discussed in one slave state and thousands are prepared for it in other states where the institution has seemed impregnable. Its advocates fail to convince the people that it is a humane, or a necessary, or even a harmless anomaly in our constitution. Nevertheless popular action is checked by alarms concerning the threatened dangers of emancipation, civil wars, and dissolution of the Union. We live in an age when the specific influences of Christianity are widely diffused, and we shrink from prosecuting even the most benevolent designs if they seem to involve the calamities of war. If we analyze the national passion of patriotism, we shall find it to consist chiefly in veneration for the constitution, and devotion to the union of the states.

The seeming indifference of the people concerning the guilt and danger of slavery has been so irksome to the impetuous that many who have been esteemed wise and patriotic citizens, have come to treat of disunion, as if it were preferable to further forbearance, or were in some way involved in the success of abolition. I trust that such sentiments will be discarded. Whatever hopes may be indulged by those who permit themselves to speculate concerning secession or nullification, we have enjoyed more abounding national prosperity, more perfect political and social equality, and more precious civil and religious liberty, by, through, and with our present constitution, than were ever before secured by any people. We can not know what portion of these blessings would be lost by dissolving the present fabric and constructing another or others in its place. Heaven forbid that we should even contemplate the experiment!

Prudence in regard to the cause of emancipation forbids the indulgence of a thought of disunion. If it be so confessedly difficult to awaken the national conscience, while the patriotism of abolitionists can not be justly questioned, it would be ruinous to suffer so noble an enterprise to be at all connected with designs which, however they may be excused or palliated, must nevertheless be seditious and treasonable.

I grant that the annexation of Texas, through the failure of concert among the opponents of slavery, vastly increases the difficulty of emancipation. But still I trust that if that great enterprise be conducted with discretion, it will advance faster than the population and political influence of the new territory. The slaveholders have enlarged the domain of our country. Let this untoward event only excite us the more. Let us rouse ourselves to the necessary effort, and enlarge indeed the "area of freedom."

Men differ much in temperament and susceptibility, and are so variously situated, that they receive from the same causes very unequal impressions. It is not in human nature that all who desire the abolition of slavery should be inflamed with equal zeal; and different degrees of fervor produce different opinions concerning the measure proper to be adopted. Great caution is necessary, therefore, to preserve mutual confidence and harmony. No cause, however just, can flourish without these. Christian Europe lost the Holy Sepulchre, which had cost so many sacrifices, less by the bravery of the Saracens, than by the mutual controversies of the Crusaders. The protestant reformation was arrested two hundred years ago, by the distraction of the reformers, and not a furlong's breadth has since been gained from the papal hierarchy.

I am far from denying that any class of abolitionists has done much good for their common cause, but I think the whole result has been much diminished by the angry conflicts between them, often on mere metaphysical questions. I sincerely hope that these conflicts may now cease. Emancipation is now a political enterprise, to be effected through the consent and action of the American people. They will lend no countenance or favor to any other than lawful and constitutional means. Nor is the range of our efforts narrowly circumscribed by the constitution.

In many of the free states there is a large mass of citizens disfranchised on the ground of color. They must be invested with the right of suffrage. Give them this right, and their influence will be immediately felt in the national councils, and it is needless to say will be cast in favor of those who uphold the cause of human liberty. We must resist unceasingly the admission of slave states, and urge and demand the abolition of slavery in the District of Columbia. We have secured the right of petition, but the federal government continues to be swerved by the influences of slavery as before. This tendency can and must be counteracted; and when one independent Congress shall have been elected, the internal slave-trade will be subjected to inquiry. Amendments to the constitution may be initiated, and the obstacles in the way of emancipation will no longer appear insurmountable.

But, gentlemen, I fear I may appear to dogmatize when I intended only to invoke concession. If I seem to do so too earnestly, it is because I feel so deeply interested in the cause to which your efforts are devoted, and because I believe with Burke, that "we ought to act in political affairs with all the moderation which does not absolutely enervate that vigor, and quench that fervency of spirit, without which the best wishes for the public good must evaporate in empty speculation." —*Letter to Hon. S. P. Chase and Others of Ohio, May*, 1845.

COMMERCE.

Public Faith.

No reason for rejecting these claims* remains, except that they have not been paid heretofore. But mere lapse of time pays no debts, and discharges no obligations. There has been no release, no waiver, no neglect, no delay, by the creditors. They have been here twenty-five times in fifty years; that is to say, they have appeared in their successive generations, before every Congress since their claims against the United States accrued. Against such claims and such creditors there is no prescription.

It is said, indeed, that the nation is unable to pay these claims now. I put a single question in reply: When will the nation be more affluent than now?

The senator [Mr. HUNTER] says, again, that, if the debts are just, we should pay the whole, and not a moiety; and that if the claims are unjust, then the bill proposes a gratuity—that in the one case the appropriation is too small, and in the other too great. This is the plea of him who, I think it was in Ephesus, despoiled the statue of Jupiter of its golden robe, saying, "Gold was too warm in summer, and too cold in winter, for the shoulders of the god."

Sir, commerce is one of the great occupations of this nation. It is the fountain of its revenues, as it is the chief agent of its advancement in civilization and enlargement of empire. It is exclusively the care of the federal authorities. It is for the protection of commerce that they pass laws, make treaties, build

* For French Spoliations.

fortifications, and maintain navies upon all the seas. But justice and good faith are surer defences than treaties, fortifications, or naval armaments. Justice and good faith constitute true national honor, which feels a stain more keenly than a wound. The nation that lives in wealth and in the enjoyment of power, and yet under unpaid obligations, dwells in dishonor and in danger. The nation that would be truly great, or even merely safe, must practise an austere and self-denying morality.

The faith of canonized ancestors, whose fame now belongs to mankind, is pledged to the payment of these debts. "Let the merchants send hither well-authenticated evidences of their claims, and proper measures shall be taken for their relief." This was the promise of Washington. The evidence is here. Let us redeem the sacred and venerable engagement. Through his sagacity and virtue, we have inherited with it ample and abundant resources, and to them we ourselves have added the newly-discovered wealth of southern plains, and the hidden treasures of the western coast. With the opening of the half century, we are entering upon new and profitable intercourse with the ancient oriental states and races, while we are grappling more closely to us the new states on our own continent. Let us signalize an epoch so important in commerce and politics, by justly discharging ourselves for ever from the yet remaining obligations of the first and most sacred of all our national engagements. While we are growing over all lands, let us be rigorously just to other nations, just to the several states, and just to every class and to every citizen; in short, just in all our administration, and just toward all mankind. So shall prosperity crown all our enterprises—nor shall any disturbance within nor danger from abroad come nigh unto us, nor alarm us for the safety of fireside, or fane, or capitol.—*Speech on French Spoliation Bill in U. S. Senate, January, 21, 1851.*

American Enterprise.

Come, then, senators, and suppose that you stand with me in the galleries of St. Stephen's chapel, on a day so long gone by as the 22d of March, 1775. A mighty debate has been going on here in this august legislature of the British empire. Insurrection against commercial restriction has broken out in the distant American colonies; a seditious assembly in Philadelphia has organized it; and a brave, patient, unimpassioned, and not untried soldier of Virginia, lies, with hastily-gathered and irregular levies, on the heights of Dorchester, waiting the coming out of the British army from Boston. The question whether Great Britain shall strike, or concede and conciliate, has just been debated and decided. Concession has been denied. A silence, brief but intense, is broken by the often fierce and violent, but now measured and solemn utterance of Burke: "My counsel has been rejected. You have determined to trample upon and extinguish a people who have, in the course of a single life, added to England as much as she had acquired by a progressive increase of improvement, brought on, by varieties of civilizing conquests and civilizing settlements, in a series of seventeen hundred years. A vision has passed before my eyes; the spirit of prophecy is upon me. Listen, now, to a revelation of the consequences which shall follow your maddened decision. Henceforth, there shall be division, separation, and eternal conflict in alternating war and peace between you and the child you have oppressed, which has inherited all your indomitable love of liberty and all your insatiable passion for power. Though still in the gristle, and not yet hardened into the bone of manhood, America will, within the short period of sixteen months, cast off your dominion and defy your utmost persecution. Perfecting the institutions you have not yet suffered to ripen, she will establish a republic, the first confederate representative commonwealth, which shall in time become the admiration and envy of the world. France, the hereditary rival whom, only twenty years ago, with the aid of your own colonies, you despoiled of her North American possessions, though they had been strengthened by the genius of Richelieu, will take sweet revenge in aiding the emancipation of those very colonies, and thus dismembering your empire. You will strike her in vain with one hand, while you stretch forth the other to reduce your colonies with equal discomfiture. And you, even you, most infatuated yet most loyal prince, will within eight years sign a treaty of peace with the royal Bourbon, and of independence with republican America! With fraud, corruption, fire and sword, you will compensate

England with conquests in the East, and within half a century they will surround the world, and the British flag shall wave over provinces covering five millions of square miles, and containing one sixth of the people of the globe. Nor shall you lose your retaliation upon your ancient enemy; for she, in the meantime, imbibing and intoxicated by the spirit of revolution in her American affiliation, shall overthrow all authority, human and divine, and, exhausting herself by twenty-five years of carnage and desolation throughout continental Europe, shall at last succumb to your victorious arms, and relapse, after ineffectual struggles, into the embraces of an inglorious military despotism. Yet, notwithstanding all these unsurpassed conquests and triumphs, shall you enjoy no certain or complete dominion. For, on the other hand, wild beasts and savage men and uncouth manners shall all disappear on the American continent; and the three millions whom you now despise, gathering to themselves increase from every European nation and island, will, within seventy-five years, spread themselves over field and forest, prairie and mountain, until, in your way to your provinces in the Bahamas, they shall meet you on the shores of the gulf of Mexico, and on your return from the eastern Indies, they will salute you from the eastern coast of the Pacific ocean. In the meantime, with genius developed by the influence of freedom, and with vigor called forth and disciplined in the subjugation of the forest, and trained and perfected in the mysteries of ship-building and navigation, by the hardy exercise of the whale fisheries under either pole, they will, in all European conflicts, with keen sagacity, assume the relation of neutrals, and thus grasp the prize of Atlantic commerce dropped into their hands by fierce belligerents. In the midst of your studies and experiments in hydraulics, steam, and electricity, they will seize the unpractised and even incomplete inventions, and cover their rivers with steamboats, and connect and bind together their widely-separated territories with canals, railroads, and telegraphs. When a long interval of peace shall have come, your merchants, combining a vast capital, will regain and hold for a time the carrying trade, by substituting capacious, buoyant, and fleet packet-ships, departing and arriving with exact punctuality; but the Americans, quickly borrowing the device, and improving on your skill, will reconquer their commerce. You will then rouse all the enterprise of your merchants, and all the spirit of your government, and wresting the new and mighty power of steam from the hands of your inveterate rival, will apply it to ocean navigation, and laying hold of the commercial and social cerrespondence between the two continents, increasing as the nations rise to higher civilization and come into more close and intimate relations, as the basis of postal revenue, you will thus restore your lost monopoly on the Atlantic, and enjoy it unmolested through a period of ten years. During that season of triumph, you will mature and perfect all the arrangements for extending this mighty device of power and revenue, so as to connect every island of the seas and every part of every continent with your capital. But just at that moment, your emulous rival will appear with steamships still more capacious, buoyant and fleet, than your own, in your harbors, and at once subverting your Atlantic monopoly, will give earnest of her vigorous renewal of the endless contest for supremacy of all the seas. When you think her expelled from the ocean, her flag will be seen in your ports, covering her charities contributed to relieve your population, stricken by famine; and while you stand hesitating whether to declare between republicanism and absolute power in continental Europe, her embassadors will be seen waiting on every battle-field to salute the triumphs of liberty; and when that cause shall be overthrown, the same constant flag shall be seen even in the straits of the Dardanelles, receiving with ovations due to conquerors the temporarily overthrown champions of freedom. Look toward Africa! there you see American colonies lifting her up from her long night of barbarism into the broad light of liberty and civilization. Look to the East, you see American missionaries bringing the people of the Sandwich islands into the family of nations, and American armaments peacefully seeking yet firmly demanding the rights of humanity in Japan Look to the equator, there are American engineers opening passages by canals and railroads across the isthmus which divides the two oceans. And last of all, look northward, and you behold American sailors penetrating the continent of ice in search of your own daring and lost navigators."

Sir, this stupendous vision has become real. All this momentous prophecy has come to pass. The man yet lives who has seen both the end and the beginning of its fulfilment. It is history. And that history shows that this enterprise of American Atlantic steam navigation was wisely and even necessarily undertaken, to maintain our present commercial independence, and the contest for the ultimate empire of the ocean. Only a word shall express the importance of these objects. International postal communication and foreign commerce are as important as domestic mails and traffic. Equality with other nations in respect to those interests is as important as freedom from restriction upon them among ourselves. Except Rome — which substituted conquest and spoliation for commeree — no nation was ever highly prosperous, really great, or even truly independent, whose foreign communications and traffic were conducted by other states; while Tyre, and Egypt, and Venice, and the Netherlands, and Great Britain, successively becoming the merchants, became thereby the masters of the world.

* * * * * * * *

I conjure you to consider, moreover, that England, without waiting for, and, I am sure, without expecting, so inglorious a retreat on our part, is completing a vast web of ocean steam navigation, based on postage and commerce, that will connect all the European ports, all our own ports, all the South American ports, all the ports in the West Indies, all the ports of Asia and Oceanica, with her great commercial capital. Thus the world is to become a great commercial system, ramified by a thousand nerves projecting from the one head at London. Yet, stupendous as the scheme is, our own merchants, conscious of equal capacity and equal resources, and relying on experience for success, stand here beseeching us to allow them to counteract its fulfilment, and ask of us facilities and aid equal to those yielded by the British government to its citizens. While our commercial history is full of presages of a successful competition, Great Britain is sunk deep in debt. We are free from debt. Great Britain is oppressed with armies and costly aristocratic institutions; industry among us is unfettered and free. But it is a contest depending not on armies, nor even on wealth, but chiefly on invention and industry. And how stands the national account in those respects? The cotton-gin, the planing-machine, steam navigation, and electrical communication—these are old achievements. England only a year ago invited the nations to bring their inventions and compare them together in a palace of iron and glass. In all the devices for the increase of luxury and indulgence, America was surpassed, not only by refined England and by chivalrous France, but even by semi-barbarian Russia. Not until after all the mortification which such a result necessarily produced, did the comparison of utilitarian inventions begin. Then our countrymen exhibited Dick's anti-friction press—a machine that moved a power greater by two hundred and forty tons than could be raised by the Brama hydraulic press, which, having been used by Sir John Stevenson in erecting the tubular bridge over the straits of Menai, had been brought forward by the British artisans as a contrivance of unrivalled merit for the generation of direct power. Next was submitted, on our behalf, the two inventions of St. John, the variation compass, which indicates the deflection of its own needle at any place, resulting from local causes; and the velocimeter, which tells, at any time, the actual speed of the vessel bearing it, and its distance from the port of departure—inventions adopted at once by the admiralty of Great Britain. Then, to say nothing of the ingeniously-constructed locks exhibited by Hobbs which defied the skill of the British artisans, while he opened all of theirs at pleasure, there was Bigelow's power-loom, which has brought down ingrain and Brussels carpets within the reach of the British mechanic and farmer. While the American ploughs took precedence of all others, M'Cormick's reaper was acknowledged to be a contribution to the agriculture of England, surpassing in value the cost of the Crystal Palace. Nor were we dishonored in the fine arts, for a well-deserved meed was awarded to Hughes for his successful incorporation in marble of the ideal of Oliver Twist; and the palm was conferred on Powers for his immortal statue of the Greek Slave. When these successes had turned away the tide of derision from our country, the yacht America entered the Thames. Skilful architects saw that she combined, in before unknown proportions, the elements of grace and motion, and her modest challenge was reluctantly accepted, and even then only for a tenth part of the prize she proposed. The trial was graced by the presence of the queen and her court, and watched with an interest created by national pride and ambition, and yet the triumph was complete.

In the very hour of this, of itself, conclusive demonstration of American superiority in utilitarian inventions, and in the art "that leads to nautical dominion," a further and irresistible confirmation was given by the arrival of American clippers from India, freighted at advanced rates with shipments, consigned by the agents of the East India company at Calcutta to their own warehouses in London. Such and so recent are the proofs, that in the capital element of invention we are equal to the contest for the supremacy of the seas. When I consider them, and consider our resources, of which those of Pennsylvania, or of the valley of the Mississippi, or of California, alone exceed the entire native wealth of Great Britain; when I consider, moreover, our yet unelicited manufacturing capacity—our great population, already nearly equal to that of the British Islands, and multiplying at a rate unknown in human progress by accessions from both of the old continents; when I consider the advantages of our geographical position, midway between them; and when I consider, above all, the expanding and elevating influence of freedom upon the genius of our people, I feel quite assured that their enterprise will be adequate to the glorious conflict, if it shall be only sustained by constancy and perseverance on the part of their government. I do not know that we shall prevail in that conflict; but for myself, like the modest hero who was instructed to charge on the artillery at Niagara, I can say that we "will try;" and that when a difficulty occurs no greater than that which meets us now, my motto shall be the words of the dying commander of the Chesapeake—"Don't give up the ship."—*Speech on American Steam Navigation, in Senate, April 27, 1852.*

The Whale Fisheries.

Mr. PRESIDENT: Some years ago, when ascending the Alabama, I saw a stag plunge into the river, and gallantly gain the western bank, while the desponding sportsman whose rifle he had escaped, sat down to mourn his ill luck under the deep magnolia forest that shaded the eastern shore. You,* sir, are a dweller in that region, and are, as all the world knows, a gentleman of cultivated taste and liberal fortunes. Perhaps then, you may have been that unfortunate hunter. Howsoever that may have been, I wish to converse with you now of the chase, and yet not of deer, or hawk, or hound, but of a chase upon the seas; and still not of angling or trolling, nor of the busy toil of those worthy fishermen who seem likely to embroil us, certainly without reluctance on our part, in a controversy about their rights in the Bay of Fundy; but of a nobler sport, and more adventurous sportsmen than Izaak Walton, or Daniel Boone, or even Nimrod, the mightiest as well as most ancient of hunters, ever dreamed of—the chase of the whale over his broad range of the universal ocean.

Do not hastily pronounce the subject out of order or unprofitable, or unworthy of this high presence. The Phœnicians, the earliest mercantile nation known to us, enriched themselves by selling the celebrated Tyrian dye, and glass made of sand taken from the sea; and they acquired not only those sources of wealth but the art of navigation itself, in the practice of their humble calling as fishermen. A thousand years ago, King Alfred was laying the foundations of empire for Young England, as we are now doing for Young America. The monarch whom men have justly surnamed the Wise as well as the Great, did not disdain to listen to Octher, who related the adventures of a voyage along the coast of Norway, "so far north as commonly the whale hunters used to travel;" nor was the stranger suffered to depart until he had submitted to the king "a most just survey and description" of the northern seas, not only as they extended upward to the North cape, but also as they declined downward along the southeast coast of Lapland, and so following the icy beach of Russia to where the river Dwina discharged its waters into the White sea, or, as it was then called, the sea of Archangel. Perhaps my poor speech may end in some similar lesson. The incident I have related is the burden of the earliest historical notice of the subjugation of the monster of the seas to the uses of man. The fishery was carried on then, and near six hundred years afterward, by the Basques, Biscayans, and Nor-

* Hon. W. R. King.

wegians, for the food yielded by the tongue, and the oil obtained from the fat of the animal. Whalebone entered into commerce in the fifteenth century, and at first commanded the enormous price of seven hundred pounds sterling per ton, exceeding a value in this age of ten thousand dollars. Those were merry times, if not for science, at least for royalty, when, although the material for stays and hoops was taken from the mouth, the law appropriated the tail of every whale taken by an English subject to the use of the queen, for the supply of the royal wardrobe. . . . .

Mr. President, I have tried to win the favor of the senate toward the national whale-fishery for a purpose. The whales have found a new retreat in the seas of Ochotsk and Anadir, south of Bhering straits, and in that part of the Arctic ocean lying north of them. In 1848, Captain Roys, in the whale-ship Superior, passed through those seas and through the straits, braving the perils of an unknown way and an inhospitable climate. He filled his ship in a few weeks, and the news of his success went abroad. In 1849, a fleet of one hundred and fifty-four sail went up to this new fishing-ground; in 1850, a fleet of one hundred and forty-four; and in 1851, a fleet of one hundred and forty-five. The vessels are manned with thirty persons each; and their value, including that of the average annual cargoes procured there, is equal to nine millions—and thus exceeds by near two millions the highest annual import from China. But these fleets are beset by not only such dangers of their calling as customarily occur on well-explored fishing grounds, but also by the multiplied dangers of shipwreck resulting from the want of accurate topographical knowledge—the only charts of those seas being imperfect and unsatisfactory. While many and deplorable losses were sustained by the fleets of 1849–'50, we have already information of the loss of eleven vessels, one thirteenth part of the whole fleet of 1851, many of which disasters might have been avoided had there been charts accurately indicating the shoals and headlands, and also places of sheltered anchorage near them. These facts are represented to us by the merchants, ship-owners, and underwriters, and are confirmed by Lieutenant Maury, who presides in this department of science in the navy, as well as in the labors and studies of the national observatory. We want, then, not bounties nor protection, nor even an accurate survey, but simply an exploration and reconnoissance of those seas, which have so recently become the theatre of profitable adventure and brave achievement by our whale-hunters. This service can be performed by officers and crews now belonging to the navy, in two or three vessels which already belong or may be added to it, and would continue, at most, only throughout two or three years. Happily, the measure involves nothing new, untried, or uncommon. To say nothing of our recent search for the lamented Sir John Franklin, nor of our great exploring expedition under Captain Wilkes, we are already engaged in triangulating a coast survey of the Atlantic shore. Charts, light-houses, and beacons, show the pilot his way, not only over that ocean and among its islands, but along all our rivers, and even upon our inland lakes. The absence of similar guides and beacons in the waters now in question, results from the fact that the Pacific coast has but recently fallen under our sway, and Behring's straits and the seas they connect have not until now been frequently navigated by the seamen of any nation. Certainly somebody must do this service. But who will? The whalers can not. No foreign nation will, for none is interested. The constitutional power and responsibility rest with the federal government, and its means are adequate.—*Speech in U. S. Senate, July* 29, 1852.

Commerce on the Pacific.

WHO does not see that every year, hereafter, European commerce, European politics, European thoughts, and European activity, although actually gaining greater force—and European connections, although actually becoming more intimate—will, nevertheless, relatively sink in importance; while the Pacific ocean, its shores, its islands, and the vast regions beyond, will become the chief theatre of events in the world's great hereafter? Who does not see that this movement must effect our own complete emancipation from what remains of European influence and prejudice, and in turn develop the American opinion and influence which shall remould constitutions, laws, and customs, in the land that is first greeted by the rising sun? Sir, although I am no socialist, no dreamer of a suddenly-coming millennium, I nevertheless can not reject the hope that peace is now to have her sway, and that as war has hitherto defaced and saddened the Atlantic world, the better passions of mankind will soon have their development in the new theatre of human activity.

Commerce is the great agent of this movement. Whatever nation shall put that commerce into full employment, and shall conduct it steadily with adequate expansion, will become necessarily the greatest of existing states; greater than any that has ever existed. Sir, you will claim that responsibility and that high destiny for our own country. Are you so sure that by assuming the one she will gain the other? They imply nothing less than universal commerce and the supremacy of the seas. We are second to England, indeed; but, nevertheless, how far are we not behind her in commerce and in extent of empire! I pray to know where you will go that you will not meet the flag of England fixed, planted, rooted into the very earth? If you go northward, it waves over half of this continent of North America, which we call our own. If you go southward, it greets you on the Bermudas, the Bahamas, and the Caribbee islands. On the Falkland islands it guards the straits of Magellan; on the South Shetland island it watches the passage round the Horn; and at Adelaide island it warns you that you have reached the Antarctic circle. When you ascend along the southwestern coast of America, it is seen at Galopagos, overlooking the isthmus of Panama; and, having saluted it there and at Vancouver, you only take leave of it in the far northwest, when you are entering the Arctic ocean. If you visit Africa, you find the same victorious cross guarding the coast of Gambia and Sierra Leone and St. Helena. It watches you at Capetown as you pass into the Indian ocean; while on the northern passage to that vast sea it demands your recognition from Gibraltar, as you enter the Mediterranean; from Malta, when you pass through the Sicilian straits; on the Ionian islands it waves in protection of Turkey; and at Aden it guards the passage from the Red sea into the Indian ocean. Wherever western commerce has gained an entrance to the continent of Asia, there that flag is seen waving over subjugated millions—

at Bombay, at Ceylon, at Singapore, at Calcutta, at Lahore, and at Hong-Kong; while Australia and nearly all the islands of Polynesia acknowledge its protection.

Sir, I need not tell you that wherever that flag waves, it is supported and cheered by the martial airs of England. But I care not for that. The sword is not the most winning messenger that can be sent abroad; and commerce, like power, upheld by armies and navies, may in time be found to cost too much. But what is to be regarded with more concern is, that England employs the steam-engine even more vigorously and more universally than her military force. Steam-engines, punctually departing and arriving between every one of her various possessions and her island-seat of power, bring in the raw material for every manufacture and supplies for every want. The steam-engine plies incessantly there day and night, converting these materials into fabrics of every variety, for the use of man. And again the steam-engine for ever and without rest moves over the face of the deep, not only distributing these fabrics to every part of the globe, but disseminating also the thoughts, the principles, the language, and religion of England. Sir, we are bold indeed to dare competition with such a power. Nevertheless, the resources for it are adequate. We have coal and iron no less than she, while corn, timber, cattle, hemp, wool, cotton, silk, oil, sugar, and the grape, quicksilver, lead, copper, silver, and gold, are all found within our own broad domain in inexhaustible profusion. What energies we have already expended, prove that we have in reserve all that are needful. What inventions we have made, prove our equality to any exigency. Our capital increases, while labor scarcely knows the burden of taxation. Our Panama route to China has a decided advantage over that of the isthmus of Suez, and, at the same time, vessels leaving that country and coming round the Horn will reach New York, always, at least five days sooner than vessels of equal speed can double the cape of Good Hope, and make the port of Liverpool.

Mr. President, we now see how conspicuous a part in the great movement of the age California and Oregon are to sustain, and that, as yet, they are separated from us and isolated. They will adhere to us only so long as our government over them shall be conducted, not for our benefit, but for their own.

Their loyalty is great, but it can not exceed that of the thirteen ancient American colonies to Great Britain; and yet the neglect and oppression of their commerce undermined that loyalty, and resulted in their independence. I hear often of dangers to the Union, and see lines of threatened separation drawn by passionate men or alarmists, on parallels of latitude; but, in my judgment, there is only one danger of severance—and that is involved in the possibility of criminal neglect of the new communities on the Pacific coast, while the summits of the Rocky mountains, and of the Snowy mountains, mark the only possible line of dismemberment. Against that danger I would guard as against the worst calamity that could befall, not only my country, at her most auspicious stage of progress, but mankind also, in the hour of their brightest hopes. I would guard against it by practising impartial justice toward the new and remote states and territories, whose political power is small, while their wants are great, and by pursuing at the same time, with liberality and constancy, the lofty course which they indicate, of an aspiring yet generous and humane national ambition.—*Speech in U. S. Senate, July* 29, 1852.

A Continental Railroad to the Pacific Ocean.—Its Commercial Advantages.

You want first and most, a communication which shall bind New Orleans, and Washington, and New York, on the Atlantic, with San Francisco, on the Pacific. The safety of your country, the safety of its Pacific posessions, demands such a communication—not over oceans exposed to all nations, and through a foreign territory occupied by a discontented, aggrieved, and probably hostile people, but inland, and altogether through your own country. You want, for your own use, for your own commerce, and for the commerce of Asia, a road which shall have the advantage of the best Atlantic and Pacific harbors which can be obtained, with one continuous connection by land, so that there shall be no necessity for reshipment between the Atlantic and Pacific ports—not a way between ports yet to be artificially made, on the Caribbean sea, and on the Pacific coast, with changes from land to water-carriage requiring breaking of bulk at least twice in the course of transit.

If you aim to erect a high commercial structure, you must lay your foundations broadly in agriculture, in mining, and manufacture; and all these within your own domain; and use the resources which God and nature have given to you, and not those which Providence has bestowed upon your neighbors. And you want, for the same reason, a passage across the continent, of your own, not shared with any foreign domain. If you will be the carriers of Europe and of Asia, if you will be the carriers in even your own interoceanic commerce, you must receive, you must convey, you must deliver merchandise, within your own temperate zone, not within that torrid zone whose heats are noxious to animal and vegetable productions, and, while so deleterious to the articles most abundant and most essential to the subsistence of man, pestilential also to human life itself. This is the communication across this continent which you want —*Speech in U. S. Senate, Feb.* 8, 1853.

MISCELLANEOUS.

The American People—Their Moral and Intellectual Development.

A KIND of reverence is paid by all nations to antiquity. There is no one that does not trace its lineage from the gods, or from those who were especially favored by the gods. Every people has had its age of gold, or Augustan age, or heroic age—an age, alas! for ever passed. These prejudices are not altogether unwholesome. Although they produce a conviction of declining virtue, which is unfavorable to generous emulation, yet a people at once ignorant and irreverential would necessarily become licentious. Nevertheless, such prejudices ought to be modified. It is untrue, that in the period of a nation's rise from disorder to refinement, it is not able to continually surpass itself. We see the present plainly, distinctly, with all its coarse outlines, its rough inequalities, its dark blots, and its glaring deformities. We hear all its tumultuous sounds and jarring discords. We see and hear the past, through a distance which reduces all its inequalities to a plane, mellows all its shades into a pleasing hue, and subdues even its hoarsest voices into harmony. In our own case, the prejudice is less erroneous than in most others. The revolutionary age was truly a heroic one. Its exigencies called forth the genius and the talents and the virtues of society, and they ripened amid the hardships of a long and severe trial. But there were selfishness, and vice, and factions, then, as now, although comparatively subdued and repressed. You have only to consult impartial history, to learn that neither public faith, nor public loyalty, nor private virtue, culminated at that period in our own country,* while a mere glance at the literature, or at the stage, or at the politics, of any European country, in any previous age, reveals the fact that it was marked, more distinctly than the present, by licentious morals and mean ambition.

Reasoning *à priori* again, as we did in another case, it is only just to infer in favor of the United States an improvement of morals from their established progress in knowledge and power; otherwise, the philosophy of society is misunderstood, and we must change all our courses, and henceforth seek safety in imbecility, and virtue in superstition and ignorance.

What shall be the test of the national morals? Shall it be the eccentricity of crimes? Certainly not; for then we must compare the criminal eccentricity of to-day with that of yesterday. The result of the comparison would be only this, that the crimes of society change with changing circumstances.

Loyalty to the state is a public virtue. Was it ever deeper-toned or more universal than it is now? I know there are ebullitions of passion and discontent, sometimes breaking out into disorder and violence; but was faction ever more effectually disarmed and harmless than it is now? There is a loyalty that springs from the affection that we bear to our native soil. This we have as strong as any people. But it is not the soil alone, nor yet the soil beneath our feet and the skies over our heads, that constitute our country. It is its freedom, equality, justice, greatness, and glory. Who among us is so low as to be insensible of an interest in them? Four hundred thousand natives of other lands every year voluntarily renounce their own sovereigns, and swear fealty to our own. Who has ever known an American to transfer his allegiance permanently to a foreign power?

The spirit of the laws, in any country, is a true index to the morals of a people, just in proportion to the power they exercise

* "I ought not to object to your reverence for your fathers, as you call them, meaning, I presume, the government, and those concerned in the direction of public affairs; much less could I be displeased at your numbering me among them. But, to tell you a very great secret, as far as I am capable of comparing the merits of different periods, I have no reason to believe that we were better than you are. We had as many poor creatures and selfish beings in proportion, among us, as you have among you; nor were there then more enlightened men, or in greater number in proportion, than there are now."—*John Adams's Letter to Josiah Quincy, Feb. 9, 1811.*

in making them. Who complains, here or elsewhere, that crime or immorality blots our statute-books with licentious enactments?

The character of a country's magistrates, legislators, and captains, chosen by a people, reflect their own. It is true that in the earnest canvassing which so frequently recurring elections require, suspicion often follows the magistrate, and scandal follows in the footsteps of the statesman. Yet, when his course has been finished, what magistrate has left a name tarnished by corruption, or what statesman has left an act or an opinion so erroneous that decent charity can not excuse, though it may disapprove? What chieftain ever tempered military triumph with so much moderation as he who, when he had placed our standard on the battlements of the capital of Mexico, not only received an offer of supreme authority from the conquered nation, but declined it?

The manners of a nation are the outward form of its inner life. Where is woman held in so chivalrous respect, and where does she deserve that eminence better? Where is property more safe, commercial honor better sustained, or human life more sacred?

Moderation is a virtue in private and in public life. Has not the great increase of private wealth manifested itself chiefly in widening the circle of education and elevating the standard of popular intelligence? With forces which, if combined and directed by ambition, would subjugate this continent at once, we have made only two very short wars—the one confessedly a war of defence, and the other ended by paying for a peace and for a domain already fully conquered.

Where lies the secret of the increase of virtue which has thus been established? I think it will be found in the entire emancipation of the consciences of men from either direct or indirect control by established ecclesiastical or political systems. Religious classes, like political parties, have been left to compete in the great work of moral education, and to entitle themselves to the confidence and affection of society, by the purity of their faith and of their morals.

I am well aware that some, who may be willing to adopt the general conclusions of this argument, will object that it is not altogether sustained by the action of the government itself, however true it may be that it is sustained by the great action of society. I can not enter a field where truth is to be sought among the disputations of passion and prejudice. I may say, however, in reply first, that the governments of the United States, although more perfect than any other, and although they embrace the great ideas of the age more fully than any other, are, nevertheless, like all other governments, founded on compromises of some abstract truths and of some natural rights.

As government is impressed by its constitution, so it must necessarily act. This may suffice to explain the phenomenon complained of. But it is true, also, that no government ever did altogether act out, purely and for a long period, all the virtues of its original constitution. Hence it is that we are so well told by Bolingbroke, that every nation must perpetually renew its constitution or perish. Hence, moreover, it is a great excellence of our system, that sovereignty resides, not in Congress and the president, nor yet in the governments of the states, but in the people of the United States. If the sovereign be just and firm and uncorrupted, the governments can always be brought back from any aberrations, and even the constitutions themselves, if in any degree imperfect, can be amended. This great idea of the sovereignty of the people over their government glimmers in the British system, while it fills our own with a broad and glowing light.

"Let not your king and parliament in one,
Much less apart, mistake themselves for that
Which is most worthy to be thought upon,
Nor think they are essentially the STATE.
Let them not fancy that the authority
And privileges on them bestowed,
Conferred, are to set up a majesty,
Or a power or a glory of their own;
But let them know it was for a deeper life
Which they but represent;
That there's on earth a yet auguster thing,
Veil'd though it be, than parliament or king."

Gentlemen, you are devoted to the pursuit of knowledge in order that you may impart it to the state. What Fenelon was to France, you may be to your country. Before you teach, let me enjoin upon you to study well the capacity and the disposition of the American people. I have tried to prove to you only that while they inherit the imperfections of humanity they are yet youthful, apt, vigorous, and virtuous, and therefore, that they are worthy, and will make noble uses of your best instructions.—*Address, Yale College, New Haven, July* 26, 1854.

Insanity.

WHAT is the human mind? It is immaterial, spiritual, immortal; an emanation of the Divine Intelligence, and if the frame in which it dwells had preserved its just and natural proportions, and perfect adaptation, it would be a pure and heavenly existence. But that frame is marred and disordered in its best estate. The spirit has communication with the world without, and acquires imperfect knowledge only through the half-opened gates of the senses. If, from original defects, or from accidental causes, the structure be such as to cramp or restrain the mind, it becomes or appears to be weak, diseased, vicious, and wicked. I know one who was born without sight, without hearing, and without speech, retaining the faculties of feeling and smell. That child was, and would have continued to be an idiot, incapable of receiving or communicating thoughts, feelings or affections; but tenderness unexampled, and skill and assiduity, unparalleled, have opened avenues to the benighted mind of Laura Bridgman, and developed it into a perfect and complete human spirit, consciously allied to all its kindred, and aspiring to Heaven. Such is the mind of every idiot, and of every lunatic, if you can only open the gates, and restore the avenues of the senses; and such is the human soul when deranged and disordered by disease, imprisoned, confounded, benighted. That disease is insanity.

Doth not the idiot eat? Doth not the idiot drink? Doth not the idiot know his father and his mother? He does all this because he is a man. Doth he not smile and weep? Do you think he smiles and weeps for nothing? He smiles and weeps because he is moved by human joys and sorrows, and exercises his reason, however imperfectly. Hath not the idiot anger, rage, revenge? Take from him his food, and he will stamp his feet and throw his chains in your face. Do you think he doth this for nothing? He does it all because he is a man, and because, however imperfectly, he exercises his reason. The lunatic does all this, and, if not quite demented, all things else that man, in the highest pride of intellect does or can do. He only does them in a different way. You may pass laws for his government. Will he conform? Can he conform? What cares he for your laws? He will not even plead; he can not plead his disease in excuse. *You* must interpose the plea for him, and if you allow it, he, when redeemed from his mental bondage, will plead for you when he shall return to your Judge and his. If you deny his plea, he goes all the sooner, freed from imperfection, and with energies restored, into the presence of that Judge. You must meet him there, and then, no longer bewildered, stricken and dumb, he will have become as perfect, clear and bright, as those who reviled him in his degradation, and triumphed in his ruin.

And now what is insanity? Many learned men have defined it for us, but I prefer to convey my idea of it in the simplest manner. Insanity is a disease of the body, and I doubt not of the brain. The world is astonished to find it so. They thought for almost six thousand years that it was an affection of the mind only. Is it strange that the discovery should have been made so late? You know that it is easier to move a burden upon two smooth rails on a level surface, than over the rugged ground. It has taken almost six thousand years to learn that. But moralists argue that insanity shall not be admitted as a physical disease, because it would tend to exempt the sufferer from responsibility, and because it would expose society to danger. But who shall know, better than the Almighty, the ways of human safety, and the bounds of human responsibility?

And is it strange that the brain should be diseased? What organ, member, bone, muscle, sinew, vessel, or nerve, is not subject to disease? What is physical man, but a frail, perishing body, that begins to decay as soon as it begins to exist? What is there of animal existence here on earth exempt from disease and decay? Nothing. The world is full of disease and that is the great agent of change, renovation, and health.

And what wrong or error can there be in supposing that the mind may be so affected by disease of the body as to relieve man from responsibility? You will answer, it would not be safe. But who has assured you of safety? Is not the way of life through dangers lurking on every side, and though you escape ten thousand perils, must you not fall at last? Human life is not safe, nor intended to be safe, against the elements. Neither is it safe, nor intended to be safe, against the moral elements of man's nature. It is not safe against pestilence, nor against war, against the thunderbolts of heaven, nor against the blow of the maniac. But comparative safety can be secured, if you will be wise. You can guard against war, if you will cultivate peace. You can guard against the lightning, if you will learn the laws of electricity, and raise the protecting rod. You will be safe against the maniac, if you will watch the causes of madness, and remove them. Yet after all, there will be danger enough from all these causes to remind you that on earth you are not immortal.

Although my definition would not perhaps be strictly accurate I should pronounce insanity to be a derangement of the mind, character, and conduct, resulting from bodily disease. I take this word derangement, because it is one in common every-day use. We all understand what is meant when it is said that anything is ranged or arranged. The houses on a street are ranged, if built upon a straight line. The fences on your farms are ranged. A single object too may be ranged. A tower, if justly built, is ranged; that is, it is ranged by the plummet. It rises in a perpendicular range from the earth. A file of men marching in a straight line are in range. "Range yourselves, men," though not exactly artistical, is not an uncommon word of command. Now what do we mean when we use the word "*de*ranged"? Manifestly that a thing is not ranged, is not arranged, is out of range. If the houses on the street be built irregularly, they are deranged. If the walls be inclined to the right or left, they are deranged. If there be an unequal pressure on either side, the tower will lean, that is, it will be deranged. If the file of men become irregular, the line will be deranged. So if a man is insane. There was a regular line which he was pursuing; not the same line which you or I follow, for all men pursue different lines, and every sane man has his own peculiar path. All these paths are straight, and all are ranged, though all divergent. It is easy enough to discover when the street, the wall, the tower, or the martial procession, is deranged. But it is quite another thing to determine when the course of an individual life has become deranged. We deal not then with geometrical or material lines, but with an imaginary line. We have no physical objects for landmarks. We trace the line backward by the light of imperfect and unsatisfactory evidence, which leaves it a matter almost of speculation whether there has been a departure or not. In some cases, indeed, the task is easy. If the fond mother becomes the murderer of her offspring, it is easy to see that she is deranged. If the pious man, whose steps were firm and whose pathway led straight to heaven, sinks without temptation into criminal debasement, it is easy to see that he is deranged. But in cases where no natural instinct or elevated principle throws its light upon our research, it is often the most difficult and delicate of all human investigations to determine when a person is deranged.

We have two tests. *First*, to compare the individual after the supposed derangement with himself as he was before. *Second*, to compare his course with those ordinary lines of human life which we expect sane persons, of equal intelligence, and similarly situated, to pursue.

If derangement, which is insanity, mean only what we have assumed, how absurd is it to be looking to detect whether memory, hope, joy, fear, hunger, thirst, reason, understanding, wit, and other faculties, remain? So long as life lasts they never cease to abide with man, whether he pursue his straight and natural way, or the crooked and unnatural course of the lunatic. If he be diseased, his faculties will not cease to act. They will only act differently. It is contended here that the prisoner is not deranged because he performed his daily task in the state-prison, and his occasional labor afterward; because he grinds his knives, fits his weapons, and handles the file, the axe, and the saw, as he was instructed, and as he was wont to do. Now, the lunatic asylum at Utica has not an idle person in it, except the victims of absolute and incurable dementia, the last and worst stage of insanity. Lunatics are almost the busiest people in the world. They have their prototypes only in children. One lunatic will make a garden, another drive the plough, another gather flowers. One writes poetry, another essays, another orations. In short, lunatics eat, drink, sleep, work, fear, love, hate, laugh, weep, mourn, die. They do all things that sane men do, but do them in some peculiar way. It is said, however, that this prisoner has hatred and anger, that he has remembered his wrongs, and nursed and cherished revenge; wherefore, he can not be insane. Cowper, a moralist who had tasted the bitter cup of insanity, reasoned otherwise: —

> "But violence can never longer sleep
> Than human passions please. In ev'ry heart
> Are sown the sparks that kindle fi'ry war,
> Occasion needs but fan them and they blaze,
> The seeds of murder in the breast of man."

Melancholy springs oftenest from recalling and brooding over wrong and suffering. Melancholy is the first stage of madness, and it is only recently that the less accurate name of monomania has been substituted in the place of melancholy. Melancholy is the foster-mother of anger and revenge.—*Argument in Defence of William Freeman, July*, 1846.

Insanity.—Some of its Causes and Circumstances.

ALL writers agree, what it needs not writers should teach, that *neglect of education* is a fruitful cause of insanity. If neglect of education produces crime, it equally produces insanity. Here was a bright, cheerful, happy child,* destined to become a member of the social state, entitled by the principles of our government to equal advantages for perfecting himself in intelligence, and even in political rights, with each of the three millions of our citizens, and blessed by our religion with equal hopes. Without his being taught to read, his mother, who lives by menial service, sends him forth at the age of eight or nine years to like employment. Reproaches are cast on his mother, on Mr. Warden, and on Mr. Lynch, for not sending him to school, but these reproaches are all unjust. How could she, poor degraded negress and Indian as she was, send her child to school? And where was the school to which Warden and Lynch should have sent him? There was no school for him. His few and wretched years date back to the beginning of my acquaintance here, and during all that time, with unimportant exceptions,

* William Freeman.—See p. 99.

there has been no school here for children of his caste. A school for colored children was never established here, and all the common schools were closed against them. Money would always procure instruction for my children, and relieve me from the responsibility. But the colored children who have from time to time been confided to my charge, have been cast upon my own care for education. When I sent them to school with my own children, they were sent back to me with a message that they must be withdrawn because they were black, or the school would cease. Here are the fruits of this unmanly and criminal prejudice. A whole family is cut off in the midst of usefulness and honors by the hand of an assassin. . . . .

Mere *imprisonment* is often a cause of insanity. Four insane persons have, on this trial, been mentioned as residing among us, all of whom became insane in the stateprison. Authentic statistics show that there are never less than thirty insane persons in each of our two great penitentiaries. In the stateprison, the prisoner was subjected to severe corporeal punishment by keepers, who mistook a decay of mind and morbid melancholy for idleness, obstinacy, and malice. Beaten, as he was, until the organs of his hearing ceased to perform their functions, who shall say that other and more important organs connected with the action of his mind did not become diseased through sympathy? Such a life, so filled with neglect, injustice, and severity, with anxiety, pain, disappointment, solicitude, and grief, would have its fitting conclusion in a madhouse. If it be true, as the wisest of inspired writers hath said, "Verily, oppression maketh a wise man mad," what may we not expect it to do with a foolish, ignorant, illiterate man! . . . . . .

There is proof, gentlemen, stronger than all this. It is silent, yet speaking. It is that *idiotic* smile which plays continually on the face of the maniac. It took its seat there while he was in the stateprison. In his solitary cell, under the pressure of his severe tasks and trials in the workshop, and during the solemnities of public worship in the chapel, it appealed, although in vain, to his taskmasters and his teachers. It is a smile, never rising into laughter, without motive or cause — the smile of vacuity. His mother saw it when he came out of prison, and it broke her heart. John Depuy saw it and knew his brother was demented. Deborah Depuy observed it and knew him for a fool. David Winner read in it the ruin of his friend, Sally's son. It has never forsaken him in his later trials. He laughed in the face of Parker, while on confession at Baldwinsville. He laughed involuntarily in the faces of Warden and Curtis, and Worden and Austin, and Bigelow and Smith, and Brigham and Spencer. He laughs perpetually here. Even when Van Arsdale showed the scarred traces of the assassin's knife, and when Helen Holmes related the dreadful story of the murder of her patrons and friends, he laughed. He laughs while I am pleading his griefs. He laughs when the attorney-general's bolts would seem to rive his heart. He will laugh when you declare him guilty. When the judge shall proceed to the last fatal ceremony, and demand what he has to say why the sentence of the law should not be pronounced upon him, although there should not be an unmoistened eye in this vast assembly, and the stern voice addressing him should tremble with emotion, he will even then look up in the face of the court and laugh, from the irresistible emotions of a shattered mind, delighted and lost in the confused memory of absurd and ridiculous associations. Follow him to the scaffold. The executioner can not disturb the calmness of the idiot. He will laugh in the agony of death. Do you not know the significance of this strange and unnatural risibility? It is a proof that God does not forsake even the poor wretch whom we pity or despise. There are in every human memory a well of joys and a fountain of sorrows. Disease opens wide the one, and seals up the other, for ever. . . .

That chaotic smile is the external derangement which signifies that the strings of the harp are disordered and broken, the superficial mark which God has set upon the tabernacle, to signify that its immortal tenant is disturbed by a divine and mysterious visitation. If you can not see it, take heed that the obstruction of your vision be not produced by the mote in your own eye, which you are commanded to remove before you consider the beam in your brother's eye. If you are bent on rejecting the testimony of those who know, by experience and by science, the deep affliction of the prisoner, beware how you misinterpret the handwriting of the Almighty.—*Argument in Defence of William Freeman*, 1846.

The Wrongs of the Negro.

I HAVE heard the greatest of American orators; I have heard Daniel O'Connell and Sir Robert Peel; but I heard John Depuy make a speech excelling them all in eloquence: "They have made William Freeman what he is, a brute beast; they don't make anything else of any of our people but brute beasts; but when we violate their laws, then they want to punish us as if we were men."

DEBORAH DEPUY is also assailed as unworthy of credit. She calls herself the wife of Hiram Depuy, with whom she has lived ostensibly in that relation for seven years, in, I believe, unquestioned fidelity to him and her children. But it appears that she has not been married with the proper legal solemnities. If she were a white woman, I should regard her testimony with caution, but the securities of marriage are denied to the African race over more than half of this country. It is within our own memory that the master's cupidity could divorce husband and wife within this state, and sell their children into perpetual bondage. Since the act of emancipation here, what has been done by the white man to lift up the race from the debasement into which he had plunged it? Let us impart to negroes the knowledge and spirit of Christianity, and share with them the privileges, dignity and hopes of citizens and Christians, before we expect of them purity and self-respect.

But, gentlemen, even in a slave state, the testimony of this witness would receive credit in such a cause, for negroes may be witnesses there, for and against persons of their *own* caste. It is only when the life, liberty, or property of the white man is invaded, that the negro is disqualified. Let us not be too severe. There was once upon the earth a Divine Teacher who shall come again to judge the world in righteousness. They brought to him a woman taken in adultery, and said to him that the law of Moses directed that such should be stoned to death, and he answered: "Let him that is without sin cast the first stone."

The testimony of SALLY FREEMAN, the mother of the prisoner, is questioned. She utters the voice of NATURE. She is the guardian whom God assigned to study, to watch, to learn, to know what the prisoner was, and is, and to cherish the memory of it for ever. She could not forget it if she would. There is not a blemish on the person of any one of us, born with us or coming from disease or accident, nor have we committed a right or wrong action, that has not been treasured up in the memory of a mother. Juror! roll up the sleeve from your manly arm and you will find a scar there of which you know nothing. Your mother will give you the detail of every day's progress of the preventive disease. — Sally Freeman has the mingled blood of the African and Indian races. She is nevertheless a woman, and a mother, and nature bears witness in every climate and in every country, to the singleness and uniformity of those characters. I have known and proved them in the hovel of the slave, and in the wigwam of the Chippewa. But Sally Freeman has been intemperate. The white man enslaved her ancestors of the one race, exiled and destroyed those of the other, and debased them all by corrupting their natural and healthful appetites. She comes honestly by her only vice. Yet when she comes here to testify for a life that is dearer to her than her own, to say she knows her own son, the white man says she is a drunkard! May Heaven forgive the white man for adding this last, this cruel injury to the wrongs of such a mother! Fortunately, gentlemen, her character and conduct are before you. No woman ever appeared with more sobriety, decency, modesty, and propriety, than she has exhibited here. No witness has dared to say or think that Sally Freeman is not a woman of truth. A witness for the prosecution, who knows her well, says, that with all her infirmities of temper and of habit, Sally "was always a truthful woman." The Roman Cornelia could not have claimed more. Let then the stricken mother testify for her son.

"I ask not, I care not, if guilt's in that heart,
I know that I love thee, whatever thou art!"

The circumstances under which this trial closes are peculiar. I have seen capital cases where the parents, brothers, sisters, friends of the accused surrounded him, eagerly hanging upon the lips of his advocate, and watching, in the countenances of the court and jury, every smile and frown which might seem to indicate his fate. But there is no such scene here. The prisoner, though in the greenness of youth, is withered, decayed, senseless, almost lifeless. He has no father here. The descendant of slaves, that father died a victim to the vices of a superior race. There is no mother here, for her child is stained and polluted with the blood of mothers and of a sleeping infant; and he "looks and laughs so that she can not bear to look upon him." There is no brother, nor sister, nor friend here. Popular rage against the accused has driven them hence, and scattered his kindred and people. On the other side, I notice the aged and venerable parents of Van Nest and his surviving children, and all around are mourning and sympathizing friends. I know not at whose instance they have come. I dare not say they ought not to be here. But I must say to you that we live in a Christian and not in a savage state, and that the affliction which has fallen upon these mourners and us, was sent to teach them and us mercy and not retaliation; that, although we may send this maniac to the scaffold, it will not recall to life the manly form of Van Nest, nor re-animate the exhausted frame of that aged matron, nor restore to life, and grace, and beauty, the murdered mother, nor call back the infant boy from the arms of his Savior. Such a verdict can do no good to the living, and carry no joy to the dead.—*Argument in Defence of William Freeman*, 1846.

The Indians—Speech of an Onondaga Chief.

GREAT FATHER: Your children, the Onondagas, have sent me to you, and they ask you to open your ears to me, and hear the talk which they have sent by me to you. . . .

Father: you are young in years; we hope you are old in counsel—so our white brethren tell us, and we believe it. And your red children would like to know what is your mind, and whether it is like our other white fathers, who have sat in council before you at the great council-fire in Albany, and who are now dead. . . .

Father: Listen once more. The chiefs, and warriors, and women of the Onondagas have had a long council—a talk of three days; and their request to their father is, that he will shut his ears, shake his head, and turn his face away from all talk to him about the sale of the lands of the Onondagas. We know he can do it, and drive them away—preserve the nation in peace—keep them together in friendship—and not scatter them like the Oneidas.

We now make our last request. Will our father think of the talk which his red children have now sent him? Will he send them his mind? Will he remember his children of the Onondagas, as our white fathers have done, and let them continue to lie under his shade, as they have done under the shade of their white fathers before him? Will he also be a father to them, and send them his mind? This is all that is sent by me, and I have done.

Governor Seward's Reply.

I HAVE considered the talk you have made to me in behalf of the sachems, chiefs, and warriors of the Onondagas. I am sorry to hear that the avarice of white men and the discontent of red men have excited alarms among your people. I rejoice, and all good white men rejoice, to hear that the Onondagas have determined to banish the use of strong water—that they assume the habits and customs of civilized life, cultivate their lands, possess oxen and horses, and desire to remain in the land of their brave and generous, though unfortunate forefathers.

Why should the Onondagas exchange their homes among us for the privations of the wilderness in the far west? They are a quiet, inoffensive, and improving people. The public welfare does not require that they should be banished from their native land. Although individuals often improve their fortunes by emigration, the removal of a whole community is always followed by calamity and distress. With temperance, industry, and education, the Onondagas may be comfortable and happy, and in time they may become good citizens of the state.

White men ought to be just and generous to your race. Indians, but a few years ago, possessed all this broad domain. Now the white men own all, except the small parcels which have been reserved as a home for the remnants of the Indian tribes. There is one common Father of all mankind. Although his ways are inscrutable, we know that his benevolence extends to all his children alike, and his blessings rest upon those who protect the defenceless and succor the unfortunate.

Say to your people that I heard their message with attention; that I approve their determination to retain their lands and remain under the protection of the state; that, so far as depends upon my exertions, the treaties made with them shall be faithfully kept; that if white men seek to obtain their lands by force or fraud, I will set my face against them; if red men propose to sell the lands, I will expostulate with them, and endeavor to convince them of their error, and that I will in no event consent to such sale, except with the free, and unbought, and uncorrupted consent of the chiefs, head men, warriors, and people of the Onondagas, and not even then without an effort to persuade them that their true happiness would be promoted by retaining their possessions, cultivating their lands, and enjoying the comforts with which our common Father has surrounded them. The Onondagas may confide in me.—*Albany, March* 6, 1840.

Letter—Reply to the Colored Citizens of Albany.

If prejudice, interest, and passion, did sometimes counsel me that what seemed to be the rights of the African race might be overlooked without compromise of principle, and even with personal advantage, yet I never have been able to find a better definition of equality than that which is contained in the Declaration of Independence, or of justice, than the form which our religion adopts. If, as the former asserts, all men are born free and equal, institutions which deny them equal political rights and advantages are unjust, and if I would do unto others as I would desire them to do unto me, I should not deny them any right on account of the hue they wear, or of the land in which they or their ancestors were born.

Only time can determine between those who have upheld, and those who have opposed the measures to which you have adverted. But I feel encouraged to wait that decision, since, in the moment when, if ever, reproaches for injustice should come, the exile does not reproach me, the prisoner does not exult in my departure, and the disfranchised and the slave greet me with their salutations. And if every other hope of my heart shall fail, the remembrance that I have received the thanks of those who have just cause to upbraid the memory of our forefathers, and to complain of our contemporaries, will satisfy me that I have not lived altogether in vain.

May that God whose impartial love knows no difference among those to whom he has imparted a portion of his own spirit, and upon whom he has impressed his own image, reward you for your kindness to me now and in times past, and sanction and bless your generous and noble efforts to regain all the rights of which you have been deprived.—*Jan.* 10, 1843.

The Militia System—Reforms proposed.*

I AM aware that the amendments I have submitted are such an innovation upon the existing militia system, as to require, if not an apology for offering them, at least an explanation of the necessity for a change of some kind. Complaints long and loud have been made of the defects of the system, and the oppressive burden it imposes upon the people; these complaints have, at length, reached the executive ear, and have drawn from the governor a recommendation to the consideration of the legislature. I do not know that I should have ventured to suggest the amendments, had not the committee of the senate, after mature deliberation, reported a bill which can be regarded in no other light but as going immediately to change the whole system, and, in the result, to abolish it. This bill originates in the deep conviction, I doubt not, of the committee, that *some* law must be proposed to relieve the people from the trouble of military duty under the present organization. I confess that it is not my object to destroy the system; but, at the same time, that I would relieve the people from the burden it imposes—I would, if possible, preserve and improve the militia, and would elevate it so that it might be what it ought to be—the ornament of the country, and the safeguard of the rights and liberties of the people.

* * * * * * * * * *

I propose as a remedy for the evils I have mentioned—

1st. To reduce the number of the militia who shall be required to perform military duty, to some much smaller number—say fifty thousand, sixty thousand, or seventy thousand; the last

* This appears to have been Mr. Seward's first parliamentary effort.—ED.

being, I believe, about the number of uniformed troops, in the present organization, and I would, I confess, prefer to sustain those whose public spirit and military ardor have induced them to assume their present organization.

2d. To make the performance of military duty voluntary, as far as practicable.

This force, if it consist of but fifty thousand men, may be subdivided into five divisions, ten brigades, fifty regiments, and five hundred companies. After what I fear has been a tedious detail of the evils and defects of the present system, it will be necessary to state, but very briefly, the advantages of the proposed system. They would be—that the force could be well and easily organized. It could be uniformed—disciplined to some considerable extent; not only the officers, but the troops could be improved in military skill. All this could be done, because there are nearly, if not quite, the requisite number of young men, who would be able and willing to encounter the expense of filling up the ranks. And if necessary that legislative encouragement should be afforded, it could be done to any requisite extent at much less expense than is now drawn from the yeomanry of the country to sustain the present defective system. Men would then seek and obtain the offices in the militia, who would have the ability and spirit necessary for the discharge of the important duties attached to them.

Adopt such a system, and I feel assured that the militia, instead of being degraded, ridiculed, and despised, will be respected, honored, and valued; men enough will *volunteer* to take its most subordinate ranks, from the patriotic desire to be among those upon whom the republic will rely for its defenders, and from the honorable ambition for military promotion. . . . .

Finally, the time has come to decide whether the militia system shall be preserved or abandoned. It can be no longer maintained without radical alteration and amendment. And though members may wish to preserve it, they will find it as hopeless as the attempt to retain the snow which melts more rapidly with the pressure of the hand.

I have looked upon the system with veneration, while I have felt and acknowledged the justice of the popular complaint against it; and, under the influence of mingled solicitude arising from both these causes, I have long endeavored to find a remedy for the evils I have mentioned. Of all which I have imagined and heard suggested, this appears to me most feasible, as well as most likely to be effectual. It is with a degree of diffidence I have ventured to give my views on the subject, which only can be overcome by a sense of my responsibility, before I can give a vote which will go to the eventual abolition of the system; to offer the best exertion in my power to procure it, and, at the same time, to meet the requirements of the people. I have always felt that the militia system is a relic of the age of the Revolution too valuable to be idly thrown away; that it is a strong and beautiful pillar of the government which ought not to be rudely torn from its base. But if no effectual remedy can be found in legislative wisdom, I shall feel myself bound, though with reluctance, to vote at all hazards for such a bill as will redress the evils the system imposes, and to trust to the exigencies of invasion, insurrection, or oppression, for a regeneration of the military spirit which brought the nation into existence, and will, if restored in its primitive purity and vigor, be able to carry us through the dark and perilous ways of national calamity yet unknown to us, but which must, at some time, be trodden by all nations.—*Speech in N. Y. Senate, Feb.* 11, 1831.

The Public Domain—The Homestead Principle.

THE aggregate quantity of the national estate is fifteen hundred and eighty-four millions of acres; of which, one hundred and thirty-four millions have been definitely appropriated, and there remain, including appropriations not yet perfected, fourteen hundred and fifty millions of acres.

Using only round numbers, these lands are distributed among the states and territories as follows:—

	Acres.
In Ohio	745,000
Indiana	2,751,000
Illinois	14,060,000
Missouri	29,216,000
Alabama	17,238,000
Mississippi	14,308,000
Louisiana	22,854,000
Michigan	24,864,000

Arkansas	27,402,000
Florida	31,801,000
Iowa	27,153,000
Wisconsin	26,321,000
Minnesota	56,000,000
Northwest Territory	376,000,000
Oregon Territory	218,536,000
Nebraska Territory	87,488,000
Indian Territory	119,789,000
California and Utah	287,162,000
New Mexico	49,727,000

The domain came to the United States encumbered with a right of possession by Indian tribes, which we are gradually extinguishing by purchase, as the necessities of advancing population require.

At the establishment of the federal government, the United States suffered from exhaustion by war, and labored under the pressure of a great national debt, while they were obliged to make large expenditures for new institutions, and to prepare for defence by land and by sea. They therefore adopted a policy which treated the domain merely as a fund or source of revenue. They divided it into townships, sections, and quarter-sections, and offered it at public sale, at a minimum price of two dollars per acre, on credit, and subsequently at private sale, on the same terms. In 1820, they abolished the credit system, and reduced the price to one dollar and twenty-five cents per acre. In 1833, they recognised a right of pre-emption in favor of actual occupants; and the system, as thus modified, still remains in form upon our statute-book. The United States, however, have, at different times, made very different dispositions of portions of the domain. Thus there have been appropriated to the new states and territories, for purposes of internal improvement, for saline reservations, for the establishment of seats of government and public buildings, and for institutions of education, as follows:

	Acres.
To Ohio	1,847,575
Indiana	2,331,690
Illinois	1,649,024
Missouri	1,793,748
Alabama	1,473,994
Mississippi	1,384,944

Louisiana	1,332,124
Michigan	1,674,598
Arkansas	1,489,220
Wisconsin	217,920
Iowa	46,720
Florida	1,553,635

Besides these appropriations, the senate will at once recall several acts of Congress, which surrendered, in the whole, seventy-nine millions of acres for bounties in the Mexican war, bounties in the war of 1812, subsequent gratuities to the soldiers in the same war and in Indian wars, cessions of swamp lands to new states, and for the construction of a railroad from Chicago to Mobile, and other internal improvements, none of which last-named cessions have yet been located.

The aggregate of revenues derived from the public domain is one hundred and thirty-five millions three hundred and thirty-nine thousand ninety-three dollars and ninety-three cents, showing an annual average revenue of one and a quarter million of dollars since the system of sales was adopted.

Mr. President, I think the time is near at hand when the United States will find it expedient to review their policy, and to consider the following principles:—

First. That lands shall be granted in limited quantities, gratuitously, to actual cultivators only.

Second. That the possessions of such grantees shall be secured against involuntary alienation.

Third. That the United States shall relinquish to the states the administration of the public lands within their limits.

If the public lands were movable merchandise, price would be the principal, if not the only subject of inquiry. On the contrary, it is only the money received by the government on sales that perishes or passes away. The lands remain fixed just where they were before the sale, and they constitute a part of the territory subject to municipal administration as much after sale as before. The possessors of the land sold become soon, if not immediately, citizens, and they will ultimately be a majority of the whole population of the country, supporting the government by their contributions, maintaining it by their arms, and wielding it for their own and the general welfare. To look, then, at this subject merely with reference to the revenue that might be derived from the sale of the lands, would be to commit the fault of that least erected spirit that fell from heaven, whose

"Looks and thoughts
Were always downward bent, admiring more
The riches of Heaven's pavement, trodden gold,
Than aught divine, or holy, else enjoyed."

All will admit—all do admit—that the power over the domain should be so exercised as to favor the increase of population, the augmentation of wealth, the cultivation of virtue, and the diffusion of happiness. . . . .

Commercial supremacy demands just such an agricultural basis as the fertile and extensive regions of the United States, when inhabited, will supply. Political supremacy follows commercial ascendency. It was by reason of the want of just such an agricultural basis that Venice, Portugal, and Holland, successively lost commerce and empire. It was for the purpose of securing just such a basis, that France, England, and Spain, seized so eagerly and held so tenaciously the large portions of this continent which they respectively occupied. It was for the purpose of supplying the loss of this basis, that England has, within the last seventy years, extended her conquests over a large portion of India.

We now possess this basis, and all that we need is to develop its capabilities as fully and as rapidly as possible. Nor ought we to overlook another great political interest. Mutual jealousies delayed a long time the establishment of the Union of these states, and have ever since threatened its dissolution. It is apparent that the ultimate security for its continuance is found in the power of the states established, and hereafter to be established, on the public domain. Those new and vigorous communities continually impart new life to the entire commonwealth, while the absolute importance of free access to the ocean will secure their loyalty, even if the fidelity of the Atlantic states shall fail. Such as these, sir, may have been some of the considerations that induced Andrew Jackson so long ago to declare his opinion, that the time was not distant when the public domain ought to cease to be regarded as a source of revenue. Such considerations may have had some influence with the late distinguished senator from South Carolina [J. C. CALHOUN], to propose a release of the public domain to the states, on their paying a small per centum of revenue to the United States; and we are at liberty to suppose that a course of reasoning not entirely unlike this, brought that eminent statesman, who is now secretary of state [DANIEL WEBSTER] to propose here, a year ago, a gratuitous appropriation of the public domain to actual settlers.—*Speech in U. S. Senate, Feb.* 27, 1851.

The Whig Party.

THE inhabitants of the banks of the Nile have a tradition that the greatest of the Egyptian pyramids was built by the antediluvians, and they venerate that great obelisk as the only work of that mighty race that has withstood the floods that changed and deformed the face of nature. Something like this is the reverence I feel toward the whig party. It was erected not this year, nor a few years ago. Its foundations were laid and its superstructure reared by the mighty men of ages now remote—by the Hampdens, the Sidneys, the Vanes, and the Miltons—by the presbyterians, the puritans, the republicans, the whigs, of England—those who first secured the responsibility of kings by bringing the tyrant Charles to the block, and the inviolability of parliaments by erecting, even in England, Scotland, and Ireland, a commonwealth. Then and there arose the whig party—that party which now, under whatever name, in every civilized country, advocates the cause of constitutional, representative government, with watchful jealousy of executive power. Of that race, who feared only God, and loved liberty, were the founders of Virginia and of New England; and the catholic founders of Maryland and the peaceful settlers of Pennsylvania were worthy associates with them. Here they established governments of which Europe was not worthy, and to perpetuate them they founded institutions for the education of children and for the worship of God.

Thus early was promulgated the pure whig creed—equal popular representative government, jealousy of executive power, the education of children, and the worship of God. When the prosperity of these colonies excited the cupidity of the parent-state, and the king and parliament invaded the rights of the

American people, there were two parties as there always have been since, and always will be hereafter. One of them adhered to the colonies through perils of confiscation and death—the other clung to the throne of England. The one was whig—and the other was—I will not call a name that the error of ultra loyalty then rendered odious, and thenceforth and for ever infamous. I desire to be understood. I by no means impute to our opponents that they have succeeded to the loyalists of the Revolution. I aver solemnly my belief that, as a general truth, all men of all parties are alike honest and patriotic citizens, and seek their country's good alone. Political life would have been unprofitable indeed if it had not taught me the virtue of candor in judging others, as well as the great error of always expecting candor in their judgments on myself. * * * *

Which, then, is the whig party? which the republican? which the true democratic party—the party of liberty, of equality, of humanity—the party of hope, of progress, and of civilization? Let the history of the past, let the developments of the future, determine. The whig party has committed errors. Human nature can not but err. Individuals often err, and masses still more frequently. But the errors of the whig party are always on the side of law, of order, and of popular liberty. Let us take care to correct all our errors, and let us take care that no errors of conduct, no partial or temporary interests, no prejudices unworthy of freemen or of men, retard the progress of this great party of our hopes and our affections. Let it continue to occupy all its broad foundations—to offer security, protection, improvement, and elevation, to all conditions of men, as all conditions of men alike enjoy the impartial favor of God, and are entitled to impartial representation in government.—*Speech, Auburn, Feb.* 22, 1844.

The Albany Regency in 1824.*

HONEST and honorable men are convinced that a combination exists in this state, enjoys its honors, and wields its power, whose

* This address is among Mr. Seward's earliest political efforts. At the time it was written (1824) he was but twenty-three years old. A more faithful portrait of the "Albany Regency" could scarcely have been drawn by a practised hand or at a later period.

principles and practices are at war with its best interest, its prosperity, and its fame.

The history of this combination begins when, taking advantage of the strong current of popular opinion in favor of a correction of the errors of the old constitution of this state, a few men who were clamorous for reform, but whose lives had exhibited not one sacrifice for the public good, united with a few others until then unknown among us, because they had done nothing worthy of notice, and all becoming loud in their protestations of devotion to republicanism, they succeeded in obtaining seats in the late constitutional convention.

Defeated then in their efforts to retain the old council of appointment which they had hoped to wield at their pleasure, they succeeded in incorporating into the new constitutional system an institution, the evils of which are more severe than those which were produced by the justly obnoxious features of the system which was abolished — an institution which combines in one strong phalanx the officeholders, from the governor and the senators down to the justices of the peace in the most remote parts of the state — which makes the governor a subservient tool of the faction which designates him; converts the otherwise respectable judiciaries of the counties into shambles for the bargain and sale of offices; and selects justices of the peace (in whose courts are decided questions involving a greater amount of property than in all the other tribunals of the state), not from among those whom an intelligent people would choose, but from the supple and needy parasites of power, who may, and it is to be feared do, bring not only the influence but the very authority of their offices to the support of the party whose creatures they are. Thus it has come to pass that each of the several counties contains a little aristocracy of officeholders, existing independently of popular control, while they are banded together by ties of common political brotherhood.

Another part of their organization which presents serious ground of apprehension, is the caucus system. It was in vain that the framers of the constitution placed a barrier between those who should make the laws and those who should execute them. The doctrine of construction has been extended so far by ingenuity and subtlety, that their union is no longer an anomaly. Men chosen to make laws, have constituted themselves a power to appoint those by whom they shall be executed. The effect is, that these men have themselves become the subjects of barter and sale. Public and beneficent laws are seldom seen in their journals, while their pages are swollen with laws to accommodate politicians and speculators. Republican dignity and simplicity are banished from the public councils, and faction has obtruded its unblushing front into the halls of legislation. The caucus system, originally adopted for necessity, and never considered obligatory further than its nominations concurred with popular opinion, has been converted into a political inquisition. Patriotism is made to consist in a servile submission to its decrees. Offices and honors are offered to those only who will renounce their independence, and give their support to the "old and established usages of the party," while denunciations without measure are poured forth upon the heads of those who dare to question the infallibility of the decrees thus obtained. These denunciations have had their effect upon weak and timid minds, while the inducements offered on the other hand have not failed to enlist profligate politicians. These systems constitute the machinery of the Albany regency. Honest men need no such aid to maintain a just influence. The safety of the state is not to be secured, nor its welfare to be promoted, by combinations to deprive the people of their constitutional power. When in republican states men attempt to entrench themselves beyond the popular reach, their designs require investigation. Such men have for three years exercised the authority of this state. And what have they done to promote its prosperity or to add to its renown? The judiciary, once our pride, is humbled and degraded. The march of internal improvement is retarded, and the character of the state is impaired. Let the proceedings of the present legislature speak—a legislature composed of members, most of whom were pledged in their several counties, and all of whom were instructed to restore to the people their constitutional right of appointing electors of president and vice-president of the United States. Yet its journals exhibit little else than contradictory measures, affecting private corporations, together with all the practices of chicanery and open opposition to the very law they were required to pass.—*Address*, 1824.

Secret Political Societies.

If virtue yet abide among us, if there be intelligence in our fellow-citizens to appreciate the dangers which threaten their liberty, and if there be patriotism to resist and prevent them, which we most firmly believe, there can be no doubt of the result of such a contest. On the one side is an aristocratic nobility, composed of men bound together by the most terrific oaths, which conflict with the administration of justice, with private rights, and with the public security; a privileged order, claiming and securing to its members unequal advantages over their fellow-citizens, veiling its proceedings from scrutiny by pledges of secrecy, collecting funds to unknown amounts and for unknown purposes, and operating through our extended country at any time and on any subject, with all the efficacy of perfect organization, controlled and directed by unseen and unknown hands. On the other side, a portion of your fellow-citizens ask for equal rights and equal privileges among the freemen of this country. They say it is in vain that this equality of rights and privileges is secured in theory by our constitutions and laws, if, by a combination to subvert it, it is in fact no longer enjoyed. They point you to masonic oaths, and to the effects of those dreadful obligations upon our elections, upon witnesses in courts of justice, and upon jurors. They show you one of your citizens murdered under their influence, and the offenders escaping with impunity. They exhibit to you the power of your courts defied, and the administration of justice defeated, through the instrumentality of those obligations. And they ask you whether our country can any longer be described as a land "where no man is so powerful as to be above the law, and no one so humble as to be beneath its protection."—*Legislative Address*, 1831.

Relief for the Indigent Insane.—The Union and the States.

Congress has passed a bill by which ten millions of acres of the public domain are granted to the several states, with unquestioned equality, on condition that they shall accept the same, and sell the lands at not less than one dollar per acre, and safely invest the gross proceeds, and for ever apply the interest thereon to the maintenance of their indigent insane inhabitants. This grant is a contribution to the states, made from a peculiar national resource, at a time when the treasury is overflowing. It is made at the suggestion, and it is not stating the case too strongly to say, through the unaided, unpaid, and purely disinterested influence of an American woman [Miss Dix], who, while all other members of society have been seeking how to advance their own fortunes and happiness, or the prosperity and greatness of their country, has consecrated her life to the relief of the most pitiable form in which the Divine Ruler afflicts our common humanity.

The purpose of the bill has commended it to our warmest and most active sympathies. Not a voice has censured it, in either house of Congress. It is the one only purpose of legislation, sufficiently great to arrest attention, that has met with universal approbation throughout the country, during the present session. It seems as if some sad fatality attends our public action, when this measure is singled out from among all others, to be baffled and defeated by an executive veto. Such, however, is the fact. The bill has been returned by the president, with objections which it is now our constitutional duty to consider.

* * * * * * * * * *

The president expresses deep concern lest this contribution by the federal government to the states should impair their vigor and independence. But it is not easy to see how a contribution which they are at liberty to reject, and which they are to apply to a necessary and proper purpose of government, in entire independence of the federal government, can wound their self-respect, or deprive them of any of their attributes of sovereignty.

The president is moreover, deeply disturbed by an apprehension, that if the policy of this bill should be pursued, its noble purposes would be defeated, and the fountains of charity within the states would be dried up. The president must not needlessly afflict himself in this wise, on the score of humanity. Experience is against his fears. Congress has never manifested a disposition of profuse liberality toward the states. Every community that has received from the federal territory or property, military bounties or pensions is at least as brave and patriotic as it was before. Every community that has received from the same sources contributions for the purposes of internal improvement is more enterprising than before. Every community that has received aid for its schools of learning has been rendered more zealous and more munificent in the cause of education.

As in the early days of the republic, there was a school of latitudinarian construction of the constitution, which school was quite erroneous; so, also, there is now a school whose maxim is strict construction of the constitution, and this school has accumulated precedents and traditions equally calculated to extinguish the spirit of the constitution. Circumstances have altogether changed since that school was founded. The states were then rich and strong; the Union was poor and powerless. Virginia lent to the United States a hundred thousand dollars to build their capitol. But the states could not enlarge themselves. They possessed respectively either no public lands at all, or very small domains, and to such domains they have added nothing by purchase or by conquest. Charged with all the expenses of municipal administration, including the relief of the indigent, the cure of the diseased, the education of the people, and the removal of natural obstructions to trade and intercourse, they reserved, nevertheless, only the power to raise revenues by direct taxation, one which always was and always will be regarded with jealousy and dislike, and is therefore never one that can be freely exercised.

The Union, on the contrary, by conquest and purchase, has quadrupled its domain, and is in possession of superabundant revenues, derived from that domain and from imposts upon foreign commerce, while it also enjoys the power of direct taxation. Contrast the meager salaries of the officers of the states with the liberal ones enjoyed by the agents of the Union. Contrast the ancient, narrow, and cheerless capitols of Annapolis, Harrisburg, and Albany, with this magnificent edifice, amplifying itself to the north and the south, while it is surrounded by gardens traversed by spacious avenues and embellished with fountains and statuary, and you see at once that the order of things has been reversed, and that it tends now not merely to concentration, but to consolidation. I know not how others may be affected by this tendency, but I confess that it moves me to do all that I can, by a fair construction of the constitution, not to abate the federal strength, and diminish the majesty of the Union, but to invigorate and aggrandize the states, and to enable them to maintain their just equilibrium in our grand but exquisitely-contrived political system.—*Speech in U. S. Senate on the President's Message vetoing the Bill granting Lands to the several States for the Relief of the Indigent Insane, June* 19, 1854.

The True Basis of American Independence.

I AM far from supposing that we are signally deficient in independence. I know that it is a national, an hereditary, and a popular sentiment; that we annually celebrate, and always glory in our independence. We do so justly, for nowhere else does even a form or a shadow of popular independence exist; while here it is the very rock on which our institutions rest. Nevertheless, occasions for the exercise of this virtue may be neglected.

We hold in contempt, equally just and profound, him who imposes, and him who wears, a menial livery; and yet, I think, that we are accustomed to regard with no great severity, the employer who exacts, or the mechanic, clerk, or laborer, who yields, political conformity in consideration of wages. We insist, as we ought, that every citizen in the state shall be qualified by education for citizenship; but we are by no means unanimous that one citizen, or class of citizens, shall not prescribe its own creed, in the instruction of the children of others. We construct and remodel partisan formulas and platforms with changing circumstances with almost as much diligence and versatility as the Mexicans; and we attempt to enforce conformity to them, with scarcely less of zeal and intolerance, not indeed by the sword, but by the greater terror of political proscription. We resist argument, not always with argument, but often with personal denunciation, and sometimes even with combined violence. We differ, indeed, as to the particular errors of political faith, that shall be corrected by this extreme remedy; but, nevertheless, the number of those who altogether deny its necessity and suitableness in some cases, is very small.

We justly maintain that a free press is the palladium of liberty; and yet, mutually proscribing all editorial independence that is manifested by opposition to our own opinions, we have only attained a press that is free in the sense that every interest, party, faction, or sect, can have its own independent organ. If it be still maintained, notwithstanding these illustrations to the contrary, that entire social independence prevails, then, I ask, why is it so necessary to preserve with jealousy, as we justly do, the ballot, in lieu of open suffrage; for if every citizen is really free from all fear and danger, why should he mask his vote more than his face. Believe me, fellow-citizens, independence always languishes in the very degree that intolerance prevails. We smile at the vanity of the factory-girl at Lowell, who, having spent the secular part of the week in making calicoes for the use of her unsophisticated countrywomen, disdainfully arrays herself on Sundays exclusively in the tints of European dyes; and yet, we are indifferent to the fact that beside a universal consumption of foreign silks, excluding the silkworm from our country, we purchase, in England alone, one hundred and fifty millions of yards of the same stained muslins. We sustain, here and there, a rickety, or at best a contracted iron manufactory; while we import iron to make railroads over our own endless ore fields, and we carry our prejudices against our struggling manufacturers and mechanics so far as to fastidiously avoid wearing on our persons, or using on our tables, or displaying in our drawing-rooms, any fabric, of whatsoever material, texture, or color, that, in the course of its manufacture, has to our best knowledge and belief, ever come in contact with the honest hand of an American citizen. In all this, we are less independent than the Englishman, the Frenchman, or even the Siberian.

It is painful to confess the same infirmity in regard to intellectual productions. We despise, deeply and universally, the spoiled child of pretension, who, going abroad for education or observation, with a mind destitute of the philosophy of travel, returns to us with an affected tone and gait, sure indications of a craven spirit and a disloyal heart. And yet how intently do we not watch to see whether one of our countrymen obtains in Europe the honor of an aristocratic dinner, or of a presentation, in a grotesque costume, at court! How do we not suspend our judgment on the merits of the native artist, be he dancer singer, actor, limner, or sculptor, and even of the native author, inventor, orator, bishop, or statesman, until, by flattering those who habitually depreciate his country, he passes safely the ordeal of foreign criticism, and so commends himself to our own most cautious approbation. How do we not consult foreign mirrors, for our very virtues and vices, not less than for our fashions, and think ignorance, bribery, and slavery, quite justified at home, if they can be matched against oppression, pauperism, and crime, in other countries!

On occasions too, we are bold in applauding heroic struggling for freedom abroad; and we certainly have hailed with enthusiasm every republican revolution in South America, in France, in Poland, in Germany, and in Hungary. And yet how does not our sympathy rise and fall, with every change of the political temperature in Europe? In just this extent, we are not only not independent, but we are actually governed by the monarchies and aristocracies of the Old World.

You may ask impatiently, if I require the American citizen to throw off all submission to law, all deference to authority, and all respect to the opinions of mankind, and that the American Republic shall constantly wage an aggressive war against all foreign systems? I answer, no. There is here, as everywhere, a middle and a safe way. I would have the American citizen yield always a cheerful acquiescence, and never a servile adherence, to the opinions of the majority of his countrymen and of mankind, whether they be engrossed in the forms of law or not, on all questions involving no moral principle; and even in regard to such as do affect the conscience, I would have him avoid not only faction, but even the appearance of it. But I demand, at the same time, that he shall have his own matured and independent convictions, the result not of any authority, domestic or foreign, on every measure of public policy, and so, that while always temperate and courteous, he shall always be a free and outspeaking censor, upon not only opinions, customs, and administration, but even upon laws and constitutions themselves. What I thus require of the citizen, I insist, also, that he shall allow to every one of his fellow-citizens. I would have the nation also, though moderate and pacific, yet always frank, decided and firm, in bearing its testimony against error and oppression; and while abstaining from forcible intervention in foreign disputes, yet always fearlessly rendering to the cause of republicanism everywhere, by influence and example, all the aid that the laws of nations do not peremptorily, or, in their true spirit, forbid.

Do I propose in this an heretical, or even a new standard of public or private duty? All agree that the customary, and even the legal standards in other countries are too low. Must we then abide by them now and for ever? That would be to yield our independence, and to be false toward mankind. Who will maintain that the standard established at any one time by a majority in our country is infallible, and therefore final? If it be so, why have we reserved, by our constitution, freedom of speech, of the press, and of suffrage, to reverse it? No, we may change every thing, first complying, however, with constitutional conditions. Storms and commotions must indeed be avoided, but the political waters must nevertheless be agitated always, or they will stagnate. Let no one suppose that the human mind will consent to rest in error. It vibrates, however, only that it may settle at last in immutable truth and justice. Nor need we fear that we shall be too bold. Conformity is always easier than contention; and imitation is always easier than innovation. There are many who delight in ease, where there is one who chooses, and fearlessly pursues, the path of heroic duty.

Moreover, while we are expecting hopefully to see foreign customs and institutions brought, by the influence of commerce, into conformity with our own, it is quite manifest that commerce has reciprocating influences, tending to demoralize ourselves, and so to assimilate our opinions, manners, and customs, ultimately to those of aristocracy and despotism. We can not afford to err at all on that side. We exist as a free people only by force of our very peculiarities. They are the legitimate peculiarities of republicanism, and, as such, are the test of nationality.

Nationality! It is as just as it is popular. Whatever policy, interest, or institution, is local, sectional, or foreign, must be zealously watched and counteracted; for it tends directly to social derangement, and so to the subversion of our democratic constitution.

But it is seen at once that this nationality is identical with that very political independence which results from a high tone of individuality on the part of the citizen. Let it have free play, then, and so let every citizen value himself at his just worth, in body and soul; namely, not a serf or a subject of any human authority, or the inferior of any class, however great or wise, but a freeman, who is so because "Truth has made him free;" who not only, equally with all others, rules in the republic, but is also bound, equally with any other, to exercise designing wisdom and executive vigor and efficiency in the eternal duty of saving and perfecting the state. When this nationality shall prevail, we shall no more see fashion, wealth, social rank, political combination, or even official proscription, effective in suppressing the utterance of mature opinions and true convictions; and so enforcing for brief periods, with long reactions, political conformity, at the hazard of the public welfare, and at the cost of the public virtue. . . . .

Let this nationality prevail, and then we shall cease to undervalue our own farmers, mechanics, and manufacturers, and their productions; our own science, and literature, and inventions; our own orators and statesmen; in short, our own infinite resources and all-competent skill, our own virtue, and our own peculiar and justly envied freedom.—*Address, American Institute, N. Y., Oct.* 20, 1853.

Peace.

THE first want of every nation is peace, the last is peace. It wants peace always. So our forefathers understood the philosophy of government; for they established a system which dispensed with even the forces necessary for perfect defence, rather than cumber it with such as might tempt it to unnecessary collision with other states. A democratic government has no adaptation to war. War involves a nation in debt, and requires vast supplies of men and taxes, and self-taxing people will not, except when absolutely obliged by the exigencies of danger, vote either one or the other. Our government has not effective powers of conscription. No modern state has carried on, or can carry on, aggressive war without conscription. War, however brief its duration, and however light its calamities, deranges all social industry, subverts order and corrupts public morals. The first element, then, of our social happiness and security is PEACE.—*Speech, Oct.* 29, 1844.

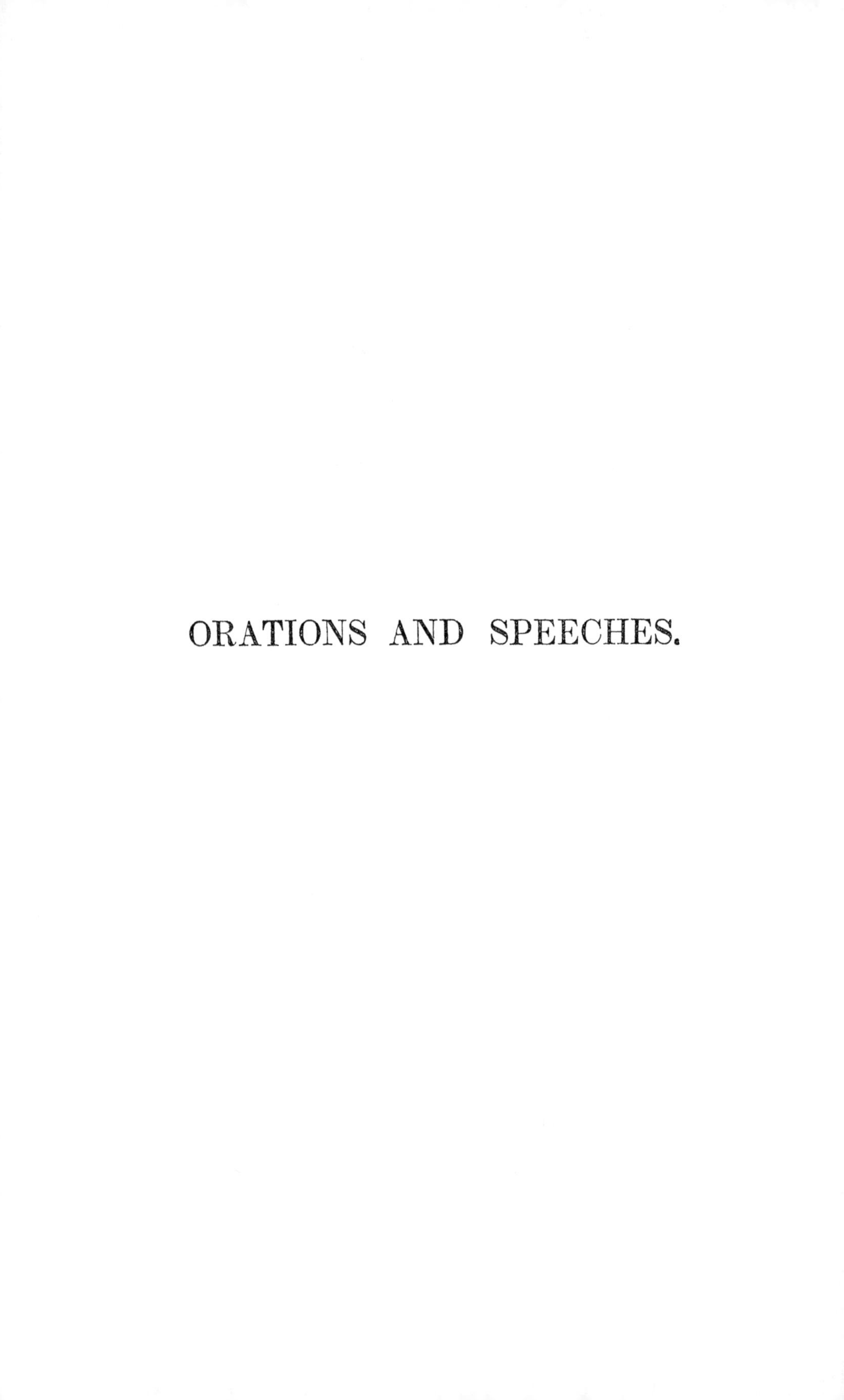

ORATIONS AND SPEECHES.

THE DESTINY OF AMERICA.*

THIS scene is new to me, a stranger in Ohio, and it must be in a degree surprising even to yourselves. On these banks of the Scioto, where the elk, the buffalo, and the hissing serpent haunted not long ago, I see now mills worked by mute mechanical laborers, and warehouses rich in the merchandise of many climes. Steeds of vapor on iron roads and electrical messengers on pathways which divide the air, attest the concentration of many novel forms of industry, while academic groves, spacious courts, and majestic domes, exact the reverence always eminently due to the chosen seats of philosophy, religion, and government.

What a change, moreover, has within the same short period come over the whole country that we love so justly and so well. High arcs of latitude and longitude have shrunk into their chords, and American language, laws, religion, and authority, once confined to the Atlantic coast, now prevail from the northern lakes to the southern gulf, and from the stormy eastern sea to the tranquil western ocean.

Nevertheless it is not in man's nature to be content with present attainment or enjoyment. You say to me therefore with excusable impatience, "Tell us not what our country is, but what she shall be. Shall her greatness increase? Is she immortal?"

I will answer you according to my poor opinion. But I pray you first, most worthy friends, to define the greatness and immortality you so vehemently desire.

* Oration at the Dedication of Capital University, Columbus, Ohio, September 14, 1853.

If the Future which you seek consists in this; that these thirty-one states shall continue to exist for a period as long as human foresight is allowed to anticipate after coming events; that they shall be all the while free; that they shall remain distinct and independent in domestic economy, and nevertheless be only one in commerce and foreign affairs; that there shall arise from among them and within their common domain even more than thirty-one other equal states, alike free, independent, and united; that the borders of the federal republic so peculiarly constituted shall be extended so that it shall greet the sun when he touches the tropic, and when he sends his glancing rays toward the polar circle, and shall include even distant islands in either ocean; that our population, now counted by tens of millions, shall ultimately be reckoned by hundreds of millions; that our wealth shall increase a thousand fold, and our commercial connections shall be multiplied, and our political influence be enhanced in proportion with this wide development, and that mankind shall come to recognise in us a successor of the few great states which have alternately borne commanding sway in the world—if this, and only this is desired, then I am free to say that if, as you will readily promise, our public and private virtues shall be preserved, nothing seems to me more certain than the attainment of this future, so surpassingly comprehensive and magnificent.

Indeed, such a future seems to be only a natural consequence of what has already been secured. Why then shall it not be attained? Is not the field as free for the expansion indicated as it was for that which has occurred? Are not the national resources immeasurably augmented and continually increasing? With telegraphs and railroads crossing the Detroit, the Niagara, the St. Johns, and the St. Lawrence rivers, with steamers on the lakes of Nicaragua, and a railroad across the isthmus of Panama, and with negotiations in progress for passages over Tehuantepec and Darien, with a fleet in Hudson's bay and another at Bhering's straits, and with yet another exploring the La Plata, and with an armada at the gates of Japan, with Mexico ready to divide on the question of annexation, and with the Sandwich islands suing to us for our sovereignty, it is quite clear to us that the motives to enlargement are even more active than they ever were heretofore, and that the public energies, instead of being relaxed, are gaining new vigor.

Is the nation to become suddenly weary and so to waver and fall off from the pursuit of its high purposes? When did any vigorous nation every become weary even of hazardous and exhausting martial conquests? Our conquests on the contrary, are chiefly peaceful, and thus far have proved productive of new wealth and strength. Is a paralysis to fall upon the national brain? On the contrary, what political constitution has ever throughout an equal period exhibited greater elasticity and capacity for endurance?

Is the union of the states to fail? Does its strength indeed grow less with the multiplication of its bonds? Or does its value diminish with the increase of the social and political interests which it defends and protects? Far otherwise. For all practical purposes bearing on the great question, the steam engine, the iron road, the electric telegraph, all of which are newer than the Union, and the metropolitan press, which is no less wonderful in its working than they, have already obliterated state boundaries and produced a physical and moral centralism more complete and perfect than monarchical ambition ever has forged or can forge. Do you reply nevertheless that the Union rests on the will of the several states, and that, no matter what prudence or reason may dictate, popular passion may become excited and rend it asunder. Then I rejoin, When did the American people ever give way to such impulses? They are practically impassive. You remind me that faction has existed, and that only recently it was bold and violent. I answer that it was emboldened by popular timidity, and yet that even then it succumbed. Loyalty to the Union is not in one or many states only, but in all the states, the strongest of all public passions. It is stronger, I doubt not, than the love of justice or even the love of equality, which have acquired a strength here never known among mankind before. A nation may well despise threats of sedition that has never known but one traitor, and this will be learned fully by those who shall hereafter attempt to arrest any great national movement by invoking from their grave the obsolete terrors of disunion.

But you apprehend foreign resistance. Well, where is our

enemy? Whence shall he come? Will he arise on this continent? Canada has great resources and begins to give signs of a national spirit. But Canada is not yet independent of Great Britain. And she will be quite too weak to be formidable to us when her emancipation shall have taken place. Moreover, her principles, interests, and sympathies, assimilate to our own just in the degree that she verges toward separation from the parent country. Canada, although a province of Great Britain, is already half annexed to the United States. She will ultimately become a member of this confederacy if we will consent, an ally if we will not allow her to come nearer. At least she can never be an adversary. Will Mexico, or Nicaragua, or Guatemala, or Ecuador, or Peru, all at once become magically cured of the diseases inherited from aboriginal and Spanish parentage, and call up armies from under the earth and navies from the depths of the sea, and thus become the Rome that shall resist and overthrow this overspreading Carthage of ours? Or are we to receive our death-stroke at the hand of Brazil, doubly cursed as she is above all other American states by her adoption of the two most absurd institutions remaining among men, European monarchy and American slavery.

Is an enemy to come forth from the islands in adjacent seas? Where then shall we look for him? On the Antilles, or on the Bermudas, or on the Bahamas? Which of the conflicting social elements existing together, yet unmixed, there, is ultimately to prevail? Will it be Caucasian or African? Can those races not only combine but become all at once aggressive and powerful?

Shall we look for an adversary in Europe? Napoleon said at St. Helena, "America is a fortunate country. She grows by the follies of our European nations." Since when have those nations grown wise? If they have at last become wise, how is it that America has nevertheless not ceased to grow? But what European state will oppose us? Will Great Britain? If she fears to grapple with Russia advancing toward Constantinople on the way to India, though not only her prestige, but even her empire is threatened, will she be bold enough to come out of her way to seek an encounter with us? Who will feed and pay her artisans while she shall be engaged in destroying her American debtors and the American consumers of her fabrics? Great

Britain has enough to do in replacing in Ireland the population that island has yielded to us, in subjecting Africa, in extending her mercantile dominion in Asia, and in perpetually readjusting the crazy balance of power in Europe, so essential to her safety. We have fraternal relations with Switzerland, the only republic yet lingering on that continent. Which of the despotic powers existing there in perpetual terror of the contagion of American principles will assail us and thus voluntarily hasten on that universal war of opinion which is sure to come at some future time, and which whenever it shall have come, whether it be sooner or later, can end only in the subversion of monarchy and the establishment of republicanism on its ruins throughout the world?

Certainly no one expects the nations of Asia to be awakened by any other influences than our own from the lethargy into which they sunk nearly three thousand years ago, under the spells of superstition and caste. If they could be roused and invigorated now, would they spare their European oppressors and smite their American benefactors? Nor has the time yet come, if indeed it shall come within many hundred years, when Africa, emerging from her primeval barbarism, shall vindicate the equality of her sable races in the rights of human nature, and visit upon us the latest, the least guilty and the most repentant of all offenders, the wrongs she has so long suffered at the hands of so many of the Caucasian races.

No! no, we can not indeed penetrate the eternal counsels, but reasoning from what is seen to what is unseen, deducing from the past probable conjectures of the future, we are authorized to conclude that if the national virtue shall prove sufficient the material progress of the United States which equally excites our own pride and the admiration of mankind, is destined to indefinite continuance.

But is this material progress even to the point which has been indicated the whole of the future which we desire? It is seen at once that it includes no high intellectual achievement, and no extraordinary refinement of public virtue, while it leaves entirely out of view the improvement of mankind. Now there certainly is a political philosophy which teaches that nations like individuals are equal, moral, social, responsible persons, existing not for objects of merely selfish advantage and enjoyment, but for the performance of duty, which duty consists in elevating themselves and all mankind as high as possible in knowledge and virtue; that the human race is one in its origin, its rights, its duties, and its destiny, that throughout the rise, progress, and decline of nations, one divine purpose runs—the increasing felicity and dignity of human nature—and that true greatness or glory, whether of individuals or of nations, is justly measured, not by the territory they compass, or the wealth they accumulate, or the fear they inspire, but by the degree in which they promote the accomplishment of that great and beneficent design of the Creator of the universe.

"The great end and object of life," said Socrates, "is the perfection of the intellect, the great moral duty of man is knowledge, and the object of all knowledge is one, namely, Truth, the Good, the Beautiful, the Divine Reason."

So also Plato taught that "Man ought to strive after and devote himself to the contemplation of the ONE, the ETERNAL, the INFINITE."

Cicero wrote, "There are those who deny that any bond of law or of association for purposes of common good exists among citizens. This opinion subverts all union in a state. There are those who deny that any such bond exists between themselves and strangers, and this opinion destroys the community of the Human Race."

Bacon declared that there was in man's nature "a secret love of others, which if not contracted, would expand and embrace all men."

These maxims proceed on the principle of the unity of the race, and of course of a supreme law regulating the conduct of men and nations upon the basis of absolute justice and equality. Locke adopted them when he inculcated that while there was a "law of popular opinion or reputation," which in society was "the measure of virtue and vice," and while there was a civil law which in the state was "the measure of crime and innocence," there was also a divine law which extended over "all society and all states, and which was the only touchstone of moral rectitude."

Guizot closed his recital of the decline of Roman civilization, with these equally true and momentous reflections: "Had not the Christian church existed at this time the whole world must have fallen a prey to mere brute force. The Christian church alone possessed a moral power. It maintained and promulgated the idea of a precept, of a law superior to all human authority. It proclaimed that great truth, which forms the only foundation of our hope for humanity, that there exists a law above all human laws, which by whatever name it may be called, whether reason, the law of God, or what not, is at all times and in all places the same, under different names."

It ought not to excite any surprise when I aver that this philosophy worked out the American Revolution. "Can anything," said John Adams, in replying to one who had apologized for the stamp-act,—"Can anything not abominable have provoked you to commence, an enemy to human nature?"

Alexander Hamilton, though less necessary to the Revolution than John Adams, was even more necessary to the reconstruction of society. He directed against the same odious stamp-act the authority of British law as he found it written down by Blackstone. "The law of nature being coeval with God himself is of course superior to any other. It is binding over all the globe, in all countries, and at all time. No human laws are of any validity if contrary to this; and such of them as are valid derive all their authority mediately or immediately from this original." Then, as if despising to stand on any mere human authority, however high, the framer of the American constitution proceeded, "The sacred rights of mankind are not to be rummaged for among old parchments or musty records. They are written as with a sunbeam in the whole volume of human nature, and can never be erased or obscured by mortal power."

How justly Knox conceived the true character of the chief personage of the Revolution, even at its very beginning, "The great and good Washington, a name which shall shine with distinguished lustre in the annals of history, a name dear to the friends of the liberties of mankind."

La Fayette closed his review of the Revolution when returning to France with this glowing apostrophe: "May this great temple which we have just erected to liberty always be an instruction to oppressors, an example to the oppressed, a refuge for the rights of the human race, and an object of delight to the manes of its founders."

"Happy," said Washington when announcing the treaty of peace to the army, "thrice happy shall they be pronounced hereafter, who shall have contributed anything, who shall have performed even the meanest office in erecting this stupendous fabric of freedom and empire on the broad basis of independency, who shall have assisted in protecting the rights of human nature and establishing an asylum for the poor and oppressed of all nations and religions."

You remember well that the Revolutionary Congress in the Declaration of Independence placed the momentous controversy between the colonies of Great Britain on the absolute and inherent equality of all men. It is not however so well understood that that body closed its existence on the adoption of the federal constitution with this solemn injunction addressed to the People of the United States, "Let it be remembered that it has ever been the pride and boast of America, that the rights for which she contended were the rights of human nature."

No one will contend that our fathers after effecting the Revolution and the independence of their country by proclaiming this system of beneficent political philosophy, established an entirely different one in the constitution assigned to its government. This philosophy then, is the basis of the American constitution.

It is moreover a true philosophy, deduced from the nature of man and the character of the Creator. If there were no supreme law, then the world would be a scene of universal anarchy, resulting from the eternal conflict of peculiar institutions and antagonistic laws. There being such a universal law, if any human constitutions and laws differing from it could have any authority, then that universal law could not be supreme. That supreme law is necessarily based on the equality of nations of races and of men. It is a simple, self-evident basis. One nation, race, or individual, may not oppress or injure another, because the safety and welfare of each is essential to the common safety and welfare of all. If all are not equal and free, then who is entitled to be free, and what evidence of his superiority can he bring from nature or revelation? All men necessarily have a common interest in the promulgation and maintenance of these principles, because it is equally in the nature of men to be content with the enjoyment of their just rights, and to be discontented under the privation of them. Just so far as these principles practically prevail, the stringency of government is safely relaxed, and peace and harmony obtained. But men can not maintain these principles, or even comprehend them, without a very considerable advance in knowledge and virtue. The law of nations, designed to preserve peace among mankind, was unknown to the ancients. It has been perfected in our own times by means of the more general dissemination of knowledge and practice of the virtues inculcated by Christianity. To disseminate knowledge and to increase virtue therefore among men, is to establish and maintain the principles on which the recovery and preservation of their inherent natural rights depend, and the state that does this most faithfully, advances most effectually the common cause of human nature.

For myself, I am sure that this cause is not a dream, but a reality. Have not all men consciousness of a property in the memory of human transactions available for the same great purposes, the security of their individual rights and the perfection of their individual happiness? Have not all men a consciousness of the same equal interest in the achievements of invention, in the instructions of philosophy, and in the solaces of music and the arts? And do not these achievements, instructions, and solaces, exert everywhere the same influences, and produce the same emotions in the bosoms of all men? Since all languages are convertible into each other by correspondence with the same agents, objects, actions, and emotions, have not all men practically one common language? Since the constitutions and laws of all societies are only so many various definitions of the rights and duties of men, as those rights and duties are learned from nature and revelation, have not all men practically one code of moral duty? Since the religions of men in their various climes are only so many different forms of their devotion toward a Supreme and Almighty Power entitled to their reverence and receiving it under the various names of Jehovah, Jove, and Lord, have not all men practically one religion? Since all men are seeking liberty and happiness for a season here, and to deserve and so to secure more perfect liberty and happiness some where in a future world, and since they all substantially agree that these temporal and spiritual objects are to be attained only through the knowledge of truth and the practice of virtue, have not mankind practically one common pursuit, through one common way, of one common and equal hope and destiny?

If there had been no such common humanity as I have insisted upon, then the American people would not have enjoyed the sympathies of mankind when establishing institutions of civil and religious liberty here, nor would their establishment here have awakened in the nations of Europe and of South America desires and hopes of similar institutions there. If there had been no such common humanity, then we should not, ever since the American Revolution, have seen human society throughout the world divided into two parties, the high and the low—the one perpetually foreboding and earnestly hoping the downfall, and the other as confidently predicting and as sincerely desiring the durability, of republican institutions. If there had been no such common humanity, then we should not have seen this tide of emigration from insular and continental Europe, flowing into our country through the channels of the St. Lawrence, the Hudson, and the Mississippi—ebbing, however, always with the occasional rise of the hopes of freedom abroad, and always swelling again into greater volume when those premature hopes subside. If there were no such common humanity, then the peasantry and the poor of Great Britain would not be perpetually appealing to us against the oppression of landlords on their farms and workmasters in their manufactories and mines: and so, on the other hand, we should not be, as we are now, perpetually framing apologies to mankind for the continuance of African slavery among ourselves. If there were no such common humanity, then the fame of Wallace would have long ago died away in his native mountains, and the name even of Washington would at most have been only a household word in Virginia, and not, as it is now, a watchword of hope and progress throughout the world.

If there had been no such common humanity, then when the civilization of Greece and Rome had been consumed by the fires of human passion, the nations of modern Europe could never have gathered from among its ashes the philosophy, the arts, and the religion, which were imperishable, and have reconstructed with those materials that better civilization which, amid the conflicts and fall of political and ecclesiastical systems, has been constantly advancing toward perfection in every succeeding age. If there had been no such common humanity, then the dark and massive Egyptian obelisk would not have everywhere reappeared in the sepulchral architecture of our own times, and the light and graceful orders of Greece and Italy would not, as now, have been the models of our villas and our dwellings, nor would the simple and lofty arch and the delicate tracery of Gothic design have been, as it now is, everywhere consecrated to the service of religion.

If there had been no such common humanity, then would the sense of the obligation of the Decalogue have been confined to the despised nation who received it from Mount Sinai, and the prophecies of Jewish seers and the songs of Jewish bards would have perished for ever with their temple, and never afterward could they have become, as they now are, the universal utterance of the spiritual emotions and hopes of mankind. If there had been no such common humanity, then certainly Europe and Africa and even new America would not, after the lapse of centuries, have recognised a common Redeemer from all the sufferings and perils of human life in a culprit who had been ignominiously executed in the obscure Roman province of Judea; nor would Europe have ever gone up in arms to Palestine to wrest from the unbelieving Turk the tomb where that culprit had slept for only three days and nights after his descent from the cross; much less would his traditionary instructions, preserved by fishermen and publicans, have become the chief agency in the renovation of human society through after-coming ages.

But, although this philosophy is undeniably true, yet it would be a great error to believe that it has ever been, or is likely soon to be, universally accepted. Mankind accept philosophy just in proportion as intellectual and moral cultivation enable them to look through proximate to ultimate consequences. While they are deficient in that cultivation, peace and order, essential to the very existence of society, are necessarily maintained by force. Those who employ that force seek to perpetuate their power, and they do this most effectually by dividing classes and castes, races and nations, and arraying them for mutual injury or destruction against each other. Despotism effects and perpetuates this division by unequal laws, subversive of those of reason and of God. Moreover, a common instinct of fear combines the oppressors of all nations in a league against the advance of that political philosophy which comes to liberate mankind. Those who inculcate this philosophy, therefore, necessarily encounter opposition and expose themselves to danger; and inasmuch as they labor from convictions of duty and motives of benevolence, with such hazards of personal safety, their principles and character are justly regarded as heroic. Adams, Hamilton, La Fayette, Knox, and Washington, although they were the champions of human nature — a cause dear to all men — were saved from the revolutionary scaffold only by the success of their treason against a king whom the very necessities of society required to reign. Milton's "Defence of the People of England," which was in truth a promulgation of the same philosophy which we have been examining, was burned by the public executioner, and its immortal author only by good fortune escaped the same punishment. The American colonists derived this philosophy chiefly from the instructions of Locke, Sidney, and Vane. Locke fled into exile, and Sidney and Vane perished as felons. Cicero, an earlier professor of the same philosophy, fell on the sword of a public assassin, and Socrates, who first inculcated it, drank the fatal hemlock, under a judicial sentence, in the jail of Athens.

Still this philosophy, although heroic, is by no means, therefore, to be regarded as unnecessary and visionary. The true heroic in human thought and conduct is only the useful in the higher regions of speculation and activity. If republicanism, or purely popular government, is the only form of political constitution which permits the development of liberty and equality, which are only other names for political justice, and if republicanism can only be established by the overthrow of despotism, then this philosophy is absolutely necessary to effect the freedom of mankind. All the citizens of this republic agree with us thus far. But with many this is rather a speculation than a vital faith, and so they hesitate to allow full activity to the principles thus acknowledged, through fear of disturbing the harmony of society and the peace of the world. Nevertheless, it is clear that the same philosophy which brings republican institutions into existence must be exclusively relied upon to defend and perpetuate them. A tree may indeed stand and grow and flourish for many seasons, although it is unsound at the heart; but just because it is so unsound, its leaves will ultimately wither, its branches will fall, and its trunk will decay. It is only the house that is built upon the rock that can surely and for ever defy the tempests and the waves. The founders of this republic knew this great truth right well, for they said: "If justice, good faith, honor, gratitude, and all the other qualities which ennoble a nation and fulfil the ends of government, shall be the fruits of our establishments, then the cause of liberty will acquire a dignity and a lustre which it has never yet enjoyed, and an example will be set which can not but have the most favorable influence on mankind. If, on the other side, our governments should be unfortunately blotted with the reverse of these cardinal virtues, then the great cause which we have engaged to vindicate will be dishonored and betrayed. The last and fairest experiment of human nature will be turned against them, and their patrons and friends will be silenced by the insults of the votaries of tyranny and oppression."*

The example of Rome is often commended to us for our emulation. Let us consider it then with becoming care. Rome had indeed forms of religion and morals and a show of philosophy and the arts, but in none of these was there more than the faintest recognition of a universal humanity. Her predecessor, Greece, had, in a brilliant but brief and precocious career, invented the worship of nature, or, in other words, the worship of deities, which were only names given to the discovered forces of nature. This religion did not indeed exalt the human mind to a just conception of the Divine, but, on the other hand, it did not altogether consign it to the sphere of sensuality. Rome unfortunately rejected even this poor religion, because it was foreign and because it was too spiritual; and in its stead she established one which practically was the worship of the state itself. The senate elected gods for Rome, and these were ex-

* Address of the Continental Congress, 1789.

pected to reward that distinguished partiality by showing peculiar and discriminating favor to the people of Rome, and the same political authority appointed creed, precepts, ritual, and priesthood. Does it need amplification to show what the character of the creed, the precepts, the ritual, and the priesthood, thus established necessarily were? All were equally licentious and corrupt.

As was the religion, so of course were the morals of Rome. Ambition was the sole motive of the state. At first every town in Italy, and afterward every nation, however remote, was regarded as an enemy to be conquered, not in retaliation for any injuries received, nor even for the purpose of amending its barbarous institutions and laws, but to be despoiled and enslaved, that Rome might be rich and might occupy the world alone. Fraud, duplicity, and treachery, might be practised against the foreigner, and every form of cruelty might be inflicted upon the captive who had resisted in self-defence or in defence of his country. Military valor not only became the highest of virtues but exclusively usurped the name of virtue. The act of parricide was the highest of crimes, not however because of its gross inhumanity, but because by a legal fiction the father was a sacred type of the Roman state. The sway of Rome, as it spread over the world as then known, nevertheless gravitated toward the city and centred in the order of Patricians. The Plebeians were degraded and despised because their ancestors were immigrants. Below the Plebeians there was yet a lower order, consisting of prisoners-of-war and their offspring, always numerous enough to endanger the safety of the state. These were slaves, and the code of domestic servitude established for the captured Africans and their descendants in some parts of our own country is a meliorated edition of that which Rome maintained for the government of slaves as various in nation, language, and religion, as the enemies she conquered. These orders, mutally hostile and aggressive, were kept asunder by discriminating laws and carefully-cherished prejudices. The Patricians divided the public domain among themselves, although Plebeian blood was shed as profusely as their own in acquiring it. The Patricians alone administered justice, and they even kept the forms of its administration a profound mystery sealed against the knowledge of those for whose safety and welfare the laws existed. The Plebeian could approach the courts only as a client in the footsteps of a Patrician patron, and for his aid in obtaining that justice which of course was an absolute debt of the state the Patrician was entitled to the support of his client in every enterprise of personal interest and ambition. Thus did Rome, while enslaving the world, blindly prepare the machinery for her own overthrow by the agency of domestic factions. Industry in Rome was dishonored. The Plebeians labored with the slaves. Patricians scorned all employments but that of agriculture and the service of the state. And so Rome rejected commerce and the arts. The person of the Patrician was inviolable, while the Plebeian forfeited liberty and for a long period even life by the failure to pay debts which his very necessities obliged him to contract. The slaves held their lives by the tenure of their masters' forbearance, and what that forbearance was we learn from the fact that they arrayed the slaves against each other, when trained as gladiators, in mortal combat for the gratification of their own pride and the amusement of the people. Punishments were graduated, not by the inherent turpitude of the crimes committed, nor by the injury or danger resulting from them to the state, but by the rank of the offender. What was that Roman liberty of which in such general and captivating descriptions we read so much? The Patrician enjoyed a licentious freedom, the Plebeian an uncertain and humiliating one, extorted from the higher order by perpetual practices of sedition. According to the modern understanding of popular rights and character, there was no people in Rome. So at least we learn from Cicero: "*Non est enim consilium in vulgo. Non ratio, non discrimen, non diligentia. Semperque sapienter ea quæ populus ferenda non laudanda.*"

The domestic affections were stifled in that wild society. The wife was a slave and might be beaten, transferred to another lord, or divorced at pleasure. The father slew his children whenever their care and support became irksome, and the state approved the act. In such a society the rich and great of course grew always richer and greater, and the poor and low always poorer and more debased; and yet throughout all her long career did Rome never establish one public charity, nor has history preserved any memorable instances of private benevolence. Such was the life of Rome under her kings and consuls. She attained the end of her ambition, and became, as her historian truly boasts, "*Populus Romanus victor dominusque omnium gentium.*" But at the same time the city trembled always at the very breathing of popular discontent, and every citizen and even the senate, generals, and consuls, were every hour the slaves of superstitious fears of the withdrawal of the favor of the gods. The people sighing for milder and more genial laws, after the lapse of many centuries recovered the lost code which the good king Numa had received from the goddess Egeria. Do we wonder that the senate interdicted its publication, lest it might produce agitation dangerous to the public peace? Or can we be surprised when we read that Cicero, whose philosophy was only less than divine, when he found that the republic was actually falling into ruins, implored his new academy to be silent?

You know well the prolonged but fearful catastrophe, the civil and the servile wars, the dictatorship, the usurpation, the empire, the military despotism, the insurrections in the provinces, the invasion by barbarians, the division and the dismemberment and the fall of the state, the extinction of the Roman name, language, and laws, and the destruction of society, and even civilization itself, not only in Italy, but throughout the world, and the consequent darkness which overshadowed the earth throughout seven centuries. This is the moral of a state whose material life is stimulated and perfected, while its spiritual life is neglected and extinguished.

And now it is seen that the future which we ought to desire for our country involves besides merely physical prosperity and aggrandizement, corresponding intellectual development and advancement in virtue also. Has our spiritual life hitherto improved equally with our material growth?

It is not easy to answer the question. We were at first a small and nearly a homogeneous people. We are now eight times more numerous, and we have incorporated large and various foreign elements in our society. We were originally a rural and agricultural people. Now one seventh of our population is found in manufacturing towns and commercial cities. We then were poor, and lived in constant apprehension of domestic disorder and of foreign danger, and we were at the same time distrustful of the capacity and stability of our novel institutions. We are now relatively rich, and all those doubts and fears have vanished. We must make allowance for this great change of circumstances, and we must remember also that it is the character of the great mass of society now existing that is to be compared with, not the heroic models of the revolutionary age, but with society at large as it then existed.

It is certain that society has not declined. Religion has, indeed, lost some of its ancient austerity, but waiving the question whether asceticism is a just test of religion, we may safely say that the change which has occurred is only a compromise with foreign elements of religion, for who will deny that those elements are purer and more spiritual here than the systems existing abroad from which they have been derived? Nor can it be denied that while the ecclesiastical systems existing among us have been, with even more than our rigorous early jealousy, kept distinct and separate from the political conduct of the state, religious institutions have been multiplied relatively with the advance of settlement and population, and are everywhere well and effectually sustained. At the era of independence we had little intellectual reputation, except what a bold and successful metaphysician and a vigorous explorer in natural philosophy had won for us. We have now, I think, a recognised and respectable rank in the republic of letters. It is true, indeed, that we have produced few great works in speculative science and polite literature; but those are not the departments which, during the last half century have chiefly engaged the human mind. A long season of political reform and recovery from exhausting wars has necessarily required intellectual activity in reducing into use the discoveries before made; and we may justly claim that in applying the elements of science to the improvement and advancement of agriculture, art, and commerce, we have not been surpassed.

I do not seek to disguise from myself, nor from you, the existence of a growing passion for territorial aggrandizement, which often exhibits a gross disregard of justice and humanity. Nevertheless, I am not one of those who think that the temper of the nation has become already unsettled. Accidents favoring the indulgence of that passion, have been met with a degree of self-denial that no other nation ever practised. Aggrandizement has been incidental, while society has nevertheless bestowed its chief care on developments of natural resources, reforms of political constitutions, melioration of codes, the diffusion of knowledge, and the cultivation of virtue. If this benign policy has been chiefly exercised within the domain of state authority, and has not reached our federal system, the explanation is obvious in the facts that the popular will is by virtue of the federal constitution, slower in reaching that system, and that we inherited fears which seemed patriotic, of the danger of severance of the Union, to result from innovation. If we have not in the federal government forsaken as widely as we ought to have done, systems of administration borrowed from countries where liberty was either unknown or was greatly abridged, and so have maintained armies, and navies, and diplomacy, on a scale of unnecessary grandeur and ostentation, it can hardly be contended that they have in any great degree corrupted the public virtue. Inquiry is now more active than it has heretofore been, and it may not be doubted that the federal action will hereafter, though with such moderation as will produce no danger and justify no alarm, be made to conform to the sentiments of prudence, enterprise, justice, and humanity, which prevail among the people.

Looking through the states which formed the confederacy in its beginning, we find as general facts, that public order has been effectually maintained, public faith has been preserved, and public tranquillity has been undisturbed, that justice has everywhere been regularly administered, and generally with impartiality. We have established a system of education, which, it is true, is surpassed by many European institutions, in regard to the instruction afforded, but which nevertheless is far more equal and universal in regard to the masses which are educated; and we are beginning to see that system adapted equally to the education of both sexes, and of all races, which is a feature altogether new even in modern civilization, and promises the most auspicious results to the cause of liberty and virtue. Our literature half a century ago was altogether ephemeral and scarcely formed an element of moral or political influence. It is now marked with our own national principles and sentiments, and exerts every day an increasing influence on the national mind. The journalist press, originally a feeble institution, often engaged in exciting the passions and alarming the fears of society, and dividing it into uncompromising and unforgiving factions, has been constantly assuming a higher tone of morality and more patriotic and humane principles of action. There are indeed gross abuses of the power of suffrage, but still our popular elections on the whole, express the will of the people, and are even less influenced by authority, prejudice, and passion, than heretofore. Slavery, an institution that was at first quite universal, has now come to be acknowledged as a peculiar one existing in only a portion of the states. And if, as I doubt not, you, like myself, are impatient of its continuance, then you will nevertheless find ground for much satisfaction in the fact that the foreign slave trade has been already by unanimous consent of all the states condemned and repudiated, that manumission has been effected in half of the states, and that, notwithstanding the great political influence which the institution has been able to organize, a healthful, constant, and growing public sentiment, nourished by the suggestions of sound economy and the instincts of justice and humanity, is leading the way with marked advance toward a complete and universal though just and peaceful emancipation.

It must be borne in mind, now, that all this moral and social improvement has been effected, not by the exercise of any authority over the people, but by the people themselves acting with freedom from all except self-imposed restraints.

Of the new states it is happily true that they have, almost without exception, voluntarily organized their governments according to the most perfect models furnished by the elder members of the confederacy, and that they have uniformly maintained law, order, and faith, while they have with wonderful forecast been even more munificent than the elder states in laying broad foundations of liberty and virtue. On the whole, we think that we may claim that, under the republican system established here, the people have governed themselves safely and wisely, and have enjoyed a greater amount of prosperity and happiness than, under any form of constitution, was ever before or elsewhere vouchsafed to any portion of mankind.

Nevertheless, this review proves only that the measure of knowledge and virtue we possess is equal to the exigency of the republic under the circumstances in which it was organized. Those circumstances are passing away, and we are entering a career of wealth, power, and expansion. In that career, it is manifest that we shall need higher intellectual attainments and greater virtue as a nation than we have hitherto possessed, or else there is no adaptation of means to ends in the scheme of the Divine government. Nay, we shall need in this new emergency intellect and virtue surpassing those of the honored founders of the republic. I am aware that this proposition will seem to you equally unreasonable and irreverent. Nevertheless, you will on a moment's reflection admit its truth. Did the invention of the nation stop with the discoveries of Fulton and Franklin? On the contrary, those philosophers, if they could now revisit the earth, would bow to the genius which has perfected the steam-engine and the telegraph with a homage as profound as that with which we honor their own great memory. So I think Jefferson, and even Washington, under the same circumstances, instead of accusing us of degeneracy, would be lost in admiration of the extent and perfection to which we have safely carried in practice the theory of self-government which they established amid so much uncertainty, and bequeathed to us with so much distrust. Shall we acquit ourselves of obligation if we rest content with either the achievements, the intelligence, or the virtue of our ancestors? If so, then the prospect of mankind is hopeless indeed, for then it must be true that not only is there an impassable stage of social perfection, but that we have reached it, and that, henceforth, not only we but all mankind must recede from it, and civilization must everywhere decline. Such a hypothesis does violence to every power of the human mind and every hope of the human heart. Moreover, these energies and aspirations are the forces of a divine nature within us, and to admit that they can be stifled and suppressed is to contradict the manifest purposes of human existence. Yet it will be quite absurd to claim that we are fulfilling these purposes, if we shall fail to produce hereafter benefactors of our race equal to Fulton, and Franklin, and Adams, and even Washington. Let us hold these honored characters indeed as models but not of unapproachable perfection. Let us, on the contrary, weigh and fully understand our great responsibilities. It is well that we can rejoice in the renown of a Cooper, an Irving, and a Bancroft, but we have yet to give birth to a Shakspere, a Milton, and a Bacon. The fame of Patrick Henry and of John Adams may suffice for the past, but the world will yet demand of us a Burke and a Demosthenes. We may repose for the present upon the fame of Morse and Fulton and Franklin, but human society is entitled to look to us, ere long, for a Des Cartes and a Newton. If we disappoint these expectations and acknowledge ourselves unequal to them, then how shall it be made to appear that freedom is better than slavery, and republicanism more conducive to the welfare of mankind than despotism? To cherish aspirations humbler than these, is equally to shrink from our responsibilities and to dishonor the memory of the ancestors we so justly revere.

And now I am sure that your hearts will sink into some depth of despondency when I ask whether American society now exhibits the influences of these higher but necessary aspirations? I think that everywhere there is confessed a decline from the bold and stern virtue which, at some previous time, was inculcated and practised in executive councils and in representative chambers. I think that we all are conscious that recently we have met questions of momentous responsibility, in the organization of governments over our newly-acquired territories, and appeals to our sympathy and aid for oppressed nations abroad in a spirit of timidity and of compromise. I think that we all are conscious of having abandoned something of our high morality, in suffering important posts of public service, at home and abroad, to fall sometimes into the hands of mercenary men, destitute of true republican spirit, and of generous aspirations to promote the welfare of our country and of mankind: —

> "Souls that no hope of future praise inflame,
> Cold and insensible to glorious fame."

I think that we are accustomed to excuse the national demoralization which has produced these results, on the ground that the practice of a sterner virtue might have disturbed the harmony of society, and endangered the safety of that fabric of union on which all our hopes depend. In this we forget that a nation must always recede if it be not actually advancing; that as hope is the element of progress, so fear admitted into public counsels betrays like treason.

But there is, nevertheless, no sufficient reason for the distrust of the national virtue. Moral forces are like material forces, subject to conflict and reaction. It is only through successive reaction that knowledge and virtue advance. The great conservative and restorative forces of society still remain, and are acquiring, all the while, even greater vigor than they have ever heretofore exercised. Whether I am right or not in this opinion, all will agree that an increase of popular intelligence and a renewal of public virtue are necessary. This is saying nothing new, for it is a maxim of political science that all nations must continually advance in knowledge and renew their constitutional virtues, or must perish. I am sure that we shall do this, because I am sure that our great capacity for advancing the welfare of mankind has not yet been exhausted, and that the promises we have given to the cause of humanity will not be suffered to fail by Him who overrules all human events to the promotion of that cause.

But where is the agency that is to work out these so necessary results? Shall we look to the press? Yes, we may hope much from the press, for it is free. It can safely inculcate truth and expose prejudice, error, and injustice. The press, moreover, is strong in its perfect mechanism, and it reaches every mind throughout this vast and ever-widening confederacy. But the press must have editors and authors — men possessing talents, education, and virtue, and so qualified to instruct, enlighten, and guide the people.

Shall we look to the sacred desk? Yes, indeed; for it is of divine institution and is approved by human experience. The ministers of Christ, inculcating divine morals, under divine authority, with divine sanctions, and sustained and aided by special co-operating influences of the Divine Spirit, are now carrying further and broadly onward the great work of the renewal of the civilization of the world, and its emancipation from superstition and despotism. But the desk, also, must have ministers —

men possessing talents, education, and virtue, and so qualified to enlighten, instruct, and guide mankind.

But however well the press, the desk, and the popular tribune, may be qualified to instruct and elevate the people, their success and consequently their influence must after all depend largely on the measure of intelligence and virtue possessed by the people when sufficiently matured to receive their instructions. Editors, authors, ministers, statesmen, and people, all are qualified for their respective posts of duty in the institutions of popular education, and the standard of these is established by that which is recognised among us by the various names of the academy, the college, and the university. We see, then, that the university holds a chief place among the institutions of the American Republic.

I may not attempt to specify at large what the university ought to teach or how it ought to impart its instructions. That has been confided to abler and more practical hands. But I may venture to insist on the necessity of having the standard of moral duty maintained at its just height by the university. That institution must be rich and full in the knowledge of the sciences which it imparts, but this is not of itself enough. It must imbue the national mind with correct convictions of the greatness and excellence to which it ought to aspire. To do this it must accustom the public mind to look beyond the mere temporary consequences of actions and events to their ultimate influence on the direction of the republic and on the progress of mankind. So it will enable men to decide between prejudice and reason, expediency and duty, the demagogue and the statesman, the bigot and the Christian.

The standard which the university shall establish must correspond to the principles of eternal truth and equal justice. The university must be conservative. It must hold fast every just principle of moral and political science that the experience of mankind has approved, but it must also be bold, remembering that in every human system there are always political superstitions upholding physical slavery in some of its modes, as there are always religious superstitions upholding intellectual slavery in some of its forms; that all these superstitions stand upon prescriptions, and that they can only be exploded where opinion is left free, and reason is ever active and vigorous. But the university must nevertheless practise and teach moderation and charity even to error, remembering that involuntary error will necessarily be mingled also even with its own best instructions, that unbridled zeal overreaches and defeats itself, and that he who would conquer in moral discussion, like him who would prevail in athletic games, must be temperate in all things.

Reverend Instructors and Benevolent Founders, this new institution by reason of its location in the centre of Ohio, itself a central one among these thirty-one united communities, must exert an influence that can scarcely be conceived, now, upon the welfare and fame of our common country. Devote it then I pray you to no mere partisan or sectarian objects. Remember that the patriot and the Christian is a partisan or a sectarian, only because the constitution of society allows him no other mode of efficient and beneficent activity. Let "Capital University" be dedicated not to the interests of the beautiful city which it adorns, nor even to the interests of the great and prosperous state whose patronage I hope it will largely enjoy, nor even to the Republic of which I trust it is destined to become a tower of strength and support. On the contrary if you would make it promote most effectually all these precious interests, dedicate it, I enjoin upon you, as our forefathers dedicated all the institutions which they established, to the cause of Human Nature.

NEBRASKA AND KANSAS.

FREEDOM AND PUBLIC FAITH.*

MR. PRESIDENT: The United States, at the close of the Revolution, rested southward on the St. Mary's, and westward on the Mississippi, and possessed a broad, unoccupied domain, circumscribed by those rivers, the Alleghany mountains, and the great northern lakes. The constitution anticipated a division of this domain into states, to be admitted as members of the Union, but it neither provided for nor foresaw any enlargement of the national boundaries. The people, engaged in reorganizing their governments, improving their social systems, and establishing relations of commerce and friendship with other nations, remained many years content within their apparently ample limits. But it was already known that the free navigation of the Mississippi would soon become an urgent public want.

France, although she had lost Canada, in chivalrous battle, on the Heights of Abraham, in 1763, nevertheless, still retained her ancient territories on the western bank of the Mississippi. She had also, just before the breaking out of her own fearful revolution, re-acquired, by a secret treaty, the possessions on the Gulf of Mexico, which, in a recent war, had been wrested from her by Spain. Her first consul, among those brilliant achievements which proved him the first statesman as well as the first captain of Europe, sagaciously sold the whole of these possessions to the United States, for a liberal sum, and thus replen-

*Speech in the United States Senate, February 17, 1854.

ished his treasury, while he saved from his enemies, and transferred to a friendly power, distant and vast regions, which, for want of adequate naval force, he was unable to defend.

This purchase of Louisiana from France by the United States, involved a grave dispute concerning the western limits of that province; and that controversy, having remained open until 1819, was then adjusted by a treaty, in which they relinquished Texas to Spain, and accepted a cession of the early-discovered and long-inhabited provinces of East Florida and West Florida. The United States stipulated, in each of these cases, to admit the countries thus annexed into the federal Union.

The acquisitions of Oregon, by discovery and occupation, of Texas, by voluntary annexation, and of New Mexico and California, including what is now called Utah, by war, completed the rapid course of enlargement, at the close of which our frontier has been fixed near the centre of what was New Spain, on the Atlantic side of the continent, while on the west, as on the east, only an ocean separates us from the nations of the old world. It is not in my way now to speculate on the question, how long we are to rest on these advanced positions.

Slavery, before the Revolution, existed in all the thirteen colonies, as it did also in nearly all the other European plantations in America. But it had been forced by British authority, for political and commercial ends, on the American people, against their own sagacious instincts of policy, and their stronger feelings of justice and humanity.

They had protested and remonstrated against the system, earnestly, for forty years, and they ceased to protest and remonstrate against it only when they finally committed their entire cause of complaint to the arbitrament of arms. An earnest spirit of emancipation was abroad in the colonies at the close of the Revolution, and all of them, except, perhaps, South Carolina and Georgia, anticipated, desired, and designed an early removal of the system from the country. The suppression of the African slave-trade, which was universally regarded as ancillary to that great measure, was, with much reluctance, postponed until 1808.

While there was no national power, and no claim or desire for national power, anywhere, to compel involuntary emancipation in the states where slavery existed, there was at the same time a very general desire and a strong purpose to prevent its introduction into new communities yet to be formed, and into new states yet to be established. Mr. Jefferson proposed, as early as 1784, to exclude it from the national domain which should be constituted by cessions from the states to the United States. He recommended and urged the measure as ancillary, also, to the ultimate policy of emancipation. There seems to have been at first no very deep jealousy between the emancipating and the non-emancipating states; and the policy of admitting new states was not disturbed by questions concerning slavery. Vermont, a non-slaveholding state, was admitted in 1793. Kentucky, a tramontane slaveholding community, having been detached from Virginia, was admitted, without being questioned, about the same time. So, also, Tennessee, which was a similar community separated from North Carolina, was admitted in 1796, with a stipulation that the ordinance which Mr. Jefferson had first proposed, and which had in the mean time been adopted for the territory northwest of the Ohio, should not be held to apply within her limits. The same course was adopted in organizing territorial governments for Mississippi and Alabama, slaveholding communities which had been detached from South Carolina and Georgia. All these states and territories were situated southwest of the Ohio river, all were more or less already peopled by slaveholders with their slaves; and to have excluded slavery within their limits would have been a national act, not of preventing the introduction of slavery, but of abolishing slavery. In short, the region southwest of the Ohio river presented a field in which the policy of preventing the introduction of slavery was impracticable. Our forefathers never attempted what was impracticable.

But the case was otherwise in that fair and broad region which stretched away from the banks of the Ohio, northward to the lakes, and westward to the Mississippi. It was yet free, or practically free, from the presence of slaves, and was nearly uninhabited, and quite unoccupied. There was then no Baltimore and Ohio railroad, no Erie railroad, no New York Central railroad, no Boston and Ogdensburgh railroad; there was no railroad through Canada; nor, indeed, any road around or across the mountains; no imperial Erie canal, no Welland canal, no lockage around the rapids and the falls of the St. Lawrence, the Mohawk, and the Niagara rivers, and no steam navigation on the lakes or on the Hudson, or on the Mississippi. There, in that remote and secluded region, the prevention of the introduction of slavery was possible; and there our forefathers, who left no possible national good unattempted, did prevent it. It makes one's heart bound with joy and gratitude, and lift itself up with mingled pride and veneration, to read the history of that great transaction. Discarding the trite and common forms of expressing the national will, they did not merely "vote," or "resolve," or "enact," as on other occasions, but they "ORDAINED," in language marked at once with precision, amplification, solemnity, and emphasis, that there "shall be neither slavery nor involuntary servitude in the said territory, otherwise than in the punishment of crime, whereof the party shall have been duly convicted." And they further ORDAINED and declared that this law should be considered a COMPACT between the original states and the people and states of said territory, and for ever remain unalterable, unless by common consent. The ordinance was agreed to unanimously. Virginia, in reaffirming her cession of the territory, ratified it, and the first Congress held under the constitution solemnly renewed and confirmed it.

In pursuance of this ordinance, the several territorial governments successively established in the northwest territory were organized with a prohibition of the introduction of slavery, and in due time, though at successive periods, Ohio, Indiana, Illinois, Michigan, and Wisconsin, states erected within that territory, have come into the Union with constitutions in their hands for ever prohibiting slavery and involuntary servitude, except for the punishment of crime. They are yet young; but, nevertheless, who has ever seen elsewhere such states as they are! There are gathered the young, the vigorous, the active, the enlightened sons of every state, the flower and choice of every state in this broad Union; and there the emigrant for conscience' sake, and for freedom's sake, from every land in Europe, from proud and all-conquering Britain, from heart-broken Ireland, from sunny Italy, from mercurial France, from spiritual Germany, from chivalrous Hungary, and from honest and brave old Sweden and Norway. Thence are already coming ample supplies of corn and wheat and wine for the manufacturers of the East, for the planters of the tropics, and even for the artisans and the armies of Europe; and thence will continue to come in long succession, as they have already begun to come, statesmen and legislators for this continent.

Thus it appears Mr. President, that it was the policy of our fathers, in regard to the original domain of the United States, to prevent the introduction of slavery, wherever it was practicable. This policy encountered greater difficulties when it came under consideration with a view to its establishment in regions not included within our original domain. While slavery had been actually abolished already, by some of the emancipating states, several of them, owing to a great change in the relative value of the productions of slave labor, had fallen off into the class of non-emancipating states; and now the whole family of states was divided and classified as slaveholding or slave states, and non-slaveholding or free states. A rivalry for political ascendency was soon developed; and, besides the motives of interest and philanthropy which had before existed, there was now on each side a desire to increase, from among the candidates for admission into the Union, the number of states in their respective classes, and so their relative weight and influence in the federal councils.

The country which had been acquired from France was, in 1804, organized in two territories, one of which, including New Orleans as its capital, was called Orleans, and the other, having St. Louis for its chief town, was called Louisiana. In 1812, the territory of Orleans was admitted as a new state, under the name of Louisiana. It had been an old slaveholding colony of France, and the prevention of slavery within it would have been a simple act of abolition. At the same time, the territory of Louisiana, by authority of Congress, took the name of Missouri; and, in 1819, the portion thereof which now constitutes the state of Arkansas was detached, and became a territory, under that name. In 1819, Missouri, which was then but thinly peopled, and had an inconsiderable number of slaves, applied for admission into the Union, and her application brought the question of extending the policy of the ordinance of 1787 to that state, and to other new states in the region acquired from France, to a direct issue. The house of representatives insisted on a prohibition against the further introduction of slavery in the state, as a condition of her admission. The senate disagreed with the house in that demand. The non-slaveholding states sustained the house, and the slaveholding states sustained the senate. The difference was radical, and tended toward revolution.

One party maintained that the condition demanded was constitutional, the other that it was unconstitutional. The public mind became intensely excited, and painful apprehensions of disunion and civil war began to prevail in the country.

In this crisis, a majority of both houses agreed upon a plan for the adjustment of the controversy. By this plan, Maine, a non-slaveholding state, was to be admitted; Missouri was to be admitted without submitting to the condition before mentioned; and in all that part of the territory acquired from France, which was north of the line of 36° 30′ of north latitude, slavery was to be for ever prohibited. Louisiana, which was a part of that territory, had been admitted as a slave state eight years before; and now, not only was Missouri to be admitted as a slave state, but Arkansas, which was south of that line, by strong implication, was also to be admitted as a slaveholding state. I need not indicate what were the equivalents which the respective parties were to receive in this arrangement, further than to say that the slaveholding states practically were to receive slaveholding states, the free states to receive a desert, a solitude, in which they might if they could, plant the germs of future free states. This measure was adopted. It was a great national transaction — the first of a class of transactions which have since come to be thoroughly defined and well understood, under the name of compromises. My own opinions concerning them are well known, and are not in question here. According to the general understanding, they are marked by peculiar circumstances and features, viz.:

First, there is a division of opinion upon some vital national question between the two houses of Congress, which division is irreconcilable, except by mutual concessions of interests and opinions, which the houses deem constitutional and just.

Secondly, they are rendered necessary by impending calamities, to results from the failure of legislation, and to be no otherwise averted than by such mutual concessions, or sacrifices.

Thirdly, such concessions are mutual and equal, or are accepted as such, and so become conditions of the mutual arrangement.

Fourthly, by this mutual exchange of conditions, the transaction takes on the nature and character of a contract, compact, or treaty, between the parties represented; and so, according to well-settled principles of morality and public law, the statute which embodies it is understood, by those who uphold this system of legislation to be irrevocable and irrepealable, except by the mutual consent of both, or of all the parties concerned. Not indeed, that it is absolutely irrepealable, but that it can not be repealed without a violation of honor, justice, and good faith, which it is presumed will not be committed.

Such was the compromise of 1820. Missouri came into the Union immediately as a slaveholding state, and Arkansas came in as a slaveholding state, sixteen years afterward. Nebraska, the part of the territory reserved exclusively for free territories and free states, has remained a wilderness ever since. And now it is proposed here to abrogate, not, indeed, the whole compromise, but only that part of it which saved Nebraska as a free territory, to be afterward divided into non-slaveholding states, which should be admitted into the Union. And this is proposed, notwithstanding a universal acquiescence in the compromise, by both parties, for thirty years, and its confirmation, over and over again, by many acts of successive Congresses, and notwithstanding that the slaveholding states have peaceably enjoyed, ever since it was made, all their equivalents, while, owing to circumstances which will hereafter appear, the non-slaveholding states have not practically enjoyed those guarantied to them.

This is the question now before the senate of the United States of America.

It is a question of transcendant importance. The proviso of 1820, to be abrogated in Nebraska, is the ordinance of the Continental Congress of 1787, extended over a new part of the national domain, acquired under our present constitution. It is rendered venerable by its antiquity, and sacred by the memory of that Congress, which in surrendering its trust, after establishing the ordinance, enjoined it upon posterity, always to remember that the cause of the United States was the cause of human nature. The question involves an issue of public faith, and national morality and honor. It will be a sad day for this republic, when such a question shall be deemed unworthy of grave discussion, and shall fail to excite intense interest. Even if it were certain that the inhibition of slavery in the region concerned was unnecessary, and if the question were thus reduced to a mere abstraction, yet even that abstraction would involve the testimony of the United States on the expediency, wisdom, morality, and justice, of the system of human bondage, with which this and other portions of the world have been so long afflicted; and it will be a melancholy day for the republic and for mankind, when her decision on even such an abstraction shall command no respect, and inspire no hope into the hearts of the oppressed. But it is no such abstraction. It was no unnecessary dispute, no mere contest of blind passion, that brought that compromise into being. Slavery and Freedom were active antagonists, then seeking for ascendency in this Union. Both Slavery and Freedom are more vigorous, active, and self-aggrandizing now, than they were then, or ever were before or since that period. The contest between them has been only protracted, not decided. It will be a great feature in our national Hereafter. So the question of adhering to or abrogating this compromise is no unmeaning issue, and no contest of mere blind passion now.

To adhere, is to secure the occupation by freemen, with free labor, of a region in the very centre of the continent, capable of sustaining, and in that event destined, though it may be only after a far-distant period, to sustain ten, twenty, thirty, forty millions of people and their successive generations for ever!

To abrogate, is to resign all that vast region to chances which mortal vision can not fully foresee; perhaps to the sovereignty of such stinted and short-lived communities as those of which Mexico and South America and the West India islands present us with examples; perhaps to convert that region into a scene of long and desolating conflicts between not merely races, but castes, to end, like a similar conflict in Egypt, in a convulsive exodus of the oppressed people, despoiling their superiors; perhaps, like one not dissimilar in Spain, in the forcible expulsion of the inferior race, exhausting the state by the sudden and complete suppression of a great resource of national wealth and labor; perhaps in the disastrous expulsion, even of the superior race itself, by a people too suddenly raised from slavery to liberty, as in St. Domingo. To adhere is to secure for ever the presence here, after some lapse of time, of two, four, ten, twenty, or more senators, and of representatives in larger proportions, to uphold the policy and interests of the non-slaveholding states, and balance that ever-increasing representation of slaveholding states, which past experience, and the decay of the Spanish-American states, admonish us has only just begun; to save what the non-slaveholding states have in mints, navy-yards, the military academy and fortifications, to balance against the capital and federal institutions in the slaveholding states; to save against any danger from adverse or hostile policy, the culture, the manufactures, and the commerce, as well as the just influence and weight of the national principles and sentiments of the slaveholding states. To adhere is to save to the non-slaveholding states, as well as to the slaveholding states, always, and in every event, a right of way and free communication across the continent, to and with the states on the Pacific coasts, and with the rising states on the islands in the South sea, and with all the eastern nations on the vast continent of Asia.

To abrogate, on the contrary, is to commit all these precious interests to the chances and hazards of embarrassment and injury by legislation, under the influence of social, political, and commercial jealousy and rivalry; and in the event of the secession of the slaveholding states, which is so often threatened in their name, but I thank God without their authority, to give to a servile population a La Vendee at the very sources of the Mississippi, and in the very recesses of the Rocky Mountains.

Nor is this last a contingency against which a statesman, when engaged in giving a constitution for such a territory, so situated, must veil his eyes. It is a statesman's province and duty to look before as well as after. I know, indeed, the present loyalty of the American people, North and South, and East and West. I know that it is a sentiment stronger than any sectional interest or ambition, and stronger than even the love of equality in the non-slaveholding states; and stronger, I doubt not, than the love of slavery in the slaveholding states. But I do not know, and no mortal sagacity does know, the seductions of interest and ambition, and the influences of passion, which are yet to be matured in every region. I know this, however— that this Union is safe now, and that it will be safe so long as impartial political equality shall constitute the basis of society, as it has heretofore done, in even half of these states, and they shall thus maintain a just equilibrium against the slaveholding states. But I am well assured, also, on the other hand, that if ever the slaveholding states shall multiply themselves, and extend their sphere, so that they could, without association with the non-slaveholding states, constitute of themselves a commercial republic, from that day their rule, through the executive, judicial, and legislative powers of this government, will be such as will be hard for the non-slaveholding states to bear; and their pride and ambition, since they are congregations of men, and are moved by human passions, will consent to no union in which they shall not so rule.

The slaveholding states already possess the mouths of the Mississippi, and their territory reaches far northward along its banks, on one side to the Ohio, and on the other even to the confluence of the Missouri. They stretch their dominion now from the banks of the Delaware, quite around bay, headland, and promontory, to the Rio Grande. They will not stop, although they now think they may, on the summit of the Sierra Nevada; nay, their armed pioneers are already in Sonora, and their eyes are already fixed, never to be taken off, on the island of Cuba, the queen of the Antilles. If we of the non-slaveholding states surrender to them now the eastern slope of the Rocky Mountains, and the very sources of the Mississippi, what territory will be secure, what territory can be secured hereafter, for the creation and organization of free states, within our ocean-bound domain? What territories on this continent will remain unappropriated and unoccupied, for us to annex? What territories, even if we are able to buy or conquer them from Great Britain or Russia, will the slaveholding states suffer, much less aid, us to annex, to restore the equilibrium which, by this unnecessary measure, we shall have so unwisely, so hurriedly, so suicidally subverted?

Nor am I to be told that only a few slaves will enter into this vast region. One slaveholder in a new territory, with access to the executive ear at Washington, exercises more political influence than five hundred freemen. It is not necessary that all or a majority of the citizens of a state shall be slaveholders, to constitute a slaveholding state. Delaware has only two thousand slaves, against ninety-one thousand freemen; and yet Delaware is a slaveholding state. The proportion is not substantially different in Maryland and in Missouri; and yet they are slaveholding states. These, sir, are the stakes in this legislative game, in which I lament to see, that while the representatives of the slaveholding states are unanimously and earnestly playing to win, so many of the representatives of the non-slaveholding states are, with even greater zeal and diligence, playing to lose.

Mr. President, the committee who have recommended these twin bills for the organization of the territories of Nebraska and Kansas, hold the affirmative in the argument upon their passage.

What is the case they present to the senate and the country?

They have submitted a report; but that report, brought in before they had introduced or even conceived this bold and daring measure of abrogating the Missouri Compromise, directs all its arguments against it.

The committee say, in their report: —

"Such being the character of the controversy, in respect to the territory acquired from Mexico, a similar question has arisen in regard to the right to hold slaves in the proposed territory of Nebraska, when the Indian laws shall be withdrawn, and the country thrown open to emigration and settlement. By the eighth section of 'An Act to authorize the People of the Missouri Territory to form a Constitution and State Government, and for the Admission of such State into the Union on an equal Footing with the original States, and to prohibit Slavery in certain Territories,' approved March 6, 1820, it was provided: 'That in all that territory ceded by France to the United States under the name of Louisiana, which lies north of thirty-six degrees and thirty minutes north latitude, not included within the limits of the state contemplated by this act, slavery and involuntary servitude, otherwise than in the punishment of crimes, whereof the parties shall have been duly convicted, shall be, and is hereby, for ever prohibited: *Provided, always*, That any person escaping into the same, from whom labor or service is lawfully claimed in any state or territory of the United States, such fugitive may be lawfully reclaimed, and conveyed to the person claiming his or her labor or service, as aforesaid.'

"Under this section, as in the case of the Mexican law in New Mexico and Utah, it is a disputed point whether slavery is prohibited in the Nebraska country by *valid* enactment. The decision of this question involves the constitutional power of Congress to pass laws prescribing and regulating the domestic institutions of the various territories of the Union. In the opinion of those eminent statesmen who hold that Congress is invested with no rightful authority to legislate upon the subject of slavery in the territories, the eighth section of the act preparatory to the admission of Missouri is null and void; while the prevailing sentiment in large portions of the Union sustains the doctrine that the constitution of the United States secures to every citizen an inalienable right to move into any of the territories with his property, of whatever kind and description, and to hold and enjoy the same under the sanction of the law. Your committee do not feel themselves called upon to enter into the discussion of these controverted questions. They involve the same grave issues which produced the agitation, the sectional strife, and the fearful struggle of 1850. As Congress deemed it wise and prudent to refrain from deciding the matters in controversy then, either by affirming or repealing the Mexican laws, or by an act declaratory of the true intent of the constitution, and the extent of the protection afforded by it to slave property in the territories, so your committee are not prepared now to recommend a departure from the course pursued on that memorable occasion, either by affirming or repealing the eighth section of the Missouri act, or by any act declaratory of the meaning of the constitution in respect to the legal points in dispute."

This report gives us the deliberate judgment of the committee on two important points. First, that the compromise of 1850 did not, by its letter or by its spirit, repeal, or render necessary, or even propose, the abrogation of the Missouri Compromise; and, secondly, that the Missouri Compromise ought not now to be abrogated. And now, sir, what do we next hear from this committee? First, two similar and kindred bills, actually abrogating the Missouri Compromise, which, in their report, they had told us ought not to be abrogated at all. Secondly, these bills declare on their face, in substance, that that compromise was already abrogated by the spirit of that very compromise of 1850 which, in their report they had just shown us, left the compromise of 1820 absolutely unaffected and unimpaired. Thirdly, the committee favor us, by their chairman, with an oral explanation, that the amended bills abrogating the Missouri Compromise are identical with their previous bill, which did not abrogate it, and are only made to differ in phraseology, to the end that the provisions contained in their previous, and now discarded, bill, shall be absolutely clear and certain.

I entertain great respect for the committee itself, but I must take leave to say that the inconsistencies and self-contradictions contained in the papers it has given us, have destroyed all claims, on the part of those documents, to respect, here or elsewhere.

The recital of the effect of the compromise of 1850, upon the compromise of 1820, as finally revised, corrected, and amended, here in the face of the senate, means after all substantially what that recital meant as it stood before it was perfected, or else it means nothing tangible or worthy of consideration at all. What if the spirit, or even the letter, of the compromise laws of 1850 did conflict with the compromise of 1820? The compromise of 1820 was, by its very nature, a compromise irrepealable and unchangeable, without a violation of honor, justice, and good faith. The compromise of 1850, if it impaired the previous compromise to the extent of the loss to free labor of one acre of the territory of Nebraska, was either absolutely void, or ought, in all subsequent legislation, to be deemed and held void.

What if the spirit or the letter of the compromise was a violation of the compromise of 1820? Then, inasmuch as the compromise of 1820 was inviolable, the attempted violation of it shows that the so-called compromise of 1850 was to that extent not a compromise at all, but a factitious, spurious, and pretended compromise. What if the letter or the spirit of the compromise of 1850 did supersede or impair, or in any way, in any degree, conflict with the compromise of 1820? Then that is a reason for abrogating, not the irrepealable and inviolable compromise of 1820, but the spurious and pretended compromise of 1850

Mr. President, why is this reason for the proposed abrogation of the compromise of 1820 assigned in these bills at all? It is unnecessary. The assignment of a reason adds nothing to the force or weight of the abrogation itself. Either the fact alleged as a reason is *true* or it is *not* true. If it be untrue, your asserting it here will not make it true. If it be true, it is apparent in the text of the law of 1850, without the aid of legislative exposition now. It is unusual. It is unparliamentary. The language of the lawgiver, whether the sovereign be democratic, republican, or despotic, is always the same. It is mandatory, imperative. If the lawgiver explains at all in a statute the reason for it, the reason is that it is his pleasure—*sic volo, sic jubeo.* Look at the compromise of 1820. Does it plead an excuse for its commands? Look at the compromise of 1850, drawn by the master-hand of our American Chatham. Does that bespeak your favor by a quibbling or shuffling apology? Look at your own, now rejected, first Nebraska bill, which, by conclusive implication, saved the effect of the Missouri Compromise. Look at any other bill ever reported by the committee on territories. Look at any other bill now on your calendar. Examine all the laws on your statute-books. Do you find any one bill or statute which ever came bowing, stooping, and wriggling into the senate, pleading an excuse for its clear and explicit declaration of the sovereign and irresistible will of the American people? The departure from this habit in this solitary case betrays self-distrust, and an attempt on the part of the bill to divert the public attention, to raise complex and immaterial issues, to perplex and bewilder and confound the people by whom this transaction is to be reviewed. Look again at the vacillation betrayed in the frequent changes of the structure of this apology. At first the recital told us that the eighth section of the compromise act of 1820 was superseded by the principles of the compromise laws of 1850—as if any one had ever heard of a supersedeas of one local law by the mere *principles* of another local law, enacted for an altogether different region, thirty years afterward. On another day we were told, by an amendment of the recital, that the compromise of 1820 was not superseded by the compromise of 1850 at all, but was only "inconsistent with" it—as if a local act which was irrepealable was now to be abrogated, because it was inconsistent with a subsequent enactment, which had no application whatever within the region to which the first enactment was confined. On a third day the meaning of the recital was further and finally elucidated by an amendment, which declared that the first irrepealable act protecting Nebraska from slavery was now declared "inoperative and void," because it was inconsistent with the present purposes of Congress not to legislate slavery into any territory or state, nor to exclude it therefrom.

But take this apology in whatever form it may be expressed, and test its logic by a simple process.

The law of 1820 secured free institutions in the regions acquired from France in 1803, by the wise and prudent foresight of the Congress of the United States. The law of 1850, on the contrary, committed the choice between free and slave institutions in New Mexico and Utah—territories acquired from Mexico nearly fifty years afterward—to the interested cupidity or the caprice of their earliest and accidental occupants. Free institutions and slave institutions are equal, but the interested cupidity of the pioneer is a wiser arbiter, and his judgment a surer safeguard, than the collective wisdom of the American people and the most solemn and time-honored statute of the American Congress. Therefore, let the law of freedom in the territory acquired from France be now annulled and abrogated, and let the fortunes and fate of freedom and slavery, in the region acquired from France, be, henceforward and for ever, determined by the votes of some seven hundred camp followers around Fort Leavenworth, and the still smaller number of trappers, government school-masters, and mechanics, who attend the Indians in their seasons of rest from hunting in the passes of the Rocky mountains. Sir, this syllogism may satisfy you and other senators; but as for me, I must be content to adhere to the earlier system. *Stare super antiquas vias.*

There is yet another difficulty in this new theory. Let it be granted that, in order to carry out a new principle recently adopted in New Mexico, you can supplant a compromise in Nebraska, yet there is a maxim of public law which forbids you from supplanting that compromise, and establishing a new system *there,* until you first restore the parties in interest there to their *statu quo* before the compromise to be supplanted was established. First, then, remand Missouri and Arkansas back to the unsettled condition, in regard to slavery, which they held before the compromise of 1820 was enacted, and then we will hear you talk of rescinding that compromise. You can not do this. You ought not to do it, if you could; and because you can not and ought not to do it, you can not, without violating law, justice, equity, and honor, abrogate the guarantee of freedom in Nebraska.

There is still another and not less serious difficulty. You call the slavery laws of 1850 a compromise between the slaveholding and non-slaveholding states. For the purposes of this argument, let it be granted that they were such a compromise. It was nevertheless a compromise concerning slavery in the territories acquired from Mexico, and by the letter of the compromise it extended no further. Can you now, by an act which is not a compromise between the same parties, but a mere ordinary law, extend the force and obligation of the principles of that compromise of 1850 into regions not only excluded from it, but absolutely protected from your intervention there by a solemn compromise of thirty years' duration, and invested with a sanctity scarcely inferior to that which hallows the constitution itself?

Can the compromise of 1850, by a mere ordinary act of legislation, be extended beyond the plain, known, fixed intent and understanding of the parties at the time that contract was made, and yet be binding on the parties to it, not merely legally, but in honor and conscience? Can you abrogate a compromise by passing any law of less dignity than a compromise? If so, of what value is any one or the whole of the compromises? Thus you see that these bills violate both of the compromises — not more that of 1820 than that of 1850.

Will you maintain in argument that it was understood by the parties interested throughout the country, or by either of them, or by any representative of either, in either house of Congress, that the principle then established should extend beyond the limits of the territories acquired from Mexico, into the territories acquired nearly fifty years before, from France, and then reposing under the guaranty of the compromise of 1820? I know not how senators may *vote*, but I do know what they will *say*. I appeal to the honorable senator from Michigan [Mr. Cass], than whom none performed a more distinguished part in establishing the compromise of 1850, whether he so intended or understood. I appeal to the honorable and candid senator, the senior representative from Tennessee [Mr. Bell], who performed a distinguished part also. Did he so understand the compromise of 1850? He is silent. I appeal to the gallant senator from Illinois [Mr. Shields]? He, too, is silent. I now throw my gauntlet at the feet of every senator now here, who was in the senate in 1850, and challenge him to say that he then knew, or thought, or dreamed, that, by enacting the compromise of 1850, he was directly or indirectly abrogating, or in any degree impairing, the Missouri Compromise? No one takes it up. I appeal to that very distinguished—nay, sir, that expression falls short of his eminence—that illustrious man, the senator from Missouri [Mr. BENTON], who led the opposition here to the compromise of 1850. Did he understand that that compromise in any way overreached or impaired the compromise of 1820? Sir, that distinguished person, while opposing the combination of the several laws on the subject of California and the territories, and slavery, together, in one bill, so as to constitute a compromise, nevertheless voted for each one of those bills, severally; and in that way, and that way only, they were passed. Had he known or understood that any one of them overreached and impaired the Missouri Compromise, we all know he would have perished before he would have given it his support.

Sir, if it were not irreverent, I would dare to call up the author of both of the compromises in question, from his honored, though yet scarcely grass-covered grave, and challenge any advocate of this measure to confront that imperious shade, and say that, in making the compromise of 1850, Henry Clay intended or dreamed that he was subverting, or preparing the way for a subversion of, his greater work of 1820. Sir, if that eagle spirit is yet lingering here over the scene of its mortal labors, and watching over the welfare of the republic it loved so well, it is now moved with more than human indignation against those who are perverting its last great public act from its legitimate uses, not merely to subvert the column, but to wrench from its very bed the base of the column that perpetuates its fame.

And that other proud and dominating senator, who, sacrificing himself, gave the aid without which the compromise of 1850 could not have been established—the statesman of New England, and the orator of America—who dare assert here, where his memory is yet fresh, though his unfettered spirit may be wandering in spheres far hence, that he intended to abrogate, or dreamed that, by virtue of or in consequence of that transaction, the Missouri compromise would or could ever be abrogated? The portion of the Missouri compromise you propose to abrogate is the ordinance of 1787 extended to Nebraska. Hear what Daniel Webster said of that ordinance itself, in 1830, in this very place, in reply to one who had undervalued it and its author: —

"I spoke, sir, of the ordinance of 1787, which prohibits slavery, in all future time, northwest of the Ohio, as a measure of great wisdom and forethought, and one which has been attended with highly beneficial and permanent consequences."

And now hear what he said here, when advocating the compromise of 1850: —

"I now say, sir, as the proposition upon which I stand this day, and upon the truth and firmness of which I intend to act until it is overthrown, that there is not at this moment in the United States, or any territory of the United States, one single foot of land, the character of which, in regard to its being free territory or slave territory, is not fixed by some law, and some IRREPEALABLE law, beyond the power of the action of this government."

What *irrepealable* law, or what law of any kind, fixed the character of Nebraska as free or slave territory, except the Missouri compromise act?

And now hear what Daniel Webster said when vindicating the compromise of 1850, at Buffalo, in 1851: —

"My opinion remains unchanged, that it was not within the original scope or design of the constitution to admit new states out of foreign territory; and for one, whatever may be said at the Syracuse convention or any other assemblage of insane persons, I never would consent, and never have consented, that there should be one foot of slave territory beyond what the old thirteen states had at the time of the formation of the Union! Never! Never!

"The man can not show his face to me and say he can prove that I ever departed from that doctrine. He would sneak away, and slink away, or hire a mercenary press to cry out, What an apostate from liberty Daniel Webster has become! But he knows himself to be a hypocrite and a falsifier."

That compromise was forced upon the slaveholding states and upon the non-slaveholding states as a mutual exchange of equivalents. The equivalents were accurately defined, and carefully scrutinized and weighed by the respective parties, through a period of eight months. The equivalents offered to the non-slaveholding states were: 1st, the admission of California; 2d, the abolition of the public slave-trade in the District of Columbia. These, and these only, were the boons offered to them, and the only sacrifices which the slaveholding states were required to make. The waiver of the Wilmot proviso in the incorporation of New Mexico and Utah, and a new fugitive slave law, were the only boons proposed to the slaveholding states, and the only sacrifices exacted of the non-slaveholding states. No other questions between them were agitated, except those which were involved in the gain or loss of more or less of free territory or of slave territory in the determination of the boundary between Texas and New Mexico, by a line that was at last arbitrarily made, expressly saving, even in *those territories*, to the respective parties, their respective shares of free soil and slave soil, according to the articles of annexation of the republic of Texas. Again: There were alleged to be five open, bleeding wounds in the federal system, and *no more*, which needed surgery, and to which the compromise of 1850 was to be a cataplasm. We all know what they were: California without a constitution; New Mexico in the grasp of military power; Utah neglected; the District of Columbia dishonored; and the rendition of fugitives denied. Nebraska was not even thought of in this catalogue of national ills. And now, sir, did the Nashville convention of secessionists understand that, besides the enumerated boons offered to the slaveholding states, they were to have also the obliteration of the Missouri compromise line of 1820? If they did, why did they reject and scorn and scout at the compromise of 1850? Did the legislatures and public assemblies of the non-slaveholding states, who made your table groan with their remonstrances, understand that Nebraska was an additional wound to be healed by the compromise of 1850? If they did, why did they omit to remonstrate against the healing of that, too, as well as of the other five, by the cataplasm, the application of which they resisted so long?

Again: Had it been then known that the Missouri compromise was to be abolished, directly or indirectly, by the compromise of 1850, what representative from a non-slaveholding state would, at that day, have voted for it? Not one. What senator from a slaveholding state would not have voted for it? Not one. So entirely was it then unthought of that the new compromise was to repeal the Missouri compromise line of 36° 30′ in the region acquired from France, that one half of that long debate was spent on propositions made by representatives from slaveholding states, to extend the line further on through the new territory we had acquired so recently from Mexico, until it should disappear in the waves of the Pacific ocean, so as to secure actual toleration of slavery in all of this new territory that should be south of that line; and these propositions were resisted strenuously and successfully to the last by the representatives of the non-slaveholding states, in order, if it were possible, to save the whole of those regions for the theatre of free labor.

I admit that these are only negative proofs, although they are pregnant with conviction. But here is one which is not only affirmative, but positive, and not more positive than conclusive:—

In the fifth section of the Texas boundary bill, one of the acts constituting the compromise of 1850, are these words:—

"*Provided,* That nothing herein contained shall be construed to impair or qualify anything contained in the third article of the second section of the joint resolution for annexing Texas to the United States, approved March 1, 1845, either as regards the number of states that may hereafter be formed out of the state of Texas, or otherwise."

What was that third article of the second section of the joint resolution for annexing Texas? Here it is:—

"New states, of convenient size, not exceeding four in number, in addition to said state of Texas, having sufficient population, may hereafter, by the consent of said state, be formed out of the territory thereof, which shall be entitled to admission under the provisions of the federal constitution. And such states as may be formed out of that portion of said territory lying south of 36° 30′ north latitude, commonly known as the Missouri compromise line, shall be admitted into the Union with or without slavery, as the people of each state asking admission may desire. And in such state or states as shall be formed out of said territory north of said Missouri compromise line, slavery or involuntary servitude (except for crime) shall be prohibited."

This article saved the compromise of 1820, in express terms, overcoming any implication of its abrogation, which might, by accident or otherwise, have crept into the compromise of 1850; and any inferences to that effect, that might be drawn from any such circumstance as that of drawing the boundary line of Utah so as to trespass on the territory of Nebraska, dwelt upon by the senator from Illinois.

The proposition to abrogate the Missouri compromise, being

thus stripped of the pretence that it is only a reiteration or a reaffirmation of a similar abrogation in the compromise of 1850, or a necessary consequence of that measure, stands before us now upon its own merits, whatever they may be.

But here the senator from Illinois challenges the assailants of these bills, on the ground that they all were opponents of the compromise of 1850, and even of that of 1820. Sir, it is not my purpose to answer in person to this challenge. The necessity, reasonableness, justice, and wisdom of those compromises, are not in question here now. My own opinions on them were, at a proper time, fully made known. I abide the judgment of my country and mankind upon them. For the present, I meet the committee who have brought this measure forward, on the field they themselves have chosen, and the controversy is reduced to two questions: 1st. Whether, by letter or spirit, the compromise of 1850 abrogated or involved a future abrogation of the compromise of 1820? 2d. Whether this abrogation can now be made consistently with honor, justice, and good faith? As to my right, or that of any other senator, to enter these lists, the credentials filed in the secretary's office settle that question. Mine bear a seal, as broad and as firmly fixed there as any other, by a people as wise, as free, and as great, as any one of all the thirty-one republics represented here.

But I will take leave to say, that an argument merely *ad personam,* seldom amounts to anything more than an argument *ad captandum.* A life of approval of compromises, and of devotion to them, only enhances the obligation faithfully to fulfil them. A life of disapprobation of the policy of compromises only renders one more earnest in exacting fulfilment of them, when good and cherished interests are secured by them.

Thus much for the report and the bills of the committee, and for the positions of the parties in this debate. A measure so bold, so unlooked-for, so startling, and yet so pregnant as this, should have some plea of necessity. Is there any such necessity? On the contrary, it is not necessary now, even if it be altogether wise, to establish territorial governments in Nebraska. Not less than eighteen tribes of Indians occupy that vast tract, fourteen of which, I am informed, have been removed there by our own act, and invested with a fee simple to enjoy a secure and perpetual home, safe from the intrusion and the annoyance, and even from the *presence* of the white man, and under the paternal care of the government, and with the instruction of its teachers and mechanics, to acquire the arts of civilization and the habits of social life. I will not say that this was done to prevent that territory, because denied to slavery, from being occupied by free white men, and cultivated with free white labor; but I will say, that this removal of the Indians there, under such guaranties, has had that effect. The territory can not be occupied now, any more than heretofore, by savages and white men, with or without slaves, together. Our experience and our Indian policy alike remove all dispute from this point. Either these preserved ranges must still remain to the Indians hereafter, or the Indians, whatever temporary resistance against removal they may make, must retire.

Where shall they go? Will you bring them back again across the Mississippi? There is no room for Indians here. Will you send them northward, beyond your territory of Nebraska, toward the British border? That is already occupied by Indians; there is no room there. Will you turn them loose upon Texas and New Mexico? There is no room there.

Will you drive them over the Rocky mountains? They will meet a tide of immigration there, flowing into California from Europe and from Asia. Whither, then, shall they, the dispossessed, unpitied heirs of this vast continent, go? The answer is, *nowhere*. If they remain in Nebraska, of what use are your charters? Of what harm is the Missouri compromise in Nebraska, in that case? Whom doth it oppress? No one.

Who, indeed, demands territorial organization in Nebraska at all. The Indians? No. It is to them the consummation of a long-apprehended doom. Practically, no one demands it. I am told that the whole white population, scattered here and there throughout those broad regions, exceeding in extent the whole of the inhabited part of the United States at the time of the Revolution, is less than fifteen hundred, and that these are chiefly trappers, missionaries, and a few mechanics and agents employed by the government, in connection with the administration of Indian affairs, and other persons temporarily drawn around the post of Fort Leavenworth. It is clear, then, that this abrogation of the Missouri compromise is not necessary for the purpose of establishing territorial governments in Nebraska, but that, on the contrary, these bills, establishing such governments, are only a vehicle for carrying, or a pretext for carrying, that act of abrogation.

It is alleged that the non-slaveholding states have forfeited their rights in Nebraska, under the Missouri compromise, by first breaking that compromise themselves. The argument is, that the Missouri compromise line of 36° 30′, in the region acquired from France, although confined to that region which was our westernmost possession, was, nevertheless, understood as intended to be prospectively applied also to the territory reaching thence westward to the Pacific ocean, which we should afterward acquire from Mexico; and that when afterward, having acquired these territories, including California, New Mexico, and Utah, we were engaged in 1848 in extending governments over them, the free states refused to extend that line, on a proposition to that effect made by the honorable senator from Illinois.

It need only be stated, in refutation of this argument, that the Missouri compromise law, like any other statute, was limited by the extent of the subject of which it treated. This subject was the territory of Louisiana, acquired from France, whether the same were more or less, then in our lawful and peaceful possession. The length of the line of 36° 30′ established by the Missouri compromise, was the distance between the parallels of longitude which were the borders of that possession. Young America—I mean aggrandizing, conquering America—had not yet been born; nor was the statesman then in being who dreamed that, within thirty years afterward, we should have pushed our adventurous way, not only across the Rocky mountains, but also across the Snowy mountains. Nor did any one then imagine, that, even if we should have done so within the period I have named, we were then prospectively carving up and dividing, not only the mountain-passes, but the Mexican empire on the Pacific coast, between Freedom and Slavery. If such a proposition had been made then, and persisted in, we know enough of the temper of 1820 to know this, viz.: that Missouri and Arkansas would have stood outside of the Union until even this portentous day

The time, for aught I know, may not be thirty years distant, when the convulsions of the Celestial empire and the decline of British sway in India will have opened our way into the regions beyond the Pacific ocean. I desire to know now, and be fully certified, of the geographical extent of the laws we are now passing, so that there may be no such mistake hereafter as that now complained of here. We are now confiding to territorial legislatures the power to legislate on slavery. Are the territories of Nebraska and Kansas alone within the purview of these acts? Or do they reach to the Pacific coast, and embrace also Oregon and Washington? Do they stop there, or do they take in China, and India, and Affghanistan, even to the gigantic base of the Himalaya mountains? Do they stop there, or, on the contrary, do they encircle the earth, and, meeting us again on the Atlantic coast, embrace the islands of Iceland and Greenland, and exhaust themselves on the barren coasts of Greenland and Labrador?

Sir, if the Missouri compromise neither is in its spirit nor by its letter extended to the line of 36° 30′ beyond the confines of Louisiana, or beyond the then confines of the United States—for the terms are equivalent—then it was no violation of the Missouri compromise in 1848 to refuse to extend it to the subsequently-acquired possessions of Texas, New Mexico, and California.

But suppose we did refuse to extend it; how did that refusal work a forfeiture of our vested rights under it? I desire to know that.

Again: If this forfeiture of Nebraska occurred in 1848, as the senator charges, how does it happen that he not only failed in 1850, when the parties were in court here, adjusting their mutual claims, to demand judgment against the free states, but, on the contrary, even urged that the same old Missouri compromise line, yet held valid and sacred, should be extended through to the Pacific ocean?

I come now to the chief ground of the defence of this extraordinary measure, which is, that it abolishes a geographical line of division between the proper fields of free labor and slave labor, and refers the claim between them to the people of the territories. Even if this great change of policy was actually wise and necessary, I have shown that it is not necessary to make it now, in regard to the territory of Nebraska. If it would be just elsewhere, it would be unjust in regard to Nebraska, simply because, for ample and adequate equivalents, fully received, you have contracted in effect not to abolish that line there.

But why is this change of policy wise or necessary? It must be because either that the extension of slavery is no evil, or that you have not the power to prevent it at all, or because the maintenance of a geographical line is no longer practicable.

I know that the opinion is sometimes advanced, here and elsewhere, that the extension of slavery, abstractly considered, is not an evil; but our laws prohibiting the African slave-trade are still standing on the statute-book, and express the contrary judgment of the American Congress and of the American people. I pass on, therefore, from that point.

Sir, I do not like, more than others, a geographical line between Freedom and Slavery. But it is because I would have, if it were possible, all our territory free. Since that can not be, a line of division is indispensable; and any line is a geographical line.

The honorable and very acute senator from North Carolina [Mr. BADGER] has wooed us most persuasively to waive our objections to the new principle, as it is called, of non-intervention, by assuring us that the slaveholder can only use slave-labor where the soils and climates favor the culture of tobacco, cotton, rice, and sugar. To which I reply: None of these find congenial soils or climates at the sources of the Mississippi, or in the valley of the Rocky mountains. Why, then, does he want to remove the inhibition there?

But again: That senator reproduces a pleasing fiction of the character of slavery from the Jewish history, and asks, Why not allow the *modern patriarchs* to go into new regions with their slaves, as their ancient prototypes did, to make them more comfortable and happy? And he tells us, at the same time, that this indulgence will not increase the number of slaves. I reply by asking, first, Whether slavery has gained or lost strength by the diffusion of it over a larger surface than it formerly covered? Will the senator answer that? Secondly, I admire the simplicity of the patriarchal times. But they, nevertheless, exhibited some peculiar institutions quite incongruous with modern republicanism, not to say Christianity, namely, that of a latitude of construction of the marriage contract, which has been carried by one class of so-called patriarchs into Utah. Certainly, no one would desire to extend that peculiar institution into Nebraska. Thirdly, slaveholders have also a peculiar institution, which makes them *political* patriarchs. They reckon five of their slaves as equal to three freemen in forming the basis of federal representation. If these patriarchs insist upon carrying their institution into new regions, north of 36° 30′, I respectfully submit, that they ought to resume the modesty of their Jewish predecessors, and relinquish this political feature of the system they thus seek to extend. Will they do that?

Some senators have revived the argument that the Missouri compromise was unconstitutional. But it is one of the peculiarities of compromises, that constitutional objections, like all others, are buried under them by those who make and ratify them, for the obvious reason that the parties at once waive them, and receive equivalents. Certainly, the slaveholding states, which waived their constitutional objections against the compromise of 1820, and accepted equivalents therefor, can not be allowed to revive and offer them now as a reason for refusing to the non-slaveholding states their rights under that compromise, without first restoring the equivalents which they received on condition of surrendering their constitutional objections.

For argument's sake, however, let this reply be waived, and let us look at this constitutional objection. You say that the exclusion of slavery by the Missouri compromise reaches through and beyond the existence of the region organized as a territory, and prohibits slavery FOR EVER even in the states to be organized out of such territory, while, on the contrary, the states, when admitted, will be sovereign, and must have exclusive jurisdiction over slavery for themselves. Let this, too, be granted. But Congress, acording to the constitution, "may admit new states." If Congress may admit, then Congress may also refuse to admit — that is to say, may reject new states. The greater includes the less; therefore, Congress may admit, on condition that the states shall exclude slavery. If such a condition should be accepted, would it not be binding?

It is by no means necessary, on this occasion, to follow the argument further, to the question, whether such a condition is in conflict with the constitutional provision, that the new states received shall be admitted on an equal footing with the original states, because, in this case, and at present, the question relates not to the admission of a *State*, but to the organization of a territory, and the exclusion of slavery within the territory while its *status* as a territory shall continue, and no further. Congress have power to exclude slavery in territories, if they have any power to create, control, or govern territories at all, for this simple reason: that find the authority of Congress over the territories wherever you may, there you find no exception from that general authority in favor of slavery. If Congress has no authority over slavery in the territories, it has none in the District of Columbia. If, then, you abolish a law of Freedom in Nebraska, in order to establish a new policy of abnegation, then true consistency requires that you shall also abolish the slavery laws in the District of Columbia, and submit the question of the toleration of slavery within the district to its inhabitants.

If you reply, that the District of Columbia has no local or territorial legislature, then I rejoin, so also has not Nebraska, and so also has not Kansas. You are calling a territorial legislature into existence in Nebraska, and another in Kansas, to assume the jurisdiction on the subject of slavery, which you renounce. Then consistency demands that you call into existence a territorial legislature in the District of Columbia, to assume the jurisdiction here, which you must also renounce. Will you do this? We shall see.

To come closer to the question: What is this principle of abnegating national authority, on the subject of slavery, in favor of the people? Do you abnegate all authority, whatever, in the territories? Not at all; you abnegate only authority over slavery there. Do you abnegate even that? No; you do not and you can not. In the very act of abnegating you legislate, and enact that the states to be hereafter organized shall come in whether slave or free, as their inhabitants shall choose. Is not this legislating not only on the subject of slavery in the territories, but on the subject of slavery in the future states? In the very act of abnegating, you call into being a legislature which shall assume the authority which you are renouncing. You not only exercise authority in that act, but you exercise authority over slavery, when you confer on the territorial legislature the power to act upon that subject. More than this: In the very act of calling that territorial legislature into existence, you exercise authority in prescribing who may elect and who may be elected. You even reserve to yourselves a veto upon every act that they can pass as a legislative body, not only on all other subjects, but even on the subject of slavery itself. Nor can you relinquish that veto; for it is absurd to say that you can create an agent, and depute to him the legislative authority of the United States, which agent you can not at your own pleasure remove, and whose acts you can not at your own pleasure disavow and repudiate. The territorial legislature is your agent. Its acts are your own. Such is the principle that is to supplant the ancient policy—a principle full of absurdities and contradictions.

Again: You claim that this policy of abnegation is based upon a democratic principle. A democratic principle is a principle opposed to some other that is despotic or aristocratic. You claim and exercise the power to institute and maintain government in the territories. Is this comprehensive power aristocratic or despotic? If it be not, how is the partial power aristocratic or despotic? You retain authority to appoint governors, without whose consent no laws can be made on any subject, and judges, without whose consideration no laws can be executed, and you retain the power to change them at pleasure. Are these powers, also, aristocratic or despotic? If they are not, then the exercise of legislative power by yourselves is not. If they are, then why not renounce them also? No, no. This is a far-fetched excuse. Democracy is a simple, uniform, logical system, not a system of arbitrary, contradictory, and conflicting principles!

But you must nevertheless renounce national authority over slavery in the territories, while you retain all other powers. What is this but a mere evasion of solemn responsibilities? The general authority of Congress over the territories is one wisely confided to the national legislature, to save young and growing communities from the dangers which beset them in their state of pupilage, and to prevent them from adopting any policy that shall be at war with their own lasting interests, or with the general welfare of the whole republic. The authority over the subject of slavery is that which ought to be renounced last of all, in favor of territorial legislatures, because, from the very circumstances of the territories, those legislatures are likely to yield too readily to ephemeral influences, and interested offers of favor and patronage. They see neither the great Future of the territories, nor the comprehensive and ultimate interests of the whole republic, as clearly as you see them, or ought to see them.

I have heard sectional excuses given for supporting this measure. I have heard senators from the slaveholding states say that they ought not to be expected to stand by the non-slaveholding states, when they refuse to stand by themselves; that they ought not to be expected to refuse the boon offered to the slaveholding states, since it is offered by the non-slaveholding states themselves. I not only confess the plausibility of these excuses, but I feel the justice of the reproach which they imply against the non-slaveholding states, as far as the assumption is true. Nevertheless, senators from the slaveholding states must consider well whether that assumption is, in any considerable degree, founded in fact. If one or more senators from the North decline to stand by the non-slaveholding states, or offer a boon in their name, others from that region do, nevertheless, stand firmly on their rights, and protest against the giving or the acceptance of the boon. It has been said that the North does not speak out, so as to enable you to decide between the conflicting voices of her representatives. Are you quite sure you have given her timely notice? Have you not, on the contrary, hurried this measure forward, to anticipate her awaking from the slumber of conscious security into which she has been lulled by your last compromise! Have you not heard already the quick, sharp protest of the legislature of the smallest of the non-slaveholding states, Rhode Island? Have you not already heard the deep-toned and earnest protest of the greatest of those states, New York? Have you not already heard remonstrances from the metropolis, and from the rural districts? Do you doubt that this is only the rising of the agitation that you profess to believe is at rest for ever? Do you forget that, in all such transactions as these, the people have a reserved right to review the acts of their representatives, and a right to demand a reconsideration; that there is in our legislative practice a form of RE-ENACTMENT, as well as an act of *repeal;* and that there is in our political system provision not only for *abrogation*, but for RESTORATION also? And when the process of repeal has begun, how many and what laws will be open to repeal, equally with the Missouri Compromise? There will be this act, the fugitive slave laws, the articles of Texas annexation, the territorial laws of New Mexico and Utah, the slavery laws in the District of Columbia.

Senators from the slaveholding states: You are politicians as well as statesmen. Let me remind you, therefore, that political movements in this country, as in all others, have their times of action and reaction. The pendulum moved up the side of freedom in 1840, and swung back again in 1844 on the side of slavery, traversed the dial in 1848, and touched even the mark of the Wilmot proviso, and returned again in 1852, reaching even the height of the Baltimore platform. Judge for yourselves whether it is yet ascending, and whether it will attain the height of the abrogation of the Missouri compromise. That is the mark you are fixing for it. For myself, I may claim to know something of the North. I see in the changes of the times only the vibrations of the needle, trembling on its pivot. I know that in due time it will settle; and when it shall have settled, it will point, as it must point for ever, to the same constant polar star, that sheds down influences propitious to freedom as broadly as it pours forth its mellow but invigorating light.

Mr. President, I have nothing to do, here or elsewhere, with personal or party motives. But I come to consider the motive which is publicly assigned for this transaction. It is a desire to secure permanent peace and harmony on the subject of slavery, by removing all occasion for its future agitation in the federal legislature. Was there not peace already here? Was there not harmony as perfect as is ever possible in the country, when this measure was moved in the senate a month ago? Were we not, and was not the whole nation, grappling with that one great, common, universal interest, the opening of a communication between our ocean frontiers, and were we not already reckoning upon the quick and busy subjugation of nature throughout the interior of the continent to the uses of man, and dwelling with almost rapturous enthusiasm on the prospective enlargement of our commerce in the East, and of our political sway throughout the world? And what have we now here but the oblivion of death, covering the very memory of those great enterprises, and prospects, and hopes?

Senators from the non-slaveholding states: You want peace. Think well, I beseech you, before you yield the price now demanded, even for peace and rest from slavery agitation. France has got peace from republican agitation by a similar sacrifice. So has Poland; so has Hungary; and so, at last, has Ireland. Is the peace which either of those nations enjoys worth the price it cost? Is peace, obtained at such cost, ever a lasting peace?

Senators from the slaveholding states: You, too, suppose that you are securing peace as well as victory in this transaction. I tell you now, as I told you in 1850, that it is an error, an unnecessary error, to suppose, that because you exclude slavery from these halls to-day, that it will not revisit them to-morrow. You buried the Wilmot proviso here then, and celebrated its obsequies with pomp and revelry. And here it is again to-day, stalking through these halls, clad in complete steel as before. Even if those whom you denounce as factionists in the North would let it rest, you yourselves must evoke it from its grave. The reason is obvious. Say what you will, do what you will, here, the interests of the non-slaveholding states and of the slaveholding states remain just the same; and they will remain just the same, until you shall cease to cherish and defend slavery, or we shall cease to honor and love freedom! You will not cease to cherish slavery. Do you see any signs that we are becoming indifferent to freedom? On the contrary, that old, traditional, hereditary sentiment of the North is more profound and more universal now than it ever was before. The slavery agitation you deprecate so much is an eternal struggle between Conservatism and Progress, between Truth and Error, between Right and Wrong. You may sooner, by act of Congress, compel the sea to suppress its upheavings, and the round earth to extinguish its internal fires, than oblige the human mind to cease its inquirings, and the human heart to desist from its throbbings.

Suppose then, for a moment, that this agitation must go on hereafter as heretofore. Then, hereafter as heretofore, there will be need, on both sides, of moderation; and, to secure moderation, there will be need of mediation. Hitherto you have secured moderation by means of compromises, by tendering which, the great mediator, now no more, divided the people of the North. But then those in the North who did not sympathize with you in your complaints of aggression from that quarter, as well as those who did, agreed that if compromises should be effected, they would be chivalrously kept on your part. I cheerfully admit that they have been so kept until now. But hereafter, when having taken advantage, which in the North will be called fraudulent, of the last of those compromises, to become, as you will be called, the aggressors, by breaking the other, as will be alleged, in violation of plighted faith and honor, while the slavery agitation is rising higher than ever before, and while your ancient friends, and those whom you persist in regarding as your enemies, shall have been driven together by a common and universal sense of your injustice, what new mode of restoring peace and harmony will you then propose? What statesman will there be in the South, then, who can bear the flag of truce? What statesman in the North who can mediate the acceptance of your new proposals? I think it will not be the senator from Illinois.

If, however, I err in all this, let us suppose that you succeed in suppressing political agitation of slavery in national affairs. Nevertheless, agitation of slavery must go on in some form; for all the world around you is engaged in it. It is, then, high time for you to consider where you may expect to meet it next. I much mistake if, in that case, you do not meet it there where we, who once were slaveholding states, as you now are, have met, and, happily for us, succumbed before it—namely, in the legislative halls, in the churches and schools, and at the fireside, within the states themselves. It is an angel of mercy with which, sooner or later, every slaveholding state must wrestle, and by which it must be overcome. Even if, by reason of this measure, it should the sooner come to that point, and although I am sure that you will not overcome freedom, but that freedom will overcome you, yet I do not look even then for disastrous or unhappy results. The institutions of our country are so framed, that the inevitable conflict of opinion on slavery, as on every other subject, can not be otherwise than peaceful in its course and beneficent in its termination.

Nor shall I "bate one jot of heart or hope," in maintaining a just equilibrium of the non-slaveholding states, even if this ill-starred measure shall be adopted. The non-slaveholding states are teeming with an increase of freemen—educated, vigorous, enlightened, enterprising freemen—such freemen as neither England, nor Rome, nor even Athens, ever reared. Half a million of freemen from Europe annually augment that increase; and ten years hence half a million, twenty years hence a million, of freemen from Asia will augment it still more. You may obstruct, and so turn the direction of those peaceful armies away from Nebraska. So long as you shall leave them room on hill or prairie, by river-side or in the mountain-fastnesses, they will dispose of themselves peacefully and lawfully in the places you shall have left open to them; and there they will erect new states upon free soil, to be for ever maintained and defended by free arms, and aggrandized by free labor. American slavery, I know, has a large and ever-flowing spring, but it can not pour forth its blackened tide in volumes like that I have described. If you are wise, these tides of freemen and of slaves will never meet, for they will not voluntarily commingle; but if, nevertheless, through your own erroneous policy, their repulsive currents must be directed against each other, so that they needs must meet, then it is easy to see, in that case, which of them will overcome the resistance of the other, and which of them, thus overpowered, will roll back to drown the source which sent it forth.

"Man proposes, and God disposes." You may legislate, and abrogate, and abnegate, as you will; but there is a Superior Power that overrules all your actions, and all your refusals to act; and, I fondly hope and trust, overrules them to the advancement of the happiness, greatness, and glory of our country—that overrules, I know, not only all your actions, and all your refusals to act, but all human events, to the distant but inevitable result of the equal and universal liberty of all men.

NEBRASKA AND KANSAS.

SECOND SPEECH.

Mr. President: I rise with no purpose of further resisting or even delaying the passage of this bill. Let its advocates have only a little patience, and they will soon reach the object for which they have struggled so earnestly and so long. The sun has set for the last time upon the guarantied and certain liberties of all the unsettled and unorganized portions of the American continent that lie within the jurisdiction of the United States. To-morrow's sun will rise in dim eclipse over them.* How long that obscuration shall last, is known only to the Power that directs and controls all human events. For myself, I know only this — that now no human power will prevent its coming on, and that its passing off will be hastened and secured by others than those now here, and perhaps by only those belonging to future generations.

Sir, it would be almost factious to offer further resistance to this measure here. Indeed, successful resistance was never expected to be made in this hall. The senate floor is an old battle-ground, on which have been fought many contests, and always, at least since 1820, with fortune adverse to the cause of equal and universal freedom. We were only a few here who engaged in that cause in the beginning of this contest. All that we could hope to do — all that we did hope to do — was to organize and to prepare the issue for the house of representatives, to which the country would look for its decision as authoritative, and to awaken the country that it might be ready for the appeal which would be made, whatever the decision of Congress might be. We are no stronger now. Only fourteen at the first, it

* It will be remembered that an almost total eclipse of the sun actually occurred on that day — the 26th of May, 1854.—Ed.

will be fortunate if, among the ills and accidents which surround us, we shall maintain that number to the end.

We are on the eve of the consummation of a great national transaction — a transaction which will close a cycle in the history of our country — and it is impossible not to desire to pause a moment and survey the scene around us and the prospect before us. However obscure we may individually be, our connection with this great transaction will perpetuate our names for the praise or for the censure of future ages, and perhaps in regions far remote. If, then, we had no other motive for our actions but that of an honest desire for a just fame, we could not be indifferent to that scene and that prospect. But individual interests and ambition sink into insignificance in view of the interests of our country and of mankind. These interests awaken, at least in me, an intense solicitude.

It was said by some in the beginning, and it has been said by others later in this debate, that it was doubtful whether it would be the cause of slavery or the cause of freedom that would gain advantages from the passage of this bill. I do not find it necessary to be censorious, nor even unjust to others, in order that my own course may be approved. I am sure that the honorable senator from Illinois [Mr. Douglas] did not mean that the slave states should gain an advantage over the free states, for he disclaimed it when he introduced the bill. I believe, in all candor, that the honorable senator from Georgia [Mr. Toombs], who comes out at the close of the battle as one of the chiefest leaders of the victorious party, is sincere in declaring his own opinion that the slave states will gain no unjust advantage over the free states, because he disclaims it as a triumph in their behalf. Notwithstanding all this, however, what has occurred here and in the country, during this contest, has compelled a conviction that slavery will gain something, and freedom will endure a severe, though I hope not an irretrievable loss. The slaveholding states are passive, quiet, content, and satisfied with the prospective boon, and the free states are excited and alarmed with fearful forebodings and apprehensions. The impatience for the speedy passage of the bill manifested by its friends betrays a knowledge that this is the condition of public sentiment in the free states. They thought in the beginning that it was necessary to guard the measure by inserting the Clayton amendment, which would exclude unnaturalized foreign inhabitants of the territories from the right of suffrage. And now they seem willing, with almost perfect unanimity, to relinquish that safeguard, rather than to delay the adoption of the principal measure for at most a year, perhaps for only a week or a day. Suppose that the senate should adhere to that condition, which so lately was thought so wise and so important — what then? The bill could only go back to the house of representatives, which must either yield or insist! In the one case or in the other, a decision in favor of the bill would be secured, for even if the house should disagree, the senate would have time to recede. But the majority will hazard nothing, even on a prospect so certain as this. They will recede at once, without a moment's further struggle, from the condition, and thus secure the passage of this bill, now to-night. Why such haste? Even if the question were to go to the country before a final decision here, what would there be wrong in that? There is no man living who will say that the country anticipated, or that *he* anticipated, agitation of this measure in Congress, when this Congress was elected, or even when it assembled in December last.

Under such circumstances, and in the midst of agitation, and excitement, and debates, it is only fair to say that certainly the country has not decided in favor of the bill. The refusal, then, to let the question go to the country, is a conclusive proof that the slave states, as represented here, expect from the passage of this bill what the free states insist that they will lose by it, an advantage, a material advantage, and not a mere abstraction. There are men in the slave states, as in the free states, who insist always too pertinaciously upon mere abstractions. But that is not the policy of the slave states to-day. They are in earnest in seeking for and securing an object, and an important one. I believe they are going to have it. I do not know how long the advantage gained will last, nor how great or comprehensive it will be. Every senator who agrees with me in opinion must feel as I do — that under such circumstances he can forego nothing that can be done decently, with due respect to difference of opinion, and consistently with the constitutional and settled rules of legislation, to place the true merits of the question before the country. Questions sometimes occur, which seem to have two right sides. Such were the questions that divided the English nation between Pitt and Fox—such the contest between the assailant and the defender of Quebec. The judgment of the world was suspended by its sympathies, and seemed ready to descend in favor of him who should be most gallant in conduct. And so, when both fell with equal chivalry on the same field, the survivors united in raising a common monument to the glorious but rival memories of Wolfe and Montcalm. But this contest involves a moral question. The slave states so present it. They maintain that African slavery is not erroneous, not unjust, not inconsistent with the advancing cause of human nature. Since they so regard it, I do not expect to see statesmen representing those states indifferent about a vindication of this system by the Congress of the United States. On the other hand, we of the free states regard slavery as erroneous, unjust, oppressive, and therefore absolutely inconsistent with the principles of the American constitution and government. Who will expect us to be indifferent to the decisions of the American people and of mankind on such an issue?

Again: there is suspended on the issue of this contest the political equilibrium between the free and the slave states. It is no ephemeral question, no idle question, whether slavery shall go on increasing its influence over the central power here, or whether freedom shall gain the ascendency. I do not expect to see statesmen of the slave states indifferent on so momentous a question, and as little can it be expected that those of the free states will betray their own great cause. And now it remains for me to declare, in view of the decision of this controversy so near at hand, that I have seen nothing and heard nothing during its progress to change the opinions which at the earliest proper period I deliberately expressed. Certainly, I have not seen the evidence then promised, that the free states would acquiesce in the measure. As certainly, too, I may say, that I have not seen the fulfilment of the promise that the history of the last thirty years would be revised, corrected, and amended, and that it would then appear that the country, during all that period, had been resting in prosperity and contentment and peace, not upon a valid, constitutional, and irrevocable compromise between the slave states and the free states, but upon an unconstitutional and false, and even infamous, act of congressional usurpation.

On the contrary, I am now, if possible, more than ever satisfied that, after all this debate, the history of the country will go down to posterity just as it stood before, carrying to them the everlasting facts that until 1820 the Congress of the United States legislated to prevent the introduction of slavery into new territories whenever that object was practicable; and that in that year they so far modified that policy, under alarming apprehensions of civil convulsion, by a constitutional enactment in the character of a compact, as to admit Missouri a new slave state; but upon the express condition, stipulated in favor of the free states, that slavery should be for ever prohibited in all the residue of the existing and unorganized territory of the United States lying north of the parallel of 36° 30′ north latitude. Certainly, I find nothing to win my favor toward the bill in the proposition of the senator from Maryland [Mr. PEARCE], to restore the Clayton amendment, which was struck out in the house of representatives. So far from voting for that proposition, I shall vote against it now, as I did when it was under consideration here before, in accordance with the opinion adopted as early as any political opinions I ever had, and cherished as long, that the right of suffrage is not a mere conventional right, but an inherent natural right, of which no government can rightly deprive any adult man who is subject to its authority, and obligated to its support.

I hold, moreover, sir, that inasmuch as every man is, by force of circumstances beyond his own control, a subject of government somewhere, he is, by the very constitution of human society, entitled to share equally in the conferring of political power on those who wield it, if he is not disqualified by crime; that in a despotic government he ought to be allowed arms, in a free government the ballot or the open vote, as a means of self-protection against unendurable oppression. I am not likely, therefore, to restore to this bill an amendment which would deprive it of an important feature imposed upon it by the house of representatives, and that one, perhaps, the only feature that harmonizes with my own convictions of justice. It is true that the house of representatives stipulate such suffrages for white men as a condition for opening it to the possible proscription and slavery of the African. I shall separate them. I shall vote for the former, and against the latter, glad to get universal suffrage of white men, if only that can be gained now, and working right on, full of hope and confidence, for the prevention or the abrogation of slavery in the territories hereafter.

Sir, I am surprised at the pertinacity with which the honorable senator from Delaware, mine ancient and honorable friend [Mr. CLAYTON], perseveres in opposing the granting of the right of suffrage to the unnaturalized foreigner in the territories. Congress can not deny him that right. Here is the third article of that convention by which Louisiana, including Kansas and Nebraska, was ceded to the United States:—

> "The inhabitants of the ceded territory shall be incorporated in the Union of the United States, and admitted as soon as possible, according to the principles of the federal constitution, to the enjoyment of the rights, privileges, and immunities, of citizens of the United States; and in the meantime they shall be maintained and protected in the free enjoyment of their liberty, property, and the religion they profess."

The inhabitants of Kansas and Nebraska are citizens already, and by force of this treaty must continue to be, and as such to enjoy the right of suffrage, whatever laws you may make to the contrary. My opinions are well known, to wit: That slavery is not only an evil, but a local one, injurious and ultimately pernicious to society, wherever it exists, and in conflict with the constitutional principles of society in this country. I am not willing to extend nor to permit the extension of that local evil into regions now free within our empire. I know that there are some who differ from me, and who regard the constitution of the United States as an instrument which sanctions slavery as well as freedom. But if I could admit a proposition so incongruous with the letter and spirit of the Federal Constitution, and the known sentiments of its illustrious founders, and so should conclude that slavery was national, I must still cherish the opinion that it is an evil; and because it is a national one, I am the more firmly held and bound to prevent an increase of it, tending, as I think it manifestly does, to the weakening and ultimate overthrow of the constitution itself, and therefore to the injury of all mankind. I know there have been states which have endured long, and achieved much, which tolerated slavery; but that was not the slavery of caste, like African slavery. Such slavery tends to demoralize equally the subjected race and the superior one. It has been the absence of such slavery from Europe that has given her nations their superiority over other countries in that hemisphere. Slavery, wherever it exists, begets fear, and fear is the parent of weakness. What is the secret of that eternal, sleepless anxiety in the legislative halls, and even at the firesides, of the slave states, always asking new stipulations, new compromises and abrogations of compromises, new assumptions of power and abnegations of power, but fear? It is the apprehension that, even if safe now, they will not always or long be secure against some invasion or some aggression from the free states. What is the secret of the humiliating part which proud old Spain is acting at this day, trembling between alarms of American intrusion into Cuba on one side, and British dictation on the other, but the fact that she has cherished slavery so long, and still cherishes it, in the last of her American colonial possessions? Thus far, Kansas and Nebraska are safe, under the laws of 1820, against the introduction of this element of national debility and decline. The bill before us, as we are assured, contains a great principle, a glorious principle; and yet that principle, when fully ascertained, proves to be nothing less than the subversion of that security, not only within the territories of Kansas and Nebraska, but within all the other present and future new territories of the United States. Thus it is quite clear that it is not a principle alone that is involved, but that those who crowd this measure with so much zeal and earnestness, must expect that either freedom or slavery shall gain something by it in those regions. The case, then, stands thus in Kansas and Nebraska: Freedom may lose, but certainly can gain nothing; while slavery may gain, but as certainly can lose nothing.

So far as I am concerned, the time for looking on the dark side has passed. I feel quite sure that slavery at most can get nothing more than Kansas; while Nebraska, the wider northern region, will, under existing circumstances, escape, for the reason that its soil and climate are uncongenial with the staples of slave culture — rice, sugar, cotton, and tobacco. Moreover, since the public attention has been so well and so effectually directed toward the subject, I cherish a hope that slavery may be prevented even from gaining a foothold in Kansas. Congress only gives consent, but it does not and can not introduce slavery there. Slavery will be embarrassed by its own over-grasping spirit. No one, I am sure, anticipates the possible re-establishment of the African slave trade. The tide of emigration to Kansas is therefore to be supplied there solely by the domestic fountain of slave production. But slavery has also other regions besides Kansas to be filled from that fountain. There are all of New Mexico and all of Utah already within the United States; and then there is Cuba, that consumes slave labor and life as fast as any one of the slaveholding states can supply it; and besides these regions, there remains all of Mexico down to the isthmus. The stream of slave labor flowing from so small a fountain, and broken into several divergent channels, will not cover so great a field; and it is reasonably to be hoped that the part of it nearest to the north pole will be the last to be inundated. But African slave emigration is to compete with free emigration of white men, and the source of this latter tide is as ample as the civilization of the two entire continents. The honorable senator from Delaware mentioned, as if it were a startling fact, that twenty thousand European immigrants arrived in New York in one month. Sir, he has stated the fact with too much moderation. On my return to the capital, a day or two ago, I met twelve thousand of these immigrants who had arrived in New York on one morning, and who had thronged the churches on the following sabbath, to return thanks for deliverance from the perils of the sea, and for their arrival in the land, not of slavery, but of liberty. I also thank God for their escape, and for their coming. They are now on their way westward, and the news of the passage of this bill, preceding them, will speed many of them toward Kansas and Nebraska. Such arrivals are not extraordinary — they occur almost every week; and the immigration from Germany, from Great Britain, and from Norway, and from Sweden, during the European war, will rise to six or seven hundred thousand souls in a year. And with this tide is to be mingled one rapidly swelling from Asia and from the islands of the South seas. All the immigrants, under this bill as the house of representatives overruling you have ordered, will be good, loyal, liberty-loving, slavery-fearing citizens. Come on, then, gentlemen of the slave states. Since there is no escaping your challenge, I accept it in behalf of the cause of freedom. We will engage in competition for the virgin soil of Kansas, and God give the victory to the side which is stronger in numbers as it is in right.

There are, however, earnest advocates of this bill, who do not expect, and who, I suppose, do not desire, that slavery shall gain possession of Nebraska. What do they expect to gain? The honorable senator from Indiana [Mr. PETTIT] says that by thus obliterating the Missouri Compromise restriction, they will gain a *tabula rasa,* on which the inhabitants of Kansas and Nebraska may write whatever they will. This is the great principle of the bill, as he understands it. Well, what gain is there in that? You obliterate a constitution of freedom. If they write a new constitution of freedom, can the new be better than the old? If they write a constitution of slavery, will it not be a worse one? I ask the honorable senator that! But the honorable senator says that the people of Nebraska will have the privilege of establishing institutions for themselves. They have now the privilege of establishing free institutions. Is it a privilege, then, to establish slavery? If so, what a mockery are all our constitutions, which prevent the inhabitants from capriciously subverting free institutions and establishing institutions of slavery? Sir, it is a sophism, a subtlety, to talk of conferring upon a country, already secure in the blessings of freedom, the power of self-destruction.

What mankind everywhere want, is not the removal of the constitutions of freedom which they have, that they may make at their pleasure constitutions of slavery or of freedom, but the privilege of retaining constitutions of freedom when they already have them, and the removal of constitutions of slavery when they have them, that they may establish constitutions of freedom in their place. We hold on tenaciously to all existing constitutions of freedom. Who denounces any man for diligently adhering to such constitutions? Who would dare to denounce any one for disloyalty to our existing constitutions, if they were constitutions of despotism and slavery? But it is supposed by some that this principle is less important in regard to Kansas and Nebraska than as a general one—a general principle applicable to all other present and future territories of the United States. Do honorable senators then indeed suppose they are establishing a principle at all? If so, I think they egregiously err, whether the principle is either good or bad, right or wrong. They are not establishing it, and can not establish it in this way. You subvert one law capriciously, by making another law in its place. That is all. Will your law have any more weight, authority, solemnity, or binding force on future Congresses than the first had? You abrogate the law of your predecessors—others will have equal power and equal liberty to abrogate yours. You allow no barriers around the old law, to protect it from abrogation. You erect none around your new law, to stay the hand of future innovators.

On what ground do you expect the new law to stand? If you are candid, you will confess that you rest your assumption on the ground that the free states will never agitate repeal, but always *acquiesce.* It may be that you are right. I am not going to predict the course of the free states. I claim no authority to speak for them, and still less to say what they will do. But I may venture to say, that if they shall not repeal this law, it will not be because they are not strong enough to do it. They have power in the house of representatives greater than that of the slave states, and, when they choose to exercise it, a power greater even here in the senate. The free states are not dull scholars, even in practical political strategy. When you shall have taught them that a compromise law establishing freedom can be abrogated, and the Union nevertheless stand, you will have let them into another secret, namely: that a law permitting or establishing slavery can be repealed, and the Union nevertheless remain firm. If you inquire why they do not stand by their rights and their interests more firmly, I will tell you to the best of my ability. It is because they are conscious of their strength, and therefore unsuspecting, and slow to apprehend danger. The reason why you prevail in so many contests, is because you are in perpetual fear.

There can not be a convocation of abolitionists, however impracticable, in Faneuil Hall or the Tabernacle, though it consists of men and women who have separated themselves from all effective political parties, and who have renounced all political agencies, even though they resolve that they will vote for nobody, not even for themselves, to carry out their purposes, and though they practise on that resolution, but you take alarm, and your agitation renders necessary such compromises as those of 1820 and 1850. We are young in the arts of politics; you are old. We are strong; you are weak. We are, therefore, over-confident, careless, and indifferent; you are vigilant and active. These are traits that redound to your praise. They are mentioned not in your disparagement. I say only that there may be an extent of intervention, of aggression, on your side, which may induce the North, at some time, either in this or in some future generation, to adopt your tactics and follow your example. Remember now, that by unanimous consent, this new law will be a repealable statute, exposed to all the chances of the Missouri compromise. It stands an infinitely worse chance of endurance than that compromise did.

The Missouri Compromise was a transaction which wise, learned, patriotic statesmen agreed to surround and fortify with the principles of a compact for mutual considerations, passed and executed, and therefore, although not irrepealable in fact, yet irrepealable in honor and conscience; and, down at least until this very session of the Congress of the United States, it has had the force and authority not merely of an act of Congress, but of a covenant between the free states and the slave states, scarcely less sacred than the constitution itself. Now, then, who are your contracting parties in the law establishing governments in Kansas and Nebraska, and abrogating the Missouri Compromise? What are the equivalents in this law? What has the North given, and what has the South got back, that makes this a contract? Who pretends that it is anything more than an ordinary act of ordinary legislation? If, then, a law which has all the forms and solemnities recognised by common consent as a compact, and is covered with traditions, can not stand amid this shuffling of this balance between the free states and the slave states, tell me what chance this new law that you are passing will have?

You are, moreover setting a precedent which abrogates all

compromises. Four years ago, you obtained the consent of a portion of the free states—enough to render the effort at immediate repeal or resistance alike impossible—to what we regarded as an unconstitutional act for the surrender of fugitive slaves. That was declared, by the common consent of the persons acting in the name of the two parties, the slave states and the free states in Congress, an irrepealable law—not even to be questioned, although it violated the constitution. In establishing this new principle, you expose that law also to the chances of repeal. You not only so expose the fugitive slave law, but there is no solemnity about the articles for the annexation of Texas to the United States, which does not hang about the Missouri compromise; and when you have shown that the Missouri compromise can be repealed, then the articles for the annexation of Texas are subject to the will and pleasure and the caprice of a temporary majority in Congress. Do you, then, expect that the free states are to observe compacts, and you to be at liberty to break them; that they are to submit to laws and leave them on the statute-book, however unconstitutional and however grievous, and that you are to rest under no such obligation? I think it is not a reasonable expectation. Say, then, who from the North will be bound to admit Kansas, when Kansas shall come in here, if she shall come as a slave state?

The honorable senator from Georgia, [Mr. TOOMBS,] and I know he is as sincere as he is ardent, says if he shall be here when Kansas comes as a free state, he will vote for her admission. I doubt not that he would; but he will not be here, for the very reason, if there be no other, that he would vote that way. When Oregon or Minnesota shall come here for admission—within one year, or two years, or three years from this time—we shall then see what your new principle is worth in its obligation upon the slaveholding states. No; you establish no principle, you only abrogate a principle which was established for your own security as well as ours; and while you think you are abnegating and resigning all power and all authority on this subject into the hands of the people of the territories, you are only getting over a difficulty in settling this question in the organization of two new territories, by postponing it till they come here to be admitted as states, slave or free.

Sir, in saying that your new principle will not be established by this bill, I reason from obvious, clear, well-settled principles of human nature. Slavery and Freedom are antagonistical elements in this country. The founders of the constitution framed it with a knowledge of that antagonism, and suffered it to continue, that it might work out its own ends. There is a commercial antagonism, an irreconcilable one, between the systems of free labor and slave labor. They have been at war with each other ever since the government was established, and that war is to continue for ever. The contest, when it ripens between these two antagonistic elements, is to be settled somewhere; it is to be settled in the seat of central power, in the federal legislature. The constitution makes it the duty of the central government to determine questions as often as they shall arise in favor of one or the other party, and refers the decision of them to the majority of the votes in the two houses of Congress. It will come back here, then, in spite of all the efforts to escape from it. This antagonism must end either in a separation of the antagonistic parties—the slaveholding states and the free states—or, secondly, in the complete establishment of the influence of the slave power over the free—or else on the other hand, in the establishment of the superior influence of Freedom over the interests of slavery. It will not be terminated by a voluntary secession of either party. Commercial interests bind the slave states and the free states together in links of gold that are riveted with iron, and they can not be broken by passion or by ambition. Either party will submit to the ascendency of the other, rather than yield to the commercial advantages of this Union. Political ties bind the Union together—a common necessity, and not merely a common necessity, but the common interests of empire—of such empire as the world has never before seen. The control of the national power is the control of the great western continent; and the control of this continent is to be in a very few years the controlling influence in the world. Who is there North, that hates slavery so much, or who, South, that hates emancipation so intensely, that he can attempt, with any hope of success, to break a Union thus forged and welded together? I have always heard, with equal pity and disgust, threats of disunion in the free states, and similar threats in the slaveholding states. I know that men may rave in the heat of passion, and under great political excitement; but I know that when it comes to a question whether this Union shall stand, either with Freedom or with Slavery, the masses will uphold it, and it will stand until some inherent vice in its constitution, not yet disclosed, shall cause its dissolution. Now, entertaining these opinions there are for me only two alternatives, viz.: either to let slavery gain unlimited sway, or so to exert what little power and influence I may have, as to secure, if I can, the ultimate predominance of freedom.

In doing this, I do no more than those who believe the slave power is rightest, wisest, and best, are doing, and will continue to do, with my free consent, to establish its complete supremacy. If they shall succeed, I still shall be, as I have been, a loyal citizen. If we succeed, I know they will be loyal also, because it will be safest, wisest, and best, for them to be so. The question is one, not of a day, or of a year, but of many years, and for aught I know, many generations. Like all other great political questions, it will be attended sometimes by excitement, sometimes by passion, and sometimes, perhaps, even by faction; but it is sure to be settled in a constitutional way, without any violent shock to society, or to any of its great interests. It is, moreover, sure to be settled rightly; because it will be settled under the benign influences of republicanism and Christianity, according to the principles of truth and justice, as ascertained by human reason. In pursuing such a course, it seems to me obviously as wise as it is necessary to save all existing laws and constitutions which are conservative of Freedom, and to permit, as far as possible, the establishment of no new ones in favor of slavery; and thus to turn away the thoughts of the states which tolerate slavery from political efforts to perpetuate what in its nature can not be perpetual, to the more wise and benign policy of emancipation.

This, in my humble judgment, is the simple, easy path of duty for the American statesman. I will not contemplate that other alternative — the greater ascendency of the slave power. I believe that if it ever shall come, the voice of Freedom will cease to be heard in these halls, whatever may be the evils and dangers which slavery shall produce. I say this without disrespect for representatives of slave states, and I say it because the rights of petition and of debate on that subject are effectually suppressed—necessarily suppressed—in all the slave states, and because they are not always held in reverence even now, in the two houses of Congress. When freedom of speech on a subject of such vital interest shall have ceased to exist in Congress, then I shall expect to see slavery not only luxuriating in all new territories, but stealthily creeping even into the free states themselves. Believing this, and believing, also, that complete responsibility of the government to the people is essential to public and private safety, and that decline and ruin are sure to follow, always, on the train of slavery, I am sure that this will be no longer a land of freedom and constitutional liberty when slavery shall have thus become paramount. *Auferre trucidare falsis nominibus imperium atque ubi solitudinem faciunt pacem appellant.*

Sir, I have always said that I should not despond, even if this fearful measure should be effected; nor do I now despond. Although, reasoning from my present convictions, I should not have voted for the compromise of 1820, I have labored, in the very spirit of those who established it, to save the landmark of Freedom which it assigned. I have not spoken irreverently, even of the compromise of 1850, which, as all men know, I opposed earnestly and with diligence. Nevertheless, I have always preferred the compromises of the constitution, and have wanted no others. I feared all others. This was a leading principle of the great statesman of the South [Mr. CALHOUN]. Said he:—

"I see my way in the constitution; I can not in a compromise. A compromise is but an act of Congress. It may be overruled at any time. It gives us no security. But the constitution is a statute. It is a rock on which we can stand, and on which we can meet our friends from the non-slaveholding states. It is a firm and stable ground, on which we can better stand in opposition to fanaticism than on the shifting sands of compromise. Let us be done with compromises. Let us go back and stand upon the constitution."

I stood upon this ground in 1850, defending freedom upon it as Mr. CALHOUN did in defending slavery. I was overruled then, and I have waited since without proposing to abrogate any compromises.

It has been no proposition of mine to abrogate them now; but the proposition has come from another quarter—from an adverse one. It is about to prevail. The shifting sands of compromise are passing from under my feet, and they are now, without agency of my own, taking hold again on the rock of the constitution. It shall be no fault of mine if they do not remain firm. This seems to me auspicious of better days and wiser legislation. Through all the darkness and gloom of the present hour, bright stars are breaking, that inspire me with hope, and excite me to perseverance. They show that the day of compromises has passed for ever, and that henceforward all great questions between freedom and slavery legitimately coming here—and none other can come—shall be decided, as they ought to be, upon their merits, by a fair exercise of legislative power, and not by bargains of equivocal prudence, if not of doubtful morality.

The house of representatives has, and it always will have, an increasing majority of members from the free states. On this occasion, that house has not been altogether faithless to the interests of the free states; for although it has taken away the charter of freedom from Kansas and Nebraska, it has at the same time told this proud body, in language which compels acquiescence, that in submitting the question of its restoration, it would submit it not merely to interested citizens, but to the alien inhabitants of the territories also. So the great interests of humanity are, after all, thanks to the house of representatives, and thanks to God, submitted to the voice of human nature.

Sir, I see one more sign of hope. The great support of slavery in the South has been its alliance with the democratic party of the North. By means of that alliance it obtained paramount influence in this government about the year 1800, which, from that time to this, with but few and slight interruptions, it has maintained. While democracy in the North has thus been supporting slavery in the South, the people of the North have been learning more profoundly the principles of republicanism and of free government. It is an extraordinary circumstance, which you, sir, the present occupant of the chair [Mr. STUART], I am sure, will not gainsay, that at this moment, when there seems to be a more complete divergence of the federal government in favor of slavery than ever before, the sentiment of universal liberty is stronger in all free states than it ever was before. With that principle the present democratic party must now come into a closer contest. Their prestige of democracy is fast waning, by reason of the hard service which their alliance with their slaveholding brethren has imposed upon them. That party perseveres, as indeed it must, by reason of its very constitution, in that service, and thus comes into closer conflict with elements of true democracy, and for that reason is destined to lose, and is fast losing the power which it has held so firmly and so long. That power will not be restored until the principle established here now shall be reversed, and a constitution shall be given, not only to Kansas and Nebraska, but also to every other national territory, which will be, not a *tabula rasa*, but a constitution securing equal, universal, and perpetual freedom.

APPENDIX.

SINCE the preceding pages were sent to the press, Mr. SEWARD has been re-elected to the Senate of the United States for the term of six years commencing the 4th day of March, 1855. The votes stood in the Senate as follows:—

For WILLIAM H. SEWARD	18
Daniel S. Dickinson	5
William F. Allen	2
Millard Fillmore	1
Ogden Hoffman	1
Preston King	1
Daniel Ullmann	1
George R. Babcock	1
Sanford E. Church	1

The Senators who voted for Mr. SEWARD were—

Hon. WILLIAM H. ROBERTSON, of Westchester county.
" ROBERT A. BARNARD, of Columbia "
" ELIAKIM SHERRILL, of Ulster "
" CLARKSON F. CROSBY, of Albany "
" ELISHA N. PRATT, of Rensselaer "
" JAMES C. HOPKINS, of Washington "
" GEORGE RICHARDS, of Warren "
" GEORGE YOST, of Montgomery "
" DANIEL G. DORRANCE, of Oneida "
" JAMES MUNROE, of Onondaga "
" GEORGE W. BRADFORD, of Cortland "
" WILLIAM CLARK, of Wayne "
" JOSIAH B. WILLIAMS, of Tompkins "
" ANDREW B. DICKINSON, of Steuben "
" WILLIAM S. BISHOP, of Monroe "
" BENJAMIN FIELD, of Orleans "
" MARTIN BUTTS, of Allegany "
" ALVAH H. WALKER, of Chautauque "

In the Assembly the votes were as follows:—

For WILLIAM H. SEWARD	69
Daniel S. Dickinson	14
Horatio Seymour	12
Washington Hunt	9
John A. Dix	7
Millard Fillmore	4
Scattering	11

The members of the Assembly who voted for Mr. SEWARD were as follows:—

NAMES. COUNTIES.

Hon. Silas Baldwin, of St. Lawrence.
" Hezekiah Baker, Montgomery.
" H. H. Beecher, of Oneida.
" James Bennett, of Orange.
" J. P. Bennett, of Wayne.
" Samuel Beyea, of Orange.
" Levi Blakeslee, of Oneida.
" R. M. Blatchford, of New York.
" N. C. Boynton, of Essex.
" Aaron B. Brush, of Madison.
" Elisha W. Bushnell, Columbia.
" A. Churchill, of Otsego.
" J. V. H. Clark, of Onondaga.
" Edmond Cole, of Rensselaer.
" S. B. Cole, of Steuben.
" Robert B. Coleman, New York.
" W. Comstock, of Otsego.
" Alexander Davidson, of Albany.
" James Donnan, of Schenectady.
" F. S. Dumont, of Tompkins.
" Moses Eames, of Jefferson.
" Jonathan Edwards, Rensselaer.
" Josiah T. Everest, of Clinton.
" Lewis Fairchilds, of Chenango.
" Edward Fitch, of Franklin.
" Wesley Gleason, Fulton and Hamilton.
" A. W. Hull, of Montgomery.
" Daniel Hunt, of Westchester.
" R. J. Jimmerson, of New York.
" C. P. Johnson, of Tioga.

NAMES. COUNTIES.

Hon. C. Littlefield, of Jefferson.
" D. W. C. Littlejohn, of Oswego.
" James I. Lourie, of Washington.
" W. I. Machan, of Onondaga.
" P. H. Maguire, of New York.
" Charles M'Kinney, of Broome.
" David Mallory, of Genesee.
" Joshua Main, of Jefferson.
" Lucius S. May, of Allegany.
" C. Miller, of Delaware.
" James M. Munro, of Onondaga.
" John C. Paine, of Wyoming.
" D. Palmer, of Chenango.
" J. P. Pennoyer, of Tompkins.
" Dudley P. Phelps, Onondaga.
" David Platt, of Suffolk.
" J. H. Ramsey, of Schoharie.
" John F. Raymond, Richmond.
" M. L. Rickerson, of Greene.
" David Rhoda, of Columbia.
" Orrin Robinson, of Chemung.
" Cornelius Schuyler, of Saratoga.
" B. Smith, of Monroe.
" S. Smith, of Steuben.
" J. W. Stebbins, of Monroe.
" John Terhune, of Saratoga.
" Gilbert Tompkins, of Madison.
" Ira Tompkins, of Niagara.
" J. B. Van Osdol, of Yates.
" Daniel Walker, of Oneida.
" Reuben Wells, of Warren.

NAMES. COUNTIES.	NAMES. COUNTIES.
Hon. L. B. Johnson, of Allegany.	Hon. G. D. Williams, of Oneida.
" John H. Knapp, of Cortland.	" W. Wilsey, of Schoharie.
" James Kirkland, Cattaraugus.	" James T. Wisner, of Wayne.
" C. C. Leigh of New York.	" William B. Woodin, of Cayuga.

The manner of electing a senator by the legislature of New York is seen by the following report of the proceedings of both branches on Tuesday, February 6, 1855:—

SENATE-CHAMBER, TUESDAY, FEBRUARY 6, 12 M.

Special Order, the Nomination of United States Senator.

THE roll having been called, each senator, as his name was called, named his candidate, as follows:—

WILLIAM H. SEWARD was nominated by [as before stated].

Daniel S. Dickinson was nominated by Messrs. Barr, Danforth, Halsey, Hutchins, and Watkins—5.

Ogden Hoffman was nominated by Mr. Brooks—1.

Preston King was nominated by Mr. Z. Clark—1.

Daniel Ullmann was nominated by Mr. Goodwin—1.

William F. Allen was nominated by Messrs. Hitchcock and Lansing—2.

George R. Babcock was nominated by Mr. Putnam—1.

Sanford E. Church was nominated by Mr. Spencer—1.

Millard Fillmore was nominated by Mr. Whitney—1. Mr. Storing was absent.

Mr. Robertson moved that the message be sent to the assembly, to inform that body of the nomination of a candidate for United States senator by this body, and that the senate was ready to compare nominations, which motion was agreed to.

A committee from the assembly informed the senate that the assembly had made a nomination for United States senator, and were ready to meet the members of the senate in the assembly-chamber, to compare nominations.

Under the lead of the sergeant-at-arms, the senate proceeded to the assembly-chamber.

On returning from the assembly-chamber—

The president announced that the nominations of the two houses were found to agree, and that WILLIAM H. SEWARD had been declared duly elected United States senator from this state for six years from the 4th of March next.

ASSEMBLY, TUESDAY, FEBRUARY 6.

AT twelve o'clock, the house proceeded to nominate a candidate for the office of senator.

WILLIAM H. SEWARD was nominated by [as before stated].

Daniel S. Dickinson was nominated by Messrs. Aitken, Allen, Buckley, Covey, Dixon, Ivans, Munday, Odell, Searing, Seymour, Smalley, Stevens, Storrs, and Waterbury—14.

Washington Hunt was nominated by Messrs. Blessing, Chester, Gates, Lamport, F. W. Palmer, Peck, Petty, Rhodes, and Van Etten—9.

Horatio Seymour was nominated by Messrs. Bridenbocker, Conger, Davy, Devening, M'Laughlin, O'Keefe, Parsons, Seagrist, E. L. Smith, W. B. Smith, Wager, and Ward—12.

John A. Dix was nominated by Messrs. Chapin, Green, J. C. Parker, Rider, Selden, Staunton, and S. S. Whallon—7.

Horatio Seymour, jr., of Erie, was nominated by Messrs. Kendig and E. S. Whalen—2.

Preston King was nominated by Mr. L. Miller—1.

Millard Fillmore was nominated by Messrs. Cocks, Emans, W. W. Weed, and A. G. Williams—4.

W. W. Campbell was nominated by Mr. Headley—1.

Benjamin F. Butler was nominated by Mr. Masters—1.

John D. Howell was nominated by Mr. Wygant—1.

Albert Lester was nominated by Mr. Chase—1.

L. Wait was nominated by Mr. J. A. Smith—1.

Greene C. Bronson was nominated by Mr. Dodge—1.

Ogden Hoffman was nominated by Mr. Ferdon—1.

S. G. Haven was nominated by Mr. Goddard—1.

Absent, Messrs. Stuyvesant and Campbell.

The clerk having announced the result—

The speaker declared William H. Seward nominated.

Mr. Blatchford moved that a committee be appointed to inform the senate that the house was prepared to meet that body in joint convention, to compare nominations for United States senator.

The speaker named Messrs. Blatchford and Aitken as such committee.

On the return of the committee—

The senate appeared and took their seats in the front circle, when

The lieutenant-governor called the joint convention to order, and

The clerk of the senate announced the nomination of William H. Seward on the part of the senate, and

The clerk of the house announced the nomination of William H. Seward on the part of the house. Whereupon—

Lieutenant Governor Raymond declared WILLAM H. SEWARD elected senator of the United States, from this state, for six years from the 4th of March next, to fill the vacancy which will then occur by the expiration of his present term. [This announcement was followed by long-continued cheers from the galleries and lobbies, by waving of handkerchiefs in the ladies' gallery, and by applause on the floor of the house.]

The senate then retired, when

The speaker formally announced the result of the joint convention.

INDEX.

THE END.

THE

WORKS OF WILLIAM H. SEWARD,

EDITED BY GEORGE E. BAKER.

IN THREE VOLUMES, 8VO.

GENERAL DIVISION OF CONTENTS.

VOLUME I.

I.—BIOGRAPHICAL MEMOIR.
II.—SPEECHES IN THE SENATE OF NEW YORK.
III.—SPEECHES IN THE UNITED STATES SENATE.
IV.—DEBATES IN THE UNITED STATES SENATE.
V.—FORENSIC ARGUMENTS.

VOLUME II.

VI.—NOTES ON NEW YORK.
VII.—ANNUAL MESSAGES TO THE LEGISLATURE.
VIII.—SPECIAL MESSAGES TO THE LEGISLATURE.
IX.—OFFICIAL CORRESPONDENCE.
X.—PARDON PAPERS.

VOLUME III.

XI.—ORATIONS AND DISCOURSES.
XII.—OCCASIONAL SPEECHES AND ADDRESSES.
XIII.—EXECUTIVE SPEECHES.
XIV.—POLITICAL WRITINGS.
XV.—GENERAL CORRESPONDENCE.
XVI.—LETTERS FROM EUROPE.
XVII.—SPEECHES IN THE SENATE OF THE U. S., *continued.*

Prices—$2.50 per Volume in Cloth.
3.75 per Volume in Half-Calf.
4.50 per Volume in Full-Calf.

J. S. REDFIELD, Publisher,
110 & 112 NASSAU STREET, NEW YORK.

It has been well said that there is no living American statesman whose works embody so much that will fix and reward the attention of the student, the statesman, and the philanthropist, as those of Governor Seward. To the general reader—to those who wish to know who and what Governor Seward is, and especially to all who desire to obtain a complete history of the times for the last quarter of a century—these volumes are of the highest interest.

Popular Education in all its phases; Internal Improvements, embracing the entire history of the origin, completion, and proposed enlargement of the Erie canal, and of the New York and Erie and other railroads; Slavery, its rights and prerogatives, the duties and obligations of the free States in regard to it; the Public Land question, with a history and discussion of the Anti-Rent troubles in this state; Crime and its penalties; Political Economy, in its adaptation to our national condition; the Fugitive-Slave Law; the Annexation of Cuba; the Maintenance of the National Honor; the Protection of American Rights; the Public Lands, &c., &c., have all been discussed with a freedom, vigor, and clearness, seldom if ever equalled, and afford information to all who wish to understand or discuss the great questions of the day.

In the execution of the mechanical portion of the work, it has been the aim of the Publisher that nothing shall be left to be desired.

The volumes contain a *Portrait of Governor Seward, a View of his Birth-place at Florida, N. Y., and his present Residence at Auburn*—all engraven in the best style of the art.

The Works have been received with unusual favor by all parties and shades of parties, as may be seen in the following extracts from the principal newspapers in the United States:—

The *Utica Herald* says: "The type is plain and neat, the paper fine and white, the binding tasteful and durable, and each volume is ornamented with an engraving."

The *National Era* speaks of them as "three large volumes, containing in the aggregate near two thousand pages, giving evidence of great industry, thorough investigation, patient and laborious thought, excellent scholarship, and a wide range of ideas—possessing an interest and value independent of time and place."

The *New York Times* says: "The first volume might be appropriately lettered—'W. H. SEWARD, THE ORATOR.' The second might stand by its side, in like manner—'W. H. SEWARD, THE PRACTICAL STATESMAN,' containing, as it does, his messages as governor, his pardon papers, official correspondence, and various writings upon political topics of state moment. The third volume, were we publisher, should be designated—'W. H. SEWARD, THE SCHOLAR,' for in its pages appear his classical eulogies and agricultural discourses—selections from his general correspondence and notes of European travel. And yet there is not a speech, a paper, or a letter, in either volume, from which the critic could not discover the three characteristics of a scholar, orator, and statesman."

The *Louisville (Ky.) Courier* says: "Mr. Seward deserves distinction, not only as a politician or statesman, but also as a moral essayist, a philanthropist, a stanch friend of popular education, and a writer of great force and eloquence."

The *National Intelligencer* says: "The Works of William H. Seward are able works, and give evidence of great intellect, of study, taste, and generous feelings."

The *Phrenological Journal* says: "These elegant volumes form a collection of writings on subjects of universal moment and interest, and in every respect may be regarded as one of the most valuable publications of the day."

The *Providence Journal* adds: "It is of much importance to commend these works to the young men of the country; they need them."

The eminent critic of the *New York Tribune*, in an elaborate review, says, "During a career which embraces but little more than half a century from his birth, Gov. Seward has furnished materials for this voluminous work, alike honorable to his ability, industry, and native nobleness of character. It comprises a range of subjects of remarkable extent—not limited to local or temporary interests."

The literary editor of the *New York Herald* describes Mr. Seward's speeches in the senate as "masterly historical dissertations, comprehensive, exhausting, and pertinent."

A writer in *Putnam's Monthly* says: "The volumes contain nearly everything that has come from his prolific pen; nor is there any want of variety in the topics of which they treat."

The *Christian Inquirer* says: "We have received three noble octavos, containing the chief works of our principal liberalist statesman, Seward. They exhibit a vast variety alike of subject and occasion."

The *New York Evangelist* remarks that "few persons are aware how large a portion of his public efforts have been directed toward moral and social reforms, in which he has appeared much more the philanthropist than the politician."

The *Northern Christian Advocate* pronounces them "three of the most useful and elegant volumes ever issued from the American press."

The *Christian Intelligencer* says: "The contents of these sumptuous volumes have been arranged with careful deference to order, with explanatory prefaces, &c., and will form a substantial addition to our political literature."

The *Christian Ambassador* says: "Whoever will candidly peruse the works will find that their author is a statesman in the highest sense of the word."

The *Boston Commonwealth* observes that, "aside from the interest which their personal character will create, they throw much light upon the great questions of our times, and exhibit the reasons which have prompted the course of many eminent men."

The *Washington Republic* says: "The New York senator has figured too largely in the politics of the country, not to make this collection a desideratum to the American statesman, however he may disapprove of much that the author has said and done."

The *Boston Transcript* says: "It is sufficient honor to Mr. Seward, that his works are necessary to any good American library."

The *Buffalo Commercial Advertiser* says: These "three handsome octavos, of six or seven hundred pages each, can not but be regarded as an important contribution to political literature."

The *Literary World*, in a long article, says: "It is rarely our province to find so much 'completeness' in the publication of a work, as appears in the volumes before us."

The *Ontario Times* says: "The work is sufficiently minute to serve as a book of reference for the politician or student, and yet of such interest in its arrangement, subjects, and style, as to be read with no less pleasure than profit by all."

The *Hartford (Ct.) Republican* says: "The volumes are edited with excellent judgment, taste, and skill, and will find their way into every library in the country. We think that many of the readers of these volumes will be surprised to find that Mr. Seward is so little of a political partisan.

The *Buffalo Express* says: "Not one of these volumes could have been spared—no page could have been abbreviated or suppressed without loss to the public, or injustice to the fame of the great man whose labors in behalf of his race these books durably record. What has been deemed a fault in the editor, or seemed to be but an author's purpose to accomplish, an appointed quantity of work, proves to be a judicious selection from the correspondence of Mr. Seward, and from his minor writings, to illustrate qualities of his character as a statesman, politician, or moralist, and to show his connection with all the important efforts made by the Americans of this day to improve their civil and social condition, and to establish Justice and Fraternity. The fullest and most reliable evidence of a man's character and principles is to be found in his letters to his intimate friends—particularly when they are written in reply to reproaches, or argumentative remonstrances against his conduct.

The entire works are an invaluable contribution to American literature, to the history of American politics, and to the science of government. They are indispensable to the politician, and should be in the library of every scholar in the country. In the discussion of measures of public policy, Mr. Seward is methodical and thorough. He exhausts his subjects, and that in the frankest and fairest manner. The most striking characteristic of his forensic efforts, and of the argumentation in his messages and addresses, is truthfulness. He is deeply in earnest at every word. There is not a sophistry, there is not an evasion, not an indecision, to denote to you that the statesman is not perfectly persuaded that the policy he advocates is not such as a wise and good man should indicate, and a brave man pursue. There is no risk of confounding this earnest truthfulness at any time with the hardihood of a public man resolute to appear consistent. Pride is not in it, nor factiousness, nor compliance with the usages or requirements of party. On occasions of great moment, and under the most trying circumstances, has this indispensable quality of a true and great man been displayed. False and hollow men would have sought in silence a refuge from Faction and Hate, and a safeguard to well-nursed or lucky reputations. But more than once has Mr. Seward, at the hazard of alienating his friends and the hazard of destruction by his enemies, spoken the truth and defended the right. He has ever filled, full to overflowing, the measure of the duties of a representative to his constituents, and of a statesman to a people. This lustrous quality of sincerity runs like a vein of silver through all his writings. All candid readers must be struck with this: and if one were disposed to speculate upon the awards of History upon the characters of public men of this day, he would inevitably say that the judgment upon William H. Seward would be, '*This* man was honest.' That it will also pronounce him to have been wise and just, in a higher degree than were any of his contemporaries in executive or senatorial office, we also believe."

The *Christian (Baptist) Review* says: "His works are an honor to American statesmanship, as well as a contribution to American literature, and will serve to raise the reputation which he has acquired both at home and abroad. We admire his abilities and respect his integrity. Often opposing himself to the prejudices of the masses, always in advance of his time, he never shrinks from a measure because it is unpopular. Certainly no man ever deserved the epithet of demagogue less."

REGAL ROME; an Introduction to Roman History. By Francis W. Newman. 1 vol. 12mo, cloth,....... $0 63
MEN OF THE TIME; or, Sketches of Living Notables. 1 vol. 12mo, cloth,....... 1 50
YOU HAVE HEARD OF THEM; being Sketches of Distinguished Artists, Composers, Actors, Singers, &c. By Q. With Portraits on steel of Horace Vernet and Julia Grisi. 12mo, cloth,....... 1 00
LADIES OF THE COVENANT. Memoirs of distinguished Scottish Females, embracing the period of the Covenant and Persecution. By Rev. James Anderson. 1 vol. 12mo, cloth, second edition,....... 1 25
MEMOIRS OF A DISTINGUISHED FINANCIER.—VINCENT NOLTE'S FIFTY YEARS IN BOTH HEMISPHERES; or, Reminiscences of a Merchant's Life. 1 vol. 12mo, cloth,....... 1 25
MEN AND WOMEN OF THE EIGHTEENTH CENTURY. By Arsène Houssaye. 2 vols. 12mo, on extra superfine paper, 450 pages each, cloth, second edition,.... 2 50
PHILOSOPHERS AND ACTRESSES. By Arsène Houssaye, author of "Men and Women of the Eighteenth Century." 2 vols. 12mo, cloth, second edition,....... 2 50
SKETCHES OF THE IRISH BAR. By the Right Hon. Richard Lalor Sheil, M.P. With a Memoir and Notes by Dr. R. Shelton Mackenzie. 2 vols. 12mo, cloth, portrait and autograph letter,....... 2 00
BARRINGTON'S SKETCHES. Personal Sketches and Memoirs of his own Time. By Sir Jonah Barrington. With Illustrations by Darley,....... 1 25
MOORE'S LIFE OF SHERIDAN. Memoirs of the Life of the Right Hon. Richard Brinsley Sheridan. By Thomas Moore. 2 vols. 12mo, cloth,....... 2 00
LORENZO BENONI; or, Passages in the Life of an Italian. Edited by a Friend. 12mo, cloth,....... 1 00
THE WORKING-MAN'S WAY IN THE WORLD; being the Autobiography of a Journeyman Printer. 12mo, cloth,....... 1 00
CLASSIC AND HISTORIC PORTRAITS. By James Bruce. 12mo, cloth,....... 1 00
NARRATIVES OF SORCERY AND MAGIC. From the most authentic sources. By Thomas Wright, M.A., F.S.A., &c. 1 vol. 12mo, cloth,....... 1 25
ART AND INDUSTRY, as represented in the Exhibition at the Crystal Palace, New-York, 1853-54. Revised and edited by Horace Greeley. 12mo, paper covers, 50 cents; cloth, fine paper,....... 1 00
MINNESOTA AND ITS RESOURCES. By J. Wesley Bond. With a new Map of the Territory, a View of St. Paul's, and one of the Falls of St. Anthony. 1 vol. 12mo, cloth, 1 00
THE GRAFTED BUD; a Memoir of Angelica Irene Hawes. By Mrs. A. H. Hawes. 1 vol. 16mo, cloth, portrait,....... 0 38

VOYAGES AND TRAVELS.

A TENNESSEAN ABROAD; or, Letters from Europe, Africa, and Asia. By Randal W. MacGavock. 12mo, cloth,....... 1 00
THE RUSSIAN SHORES OF THE BLACK SEA. By Laurence Oliphant. Fourth edition, 12mo, cloth,....... 0 75
A YEAR WITH THE TURKS; or, Sketches of Travel in the European and Asiatic Dominions of the Sultan. By Warington W. Smyth. With a colored Ethnological Map of the Turkish Empire. Third edition, 12mo, cloth,....... 0 75
NARRATIVE OF A VOYAGE TO THE NORTH-WEST COAST OF AMERICA, in the years 1811, '12, '13 and '14; or the First Settlement on the Pacific. By Gabriel Franchère. Translated and edited by J. V. Huntington. 12mo, cloth, plates,....... 1 00
A MONTH IN ENGLAND. By Henry T. Tuckerman. Second edition, 12mo, cloth,. 0 75
LIFE IN THE MISSION, THE CAMP, AND THE ZENANA; or, Six Years in India. By Mrs. Colin Mackenzie. 2 vols. 12mo, cloth,....... 2 00
WHITE, RED AND BLACK; Sketches of American Society during the Visit of their Guests. By Francis and Theresa Pulszky. 2 vols. 12mo, cloth,....... 2 00
THE BLACKWATER CHRONICLE; a Narrative of an Expedition into the Land of Canaan, in Randolph County, Virginia. By "The Clerke of Oxenforde." With numerous Illustrations by Strother. 12mo, cloth,....... 1 00

BELLES-LETTRES.

CHRISTOPHER NORTH'S GREAT WORK. THE NOCTES AMBROSIANÆ. By Professor Wilson, J. G. Lockhart, James Hogg, and Dr. Maginn. Edited, with Memoirs and Notes, by Dr. R. Shelton Mackenzie. In 5 vols............................ $5 00

THE WORKS OF EDGAR ALLAN POE. 3 vols. 12mo, cloth, portrait on steel,..... 3 50

Simms' Revolutionary Tales.

Uniform Series, with Illustrations by Darley.

THE PARTISAN; a Romance of the Revolution. 12mo, cloth,.................... 1 25

MELLICHAMPE; a Legend of the Santee. 12mo, cloth,........................ 1 25

KATHARINE WALTON; or, The Rebel of Dorchester. 12mo, cloth,................ 1 25

THE SCOUT; or, The Black Riders of the Congaree. 12mo, cloth,................ 1 25

WOODCRAFT; or, the Hawks about the Dovecote. 12mo, cloth,.................. 1 25

THE YEMASSEE; a Romance of South Carolina. 12mo, cloth,.................... 1 25

Simms' New Work.

SOUTHWARD HO! A Spell of Sunshine. By William Gilmore Simms. 1 vol. 12mo, 1 25

(Dr. R. Montgomery Bird.)

CALAVAR; the Knight of the Conquest. By the late Robert Montgomery Bird. 12mo, cloth,.. 1 25

NICK OF THE WOODS; or, The Jibbenainosay: a Tale of Kentucky. By Robert M. Bird, M.D. 1 vol. 12mo, cloth,... 1 25

(William Henry Herbert.)

THE CAVALIERS OF ENGLAND; or, The Times of the Revolutions of 1642 and 1688. By Henry W. Herbert. 1 vol. 12mo, cloth, second edition,....................... 1 25

THE KNIGHTS OF ENGLAND, SCOTLAND, AND FRANCE. By Henry W. Herbert. 1 vol. 12mo, cloth,... 1 25

THE CHEVALIERS OF FRANCE; from the Crusaders to the Mareschals of Louis XIV. By H. W. Herbert, author of the "Cavaliers of England," &c., &c. 1 vol. 12mo, cloth, 1 25

MARMADUKE WYVIL; an Historical Romance of 1651. By H. W. Herbert. New and Revised Edition. 1 vol. 12mo, cloth,.................................. 1 25

(J. V. Huntington.)

THE FOREST. By J. V. Huntington, author of "Lady Alice," "Alban," &c. 1 vol. 12mo, second edition,.. 1 25

ALBAN. By J. V. Huntington, author of "Lady Alice," "The Forest," &c. A new and completely altered edition. 2 vols. 12mo, cloth,............................ 2 00

Lee's Tales of Labor.

THE MASTER BUILDER; or, Life at a Trade. By Day Kellogg Lee, author of "Summerfield; or, Life on a Farm." 12mo, cloth, second edition,...................... 1 00

MERRIMACK; or, Life at the Loom. By Day Kellogg Lee, author of "The Master Builder; or, Life at a Trade," &c. 12mo, cloth,................................. 1 00

SUMMERFIELD; or, Life on a Farm. By Day Kellogg Lee. 12mo, cloth,.......... 1 00

(Alice Carey.)

CLOVERNOOK; or, Recollections of our Home in the West. By Alice Carey. 1 vol. 12mo, cloth, seventh edition,.. 1 00

CLOVERNOOK, SECOND SERIES; or, Recollections of our Neighborhood in the West. By Alice Carey, author of "Hagar," &c., &c. 12mo, cloth,...................... 1 00

HAGAR; a Story of To-day. By Alice Carey, author of "Clovernook," "Lyra," &c. 1 vol. 12mo, cloth, second edition,.. 1 00

(Caroline Chesebro'.)

DREAM-LAND BY DAYLIGHT; a Panorama of Romance. By Caroline Chesebro'. 12mo, second edition,... 1 25

ISA; a Pilgrimage. By Caroline Chesebro', author of "Dream-Land by Daylight," &c., &c. 1 vol. 12mo, cloth, second edition,.................................. 1 00

THE CHILDREN OF LIGHT; a Theme for the Time. By Caroline Chesebro'. 1 vol. 12mo, cloth, second edition,.. 1 00

THE YOUTH OF JEFFERSON; a Chronicle of College Scrapes at Williamsburg, Virginia, A.D. 1764. 12mo, cloth, second edition,.................................. $0 75
WESTERN CHARACTERS; being Types of Border Life in the Western States. By J. L. McConnell. 12mo, cloth,.. 1 25
EASY WARREN AND HIS CONTEMPORARIES. Sketches for Home Circles. By William T. Coggeshall. 12mo, cloth,.. 1 00
A STRAY YANKEE IN TEXAS. By Philip Paxton. With Illustrations by Darley. 1 vol. 12mo, cloth,.. 1 25
VASCONSELOS; a Romance of the New World. By Frank Cooper. 12mo, cloth,... 1 25
TALES AND TRADITIONS OF HUNGARY. By Theresa Pulszky. With a portrait of the Author. 1 vol. 12mo, cloth,.. 1 25
CAP-SHEAF; a Fresh Bundle. By Louis Myrtle. 1 vol. 12mo, cloth,............... 1 00
THE LION'S SKIN AND LOVER HUNT. By Charles de Bernard. 1 vol. 12mo,.... 1 00
CHANTICLEER; a Thanksgiving Story of the Peabody Family. By Cornelius Mathews.. 0 75
THE PRETTY PLATE; a Christmas Juvenile. By John Vincent, Esq. With Illustrations by Darley. 1 vol. 18mo, cloth gilt,.................................... 0 50

MISCELLANEOUS.

THE WORKS OF THE HON. WILLIAM H. SEWARD, with a Memoir, Portrait, and other engravings on steel. 3 vols. 8vo, cloth, per volume,......................... 2 50
Do. do. do. half calf,.................................. 3 75
Do. do. do. full calf, extra,.............................. 4 50
MACAULAY'S SPEECHES. 2 vols. 12mo, cloth, second edition,..................... 2 00
MEAGHER'S SPEECHES. Speeches on the Legislative Independence of Ireland, with Introductory Notes. By Thomas Francis Meagher. 12mo, portrait,.............. 1 00
THE SUPPRESSED LETTERS OF THOMAS MOORE. Edited, with an Introductory Letter, by T. Crofton Croker, F.S.A.; four engravings on steel. 12mo, cloth,...... 1 50
EPISODES OF INSECT LIFE. By Acheta Domestica. Three series: Insects of Spring, Summer, and Autumn. 3 vols. 8vo, cloth gilt, beautifully illustrated. Each,...... 2 00
The same Work, in sets of Three Volumes, *exquisitely colored after Nature.* Extra gilt, gilt edges,.. 12 00
OUTLINES OF COMPARATIVE PHYSIOGNOMY; or, Resemblances between Men and Animals. By J. W. Redfield, M.D. With 330 Illustrations. 8vo,............. 2 00

(R. C. Trench, B. D.)

SYNONYMS OF THE NEW TESTAMENT. By Richard Chenevix Trench, B.D. 12mo, cloth,.. 0 75
ON THE STUDY OF WORDS. By Richard Chenevix Trench, B.D. 1 vol. 12mo, cloth, fifth edition. From the second London edition,.......................... 0 75
ON THE LESSONS IN PROVERBS. By Richard Chenevix Trench, B.D., author of "The Study of Words." 12mo, cloth,.. 0 50

CHARACTERS IN THE GOSPELS; illustrating Phases of Character at the Present Day. By Rev. E. H. Chapin. 1 vol. 12mo, cloth,.............................. 0 50
THE CATACOMBS OF ROME, as Illustrating the Church of the First Three Centuries. By the Right Rev. William Ingraham Kip, D.D., Missionary Bishop of California. With over 100 Illustrations. 12mo, cloth,.. 0 75
THEOLOGICAL ESSAYS. By Frederick Denison Maurice. 12mo, cloth,............ 1 00
THE DIVINE CHARACTER VINDICATED; being a Review of Dr. Beecher's "Conflict of Ages." By Rev. Moses Ballou. 12mo, cloth,............................ 1 00
THE NIGHT SIDE OF NATURE; or, Ghosts and Ghost Seers. By Catharine Crowe. 1 vol. 12mo, cloth,.. 1 00
BRONCHITIS AND KINDRED DISEASES, in language adapted to the common reader. By W. W. Hall, M.D. 1 vol. 12mo, cloth,.. 1 00
GRISCOM ON VENTILATION. The Uses and Abuses of Air. 12mo, cloth, third edition,.. 0 75
CHAPMAN'S AMERICAN DRAWING-BOOK. Three Parts published. Each........ 0 50
CHAPMAN'S DRAWING COPY-BOOKS. Per dozen 1 50

www.ingramcontent.com/pod-product-compliance
Lightning Source LLC
LaVergne TN
LVHW011156110826
845150LV00006B/1232

* 9 7 8 1 4 2 5 5 4 6 0 2 1 *